W9-BTD-337

A Field Guide
to Pacific Coast Shells

THE PETERSON FIELD GUIDE SERIES

EDITED BY ROGER TORY PETERSON

1. A Field Guide to the Birds by Roger Tory Peterson

2. A Field Guide to Western Birds by Roger Tory Peterson

3. A Field Guide to Shells of the Atlantic and Gulf Coasts and the West Indies by Percy A. Morris

4. A Field Guide to the Butterflies by Alexander B. Klots

5. A Field Guide to the Mammals by William H. Burt and Richard P. Grossenheider

6. A Field Guide to Pacific Coast Shells (including shells of Hawaii and the Gulf of California) by Percy A. Morris

7. A Field Guide to Rocks and Minerals by Frederick H. Pough

8. A Field Guide to the Birds of Britain and Europe by Roger Tory Peterson, Guy Mountfort, and P. A. D. Hollom

9. A Field Guide to Animal Tracks by Olaus J. Murie

10. A Field Guide to the Ferns and Their Related Families of Northeastern and Central North America by Boughton Cobb

11. A Field Guide to Trees and Shrubs (Northeastern and Central North America) by George A. Petrides

12. A Field Guide to Reptiles and Amphibians of the United States and Canada East of the 100th Meridian by Roger Conant

13. A Field Guide to the Birds of Texas and Adjacent States by Roger Tory Peterson

14. A Field Guide to Rocky Mountain Wildflowers by John J. Craighead, Frank C. Craighead, Jr., and Ray J. Davis

15. A Field Guide to the Stars and Planets by Donald H. Menzel

16. A Field Guide to Western Reptiles and Amphibians by Robert C. Stebbins

17. A Field Guide to Wildflowers of Northeastern and North-central North America by Roger Tory Peterson and Margaret McKenny

18. A Field Guide to the Mammals of Britain and Europe by F. H. van den Brink

19. A Field Guide to the Insects of America North of Mexico by Donald J. Borror and Richard E. White

20. A Field Guide to Mexican Birds by Roger Tory Peterson and Edward L. Chalif

QL
417
.M72
1974

THE PETERSON FIELD GUIDE SERIES

A Field Guide to Pacific Coast Shells

including shells of Hawaii and the Gulf of California

BY PERCY A. MORRIS

Peabody Museum of Natural History
Yale University

Illustrated with Photographs

LIBRARY
FLORIDA KEYS COMMUNITY COLLEGE
5901 West Junior College Road
Key West, Florida 33040

Second Edition
Revised and Enlarged

Sponsored by the National Audubon Society
and National Wildlife Federation

HOUGHTON MIFFLIN COMPANY BOSTON

Publisher's Note

With this printing the title has been modified
slightly from *A Field Guide to Shells of the Pacific
Coast and Hawaii* to *A Field Guide to Pacific Coast
Shells* in order to distinguish the volume more readily
from its East Coast counterpart, *A Field Guide
to Shells*. The text remains unchanged.

Third Printing of Second Edition   V

Copyright © 1966 by Percy A. Morris
Copyright 1952 by Percy A. Morris

All rights reserved. No part of this work may be
reproduced or transmitted in any form by any means,
electronic or mechanical, including photocopying and
recording, or by any information or retrieval system,
without permission in writing from the publisher.

Library of Congress Cataloging in Publication Data

Morris, Percy A   1899–1969
  A field guide to Pacific coast shells, including
shells of Hawaii and the Gulf of California.

  (The Peterson field guide series; 6)
  Published in 1952 and 1966 under title: A field
guide to shells of the Pacific coast and Hawaii.
  Bibliography: p.
  1. Shells — Pacific Coast (North America) — Identifi-
cation.   2. Shells — Hawaii — Identification.
I. Title.
QL417.M72   1974   594'.04'7   73-14605
ISBN 0-395-08029-0 hardbound
ISBN 0-395-18322-7 paperbound

Printed in the United States of America

Editor's Note

BUTTERFLIES have their points and so do minerals, but no natural history objects lend themselves better to the gratification of the collecting instinct than shells. Many collectors are interested in shells in the same way that one would be interested in jewels, jades, or fine porcelain. Others, aware that the shell is but the garment of a once-living animal, take the naturalist's point of view and concern themselves with classification and distribution. A growing number now inquire into the life of the living mollusk, its ecology and its habits.

Although the shells of mollusks of one sort or another (mostly very small ones) can be found in muddy ditches, under stones, and even on mountaintops, the ones that fascinate us most by their delicacy of form and color are the ones we find along the ocean beaches, treasures cast up from the sea by the surf and the tide.

Recognition always comes first. That is why the Field Guide Series was launched — as a shortcut to recognizing and naming the multitude of living things that populate America — a *Who's Who* of the outdoors. The first volume to appear, *A Field Guide to the Birds*, met with instant success. This was followed by field guides to western birds, eastern shells, butterflies, mammals, and then Percy Morris's admirable *A Field Guide to Shells of the Pacific Coast and Hawaii*.

This new edition is much expanded over the first edition, which was published in 1952. Fourteen years have seen a substantial growth in our knowledge of Pacific Coast mollusks. Mr. Morris has not only integrated this new information and streamlined it, but has also added to the area covered. He now includes the long sea to the south of our border, the Gulf of California, a favorite collecting ground of western conchologists. This has necessitated the addition of a number of new plates and a rebuilding of the old ones. Whereas the first edition had 48 plates the present one has 72. It is therefore more than a mere revision, it is really a new book.

Whether your interest in the seashore is that of a bird watcher (no seascape is devoid of birds), that of a surf fisherman, a bather basking on the sand, or merely that of a beachcomber, you cannot overlook the shells. From Alaska to Baja California stretch thousands of miles of good collecting grounds. The Hawaiian Islands offer excellent hunting and a different assortment of species;

so does the Gulf of California. Rock, sand, and mud offer radically dissimilar environments. Some specimens you will find at high-tide line where the waves have tossed them. Others will be in the tide pools. Still others you must dredge for in deep water.

Take this book with you whenever you go to the shore. Do not leave it home on your library shelf; it is a Field Guide, intended to be used.

ROGER TORY PETERSON

Acknowledgments

THE AUTHOR wishes to acknowledge his indebtedness to many who have aided materially in the production of this second edition. Shell people are notoriously friendly, and probably in no other field would an author find so many top specialists willing to give so generously of their time in answering questions relating to difficult problems. The writer wishes to express his especial gratitude to A. Myra Keen of Stanford University, who has been of inestimable help in matters of classification, distribution, and nomenclature and in providing many specimens for photographic purposes. Others who have aided in many ways include: S. Stillman Berry of Redlands, California; Rudolf Stohler of the University of California; Allyn G. Smith of Berkeley, California; Alan J. Kohn of the University of Washington; Emery F. Swan of the University of New Hampshire; Ross Hardy of Long Beach State College, California; and Willard D. Hartman of Yale University. The writer wishes to express his sincere thanks to all of these, and at the same time point out that any errors that may creep into the book are the sole responsibility of the author.

Many shell collectors have been most kind in answering questions and in providing specimens for study and photography. John Q. Burch of Los Angeles, well known to all West Coast collectors, has provided a number of specimens and much information, and the same can be said for Mrs. A. R. Wingard of Gig Harbor, Washington, who was especially helpful with the chitons. Thanks are due Mrs. Eleanor Duggan of Everett, Washington, Walter J. Eyerdam of Seattle, Washington, and Ruth A. Craine of Norwich, New York.

The writer would like to acknowledge his indebtedness also to the late Heathcote M. Woolsey of Kent, Connecticut, and the late Mrs. North McLean of Washington, Connecticut. These two ardent and veteran collectors bequeathed their extensive collections to the Division of Mollusks of the Peabody Museum of Natural History at Yale University. The Woolsey Collection was rich in California material, and the McLean Collection featured several seasons of collecting at Guaymas, Mexico.

Roger Tory Peterson, Editor of the Peterson Field Guide Series, has been ever helpful, and his many suggestions are deeply appreciated. While the author made all of the black and white photographs, the color plates were made by John Howard of Yale University. Finally, the author's sincere thanks go to Paul Brooks and Helen Phillips of Houghton Mifflin Company, for their patience and their untiring efforts in seeing the work through the press.

PERCY A. MORRIS

Introduction

OF THE many amusements for the wanderer by the seashore, one of the most rewarding is the search for shells. None but those who have given a little time to shell-collecting can conceive of the multitude of varieties which are discovered when practice sharpens the eyes.

A well-organized collection can be a joy to own. Properly cleaned shells will never be marred by insects; they are most durable, and the beautiful colors and patterns that many of them exhibit are practically permanent. While it is true that a shell will fade and lose its luster if exposed to the bright sun for a long period (the bleached examples to be seen on any beach prove this), it is also true that if kept in a cabinet or drawer away from direct sunlight the same shells will retain their beauty for years. In our great museums one can find shells that were collected more than a century ago, and they are just as colorful and fresh-appearing as specimens that are living along our shores today.

Collecting your shells: For collecting one should of course wear old clothes, and sturdy shoes. Never collect when barefooted, because many of our shells, buried in the sand, have razor-sharp edges. You will need a bag or sack in which to put specimens, a jar or two of seawater in which to put fragile specimens until you can care for them later, and a few small vials for minute forms. A stout bar of some sort for probing and overturning stones is useful; a shovel or trowel is a necessity. A pair of tweezers for handling tiny mollusks is helpful, and a small hand lens makes critical examination on the spot possible.

One scarcely needs to be told where to find shells. The beginner usually starts by walking along the shore and keeping a sharp eye for specimens that have been washed in by the tides. While many excellent shells may be obtained in this way, a large majority will be wave-worn, eroded, broken, or otherwise imperfect. Bivalve shelves will in most cases be represented by single valves, and the lips of univalves will show broken edges, or worn sculpture or damaged spires.

The young collector soon learns that to build up a really fine collection he must look for living specimens. Just as in bird study we look for certain kinds of birds in open fields, others in deep forests, and still others in marshes, so it is with the mollusks. We find that some — in fact most — show decided preferences for particular types of marine territory. A vast assemblage of different forms lives on rocky shores, clinging to or hiding under the rocks while the tide is out. Others prefer sandy flats, where they burrow into the sand during ebb tide. Many like nothing better than a muddy bottom, and the blacker and stickier the better. Some will live only in the purest seawater, tolerating no brackishness at all; whereas others seem to like it better where the water is brackish, often thriving best in partially polluted areas.

A large and interesting part of our molluscan fauna lives in what is known as the *littoral zone*, that portion of the beach between high and low tides which is exposed to the sun twice each day. Others live out beyond the low-water level, and many species are found in deep water, even up to several hundred fathoms. Temperature controls the distribution of many varieties, and we shall find a different group at San Diego from those found at Puget Sound. Yet some of the shells that may be collected close to shore in northern waters are to be found living in deeper water in the south.

On rocky coasts the receding tides leave pockets of water in all depressed areas, and in these tide pools one can find various kinds of molluscan life carrying on in a business-as-usual manner. It will reward the collector to scan these miniature aquariums carefully. The pilings and undersides of wharves are rich collecting grounds too, the logs generally being covered with a heavy growth of marine algae that conceals many of the smaller mollusks.

The best time to collect is of course at low tide, when one can get out to the low-water limits. Any stone, plank, or section of driftwood should be turned over; a host of marine creatures, including mollusks, take refuge under such objects to await the return of the next tide. A good practice is to roll the stone or log back the way it was after you are through searching, for future collecting. On sand and mudflats the presence of bivalves can usually be detected by small holes that reveal the location of the clam's siphon. As you trudge along, the mollusk draws in its siphon, commonly ejecting a thin squirt of water as it does so. The snails generally burrow just beneath the surface, producing little telltale mounds. By energetically digging in likely places while the tide is out, one should come up with a good representative collection of the shells inhabiting that particular beach, all of them "taken alive" specimens, far superior to the old and empty shells picked up along the shoreline.

Nevertheless, the collecting of dead shells is not to be neglected altogether, since some fine examples may be obtained thus. This is particularly true of the minute forms. On nearly every exposed beach you will find a long and wavy line of flotsam and jetsam known as sea wrack or beach litter that marks the high-tide limit. It will pay you to examine this debris carefully. Here you will find large pieces of seaweeds that have been torn from their moorings and washed ashore. Concealed in the folds and among the roots you may find scores of tiny mollusks that live out in deeper waters. If you gather freshly washed-up material, such as on a day following a violent storm, most of the mollusks will be live ones. Sections of sponges should be pulled apart and examined, and pieces of driftwood broken up to reveal piddocks and shipworms. Dead crustaceans and sea urchins can be looked over for parasitic mollusks. The fine material in the beach litter should be run through a sieve to eliminate most of the sand grains, and the shelly particles remaining searched for tiny pelecypods and gastropods. Most collectors take home small bags of this material to work on in the evenings or on rainy days.

Try collecting at night with a strong flashlight. Several of our snails are nocturnal, and certain species that have to be searched for under stones and in crevices during the daylight hours will be found crawling over the rocks and the sandbars after dark. It is suggested that any night collecting be done with a companion or two, for safety reasons.

One of the most exciting, as well as rewarding, types of collecting is dredging. We cannot all afford the boats, winches, and heavy gear to do this on a large scale, much as we would like to, but it does not cost much to rig up a small iron frame, attach a netting or fine wire bag, and drag it along the bottom from a rowboat in 15 to 20 feet of water. Low tide is the best time. Try all sorts of bottoms — sandy, muddy, gravelly, and so on. After dragging your scoop for several minutes, pull it up to the surface, jiggle it a bit to wash most of the mud and silt, and then haul it over the side and empty it into a basin or tub of water. It is easier to separate your catch in this way, and small, fragile shells are less likely to be injured than if you dumped the contents out onto the deck.

Preparing your shells: While the collecting of shells is sheer pleasure, the necessary cleaning and preparing comes under the label of work; but it is work that has to be done if we are to gather living material. The first thing to do is to get rid of the animal in the shell. The common practice is to place the shells in a pan of water, bring them to a boil, and let them boil for from 5 to 15 minutes. After that the bivalves present no problem: the valves gape open and the mollusk can be removed with no difficulty. One generally has to scrape briefly over the muscle scars. Valves that have an external ligament will remain attached in pairs; after the interior has been thoroughly cleaned the two valves can be closed and the whole shell wrapped with strong thread until the ligament has dried. In each tray of specimens you will want a pair of valves that are separated to show the interiors.

With univalves, the animal will have to be drawn out of its shell by a hook or bent wire. After being boiled the soft parts generally slip out without too much trouble, but sometimes the small end will break off and stay in the upper whorls. Soaking in plain water for several days will often rot and soften this part so that it can be washed out. If this fails the usual practice is to put the shell in a 10 per cent solution of formaldehyde for a few hours to harden the animal matter. Then the shell can be dried in a shady place, and after this there should be no offensive odor. Very tiny snails are generally kept in alcohol (about 70 per cent) for several days and then dried.

Many of the snails have an operculum attached to the body in such a manner that when the "foot" is withdrawn it serves as a door, effectively blocking the aperture (see p. xxxvi). Opercula may be horny, leathery, or calcareous. This structure must be cut away from the flesh and its reverse side scraped clean. When the shell is prepared and ready for the cabinet, the operculum is glued to a tuft of cotton, and then inserted in the aperture and positioned as it would be in life. In cleaning your gastropods take special care to see that each operculum is kept with its own shell.

Some of the larger bivalves, particularly of the genera *Spondylus* and *Chama*, usually have their shells more or less coated with worm tubes, barnacles, calcareous algae, and other foreign growths. They can only be cleaned by careful and painstaking work with tiny chisels, needles, and scrapers. Some collectors paint the unwanted incrustations with a weak solution of muriatic acid, and although the acid will dissolve all limy deposits it will also attack the shell itself. Therefore its use is not recommended.

The periostracum (or noncalcareous covering that protects the outside of many shells) can be removed by soaking the shell in a solution of caustic soda, about one pound to a gallon of water. Most collectors, however, prefer their specimens in a natural state. An ideal plan is to have two or three examples of each species in a tray, one denuded of its periostracum and the others as they were in life.

After your shells are cleaned, washed, and dried, and ready for their trays or the cabinet, they may be lightly rubbed with a small amount of mineral oil applied with a tuft of cotton. This will impart a slight luster to the surface, make them fresh-looking, and aid in preserving the delicate coloring. Some workers use olive oil, but that may in time become rancid, and it also may attract insects.

Arranging your shells: A collection's value is proportional to its labeling. The precise locality and date are far more important than having the shell correctly named. Any competent worker can put the correct name on your shell, at any time, but you and *only you* can provide the exact location and date. Adopt some form of label that provides space for a number (which will be entered in your catalog and written in waterproof ink on each specimen), the name, date, and locality. This last should be as exact as possible. "Southern California" does not mean very much, but "½ mile south of Point Loma, California" ties the specimen down accurately. The collector's name should be included, and most collectors can be depended upon not to neglect that. Under the entry number in the catalog you may include notes on the tide conditions, the weather, whether or not the mollusk was a living specimen or an empty shell, its relative abundance at that time and place, what it was doing, and anything else that may seem pertinent. Below is a sample label used by the writer:

```
┌─────────────────────────────────────────┐
│           YALE PEABODY MUSEUM            │
│       Division of Invertebrate Zoology   │
│                                          │
│   ...13014......                         │
│   Cardiomya...pectinata..............    │
│   .....................(Carpenter)       │
│   ..Dredged,.75.fathoms. / 214 /         │
│   ..Off..Redondo.Beach,.Calif......      │
│   Coll..John.Q..Burch.......... Date 3/10/1961 │
└─────────────────────────────────────────┘
```

The number in the small box is an accession number applying to all shells from a certain collection. For example, if we spend a day or a week collecting at a certain locality, all the shells gathered on that trip can have the same accession number; or if we purchase a complete collection from some source we may give an accession number to the whole lot. Then, although each species will eventually have its catalog number, the number in the box instantly associates each shell with a certain group.

Names of shells: The beginner is apt to be confused and at first annoyed by some of the "jawbreaking" names that have been given to shells. This is true in any branch of natural history, but is perhaps more apparent in the molluscan field, since only a few kinds have become well enough known to have acquired common or popular names. Perhaps this is a good thing, because English names are very likely to be too local in character. Thus the same shell may be called one thing in one place go under a completely different name a few miles down the coast, and in three widely separated localities the same name may be applied to three totally different shells.

Scientists have agreed upon Latin as usual for the naming of animals (and plants) for very good reasons. It is a dead language and therefore not subject to change. Serious scholars all over the world, regardless of their individual nationalities, are familiar with it, so that it is about as close as one can get to an international tongue. The name "Pismo Clam" means something to a resident of California, but it means nothing to a Frenchman or a Dutchman, or to most New Englanders. Use the bivalve's correct genus name of *Tivela*, however, and every shell enthusiast, whatever his country, knows what shell we are talking about.

In this book the common names have been given wherever they seem well established, but the serious collector is strongly urged to learn his treasures by their authentic names. Scientific names are not difficult after we become familiar with them. We use the words alligator, boa constrictor, and gorilla commonly enough without stopping to realize that they are perfectly good scientific names. In the field of flowers we all speak or write of our iris, forsythia, geranium, crocus, delphinium, and scores of others with the greatest of ease. Who can say that chrysanthemum or rhododendron is easier to say than *Murex*, *Tellina*, or *Littorina?*

It has been found convenient to give each animal two names: first, a general, or generic, name (always capitalized), indicating the group (genus) to which it belongs; second, a special, or specific, name (not capitalized), to apply to that animal alone as the *species* name. In older works, the specific name was capitalized if a proper name, but that practice has been discontinued for many years.

Thus the Pismo Clam referred to above was first described by a Mr. John Mawe — in 1823 — placed in the genus *Donax*, and given a species name, *stultorum*. The name of the person who first describes a species, known as the author, follows the scientific name; so our bivalve became *Donax stultorum* Mawe. If later research proves that a species belongs in a genus different from the one to which the author has allocated it, it is removed to the proper genus, but the species name is retained and parentheses are placed around the author's name to indicate that a change has been made from the original allocation. In this case the clam was put in the genus *Tivela*, so our name now reads *Tivela stultorum* (Mawe). The parentheses are a technicality of importance chiefly to specialists, and many books for the nonspecialists do not use them, although the International Rules of Zoological Nomenclature insist that they are a valid part of the name. A List of Authors whose names appear in this *Field Guide* can be found at the back of the book as Appendix II.

Your fellow collectors: One of the many joys connected with "shelling" is meeting others with the same interests. One cannot search the sandflats or pry under driftlogs and stones for any length of time without running into someone similarly occupied; many lasting friendships have been initiated on the beach. Shell people like to get together, and shell clubs have been organized in many localities throughout the country. In fact, their growth during the past decade has been little short of phenomenal. Most are affiliated with the American Malacological Union, which has a West Coast branch called the Pacific Division. It is strongly urged that anyone seriously collecting shells consider joining this society. The only requirement is an interest in mollusks. The membership is about one-third professional malacologists and two-thirds enthusiastic amateurs. The corresponding address of this society varies with that of the acting Secretary, but their official publication is *The Nautilus*, Academy of Natural Sciences, Philadelphia, Penna., and any inquiry about the association would receive prompt attention.

Some of the West Coast shell clubs are listed in Appendix IV. If you are within commuting distance of any, by all means get in touch with the Secretary and plan to attend one of the meetings to get acquainted. Here you will find kindred souls, perhaps enrich your own collection by exchanges, enjoy the good fellowship of local field trips, and obtain help in the identification of puzzling material. Many of these shell clubs issue a publication for the benefit of club members, possibly a bimonthly newsletter or a monthly bulletin. It may be simply a mimeographed list of members with program notes and local items, and it may include short articles about collecting and classification, or discussions on a particular genus or group. Some clubs issue a regularly printed journal with original work by some of the country's leading scientists. Two of the best are *Hawaiian Shell News* of the Hawaiian Malacological Society, and the *Veliger* of the Northern California Malacozoological Club.

The Phylum Mollusca: This group forms one of the major branches of the Animal Kingdom, including as it does the clams, oysters, and scallops, the snails and slugs, and the chitons, squids, octopuses, and some others. Close to a hundred thousand living kinds are known throughout the world, besides many thousands of fossil species, for the group is represented in the most ancient of fossil-bearing rocks. The mollusks are divided into 5 major classes, as follows:

1. The *Pelecypoda* are entirely aquatic and predominately marine, with a pair of valves joined by a hinge and held together by strong muscles within. The animal has no head, and feeds upon microscopic plant and animal matter that is drawn into the mantle cavity through the siphon. There is commonly a muscular foot for burrowing.

2. The *Gastropoda* are numerically the largest division of the Mollusca. Examples occur in marine and fresh waters, and as terrestrial air-breathing animals. There is but a single valve, usually spiral or caplike, but some are shell-less. There is a distinct head, often with eyes, and the mollusk is provided with a toothed radula, or lingual ribbon, by means of which it shreds its food. Gastropods may be either herbivorous or carnivorous.

3. The *Amphineura* are primitive mollusks of very sluggish habits, mostly preferring shallow water close to shore. The typical chiton (the common name) is an elongate, depressed mollusk, bearing a shelly armor of 8 saddle-shaped plates arranged in an overlapping series along the back. The foot is broad and flat,

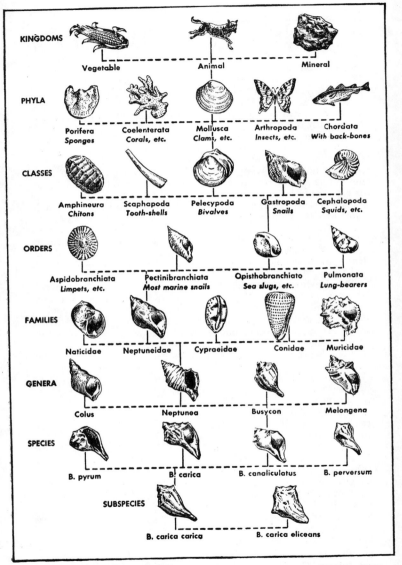

KINGDOMS
Vegetable   Animal   Mineral

PHYLA
Porifera
Sponges   Coelenterata
Corals, etc.   Mollusca
Clams, etc.   Arthropoda
Insects, etc.   Chordata
With back-bones

CLASSES
Amphineura
Chitons   Scaphopoda
Tooth-shells   Pelecypoda
Bivalves   Gastropoda
Snails   Cephalopoda
Squids, etc.

ORDERS
Aspidobranchiata
Limpets, etc.   Pectinibranchiata
Most marine snails   Opisthobranchiato
Sea slugs, etc.   Pulmonata
Lung-bearers

FAMILIES
Naticidae   Neptuneidae   Cypraeidae   Conidae   Muricidae

GENERA
Colus   Neptunea   Busycon   Melongena

SPECIES
B. pyrum   B. carica   B. canaliculatus   B. perversum

SUBSPECIES
B. carica carica   B. carica eliceans

Modified from an exhibit at the Cranbrook Institute of Science, Bloomfield Hills, Michigan

CLASSIFICATION CHART FOR THE MOLLUSKS

and serves as a creeping sole or a sucking pad by which the creature clings to the rocks. The ancestral mollusk, from which all existing forms have evolved, is believed to have been very similar to the present-day chiton.

4. The *Scaphopoda* are elongate mollusks enclosed in a tapering, conical shell open at both ends and slightly curved. From the larger end project the foot and several slender filaments. Scaphopods live in clean sand, from shallow water to considerable depths. They are commonly called tusk shells or tooth shells.

5. The *Cephalopoda* are highly specialized mollusks, keen of vision and swift in action. The head is armed with a sharp parrot-like beak, and is surrounded by long, flexible tentacles studded with sucking disks. Besides the well-known devilfishes (octopuses), this class includes the delicate Paper Argonaut and the beautiful Pearly Nautilus of Asiatic waters. *Spirula*, a delicate, white, chambered shell sometimes washed up on the beach, belongs to this class, and the beautiful *Ammonites* found in rocks of Jurassic and Cretaceous periods were cephalopods too. The cephalopods of the West Coast are without external shells, and are not included in the text.

Contents

III. West Coast Amphineurans and Scaphopods 112

IV. Gulf of California Pelecypods 118

Appendixes

Index

Illustrations

About This Book

THIS BOOK has been completely rewritten, much new material added, and old material brought up to date. The plan of listing the geographic range, habitat, description, and remarks under boldface headings should make it much easier to use than the first edition. The black and white plates have been completely rebuilt, with many new photographs, and the number of plates increased from 48 to 72. Seven of the 8 color plates are also new. A whole section has been added to include the shells of the Gulf of California, which are illustrated on 23 plates.

Scope: Despite the seven chapters of this *Field Guide*, the basic plan of the book is in three parts. The first part covers the marine shells occurring from Alaska to southern California, the range of some extending to Baja California and even to Panama; the second includes the Gulf of California, with some species that may be found as well on the Pacific coast of Baja California; and the third part deals with the shells of Hawaii. A total of 945 species are described and illustrated by one or more photographs, but it should be understood that the coverage is by no means complete. Some families actually contain hundreds of described species, many of them very rare, and often differing from each other so slightly that only a specialist can tell them apart; and not always is there complete agreement even among the specialists. The author has tried to include all of the common mollusks that the collector is likely to discover on trips to the beaches, and it is hoped that the selection herein presented will prove adequate for building a foundation of knowledge about one of the most interesting groups in nature. For more advanced identification work, the reader is referred to some of the technical works listed in the Bibliography.

Classification: Unlike books on birds or reptiles or minerals, shell books rarely agree on the arrangement of families, or, in other words, the classification of the mollusks. The accepted plan is to begin with the most primitive forms and work up to the most advanced, or complex, forms. This is determined largely by the mollusk's anatomy. The early conchologists were concerned chiefly with the characters of the shell rather than with the soft parts. Modern workers have arrived at a fairly satisfactory listing, certainly better bringing together those forms most closely related, and the classification is constantly being improved as more and more anatomical work is done.

An example: until a few years ago practically all writers began their gastropod sections with the genera *Patella* and *Acmaea* (the true limpets), followed by the keyhole limpets, *Fissurella*, *Diodora*, and so on. It is now recognized that the keyhole limpets are more primitive than the true limpets, so in modern listings they precede them. As more intensive research is done it can occasionally be demonstrated that whole genera should be taken out of one family and placed in another. We can hope that someday the classification will be stabilized, but there may never be complete agreement between equally competent malacologists.

The arrangement in this book is taken from Johannes Thiele's *Handbuch der systematischen Weichtierkunde*, Volumes 1 and 2 (Jena, 1929–35), with some modifications. It is essentially that arrangement adopted by the editors of *Indo-Pacific Mollusca*, published by the Academy of Natural Sciences, Philadelphia. The listing of species within a genus is alphabetical.

Nomenclature: The nomenclature of any branch of natural science is never static, but always subject to change. Although name changes are often annoying to the amateur collector, they are necessary if we are to abide by the rules and eventually arrive at something resembling stability. The International Commission on Zoological Nomenclature is a body set up to formulate rules and pass judgment on such matters; and perhaps the most important rule is the law of priority — the first published name must be the valid one, even if it is mispelled or is misleading. A common lucine of our East Coast carries the specific name of *pensylvanica*, with one *n*, and a helmet from the Caribbean is listed as *Cassis madagascarensis*.

Let us consider the reasons behind a recent name change in a familiar West Coast shell. The well-known Gaper is presently in the genus *Tresus*. This generic name was published by Gray in January 1853. In February, Conrad published the name *Schizothaerus* for the same genus, but of course Gray's name had priority by one month. It was subsequently discovered that the name *Tresus* had been used in 1833 by one Walckenaur for a genus of arachnid. The same generic name may not be used twice, even in different phyla. So the conchologists had to surrender the name to the entomologists. The next in line (Conrad's *Schizothaerus*) was adopted, and the shell has been listed as *"Schizothaerus nuttallii* Conrad" for many years. A few years ago it was found that the arachnid Walckenaur had named *Tresus* in 1833 had been described and named several years before. So *Tresus* became a synomyn, and as such was available to the conchologists. Now our Gaper is properly listed as *"Tresus nuttallii* (Conrad)."

The nomenclature in this *Field Guide* is believed to be as up-to-date as possible before time of publication, but in the years ahead, possibly in the months ahead, there undoubtedly will be additional name changes.

In many listings you will find species, subspecies, and varieties. A *variety* is simply a color form, or perhaps an unusually slender form, occupying the same geographic range as the *typical species*, and it has no taxonomic validity. A *subspecies*, on the other hand, differs slightly but constantly from the typical species; more important, it occupies a different geographic range, so that, except where the two forms meet and perhaps overlap a bit, there can be no intergrades. However, this rule is not absolute, for we have what is termed a *sympatric subspecies*. This is a form slightly but demonstrably different from the typical, which though occupying the same geographic range is confined to a particular ecologic niche, so that ordinarily it does not come in contact with the typical species. A good example of the latter would be the little Kelp-weed Scallop of the California coast (see p. 15). In this book subspecies are not included, except for a few that are well established, easily recognized, and well known.

Measurements: The *length of a bivalve* shell is the distance, in a straight line, from the anterior end to the posterior end. The *height* is a straight line from the dorsal margin to the ventral margin (see illustration, p. xxxii). It should be noted that with some shells, such as *Lima*, the height may be greater than the length. The *anterior end* of a bivalve is usually (but not always) the shorter; that is, it is closer to the beaks than the posterior end, and the beaks generally incline forward. In some cases, especially with orbicular shells, one has to see the interior to be sure. The foot protrudes from the anterior end and the siphons from the posterior. The pallial sinus, when present, opens toward the posterior end. Oysters, irregular in form but commonly elongate, are usually measured in length from the beaks to the opposite end.

Bivalves have *left and right valves*. When a clam is held with the dorsal margin up, and with the anterior end away from the observer, the right valve is on the right and the left valve on the left. With sessile bivalves such as oysters and jewel boxes, one usually refers to the valves as upper and lower. The same is true of some of the scallops, particularly where one valve is deeply cupped (lower) and its mate more or less flat (upper).

With *gastropods* it is always a question whether to give the distance between the apex and the opposite end as height or length. Since most of our snails customarily carry their shells in a horizontal or semihorizontal position, it is probably more correct anatomically to regard this measurement as length; but since virtually all illustrations of gastropods show them with the apex uppermost, that dimension will be given in this book as height. As with the bivalves, there will be some exceptions. With the *limpets* the height is the distance of the apex, or summit, above the place of the snail's attachment, and the length is a straight line from the anterior to the posterior end. *Cowries,* which crawl about on the apertural area and thus have an upper and lower surface, are measured from end to end as length, and length is also used for the maximum distance from apex to aperture in the elongate worm shells (see illustration opposite).

Measurements given in this book refer to average, mature shells. The collector will find many young examples that are smaller than the stated dimensions, and may obtain occasional specimens that exceed them.

Range and Habitat: The ranges cited are based on records compiled over many years by West Coast collectors and on published lists from the leading institutions of the region. Ranges may be extended from time to time as new material is collected. For the purposes of this book the term *shallow water* includes from the tidal area to a depth of about 30 feet, *moderately shallow water* from 30 to about 80 feet, *moderately deep water* from 80 to about 200 feet, and *deep water* anything beyond 200 feet.

Except for cases where space limitation prevented, the color of each shell is given on the legend page for each black and white plate. Where the periostracum is an important factor in the shell's color that fact is noted.

A Field Guide
to Pacific Coast Shells

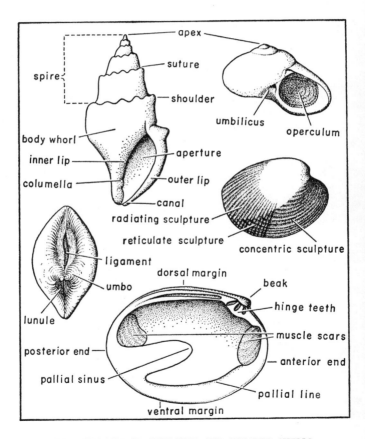

TERMINOLOGY OF UNIVALVE AND BIVALVE SHELLS

West Coast Pelecypods

Family Solemyacidae: Veiled Clams

IN this group the valves are equal and considerably elongated, gaping a little at both ends. A tough and glossy periostracum extends well beyond the margins of the shell. These are uncommon bivalves, living in the muds of from moderate to great depths; seldom to be obtained except by dredging. Commonly known as veiled clams and awning shells, they range from Canada to S. America on both our East and West Coasts.

Genus *Solemya* Lamarck 1818

SOLEMYA JOHNSONI Dall   Veiled Clam   Pl. 9
Range: Oregon to Panama.
Habitat: Deep water generally; mud bottoms.
Description: A rather delicate bivalve, with a remarkable periostracum that projects far beyond the edges of the shell. This covering is thick and tough, elastic and shiny; color greenish black. Growing to a length of 4 in., the shell is elongate and but little inflated. Both ends gently rounded, with beaks closer to the anterior end. No hinge teeth. Both ends of valves radially channeled with broad and deep grooves; glossy periostracum extends from these grooves in a fingerlike fringe; from smoother central part of the shell it projects in a ragged sheet.
Remarks: *S. valvulus* Carp. is a smaller species, about ½ in. long, that may be found closer to shore, from San Pedro, California, south.

Family Nuculidae: Nut Shells

THESE are 3-cornered or oval shells, with a row of teeth on each side of the beak cavity, but with no pit for the ligament between them. Inside pearly, with inner margins crenulate. Small shells, distributed in nearly all seas, but most abundant in cool waters.

Genus *Nucula* Lamarck 1799

NUCULA TENUIS (Mtg.)   **Smooth Nut Shell**   Pl. 9
  Range: Circumpolar; Alaska to Mexico; Greenland to Maryland; n. Europe.
  Habitat: Moderately shallow water; mud bottoms.
  Description: A small nutlike clam, oval-triangular in outline and rather plump in form. Color greenish yellow with a thin olive periostracum; surface shiny. Length only a little more than ¼ in., many specimens even smaller. Beaks small and located near anterior end. Inside of shell white, often polished; margins finely crenulate. A row of prominent teeth along the hinge, 6 before and 9 behind the beaks.
  Remarks: *N. bellottii* A. Adams (Bellott's Nut Shell; see Plate 9, No. 4) is a larger and thinner species, found chiefly in the Arctic Ocean, but ranging down to s. Alaska.

Genus *Acila* H. & A. Adams 1858

ACILA CASTRENSIS (Hinds)   **Sculptured Nut Shell**   Pl. 9
  Range: Alaska to Baja California.
  Habitat: Moderate depth; sandy mud.
  Description: One of the larger members of the Nuculidae. Most specimens just under ½ in., but some individuals larger. On inside they resemble the true *Nucula*, except that margins are not crenulate. On the outside, the shell bears an odd sculpture, being decorated with prominent raised lines that are angular, coming to points at center of the valves. These lines have been likened to a series of steep-walled tents. Color brown.
  Remarks: Formerly listed as *Nucula castrensis*. This bivalve is abundant as a fossil in the Pliocene and Pleistocene deposits of California, Oregon, and Washington.

Family Nuculanidae: Nut Shells and Yoldias

THESE were formerly classed with the Nuculidae. Shells more or less oblong, usually rounded in front and produced into an angle behind. Margins not crenulate. Two series of hinge teeth, separated by an oblique pit for the ligament. Distributed widely, chiefly in cool seas.

Genus *Nuculana* Link 1807

NUCULANA AMBLIA (Dall)   Pl. 9
  Range: Monterey, California.
  Habitat: Fairly deep water.
  Description: Nearly ¾ in. long, the shell is broadly rounded

anteriorly and slightly prolonged posteriorly, where it is bluntly truncate. Bears a greenish-brown periostracum. About 12 robust teeth in front series, and nearly 20 in back series.

NUCULANA BUCCATA (Steens.)   Pl. 9
Range: Circumpolar; south to s. Alaska.
Habitat: Deep water.
Description: A stout little shell about ¾ in. long. It is less pinched out than many of its group. Beaks moderately prominent, and hinge teeth large and sturdy. Shell fairly thick, and pale brown, with a sculpture of closely spaced concentric lines.

NUCULANA FOSSA (Baird)   **Trenched Nut Shell**   Pl. 9
Range: Alaska to Puget Sound.
Habitat: Moderately deep water.
Description: Just over ½ in. long, this is a rather plump shell, the beaks being somewhat swollen. Anterior end is regularly rounded; posterior end narrowed and prolonged, and square at tip. A line extends from beaks to the posterior tip, producing a noticeable angle on that portion of shell. Surface fairly smooth, with only weak concentric lines. Color greenish brown. Teeth of the hinge, in the usual 2 series, very robust.

NUCULANA HAMATA (Carp.)   **Hooked Nut Shell**   Pl. 9
Range: Puget Sound to cent. California.
Habitat: Deep water.
Description: An oddly shaped bivalve, the length about ¼ in. and the shell covered with a thick brownish periostracum. Anterior end regularly rounded, posterior end greatly prolonged and pinched out to a slightly upturned and squarely cut-off tip. Beaks close to anterior end. Valves sculptured with distinct concentric ridges.

NUCULANA MINUTA (Fabr.)   **Minute Nut Shell**   Pl. 9
Range: Arctic Ocean to San Diego, California; also Atlantic Coast.
Habitat: Moderately deep water.
Description: A small species, about ¼ in. long, brownish. The anterior end is broadly rounded, the posterior slightly prolonged and narrowed at the tip, where it is abruptly truncate. Very fine concentric lines decorate the valves.

NUCULANA PERNULA (Müll.)   Pl. 9
Range: Circumpolar; south to Alaska, Europe, Asia.
Habitat: Deep water.
Description: Nearly ¾ in. long, rather thin, with a short, rounded anterior end and a prolonged but only slightly narrowed posterior end. Sculpture consists of rather weak concentric lines. Color olive-green.

NUCULANA REDONDOENSIS Burch   Pl. 9
Redondo Nut Shell
  Range: California.
  Habitat: Moderately shallow water.
  Description: A solid, minute shell, its length about ¼ in. Anterior end rounded and the slightly longer posterior end is drawn to a point. Sculpture of sharp concentric lines. Color whitish. Hinge bears 18 teeth in anterior series, 14 in posterior.
  Remarks: Probably the commonest member of its group in California. Used to be confused with *N. acuta* (Con.) of the Atlantic, but Burch has demonstrated that it is different. Some authors prefer to call it *N. hindsi* (Han.), but it is not certain just where Hanley's type came from.

NUCULANA TAPHRIA (Dall)   **Grooved Nut Shell**   Pl. 9
  Range: Bodega Bay, California, to Baja California.
  Habitat: Moderately shallow water.
  Description: Broader and less elongate than most of its group, and rather plump, the length just over ½ in. It is rounded in front and pointed behind, the low beaks nearly central in position. About 12 teeth on each side of ligament pit. Valves decorated with numerous very fine concentric lines. Color white or yellowish white.

Genus *Yoldia* Möller 1842

YOLDIA COOPERI Gabb   **Cooper's Yoldia**   Pl. 9
  Range: Cent. California to Mexico.
  Habitat: Deep water.
  Description: A rather large bivalve, attaining a length of nearly 3 in., although most individuals are smaller. Shell quite thin, shiny green, and marked with distinct concentric lines. Small beaks situated near posterior end. Anterior end much the larger of the two, and broadly rounded; basal margin continues around in a gentle curve to posterior tip. Area between tip and beaks deeply concave, so that from the side this clam has a hooked appearance. Twelve V-shaped teeth in front series; 40 or more in the back.

YOLDIA LIMATULA Say   **File Yoldia**   Pl. 9
  Range: Northern seas.
  Habitat: Moderate depth; muddy bottoms.
  Description: From 2 to 3 in. long, glossy green. Shell oval, much elongated and thin, with beaks nearly central and not very prominent. Anterior and basal margins regularly rounded, posterior tip pointed and recurved. Interior bluish white, with about 20 sharp teeth on each side of the pit. This streamlined

bivalve may be recognized by its length, which is more than twice as great as its height, and by its peculiarly upturned, snoutlike tip.

Remarks: Very similar examples of this clam are found on both our coasts, as well as in Europe. On West Coast, probably does not get down below Alaska.

YOLDIA MYALIS (Couth.) **Oval Yoldia** Pl. 9
Range: Arctic Ocean to Puget Sound; also Atlantic Coast.
Habitat: Moderately deep water.
Description: A small species, in length averaging 1 in. Thin-shelled, with low beaks that are nearly central in position. Anterior end rounded, posterior bluntly pointed, the valves but little inflated. There is a dark green periostracum, arranged in darker and lighter zones in fresh specimens. Interior yellowish white, with about 12 teeth on each side of beaks.

YOLDIA SCISSURATA Dall Pl. 9
Range: Arctic Ocean to San Diego, California.
Habitat: Moderately deep water.
Description: A rather small oval shell, seldom more than 1½ in. long, the valves quite thin and compressed. Beaks tiny and central. Posterior end rather well pointed, anterior end sharply rounded. A slight hump between the tip and the beaks. Color green and surface quite shiny.

YOLDIA THRACIAEFORMIS (Stor.) **Axe Yoldia** Pl. 9
Range: Circumpolar; south to Oregon and Maine.
Habitat: Moderately shallow water; mud.
Description: About 2 in. long, a grayish-brown shell shaped something like the blade of an axe. An oblique fold extends from the beaks to posterior 3rd of shell at basal margin, giving the exterior a wavy appearance. Ligament pit under the beaks is large and spoonlike, with about 12 robust teeth on each side. A minutely wrinkled yellowish-brown periostracum; inside of shell chalky white.

Family Arcidae: Ark Shells

THE shell is rigid, strongly ribbed (cancellated), the hinge line bearing numerous teeth arranged in a line on both valves. There is usually a heavy, commonly bristly periostracum. There is no siphon. Some members of this family crawl about in sand or mud, some prefer to live among stones, attached by a silky byssus. Worldwide in distribution, from shallow water to great depths. Extremely abundant in some parts of the world, this group is poorly represented on our West Coast.

Genus *Barbatia* Gray 1847

BARBATIA BAILYI (Bar.)   **Baily's Ark**   **Pl. 9**
    Range: Santa Monica, California, to Gulf of California.
    Habitat: Stones and pebbles at low tide.
    Description: Length less than ½ in. Color yellowish white. A moderately elongate shell; anterior end short and rounded, posterior deeper and bluntly pointed. Surface decorated with strong radiating ribs. Across the hinge line is a series of well-developed comblike teeth.
    Remarks: This species has been listed as *Arca pernoides* Carp., but that name is now believed to belong to quite another shell.

Genus *Anadara* Deshayes 1830

ANADARA MULTICOSTATA (Sow.)   **Many-ribbed Ark**   **Pl. 9**
    Range: San Diego, California, south to Galápagos Is.
    Habitat: Moderately shallow water.
    Description: Nearly 4 in. long. A strong and solid clam, rather squarish, or boxlike in shape, and possessing usual row of robust teeth along the hinge. As name implies, sculptured with many prominent ribs. Color ivory-white, with a velvety brown periostracum in life.
    Remarks: This species is very common along the Mexican coast, but is rare as far north as California.

Family Glycymeridae: Bittersweet Shells

SHELL solid, usually orbicular. Teeth chevron-shaped and arranged in a curving row at the hinge. Occurring in shallow to moderately deep water, chiefly in warm seas.

Genus *Glycymeris* Da Costa 1778

GLYCYMERIS SUBOBSOLETA (Carp.)   **Bittersweet**   **Pl. 9**
    Range: Aleutian Is. to Baja California.
    Habitat: Moderate depths.
    Description: Commonest member of the genus along much of our West Coast. A fairly solid small bivalve, nearly round in shape and only slightly inflated. Diam. about ¾ in. Beaks central and rather prominent. Inside, the shell bears 2 curving rows of compressed hinge teeth and the shell margins are strongly crenulate. Color yellowish gray; a heavy periostracum during life.

Family Philobryidae: Minute Pens

MINUTE bivalves, shaped something like tiny pinnas. The shell is strong and solid for its size and is well inflated.

Genus *Philobrya* Carpenter 1872

PHILOBRYA SETOSA (Carp.)   Pl. 10
    Range: Alaska to Gulf of California.
    Habitat: Shallow water.
    Description: A very tiny clam, not much more than ⅛ in. long. Shape elongate-triangular; looks like a miniature but plump pen shell of the genus *Pinna*. Valves rather solid, varying from rich brown to salmon; interior pearly.

Family Mytilidae: Mussels

SHELLS equivalve, the hinge line long and the umbones sharp. Some members burrow in soft rock or clay, but the majority are fastened by a byssus. Many of these mussels are edible but seldom are eaten in this country. In Europe the mussel is "farmed," much the same as the oyster is here, and it forms an important item of food across the sea. Mussels are worldwide, being best represented in cool waters.

Genus *Mytilus* Linné 1758

MYTILUS CALIFORNIANUS (Con.)   **California Mussel Pl. 10**
    Range: Aleutian Is. to Socorro I., Mexico.
    Habitat: Water's edge; rocks.
    Description: A fine large mussel, attaining a length of some 5 to 7 in. Shell considerably elongated; narrow anterior margin straight and posterior margin curved. Beaks at apex of a long triangle. Ribs prominent, especially near basal margins, but not very numerous. Usual color bluish black, although young specimens often show streaks of brown and white.

MYTILUS EDULIS Linné   **Bay Mussel**   Pl. 10
    Range: Nearly worldwide; Alaska to Cedros I., Mexico.
    Habitat: Rocky situations inshore; in colonies.
    Description: Shell elongate-triangular, rather plump, with the scarcely noticeable beaks at the apex. Length about 3 in. on the average. Adult shells are deep bluish black, with a shiny periostracum; juveniles show various shades of gray, green, and brown, often exhibiting rays of color.

Remarks: Sometimes called Blue Mussel or Blue Clam. This is the edible mussel of Europe, where it is regularly cultivated for profit.

Genus *Hormomya* Mörch 1853

HORMOMYA ADAMSIANA (Dun.)   **Stearns' Mussel**   Pl. 10
  Range: Santa Barbara, California, to S. America.
  Habitat: Shallow water.
  Description: Shell fan-shaped, growing to a length of 1 in. In appearance much like the next clam, *Septifer bifurcatus*, but without small "deck" under beaks. Margins strongly crenulate, suggesting teeth along inner margin on anterior side. Color purplish brown; interior tinged with purple.
  Remarks: Common in the Gulf of California. This species is listed in older books as *Mytilus stearnsi* Pils. & Ray. Both names apparently apply to what is really a single species. Dunker's name has priority. It has also been listed as *Brachidontes adamsianus*.

Genus *Septifer* Récluz 1848

SEPTIFER BIFURCATUS (Con.)   **Platform Mussel**   Pl. 10
  Range: Crescent City, California, to Mexico.
  Habitat: Shallow water.
  Description: A small species, length averaging about 1½ in. Anterior margin considerably flattened, posterior curved. There is a small shelly platform (diaphragm) stretched across the interior of each valve, near the beaks. Surface sculptured with narrow but prominent ribs which bifurcate, or fork. Color dark purplish brown.

Genus *Modiolus* Lamarck 1799

MODIOLUS CAPAX (Con.)   **Fat Horse Mussel**   Pls. 1, 11
  Range: Santa Cruz, California, to Peru.
  Habitat: Moderately deep water.
  Description: Length averages about 4 in. The shell is elongate, considerably inflated, broadly rounded at the basal margin, and bluntly rounded at the top. Color chestnut-brown, with a thin periostracum; when this peels off the shell is often pinkish red. Interior bluish, tinged with yellow.

MODIOLUS DEMISSUS (Dill.)   **Ribbed Mussel**   Pl. 11
  Range: California coast.
  Habitat: Muddy shores.
  Description: Shell considerably elongate and moderately thin in substance. Surface bears many radiating, somewhat undu-

lating, ribs that occasionally branch. Color yellowish green, the interior silvery white.

Remarks: This is an Atlantic species introduced on the West Coast, probably with seed oysters. It appears to favor semi-brackish, even polluted waters. It is sometimes listed as *M. plicatulus* Lam., and has been placed in the genus *Brachidontes* by some authors, and in *Arcuatula* by others.

MODIOLUS FLABELLATUS (Gould)   Pl. 25
Fan-shaped Horse Mussel
  Range: Vancouver I. to San Diego, California.
  Habitat: Moderately deep water.
  Description: Attains a length of more than 7 in. Beaks elevated and set close to anterior end, which is short and abruptly rounded. Shell moderately solid and well inflated. Shell whitish lavender; periostracum dark chestnut-brown, and glossy. Interior pearly white, often with a pinkish tinge.
  Remarks: Regarded by some authorities as a subspecies of *M. rectus* (Con.).

MODIOLUS MODIOLUS (Linné)   **Horse Mussel**   Pl. 11
  Range: Worldwide in northern seas; south to Monterey, California.
  Habitat: Moderately deep water.
  Description: Brownish to deep purplish black, this mussel grows to be 7 in. long; old specimens have fairly thick and heavy shells. Tough and leathery periostracum; inside of shell more or less pearly.
  Remarks: Spreading south from the Arctic, this big mussel is found offshore in Norway and Japan, as well as on both our East and West Coasts. Throughout its wide range this mollusk is regarded as unfit food for man.

MODIOLUS RECTUS (Con.)   **Straight Horse Mussel**   Pl. 11
  Range: B.C. to Gulf of California.
  Habitat: Moderately deep water.
  Description: A straight-shelled mussel almost as big at the beak end as at other end. Valves thin and rather fragile, average length about 4 in. Near the hinge, the periostracum is glossy and dark brown; near the opposite end, paler brown and provided with numerous hairy projections. Interior white.

Genus *Musculus* Röding 1798

MUSCULUS DISCORS (Linné)   Pl. 10
  Range: Arctic Ocean to Puget Sound; also North Atlantic Coast.
  Habitat: Moderately deep water.
  Description: A plump shell, length about 1 in. Anterior end very

short, posterior end broadly rounded. Beaks moderately prominent. There are a few coarse radiating lines on front of shell, and many crowded lines at the back, with a relatively smooth area between. Periostracum shiny and nearly black; interior of shell bluish white.

Remarks: This mussel is often found adhering to the stalks of seaweeds cast up on the beach.

MUSCULUS NIGER (Gray)　**Little Black Mussel**　　**Pl. 10**
　　Range: South to Oregon; also North Atlantic Coast.
　　Habitat: Moderately deep water.
　　Description: Small, brownish black, about 1½ in. long. Shell plumply oval, slightly produced at posterior end. Beaks fairly prominent, placed some distance from anterior end. Surface bears a network of very faint, crowded growth lines and radiating lines, the latter lacking on an area midway of each valve. Periostracum rusty brown; interior pearly.

MUSCULUS SENHOUSIA (Ben.)　**Japanese Mussel**　　**Pl. 15**
　　Range: Puget Sound to San Francisco Bay.
　　Habitat: Shallow water.
　　Description: A small and fragile mussel, its length seldom more than 1 in. Beaks are low, the anterior end is short and acutely rounded, and the posterior end is long and deeply rounded. Color greenish yellow, with several wavy bars of pale brown on the posterior slope. Interior purplish gray, often with the brownish bars showing through.
　　Remarks: This bivalve is at home in Japan and the Philippine Is., but it has gained a foothold on our shores, probably having been introduced with oysters from Japan.

MUSCULUS SUBSTRIATA (Gray)　**Nestling Mussel**　　**Pl. 10**
　　Range: Arctic Ocean to Puget Sound.
　　Habitat: Moderately deep water.
　　Description: About 1 in. long, a dark yellowish-brown mussel. Shell oblong-oval, swollen, and a little broader at anterior end. Surface bears minute concentric lines, slightly excavated in a channel across middle of valve.
　　Remarks: This mussel constructs a nest of byssal threads among the stones and pebbles.

Genus *Crenella* Brown 1827

CRENELLA DECUSSATA (Mtg.)　**Netted Crenella**　　**Pl. 11**
　　Range: Arctic Ocean to San Pedro, California; also Atlantic Coast.
　　Habitat: Just off shore; mud.
　　Description: About ½ in. long. This is a well-inflated shell,

obliquely oval, swollen, and quite fragile. Surface sculptured with numerous crowded radiating lines, and often appears beaded owing to faint concentric lines. Inner surface pearly, margins crenulate. A thin yellowish-brown periostracum.

Remarks: A common shell in the stomachs of bottom-feeding fishes.

Genus *Adula* H. & A. Adams 1857

ADULA CALIFORNIENSIS (Phil.)   Pl. 11
California Pea-pod Shell

Range: Vancouver I. to San Diego, California.

Habitat: Burrows in clay.

Description: About 1 in. long; deep brownish-black color, with a heavy, smooth, and shiny periostracum. Interior bluish gray. Shell elongate and somewhat cylindrical; rounded at each end, posterior end a little broader. Beaks low and situated close to anterior end.

Remarks: This species, and *A. falcata* (below), will be found in most books under the genus *Botula* Mörch 1853, but it has recently been determined that there are no true members of that genus in our waters.

ADULA FALCATA (Gould)   **Pea-pod Shell**   Pl. 11

Range: Oregon to Baja California.

Habitat: Bores in solid rock.

Description: At least 3 in. long when fully grown, and not much more than ½ in. high. Shell fragile, with anterior end rounded and dilated, the posterior end drawn out to a lengthy blunt point. Shell covered with a thick brownish periostracum that shows numerous wrinkles. Interior white, more or less pearly.

Remarks: This delicate bivalve bores a cylindrical hole in solid rock, and lives safely ensconced in its stony home, fastened by a silky byssus. This and *A. californiensis* (above) will be found in most books under the name of *Botula* Mörch 1853, but it is generally recognized now that there are no true members of that genus in our waters.

Genus *Lithophaga* Röding 1798

LITHOPHAGA ARISTATA (Dill.)   Pl. 11

Range: La Jolla, California, to Peru.

Habitat: Bores in rocks.

Description: Pale brown and cylindrical, length about 1 in. This clam is instantly recognized by the processes that extend from the extremity of each valve and cross each other.

Remarks: Sometimes called the Scissor Date Shell.

LITHOPHAGA PLUMULA (Han.)   **Rock Borer**   Pl. 11

Range: Monterey, California, to Patagonia.

Habitat: Bores in rocks and dead shells.

Description: Length somewhat more than 1 in., color rusty brown. Shell elongate and cylindrical, rounded at posterior end and gracefully tapering at anterior end.

Remarks: This bivalve lives in neat round holes it bores in solid rock, and also in large dead shells of such as members of the genera *Chama* and *Spondylus*. Some authorities regard the northern specimens as a subspecies, restricting the typical *L. plumula* to Mexico and S. America, and list the California specimens as *L. plumula kelseyi* Hert. & Strong.

Family Isognomonidae: Purse Shells

SHELLS thin and compressed. Hinge with numerous vertical grooves for the divided ligament. Interior pearly. Confined to warm seas.

Genus *Isognomon* Solander 1786

ISOGNOMON CHEMNITZIANA (Orb.)   **Purse Shell**   Pl. 10

Range: S. California (?) to Chile.

Habitat: Shallow water; brush or stones.

Description: About 1½ in. long and some 2 in. high. Upper valve almost flat, and the lower but little arched. Hinge line straight, with vertical grooves on inside, and rest of the shell extends like a pouch from this hinge area. Surface may be smooth or scaly, color usually deep purplish black, although it may be grayish yellow. Inside of shell has a pearly layer that does not extend all the way to margins.

Remarks: There is some question as to whether or not this species is presently living in the waters of s. California. It is abundant in the Gulf of California. This group has been listed under several generic names, including *Perna*, *Melina*, and *Pedalion*. It is a colonial bivalve, generally found in congested clusters.

Family Pteriidae: Pearl Oysters

IN this group the shell is inequivalve, the lower valve with an opening, or notch, for the attachment of the byssus. Occurring in warm seas, this family includes the valuable pearl oysters.

Genus *Pteria* Scopoli 1777

PTERIA STERNA (Gould)   **Winged Oyster**   Pls. 1, 10
  Range: California to Panama.
  Habitat: Shallow water; weedy muds.
  Description: A rather thin, obliquely oval shell with a slender
  wing projecting on the posterior end that may be extremely long
  or moderately short. Beaks low and situated close to anterior
  end. Length 3 or 4 in. Color deep purplish brown, with occasional paler rays. The shell bears a wrinkled periostracum.
  Interior highly iridescent.

Family Pinnidae: Pen Shells

LARGE, wedge-shaped bivalves, thin and brittle, gaping at the
posterior end. They are attached by a large and strong byssus,
and there are large muscles in both valves. Natives of warm seas,
some members grow to a length of more than 2 ft., and occasional
specimens contain black pearls. The pen shells live buried in the
muds and gravels, secured by the silky byssus, with just the top
of the broad edge visible.

Genus *Atrina* Gray 1847

ATRINA OLDROYDII Dall   **Oldroyd's Pen Shell**   Pl. 9
  Range: S. California.
  Habitat: Moderately deep water.
  Description: Shape triangular, with the beaks at the apex.
  Ventral margin rounded, dorsal margin nearly straight. Valves
  gape somewhat. Length about 4 in. Shell thin in substance and
  almost black, and attached by a silky byssus.
  Remarks: This is a rare shell, only a few examples having been
  collected. The type locality, where the first specimen was discovered, and subsequently sent to Dall by the person whose
  name it bears, Mrs. Ida S. Oldroyd, was in 25 fathoms of water
  off San Pedro, California.

Family Pectinidae: Scallops

THESE are the scallops. The valves are commonly unequal in
shape, the lower one convex and upper one flat or concave. Surface
usually ribbed, margins scalloped. Juvenile specimens sometimes
attached by a byssus, but adults are generally free-swimming,
traveling about in a jerky manner by rapidly opening and closing
their valves. Valves powered by a single large muscle — the only
part of the scallop we eat. There is a row of tiny eyes fringing the

edge of the mantle, each complete with cornea, lens, and optic nerve. Scallops are found in all seas, from shallow water to great depths. Shells of this family have always had a certain appeal to the artistic. The Crusaders used the shell of *Pecten jacobaeus* (Linné) from the Mediterranean as a badge of honor, and at the present time a scallop shell is the well-known trademark of a great oil company.

Genus *Pecten* Müller 1776

PECTEN CAURINUS Gould   **Weathervane Scallop**   Pl. 12
   Range: Alaska to Humboldt Bay, California.
   Habitat: Moderately deep water.
   Description: Somewhat compressed, both valves but little arched, reaching a length of 6–8 in. Valves rather thick and solid, decorated with about 20 broad and sturdy ribs. Wings, or ears, nearly equal. Color purplish red on upper surface; lower valve white or pale pinkish.
   Remarks: Sometimes known as the Giant Pacific Scallop.

PECTEN DIEGENSIS Dall   **San Diego Scallop**   Pl. 13
   Range: Monterey, California, to Mexico.
   Habitat: Moderately deep water.
   Description: Another large scallop, but not as large as *P. caurinus* (above). Diam. averages about 4 in. One valve is concave, and its mate is more flat. Sculpture consists of from 16 to 20 rather squarish ribs, sometimes with faint grooves down their crests; wings about equal. The flattish valve is rosy brown, commonly more or less mottled; arched valve usually unspotted and paler in color, often white or yellowish.

Genus *Chlamys* Röding 1798

CHLAMYS HASTATUS (Sow.)   **Spear Scallop**   Pl. 14
   Range: Monterey, California, to San Diego.
   Habitat: Moderately deep water.
   Description: About 2 in. long. Wings unequal, the posterior one almost absent. Upper valve bears about 8 elevated ribs, each with a series of sharp, scalelike spines; spaces between the ribs bear smaller spiny ribs. Color ranges from red to purple to yellow.
   Remarks: A rather uncommon bivalve.

CHLAMYS HERICIUS (Gould)   **Pink Scallop**   Pls. 2, 14
   Range: Alaska to San Diego, California.
   Habitat: Moderately deep water.
   Description: About 3 in. long, generally a little less. Surface sculptured with prominent radiating ribs that are scaly, those

on the lower valve closer together than those on the upper. Lower valve is paler in tone, often white, while upper valve is handsomely marked with broad rays of pink or lavender.
Remarks: Some authors regard this scallop as a subspecies of *C. hastatus.*

CHLAMYS ISLANDICUS (Müll.)   **Iceland Scallop**   **Pl. 14**
   Range: Circumpolar; south to Puget Sound.
   Habitat: Moderately deep water.
   Description: From 3 to 4 in. long. Color ranges from pale to dark reddish brown. Upper valve a bit more convex than lower, and it bears 50 or more crowded radiating ribs that are set with tiny erect scales. Wings very unequal, the posterior one shorter.

CHLAMYS RUBIDUS (Hinds)   **Hinds' Scallop**   **Pl. 15**
   Range: Bering Sea to San Diego, California.
   Habitat: Moderately deep water.
   Description: Shell about 2 in. long, sculptured with some 25 closely set ribs with narrow interspaces. Wings unequal, posterior one considerably expanded. Color ranges from pink to white, the upper valve bearing the darkest shade.
   Remarks: This scallop has long been known as *Chlamys* (or *Pecten*) *hindsi* Carp. Unfortunately, this well-known name must now be discarded and the name given by Hinds in 1845 used instead.

Genus *Leptopecten* Verrill 1897

LEPTOPECTEN LATIAURATUS (Con.)   **Pls. 2, 15**
Kelp-weed Scallop
   Range: San Francisco Bay to Baja California.
   Habitat: Shallow water; *L. l. latiauratus* (Con.), on rocks and in sand; *L. l. monotimeris* (Con.), on seaweeds.
   Description: A colorful shell about 1 in. long. Valves thin and rather delicate, with wings that are equal in size. About 12 rounded ribs ornament the shell, but they are not very prominent. Color usually yellow-brown or orange-brown, with zigzag markings of white. The subspecies *monotimeris* is slightly smaller, with less prominent wings.

Genus *Delectopecten* Stewart 1930

DELECTOPECTEN VANCOUVERENSIS (Whit.)   **Pl. 14**
Transparent Scallop
   Range: Bering Sea to San Diego, California.
   Habitat: Moderately deep water.
   Description: A tiny scallop seldom more than $\frac{1}{4}$ in. long. Shell is equivalve and somewhat compressed, the hinge line relatively

long. Surface marked with exceedingly small, irregular, and densely crowded radiating lines. Valves thin and fragile, almost transparent, with a tinge of yellowish gray.

Genus *Propeamussium* Gregorio 1883

PROPEAMUSSIUM ALASKENSE (Dall)   **Pl. 15**
 Range: Pribilof Is. to California.
 Habitat: Deep water.
 Description: Small and distinctly fan-shaped, diam. about 1 in. Wings unequal and the hinge line short. Outer surface decorated with minute radiating lines; the inner surface bears larger and coarser radiating lines, or ribs, especially prominent near the margins. Color silvery gray.

Genus *Hinnites* Defrance 1821

HINNITES MULTIRUGOSUS (Gale)   **Pl. 15**
Giant Rock Scallop
 Range: Aleutian Is. to Baja California.
 Habitat: Moderately shallow water.
 Description: A peculiar bivalve that starts life as a free-swimming scallop, but later on settles upon some object and becomes sessile. Attached by the lower valve, and soon grows into an irregular, oblong shape. Length may be anywhere from 3 to 10 in. Shell attains considerable thickness, and is sculptured with numerous and crowded wrinkled lines. Color reddish to grayish white, but as the shell increases in size it becomes coarse and the colors tend to fade. Interior white, stained with rich purple near the hinge.
 Remarks: This scallop that has decided to live like an oyster used to be listed under the name *H. giganteus* (Gray).

Family Limidae: File Shells

SHELLS obliquely oval and winged on one side. The ends are gaping. Hinge toothless, with a triangular pit for the ligament. Color usually white. Members of this family are commonly called file shells and scoop shells. They about equal scallops in swimming ability, but they dart about in the opposite direction, with the hinge foremost, often trailing a long sheaf of filaments. They are worldwide in distribution, and there are many fossil forms.

Genus *Lima* Bruguière 1797

LIMA HEMPHILLI Hert. & Strong   **Hemphill's File**   **Pl. 11**
 Range: Monterey, California, to Mexico.
 Habitat: Shallow water.

Description: A neat shell, somewhat compressed, and obliquely oval in outline. Length about 1 in. Anterior end fairly straight and gaping, the posterior somewhat rounded. Wings very small. Pure white in color, the surface is ornamented with narrow and sharp radiating lines, like the teeth of a file.

Genus *Limatula* Wood 1839

LIMATULA SUBAURICULATA (Mtg.)   **Pl. 11**
  Range: Alaska to Mexico.
  Habitat: Shallow water.
  Description: A tiny white clam, less than $\frac{1}{2}$ in. long. Elongate-oval in shape, with the hinge at the top, and sculptured with very fine radiating lines. Two lines, or ribs, along middle of shell stronger and more conspicuous; these can usually be seen on inside of shell.

Family Ostreidae: Oysters

SHELLS irregular and inequivalve, often large and heavy. The lower valve usually adheres to some object, and the upper valve is somewhat smaller as a rule. Distribution worldwide, in temperate and warm seas.

Genus *Ostrea* Linné 1758

OSTREA LURIDA Carp.   **California Oyster**   **Pl. 9**
  Range: Alaska to Baja California.
  Habitat: Shallow water; stony bottoms.
  Description: About 2 in. long, the shape quite irregular, according to the outlines of the object on which it grows. Color brownish gray. Valves are not especially thick or heavy. There are 2 varieties: *O. l. expansa* Carp., which is roundish and often fluted at the margins, and *O. l. laticaudata* Carp., which is more slender and elongate, and often reddish in hue. Both are considered excellent eating in spite of their relatively small size.
  Remarks: This is the common native oyster along the West Coast. Two other species of oyster have been introduced in Pacific Coast waters. *Crassostrea virginica* (Gmel.), the well-known commercial shellfish of the Atlantic seaboard, and *C. gigas* (Thun.), the Japanese oyster.

Family Anomiidae: Jingle Shells

THESE are thin, more or less translucent bivalves, usually pearly within. They are attached to some solid object by a fleshy byssus that passes through a hole or notch in the lower valve. This byssus becomes calcified, and the mollusk is permanently fixed. Chiefly natives of warm and temperate seas.

Genus *Anomia* Linné 1758

ANOMIA PERUVIANA Orb.   **Jingle Shell**   Pl. 10
Range: San Diego, California, to Peru.
Habitat: Shallow water.
Description: A rather thin shell, about 1 in. long, sometimes a little more. Color pale yellowish green. Rests on its lower valve, which is perforated near the beak for passage of a muscular byssus by which the clam adheres to some stone or dead shell on ocean floor. It is the upper, concave valve that is commonly washed ashore after the mollusk dies. Irregularly circular, the shell has a waxy luster.

Genus *Pododesmus* Philippi 1837

PODODESMUS CEPIO (Gray)   **Pearly Monia**   Pls. 2, 10
Range: B.C. to Gulf of California.
Habitat: Moderately shallow water.
Description: Resembling *Anomia peruviana* (above) but much larger, up to 4 in. long. Of heavier build; lower valve the smaller of the two, and bears a large round hole for the attaching byssus. Upper valve roughly circular, although it may be distorted. Color yellowish white; surface irregularly ribbed. Interior pearly, usually tinged with green and purple around hinge; prominent dark muscle scar directly over the perforation.
Remarks: This bivalve used to be listed as *P. macroschisma* (Desh.), but that name is now restricted to a form that occurs in the extreme north.

Family Astartidae: Astartes

SMALL brownish pelecypods, usually with concentric furrows. Shell thick and solid, the soft parts commonly bright-colored. There are many species; distributed in cold seas around the world.

Genus *Astarte* Sowerby 1816

ASTARTE ALASKENSIS Dall   **Alaska Astarte**   Pl. 11
Range: Alaska to Puget Sound.
Habitat: Moderately shallow water.
Description: About 1 in. long, more or less triangular in outline, the surface bearing evenly spaced concentric ridges and furrows that cover the entire shell from the beaks to the margins. There is a dark brown periostracum; interior chalky white.

ASTARTE BOREALIS Schum.   **Northern Astarte**   Pl. 11
  Range: Circumpolar; south to s. Alaska.
  Habitat: Moderately deep water.
  Description: A somewhat larger species than *A. alaskensis*
  (above), averaging about 1¼ in. Shell is less triangular — more
  oval — than *A. alaskensis*. Beaks rather low and centrally
  located. Surface bears distinct concentric furrows on the upperpart of each valve, but they fade toward the margins. As with
  all of the astartes, color is deep brown, the interior white.

ASTARTE ESQUIMALTI Baird   **Esquimalt Astarte**   Pl. 11
  Range: Aleutian Is. to Puget Sound.
  Habitat: Moderately deep water.
  Description: A small member of the genus, about ½ in. long.
  General shape like that of other astartes, with beaks at top of a
  blunt triangle. Color rich brown. Unlike the others, this one has
  a peculiar sculpture that immediately identifies it; a number of
  irregular concentric ridges, occasionally interrupted.
  Remarks: This species could be classed as fairly uncommon.

ASTARTE FABULA Reeve   Pl. 11
  Range: Bering Sea to B.C.
  Habitat: Moderately deep water.
  Description: A small dark brown bivalve about 1 in. long.
  Shape roughly triangular, with both ends rounded, the pos-
  terior bearing a more prominent slope. Valves thick and solid;
  dull white on inside. Sculpture consists of small but sharp con-
  centric ridges, most conspicuous on upper portions of shell.

Family Carditidae: Carditas

SMALL, generally swollen shells, equivalve and usually strongly
ribbed. There is an erect, robust tooth under the umbones. These
bivalves are found in warm, temperate, and cold seas.

Genus *Cardita* Bruguière 1792

CARDITA CARPENTERI Lamy   **Carpenter's Cardita**   Pl. 11
  Range: B.C. to Baja California.
  Habitat: Water's edge; under stones.
  Description: An elongate shell, usually about ¼ in. long. Beaks
  very small. Posterior end lengthened and rounded; anterior
  short and nearly straight. Surface sculptured with strong
  radiating lines or ridges. Color brownish gray, sometimes more
  or less mottled; interior purplish.

CARDITA VENTRICOSA Gould   **Stout Cardita**   **Pl. 11**
  Range: Alaska to Coronado Is., Mexico.
  Habitat: Moderately shallow water.
  Description: Small but solid; length ¾ in. Outline circular, with very prominent, highly elevated beaks. As the name implies, the valves are well inflated. Shell decorated with about 20 radiating ribs crossed by minute concentric lines. Margins of shell scalloped. Color whitish, with a velvety-brown periostracum.
  Remarks: A similar species is found off Redondo Beach, California, which is stouter and the concentric sculpture more pronounced. This has been named *C. redondoensis* Burch (Redondo Cardita; see Plate 11, No. 18), but is believed by some authors to be *C. ventricosa stearnsi* Dall.

Genus *Miodontiscus* Dall 1903

MIODONTISCUS PROLONGATUS (Carp.)   **Pl. 17**
  Range: Alaska to San Diego, California.
  Habitat: Moderately shallow water.
  Description: A small shell, the length slightly less than ½ in. Beaks are high; shell is obliquely round, with anterior end a little longer than posterior. Shell relatively thick and solid, sculptured with about 10 broadly rounded radiating ribs with very narrow grooves between them. Color white.

Family Diplodontidae: Thyasiras

SMALL, roundish, very well inflated bivalves. The surface is smooth and polished. Also known as Ungulinidae.

Genus *Diplodonta* Bronn 1831

DIPLODONTA ORBELLA (Gould)   **Orb Diplodonta**   **Pl. 17**
  Range: Bering Sea to Gulf of California.
  Habitat: Moderately deep water.
  Description: A small, thin-shelled white clam that is so inflated it is almost globular. Length is about 1 in., outline is circular. Beaks small.
  Remarks: This mollusk often builds a nest by cementing sand grains and mucus, leaving long tubelike openings for the siphon.

Genus *Thyasira* Lamarck 1818

THYASIRA BISECTA Con.   **Cleft Thyasira**   **Pl. 11**
  Range: Alaska to Oregon.
  Habitat: Moderately deep water.
  Description: A large shell for this family, attaining a length of

about 2 in. It is a sturdy shell, with beaks at extreme anterior end, and that end is abruptly truncate. Posterior end long and rounded, with a distinct furrow, or cleft, extending from beaks to tip, so that that portion of the shell is 2-lobed. Valves moderately thick, well inflated, grayish white, and marked only by lines of growth.

THYASIRA GOULDII (Phil.)   **Gould's Thyasira**   Pl. 11
  Range: Bering Sea to San Diego, California.
  Habitat: Moderately deep water.
  Description: A small shell, less than ½ in. long as a rule. It is whitish, relatively thick and solid, and roughly triangular in shape. Beaks nearly central, the anterior end rather sharply rounded and posterior end divided by a cleft running from beaks to the tip.

Genus *Axinopsida* Chavan 1951

AXINOPSIDA SERICATA (Carp.)   **Silky Axinopsida**   Pl. 11
  Range: Alaska to Baja California.
  Habitat: Shallow water; sand and mud.
  Description: A tiny mollusk, only about ⅛ in. long. Shell almost circular, highly polished, and covered with a greenish-brown periostracum that is quite fragile when dry.
  Remarks: This genus was formerly listed as *Axinopsis* Sars.

Family Lucinidae: Lucines

SHELLS generally round, compressed, and equivalve, with beaks that are small and well formed. Members of this family are distributed in temperate, tropical, and cool seas, and are usually white.

Genus *Lucina* Bruguière 1797

LUCINA ANNULATA Reeve   **Ringed Lucina**   Pl. 16
  Range: Alaska to Coronado Is., Mexico.
  Habitat: Moderately deep water.
  Description: A fine, large clam 3 in. or more in length. Shell circular and somewhat compressed, the dorsal margins rather flat and the rest of the shell gently curving. Beaks nearly central. Valves ornamented with evenly spaced, sharp concentric ridges. Color white.

LUCINA APPROXIMATA (Dall)   Pl. 16
  Range: Monterey, California, to Panama.
  Habitat: Moderately shallow water.
  Description: Small and white, only about ¼ in. long. Circular in outline and fairly well inflated. There is a sculpture of radiating lines that are easily seen, even on such a dimunitive shell.

LUCINA NUTTALLI Con.   Nuttall's Lucina   Pl. 16
  Range: Monterey, California, to Mexico.
  Habitat: Moderately shallow water.
  Description: Diam. about 1 in. Another shell that is more or
  less circular in outline. Valves are rather solid and moderately
  inflated. Color is pure white. Surface marked with sharp lines,
  both radiating and concentric.

LUCINA TENUISCULPTA (Carp.)   Fine-lined Lucina   Pl. 16
  Range: Alaska to Baja California.
  Habitat: Shallow water.
  Description: A small white shell, nearly circular in outline, its
  length about ½ in. There is a thin gray periostracum; beneath
  this the shell is sculptured with very faint concentric lines and
  even weaker radiating lines. Beaks fairly prominent.

Genus *Epilucina* Dall 1901

EPILUCINA CALIFORNICA (Con.)   California Lucina   Pl. 16
  Range: Crescent City, California, to Baja California.
  Habitat: Moderately shallow water.
  Description: Another pure-white shell with a circular outline,
  the length about 1½ in. Surface bears concentric lines, but they
  are not sharp and distinct. As with the others of this group,
  posterior muscle scar small and round but anterior scar very
  long and narrow.

Family Chamidae: Jewel Boxes

SHELLS thick and heavy, irregular, and inequivalve. They are
attached to some solid object, the fixed valve being the larger and
more convex. Natives of warm seas.

Genus *Chama* Linné 1758

CHAMA PELLUCIDA Brod.   Agate Jewel Box   Pl. 16
  Range: Oregon to Baja California.
  Habitat: Moderately shallow water.
  Description: A very strong and robust shell, usually circular in
  outline, about 2 in. long. The mollusk lives attached to a stone
  or dead shell fastened by its left valve, beyond the low-water
  level, commonly wedged in coral growths; although the free
  valve is washed ashore frequently, one usually has to use a
  hammer and chisel to collect entire specimens. Both valves
  decorated with concentric wrinkles, some of them bladelike.
  The color may be white or cream, often with rosy rays; interior
  like white china; whole shell curiously translucent.

Genus *Pseudochama* Odhner 1917

PSEUDOCHAMA EXOGYRA (Con.)   Pl. 16
Reversed Jewel Box
  Range: Oregon to Baja California.
  Habitat: Moderately shallow water.
  Description: This bivalve has about the same size and general
  shape as *Chama pellucida* (above), but it is attached by its right
  valve, and the beaks have a sinistral twist; with *C. pellucida* the
  twist is dextral. Valves thick and solid, sculptured with irregular
  wrinkles. Color dull white, sometimes tinged with greenish.
  Remarks: This is a rather common shell near shore, but it is not
  nearly as attractive as *Chama pellucida*.

Family Leptonidae: Leptons

SMALL, smooth, and thin-shelled bivalves, chiefly nestling in small
crevices and old shells. Worldwide.

Genus *Kellia* Turton 1822

KELLIA LAPEROUSII (Desh.)   **Kelly Shell**   Pl. 17
  Range: Pribilof Is. to Panama.
  Habitat: Moderately shallow water.
  Description: A neat little shell, pale brown, smooth and shining,
  and about 1 in. long. Beaks almost central, both ends gently
  rounded. Valves are thin, but well inflated.
  Remarks: This bivalve may be found nestling in small rocky
  crevices.

Family Cardiidae: Cockles

SHELLS equivalve and heart-shaped, sometimes gaping a little at
one end. The margins are serrate, or scalloped. Native to all seas,
this family contains the cockles, or heart-clams. In Europe these
bivalves are regularly eaten, and cockle-gathering is a recognized
seaside industry, but they are not used for food to any extent in
this country.

Genus *Trachycardium* Mörch 1853

TRACHYCARDIUM QUADRAGENARIUM (Con.)   Pls. 1, 17
Giant Pacific Cockle
  Range: Santa Barbara, California, to Baja California.
  Habitat: Moderately shallow water.
  Description: Attains a length of about 5 in. Both ends rounded,
  the posterior flattened a little. Shell well inflated, and heart-

shaped when viewed from the end. Beaks moderately large. Shell decorated with about 40 strong radiating ribs that produce a markedly scalloped margin. These ribs, particularly those on the anterior end, are studded with small but sharp tubercles. Color yellow, with patches of brown; interior orange-brown.

Genus *Clinocardium* Keen 1936

CLINOCARDIUM CILIATUM (Fabr.) Iceland Cockle Pl. 16
Range: Circumpolar; south to Puget Sound.
Habitat: Moderately deep water.
Description: About 2½ in. long, the shell is rather obliquely roundish in outline, the anterior end somewhat shorter than the posterior, with both ends rounded. There are about 36 rather sharp ribs, which have rounded furrows between them. Shell is white, with a yellowish-brown periostracum that produces stiff hairlike projections on some of the ribs. Interior pale yellow in fresh specimens.
Remarks: Formerly known as *Cardium islandicum* Brug.

CLINOCARDIUM FUCANUM (Dall) Fucan Cockle Pl. 16
Range: Alaska to Monterey, California.
Habitat: Moderately deep water.
Description: A smaller cockle than *C. ciliatum* (above), the length averaging about 1½ in. A solid shell, quite plump, obliquely circular in outline, with rather low beaks. Usually more than 50 close-set radiating ribs; rest periods during shell growth leave many individuals with distinct concentric lines at occasional intervals. Interior polished white; outer surface bears a thin, grayish-brown periostracum.

CLINOCARDIUM NUTTALLII (Con.) Pl. 16
Nuttall's Cockle
Range: Bering Sea to San Diego, California.
Habitat: Moderately shallow water.
Description: Shell rather stout and thick, but quite brittle. Grows to be 4 in. long in northern sections of its range, somewhat smaller in southern. Beaks are high. Valves sculptured with about 37 strong, squarish ribs that are crossed by wavy lines as they approach the margins. Color white or yellowish white.
Remarks: This is a common cockle of the West Coast. For many years it went under the name *Cardium corbis* Mtyn.

Genus *Nemocardium* Meek 1876

NEMOCARDIUM CENTIFILOSUM (Carp.) Pl. 16
Hundred-lined Cockle
Range: Puget Sound to California.

Habitat: Moderately shallow water.
Description: A small pelecypod, not over ¾ in. long. Shell almost round, somewhat longer than high, with beaks that are central in position. Surface sculptured with numerous very fine and sharp ribs, those on posterior end cancellated by threadlike lines. Color white.

Genus *Trigoniocardia* Dall 1900

TRIGONIOCARDIA BIANGULATA (Sow.)   **Pl. 17**
Strawberry Cockle
  Range: California to Ecuador.
  Habitat: Moderately shallow water.
  Description: This shell may be described as roundly angular. Anterior end is regularly rounded, the posterior end is concavely sloping. Length about 1½ in. Shell ornamented with strong radiating ribs, some 30 in number, those on the posterior slope narrower than the rest. Color yellowish white; interior reddish purple.

Genus *Laevicardium* Swainson 1840

LAEVICARDIUM ELATUM (Sow.)   **Giant Egg Cockle**   **Pl. 17**
  Range: San Pedro, California, to Panama.
  Habitat: Moderately shallow water.
  Description: The largest of our cockles, attaining a height of more than 6 in., the length about 4. Shell moderately thin, with an obliquely oval shape. Valves well inflated. There are about 40 radiating ribs, which are quite low, so surface of the shell is relatively smooth. Color yellow; interior white.

LAEVICARDIUM SUBSTRIATUM (Con.)   **Pl. 17**
Little Egg Cockle
  Range: Catalina I., California, to Baja California.
  Habitat: Moderately shallow water.
  Description: About 1 in. long, valves thin but well inflated, the shape obliquely oval. The surface is quite smooth, although there are obscure radiating lines. Color yellowish brown; interior yellow with purple spots and blotches.

Genus *Serripes* Gould 1841

SERRIPES GROENLANDICUS (Brug.)   **Pl. 17**
Greenland Cockle
  Range: Circumpolar; south to Puget Sound.
  Habitat: Moderately deep water.
  Description: Rather large, some specimens 4 in. long. Drab gray in color; young individuals show a few zigzag lines of darker

shade. Although large, the valves are thin; shell but little inflated. Beaks about central; anterior end rounded and the posterior end partially truncate and widely gaping.

Family Veneridae: Venus Clams

THIS is the largest pelecypod family, and it has the greatest distribution, both in depth and in range. Named for the goddess Venus, this group is noted for graceful lines and beauty of color and sculpture. Shells equivalve, oblong-oval in outline as a rule, and porcelaneous in texture. The mollusks are burrowers just beneath the surface of sand and mud, and are never fixed in one place. Native to all seas, and since ancient times many of them have been used by man for both food and ornament.

Genus *Ventricolaria* Keen 1954

VENTRICOLARIA FORDI (Yates)   **Ford's Venus**   **Pl. 19**
     Range: Monterey, California, to Panama.
     Habitat: Well off shore.
     Description: Strong and rugged in character, the length is about 2½ in. Beaks are very prominent; posterior end greatly rounded and anterior end short and acutely rounded. Shell very stout; decorated with rounded concentric ribs, and by irregular radiating lines as well, so that surface may be cancellated, especially on anterior part. Color yellowish brown, commonly with rays of darker shade.

Genus *Tivela* Link 1807

TIVELA STULTORUM (Mawe)   **Pismo Clam**   **Pls. 1, 17**
     Range: Half Moon Bay, California, to Mexico.
     Habitat: Moderately shallow water.
     Description: Some 3 to 4 in. long ordinarily, although 7-in. specimens have been reported. Shell thick and solid, both ends roundly pointed. Surface is smooth, usually polished. Color grayish, often with distinct rays of brown. Hinge very rugged; shell's interior porcelaneous and white.
     Remarks: An important food mollusk in parts of California where it is sufficiently abundant.

Genus *Amiantis* Carpenter 1863

AMIANTIS CALLOSA (Con.)   **White Venus**   **Pl. 22**
     Range: Santa Monica, California, to Mexico.
     Habitat: Shallow water.
     Description: A handsome snow-white shell, pleasingly formed.

Length about 4 in. and shape a nice oval, with both ends evenly
rounded, the posterior end slightly higher. Beaks prominent,
set a bit closer to anterior end. Surface sculptured with strong,
flattened, concentric ribs, some of which divide toward the ends,
as well as occasionally at the center. Valves heavy and robust
— quite thick through the umbonal region — and covered in
life by an extremely thin grayish periostracum. The pallial
sinus is very well impressed.

Genus *Saxidomus* Conrad 1837

SAXIDOMUS NUTTALLI Con.   **Washington Clam**   **Pl. 19**
   Range: Humboldt Bay, California, to Baja California.
   Habitat: Moderately deep water.
   Description: Another sturdy clam, about 5 in. long when fully
   grown. Shell roughly oval, with prominent beaks set near
   anterior end. Color grayish white, usually with a few brownish
   scrawls near beaks. Sculpture consists of fine but sharp concentric lines. Interior white, stained with purple.
   Remarks: North of Humboldt Bay, and extending to Alaska,
   we find a slightly larger species, *S. giganteus* Desh. The concentric sculpture is less conspicuous on the valves. Color gray,
   with a polished white interior.

Genus *Chione* Mühlfeld 1811

CHIONE CALIFORNIENSIS (Brod.)   **California Venus**   **Pl. 19**
   Range: Point Mugu, California, to Panama.
   Habitat: Moderately shallow water.
   Description: A robust shell fully 2½ in. long, roundly oval in
   outline, and only moderately inflated. Surface bears a number
   of stout concentric ribs and numerous rounded radiating ridges.
   The pattern is usually quite marked on center of shell and grows
   progressively weaker toward the edges. Color dull grayish;
   interior white. Margins are crenulate.
   Remarks: Formerly listed as C. *succincta* (Val.).

CHIONE FLUCTIFRAGA (Sow.)   **Pl. 18**
Smooth California Venus
   Range: San Pedro, California, to Gulf of California.
   Habitat: Just below low-water line; mud.
   Description: Strong and solid, seldom more than 2 in. long and
   commonly just over 1. Shell roundish oval, the beaks closer to
   the anterior end. Surface bears both radiating and concentric
   ridges, usually stronger over the umbones but weak toward the
   margins. Color yellowish white, commonly with darker bands.
   Interior marked with purple at the edges; margins crenulate.

CHIONE UNDATELLA (Sow.)   Pls. 2, 19
Frilled California Venus
> **Range:** San Pedro, California, to S. America.
> **Habitat:** Shallow water; muddy bottoms.
> **Description:** Averaging in length about 2 in., this bivalve has the same general shape as *C. fluctifraga* (above), and similarly is a rugged and strong shell. Color grayish white, marked and blotched with violet-brown. Sculpture consists of numerous close-set wavy, concentric ridges, and weaker radiating lines.
> **Remarks:** This is probably the most common chione on California beaches, although in certain localities *C. fluctifraga* is more abundant. Some authorities consider it a subspecies of *C. californiensis.*

Genus *Prototbaca* Dall 1902

PROTOTHACA LACINIATA (Carp.)   **Folded Littleneck**   Pl. 18
> **Range:** Alaska to Baja California.
> **Habitat:** Moderately shallow water.
> **Description:** A roundly oval shell nearly 3 in. long. This bivalve bears a strong reticulate pattern, produced by prominent radiating and concentric lines, many of the former provided with sharp spines. Color varies from yellowish gray to pale reddish brown.
> **Remarks:** Some authorities consider this a subspecies of *P. staminea* (Con.); see below.

PROTOTHACA STAMINEA (Con.)   **Pacific Littleneck**   Pl. 18
> **Range:** Aleutian Is. to Baja California.
> **Habitat:** Moderately shallow water.
> **Description:** Length about 2 in. Both ends are rounded, the beaks somewhat closer to anterior end. Valves quite thick — the bivalve is known locally as "hard-shelled clam" — and sculptured with numerous fine radiating lines and even finer concentric lines, particularly toward the anterior end. Color ranges from creamy white to rich brown; many specimens show chevronlike markings.
> **Remarks:** Most abundant north of San Francisco. One of the few native varieties regularly found in the markets.

PROTOTHACA TENERRIMA (Carp.)   Pl. 18
Thin-shelled Littleneck
> **Range:** B.C. to Baja California.
> **Habitat:** Moderately shallow water.
> **Description:** Oval in shape and about 4 in. long. Anterior end very short and rounded, posterior end rounded and deep, constituting nearly 4/5 of shell. Valves moderately thin, grayish brown, and decorated with evenly spaced concentric ridges, as well as numerous tiny radiating lines.

Genus *Tapes* Mühlfeld 1811

TAPES JAPONICA (Desh.)   **Japanese Littleneck**   **Pl. 19**
Range: Puget Sound.
Habitat: Shallow water.
Description: About 2 in. long, this shell looks very much like an elongate *Protothaca*. Belongs in the waters of Japan and the Philippines, but has been introduced in Puget Sound, where it is now quite plentiful; each year it slightly extends range southward. More compressed than a *Protothaca*. Yellowish gray, usually more or less mottled. When abundant, it is an important food item.
Remarks: This species is listed in many books as *T. philippinarum* A. Adams & Reeve. It has also been introduced in Hawaii. See also Plate 65, No. 13.

Genus *Humilaria* Grant & Gale 1931

HUMILARIA KENNERLEYI (Reeve)   **Pl. 19**
Kennerley's Venus
Range: Alaska to Carmel Bay, California.
Habitat: Moderately shallow water.
Description: A fairly large and robust shell about 3 in. long. Shape oval; beaks situated near anterior end. Both ends rounded, the posterior somewhat longer. Color white, inside as well as outside. Surface sculptured with close-set concentric ridges.

Genus *Compsomyax* Stewart 1930

COMPSOMYAX SUBDIAPHANA (Carp.)   **Milky Venus**   **Pl. 17**
Range: Alaska to Baja California.
Habitat: Moderately shallow water.
Description: A plump shell about 1¾ in. long. Shape oval; beaks near the anterior end, and both ends are rounded. Valves rather thin, marked with very fine lines, but surface is relatively smooth. Color white or pale gray.

Genus *Irus* Oken 1815

IRUS LAMELLIFERA Con.   **Ribbed Venus**   **Pl. 18**
Range: Monterey, California, to San Diego.
Habitat: Water's edge; holes and crevices.
Description: An oddly different clam, and a favorite with collectors. Length 1½ in. Beaks very inconspicuous. Anterior end short and rounded, the posterior long and abruptly truncate. Valves quite solid, decorated with from 8 to 10 strong concentric ridges that are high and often bladelike. Color white.

Remarks: This bivalve bores into clay and soft rocks, but is more commonly found in crevices.

Family Petricolidae: Rock Dwellers

SHELLS elongate, gaping, with a weak hinge. These are boring mollusks, excavating cavities in clay, coral, limestone, and such. The cavity is generally enlarged until the clam attains adult size. Members of this family are to be found in warm and temperate seas.

Genus *Petricola* Lamarck 1801

PETRICOLA CARDITOIDES (Con.)   Pl. 22
Heart Rock Dweller
  Range: B.C. to Baja California.
  Habitat: Shallow water; claybanks.
  Description: An oblong shell from 1 to 2 in. long. Beaks low, the anterior end short and round, the posterior elongate, sloping, and partially truncate. Color chalky white, the only ornamentation fine radiating lines and wrinkles.
  Remarks: This is normally a rather plump shell, but it bores into stiff clay and some of the softer rocks, such as limestone, and many specimens will be found that are slender, or variously distorted, according to the site selected. A related species, *P. pholadiformis* Lam. (False Angel Wing; see Plate 22, No. 6) — a more slender, white form with strong radiating sculpture — has been introduced from the East Coast. It may be found in San Francisco Bay.

Genus *Cooperella* Carpenter 1864

COOPERELLA SUBDIAPHANA (Carp.)   Pl. 18
  Range: Queen Charlotte Is. to Gulf of California.
  Habitat: Mudflats.
  Description: Plump and about ½ in. long. Both ends evenly rounded, and valves very thin and delicate. Surface smooth and shining; color shiny tan.
  Remarks: Often found living in a little nest made of agglutinated sand grains.

Family Mactridae: Surf Clams

SHELLS equivalve, usually gaping a little at the ends. The hinge has a large, spoon-shaped cavity for an internal ligament. Native to all seas, surf clams live in sandy situations, especially in the surf.

Genus *Mactra* Linné 1767

MACTRA CALIFORNICA Con.   **California Surf Clam**   Pl. 20
Range: Puget Sound to Panama.
Habitat: Shallow water.
Description: A rather fragile shell, whitish in color, attaining a length of about 1½ in. Oval-triangular in outline, with a smooth surface, marked by concentric undulations on the beaks.

MACTRA NASUTA Gould   **Pacific Surf Clam**   Pl. 20
Range: San Pedro, California, to Mazatlán, Mexico.
Habitat: Moderately shallow water; sand.
Description: Strong and rather solid, the length from 3 to 4 in. Both ends rounded, the anterior somewhat more acutely. Beaks prominent and nearly central, and the strong hinge features a large triangular pit for the ligament. Color yellowish white, with a shiny yellowish periostracum.
Remarks: In the following genus, *Spisula*, the hinge pit is not set off from the ligament by a shelly plate, whereas in *Mactra* such a plate is present.

Genus *Spisula* Gray 1837

SPISULA ALASKANA Dall   **Alaska Surf Clam**   Pl. 20
Range: Arctic Ocean to Puget Sound.
Habitat: Moderately deep water; sand.
Description: A large and rugged shell, its length 4 or 5 in. Valves thick and strong, but somewhat compressed. Beaks large and central, with anterior end slightly the shorter of the two. Color chalky white; there is a grayish periostracum that bears heavy wrinkles at the two ends.
Remarks: Some malacologists believe that this species is the same as *S. polynyma* Stim. of the North Atlantic Coast.

SPISULA DOLABRIFORMIS (Con.)   Pl. 20
Mattock Surf Clam
Range: Redondo Beach, California, to Baja California.
Habitat: Moderately shallow water.
Description: Smooth and polished, attaining a length of about 3 in. Shape somewhat triangular, the beaks about central in position. Both ends slope, and the basal margin is evenly rounded. Posterior end slightly more pointed than anterior. Color white, under a brownish periostracum.

SPISULA FALCATA (Gould)   **Hooked Surf Clam**   Pl. 20
Range: Puget Sound to California.
Habitat: Just off shore; sand.
Description: Length about 3 in. Anterior end narrower and

longer than posterior, the upper margin of that end slightly concave. There is a thin pale brown periostracum that is easily rubbed off and reveals a somewhat chalky exterior.

SPISULA HEMPHILLI Dall   **Hemphill's Surf Clam**   Pl. 20
Range: Redondo Beach, California, to Nicaragua.
Habitat: Moderately deep water; sand.
Description: Large but thin-shelled, the length fully 6 in. Shell well inflated, anterior end rounded and posterior end sloping and bluntly pointed. Beaks large and central. Color yellowish white, with a thin yellowish periostracum that is quite wrinkled on the posterior slope.

SPISULA PLANULATA (Con.)   **Flat Surf Clam**   Pl. 20
Range: Monterey, California, to Cape San Lucas, Baja California.
Habitat: Just off shore; sand.
Description: Grayish white and only 1½ in. long. Shell is rather thin, the anterior end regularly rounded and the posterior sloping to a rounded point. Beaks slightly closer to the front end. There is a thin brownish periostracum.

Genus *Tresus* Gray 1853

TRESUS NUTTALLII (Con.)   **Gaper**   Pl. 24
Range: Bolinas Bay, California, to Baja California.
Habitat: Near low-water line; deep in mud.
Description: Probably the largest bivalve found along the West Coast. It attains a length of 8 in., although most specimens are not that large. Shell roughly oval and well inflated, rounded at anterior end and sloping and truncate at posterior end. Both ends gape, the posterior end broadly. A deep triangular pit on inside of the shell, under the beaks. Color white or gray, with a thin brownish periostracum.
Remarks: This species was long listed under the genus *Schizothaerus* Con. 1853. A subspecies, *T. n. capax* Gould, is a higher and stouter shell occurring from Alaska to n. California. This bivalve reaches a length of full 10 in.

Family Tellinidae: Tellins

THE shells of this family are generally equivalve and rather compressed, often somewhat curved. Anterior end is rounded, and the posterior end more or less pointed. The animals are noted for the length of their siphons. Native to all seas, several hundred species have been described. Within this group we find some of the most colorful, highly polished, and graceful of the bivalves.

Genus *Tellina* Linné 1758

TELLINA BODEGENSIS Hinds   **Bodega Tellin**   **Pl. 21**
Range: B.C. to Baja California.
Habitat: Shallow bays and coves.
Description: A slender species attaining a length of 2 in., with the average specimen somewhat less. Anterior end nicely rounded, posterior rather sharply pointed. Color yellowish white, the surface smooth and polished but with minute concentric lines.

TELLINA CARPENTERI Dall   **Carpenter's Tellin**   **Pl. 21**
Range: Alaska to Baja California.
Habitat: Shallow water; muddy bottoms.
Description: Length about ¾ in. Valves thin and compressed and oval in outline, the posterior end slightly the shorter and more pointed. Surface glossy. Color ranges from deep pink to pinkish white.

TELLINA IDAE Dall   **Ida's Tellin**   **Pl. 21**
Range: Santa Barbara, California, to San Diego.
Habitat: Moderately deep water.
Description: An interesting shell about 2 in. long. Beaks are central; anterior end is gracefully rounded, and posterior end is rather sharply pointed. A distinct ridge, or fold, extends from just behind the beaks to posterior tip. Sculpture consists of fine but sharp concentric lines. Color pure white.

TELLINA LUTEA Wood   **Great Alaskan Tellin**   **Pl. 21**
Range: Circumpolar; south to Cook Inlet, Alaska.
Habitat: Moderately deep water.
Description: One of the largest tellins on our West Coast, reaching a length of 4 in. Valves somewhat compressed, the posterior tip twisting a little to the left. Beaks about central, and there is a prominent posterior slope. Color white, sometimes pinkish, and the surface is usually rather dull.

TELLINA MODESTA (Carp.)   **Modest Tellin**   **Pl. 21**
Range: Alaska to Gulf of California.
Habitat: Moderately shallow water.
Description: About 1 in. long and white, this bivalve has an anterior end that is long and gently rounded and a posterior end that is short and rather sharply pointed. Valves compressed, with a distinct slope from the beaks to the tip. Surface bears numerous very fine lines, but it appears smooth and glossy.

TELLINA SALMONEA Carp.   **Salmon Tellin**   **Pl. 21**
Range: Alaska to San Pedro, California.
Habitat: Moderately shallow water.

Description: A small shell, only about ½ in. long. It is rather stout, and somewhat triangular in outline. Beaks set close to posterior end. Surface shiny, creamy white, often with zones of darker hue; the inside a delicate salmon-pink.

Genus *Macoma* Leach 1819

MACOMA BALTHICA (Linné)   **Baltic Macoma**   Pl. 21
  Range: Circumpolar; Bering Sea to Monterey, California; also Atlantic Coast and Norway and Sweden.
  Habitat: Muddy bays and coves.
  Description: Pinkish white and about 1 in. long. Shell moderately thin, with a rounded outline, the posterior end somewhat constricted. Beaks rather prominent and nearly central in position. Surface bears numerous very fine concentric lines of growth, and there is a thin olive-brown periostracum that is usually lacking on upperparts of shell.
  Remarks: This small clam sometimes travels partway up creeks and rivers.

MACOMA BROTA Dall   Pl. 21
  Range: Bering Sea to Puget Sound.
  Habitat: Coves and bays.
  Description: A sizable shell, its length about 3 in. Shape more or less oval. A fairly solid shell, moderately inflated. Color grayish white.

MACOMA CALCAREA (Gmel.)   **Chalky Macoma**   Pl. 21
  Range: Circumpolar; south to Monterey, California.
  Habitat: Bays and coves.
  Description: Length sometimes approaches 2 in., generally less. Dull chalky white inside and outside; oval-elongate shape. Posterior end narrowed and slightly twisted. Periostracum dull gray, and generally present only toward base of shell.

MACOMA CARLOTTENSIS Whit.   Pl. 21
Queen Charlotte Macoma
  Range: Arctic Ocean to Baja California.
  Habitat: Moderately shallow water.
  Description: Rather small and delicate, its length seldom more than 1 in. Shell moderately inflated, gently sloping at ends, with beaks near center. Color grayish white. In life, has a thin glossy periostracum that is greenish.

MACOMA INCONGRUA (Mart.)   Pl. 21
Incongruous Macoma
  Range: Arctic Ocean to San Diego, California.
  Habitat: Moderately shallow water.

Description: A rather small white shell, the anterior end rounded and slightly longer than the more pointed posterior end. Length 1½ in. Valves moderately thin. During life there is a thin grayish periostracum.

MACOMA INCONSPICUA (Brod. & Sow.)   Pl. 21
Inconspicuous Macoma
   Range: Arctic Ocean to San Diego, California.
   Habitat: Moderately deep water.
   Description: Small, usually less than 1 in. long. Color white or pinkish white. Shell less elongate than many of the group, and rather well inflated. Anterior end is evenly rounded, the slightly longer posterior end bluntly pointed.

MACOMA IRUS (Han.)   **Irus Macoma**   Pl. 21
   Range: Alaska to San Pedro, California.
   Habitat: Moderately shallow water.
   Description: The length of this shell averages about 1½ in. Valves compressed; beaks a little closer to posterior end. Anterior end very broadly rounded; the posterior sloping and rather bluntly pointed. Color grayish white, with a thin periostracum.
   Remarks: Formerly called *M. inquinata* (Desh.).

MACOMA NASUTA (Con.)   **Bent-nosed Macoma**   Pls. 2, 21
   Range: Alaska to Baja California.
   Habitat: Shallow water; muddy bottoms.
   Description: Some 2 in. long. Color grayish white, with a very thin periostracum. Anterior end broadly rounded; posterior end bluntly pointed, partially truncate, and noticeably bent to one side. The beaks are nearly central.

MACOMA PLANIUSCULA Grant & Gale   Pl. 21
   Range: Arctic Ocean to Puget Sound.
   Habitat: Moderately deep water.
   Description: An oval shell slightly more than 1 in. long. Beaks about central. Anterior end evenly and broadly rounded, posterior end bluntly pointed. Inner surface is shiny, and the shell bears a yellowish-gray periostracum.
   Remarks: Rare south of Alaska.

MACOMA SECTA (Con.)   **White Sand Macoma**   Pl. 21
   Range: Vancouver I. to Baja California.
   Habitat: Shallow water; sandflats.
   Description: The largest member of the genus on West Coast, attaining a length of 4 in. Valves not well inflated, and the general shape is oval. Anterior end long and rounded; posterior

end short and partially truncate, with a distinct angulation extending from the beaks to the tip. Valves thin and glossy white, and generally have a fringe of periostracum at the edges.

MACOMA YOLDIFORMIS Carp.   Pl. 21
Range: Alaska to San Diego, California.
Habitat: Shallow water.
Description: About ¾ in. long, the anterior end long and broadly rounded; the posterior shorter and narrower, with an acutely rounded tip. The valves are thin and glossy white.

Family Donacidae: Bean Clams

GENERALLY small wedge-shaped clams, the posterior end prolonged and acutely rounded, and the anterior end short and sloping. Distributed in all seas that are warm, where they live in the sand close to shore. Sometimes called wedge shells.

Genus *Donax* Linné 1758

DONAX CALIFORNICA Con.   **California Bean Clam**   Pl. 22
Range: Santa Barbara, California, to Baja California.
Habitat: Shoreline; sand.
Description: Length just under 1 in. Posterior end long and rather pointed, anterior end short and sloping. Surface quite smooth. Color yellowish white; interior with a purplish stain at the dorsal margin.

DONAX GOULDII Dall   **Little Bean Clam**   Pl. 22
Range: San Luis Obispo, California, to Mexico.
Habitat: Shoreline; sand.
Description: A wedge-shaped clam nearly 1 in. long. Anterior end short and sharply rounded the posterior considerably lengthened and bluntly rounded. Surface bears faint radiating lines; inner basal margin strongly crenulate. Color varies from white to purple, with most specimens exhibiting a pattern of lilac or rosy rays.
Remarks: Despite its small size, this clam is extensively gathered for making soup.

Family Sanguinolariidae: Gari Shells

SHELLS somewhat like the tellins, with which they used to be grouped. The animals have very long siphons. Distributed chiefly in warm seas.

Genus *Sanguinolaria* Lamarck 1799

SANGUINOLARIA NUTTALLII Con.   **Purple Clam**   **Pls. 2, 23**
Range: San Pedro, California, to Baja California.
Habitat: Bays and estuaries; mud.
Description: A shiny purplish-brown shell about 3 in. long.
Valves quite compressed, oval in outline; both ends rounded, the
posterior slightly longer and less broad. Beaks very small.
Color whitish lavender, often with purplish rays, but fresh
specimens are covered with a rich brown periostracum that is
very glossy. Interior purplish.

Genus *Heterodonax* Mörch 1853

HETERODONAX BIMACULATA (Linné)   **False Donax**   **Pl. 22**
Range: Monterey, California, to Mexico; also s. Florida and
the West Indies.
Habitat: Moderately shallow water.
Description: Rather solid and triangular in shape, the posterior
end short and squarish, the anterior more rounded. About 1 in.
long when fully grown. Color bluish white, and most valves
bear 2 red or purple blotches; in addition there may be rays of
purplish.

Genus *Gari* Schumacher 1817

GARI CALIFORNICA (Con.)   **Sunset Shell**   **Pl. 1**
Range: Alaska to San Diego, California.
Habitat: Just off shore; sand.
Description: A handsome shell some 3 in. long. Valves rather
compressed, with very small beaks that are nearly central in
position. Both ends rounded, the anterior end partially truncate
above. Surface rather smooth, creamy white, and usually with
pinkish rays extending from the beaks. Interior pure white.

Genus *Tagelus* Gray 1847

TAGELUS CALIFORNIANUS (Con.)   **Jackknife Clam**   **Pl. 25**
Range: Monterey, California, to Panama.
Habitat: Sandy mud between tides.
Description: An elongate shell, 2 to 3 in. long. Beaks central,
both ends bluntly rounded. Valves rather thin, dull white, and
partly covered with a yellowish periostracum that bears wrinkles
on the posterior slope.

Family Semelidae: Semeles

SHELLS rounded oval in shape and but little inflated, with more or less obscure folds on the posterior end. The pallial sinus is deep and well impressed. Confined chiefly to warm seas.

Genus *Semele* Schumacher 1817

SEMELE DECISA Con.   Bark Semele   Pl. 22
   Range: San Pedro, California, to Mexico.
   Habitat: Moderately shallow water; rocky bottoms.
   Description: An attractive mollusk and a large one, its length between 4 and 5 in. Shell is nearly circular, with a short slope from the beaks to the posterior end, where the tip is abruptly cut off. Valves rather solid, brownish white, and sculptured with wrinkled concentric lines and furrows. The interior is like white china, with a rosy tinge around the edges; pallial sinus very deep and prominent.

SEMELE RUBROPICTA Dall   Rose-petal Semele   Pl. 22
   Range: Alaska to Mexico.
   Habitat: Moderately shallow water.
   Description: Nearly 2 in. long, this is a roundly oval shell, with beaks closer to the posterior end. There is a weak sculpture of radiating and concentric lines, but surface is usually rather smooth. Color grayish white; interior shining white, with a touch of yellowish brown at each end of hinge.

SEMELE RUPICOLA Dall   Rock-dwelling Semele   Pl. 22
   Range: Santa Cruz, California, to Baja California.
   Habitat: Moderately shallow water; rocky bottoms.
   Description: A rather thick shell about 1½ in. long. Shape nearly circular, with anterior end quite rounded and basal margin rather flat. Color grayish; surface roughened by numerous concentric growth lines. Interior often colored purple at the margins.

Genus *Cumingia* Sowerby 1833

CUMINGIA CALIFORNICA Con.   Pl. 21
California Cuming Shell
   Range: Monterey, California, to Baja California.
   Habitat: Shallow water.
   Description: Rather variable in shape and about ¾ in. long. Somewhat triangular in outline, the beaks almost central. Anterior end rounded, posterior pointed and sometimes twisted

slightly to one side. Surface lined concentrically. Color dingy white.

Remarks: This small clam likes to live in rock crevices, and as a result the valves are apt to be more or less distorted.

Family Solenidae: Razor Clams

MEMBERS of this family are the true razor clams, and they are so called wherever they occur. The shells are equivalve, usually considerably elongated, and they gape at both ends. Distributed in the sandy bottoms of coastal waters in nearly all seas. All are considered edible.

Genus *Siliqua* Mühlfeld 1811

SILIQUA LUCIDA (Con.)   **Transparent Razor Clam**   Pl. 23
   Range: Bolinas Bay, California, to Mexico.
   Habitat: Sandbars.
   Description: An elongate shell of about 2 in., sometimes a bit longer. Valves rather thin and fragile, and often translucent. Both ends are rounded, the beaks nearly central in position. Interior reinforced by a stout vertical rib which begins under the beaks and extends halfway across the shell, where it becomes lost near the margin. Color bluish white, with darker concentric zones; there is a strong greenish-brown periostracum.

SILIQUA PATULA (Dixon)   **Pacific Razor Clam**   Pls. 1, 23
   Range: Aleutian Is. to Pismo, California.
   Habitat: Muds and sands between tides.
   Description: A fine large shell, very oval in shape, flatly compressed, and up to 6 in. long. Beaks about central. Interior rib is very well developed. Color whitish, with concentric markings, but in life this is concealed by a shining yellowish-brown periostracum. Interior white, tinted with pinkish.
   Remarks: Also known as the Giant Pod, this bivalve is regarded as excellent eating, and is regularly canned on the California coast.

Genus *Solen* Linné 1758

SOLEN ROSACEUS Carp.   **Rosy Razor Clam**   Pl. 23
   Range: Santa Barbara, California, to Gulf of California.
   Habitat: Between tides.
   Description: About 2 in. long and rather blunt at both ends. Valves but little inflated, not very much curved. Color pinkish white, with a yellowish-gray periostracum that is smooth and glossy.

SOLEN SICARIUS Gould   **Blunt Razor Clam**   Pl. 23
  Range: Vancouver I. to Mexico.
  Habitat: Between tides.
  Description: Another elongate bivalve from 2 to 3 in., and less
than 1 in. high. Valves thin but well inflated. Beaks set at
extreme anterior end, and that end seems to be chopped off
abruptly. Color white, with a glossy yellowish-green periostracum.

Genus *Ensis* Schumacher 1817

ENSIS MYRAE Berry   **Myra's Razor Clam**   Pl. 23
  Range: Monterey, California, to n. Baja California.
  Habitat: Between tides.
  Description: A small and slender clam, with sides nearly par-
allel. Length is about 2 in. Beaks nearer to anterior end, and
both ends are squarish. The elongate shell is slightly curved.
Color greenish.
  Remarks: Formerly listed as *E. californicus* Dall, which is a
more southern species occurring from Magdalena Bay throughout
the Gulf of California and south to Colima, Mexico.

Family Hiatellidae: Giant Clams

SHELLS usually elongate and inequivalve. Members of this family
commonly bore into sponge, coral, and limestone. The surface of
the shell is irregular and rough, and the valves gape widely. The
range is from the Arctic to the Tropics, and some examples grow
to a very large size.

Genus *Hiatella* Daudin 1801

HIATELLA ARCTICA (Linné)   **Arctic Rock Borer**   Pl. 25
  Range: Circumpolar; Alaska to Panama.
  Habitat: Bores in clay, or limestone.
  Description: An oblong-oval shell, rather squarish in appearance,
length about 1 in. Anterior end short and posterior long, with
both ends bluntly rounded. Surface marked by coarse lines of
growth and numerous wrinkles. Color white, with a dingy yellowish periostracum, the texture chalky.
  Remarks: In 1802 Fleuriau de Bellevue named this genus *Saxi-
cava*, and it is so listed in many shell books. However, the
name *Hiatella* has a one-year priority.

HIATELLA PHOLADIS (Linné)   Pl. 25
  Range: Arctic Ocean to Panama.
  Habitat: Bores in the softer rocks.

Description: An elongate shell of about 1½ in. Anterior end very short and rounded, the posterior lengthened and truncate at the tip. Valves thin, and marked by coarse wrinkles. Color chalky white; yellowish-brown periostracum.

Genus *Panomya* Gray 1857

PANOMYA AMPLA Dall   **Ample Panomya**   Pl. 25
Range: Aleutian Is. to Puget Sound.
Habitat: Gravelly shores between tides.
Description: A rough and sturdy shell some 3 in. long. Posterior end squarely cut off; anterior end slopes to a rounded point, then rounds to the basal margin, which is straight. Color chalky white, with a dark, almost black, periostracum that peels easily from the shell, so even living specimens are rarely covered. Posterior end gapes widely, and valves fail to encase the animal completely.

Genus *Panope* Ménard 1807

PANOPE GENEROSA Gould   **Gweduc**   Pl. 24
Range: Alaska to Baja California.
Habitat: Moderately shallow water; deep in mud.
Description: A large bivalve, the shell measuring in length up to 8 in.; but even so it does not completely contain the mollusk's huge siphon. Valves bluntly oval; anterior end rounded and posterior end truncate and widely gaping. Color dull grayish white; interior somewhat pearly in fresh specimens.
Remarks: This clam buries itself some 3 ft. in the mud, its long siphon reaching to the surface. In the North it goes by the name of "geoduck" or "gooey-duck," from the Indian name *Gweduc*.

Family Myacidae: Soft-shelled Clams

SHELLS usually inequivalve and gaping. The left valve contains a spoonlike structure called a chondrophore, which fits into a corresponding groove in the right valve. These clams live buried in sands, muds, and gravels, and are to be found in nearly all seas.

Genus *Mya* Linné 1758

MYA ARENARIA Linné   **Soft-shelled Clam**   Pl. 25
Range: Alaska to San Francisco Bay.
Habitat: Between tides.
Description: This is an introduced clam, brought here from our Atlantic Coast, where it is an important commercial mollusk.

It grows to be 4 or 5 in. long, but persistent clamming has made examples that large hard to find. Shell is moderately thin, and it gapes at both ends. Pallial line with deep sinus. Dull gray or chalky white in color, the surface is roughened and somewhat wrinkled by lines of growth. Anterior end rounded, the posterior slightly pointed. An erect chondrophore is located in the left valve.

Remarks: This succulent clam lies buried with just the tip of its siphon at the surface. As one walks over its territory when the tide is out the mollusk's position is revealed by a vertical spurt of water that is ejected as the alarmed mollusk suddenly withdraws its "neck." This Atlantic pelecypod is also well known on European beaches.

MYA TRUNCATA Linné   **Truncated Mya**   Pl. 25
   Range: Circumpolar; south to Puget Sound.
   Habitat: Between tides.
   Description: A dingy-white shell about 2½ in. long, sometimes slightly longer. Shell is oblong, rounded at anterior end and abruptly truncate at posterior end, the truncated edges flaring to some degree. There is a thick and tough yellowish-brown periostracum.

Genus *Cryptomya* Conrad 1849

CRYPTOMYA CALIFORNICA (Con.)   Pl. 25
California Soft-shelled Clam
   Range: Alaska to Mexico.
   Habitat: Between tides.
   Description: A rather small shell, only 1½ in. long. Outline oval. Valves thin and ashy gray, gaping slightly at one end. Posterior end noticeably curved. Surface smooth, marked only by lines of growth. Inside, the pallial line is entire, since there is no pallial sinus; this lack immediately distinguishes it from young specimens of *Mya arenaria* discussed above.

Genus *Platyodon* Conrad 1837

PLATYODON CANCELLATUS Con.   **Chubby Mya**   Pls. 2, 25
   Range: Queen Charlotte Is. to San Diego, California.
   Habitat: Between tides.
   Description: A fair-sized clam, attaining a length of 3 in. Well inflated, the valves moderately thick and solid. Posterior end long and bluntly rounded, the anterior short and abruptly truncate. Chondrophore in left valve. Color gray; shell sculptured with fine but sharp concentric lines. There is a thin yellowish-brown periostracum.

Family Corbulidae: Basket Clams

SHELLS small but solid, very inequivalve, one valve generally overlapping its mate. Often slightly gaping at the anterior end. White, and often concentrically ribbed. An upright conical tooth is present in each valve. These little bivalves are distributed in nearly all seas.

Genus *Corbula* Bruguière 1797

CORBULA LUTEOLA Carp. **Basket Clam** Pl. 23
  Range: Monterey, California, to La Paz, Mexico.
  Habitat: Shallow water; rocky bottoms.
  Description: Usually less than ½ in. long, this is a sturdy little fellow, somewhat squarish in shape. Anterior end is bluntly rounded and the posterior is sloping, rather pointed, and bears a distinct line running from the beaks to the posterior tip. Color ordinarily yellow, but pink and rosy individuals are sometimes found.
  Remarks: This group has been listed as *Aloides* Mühl. 1811.

Family Pholadidae: Piddocks

BORING clams capable of penetrating wood, coral, and moderately hard stone. The shells are white, thin, brittle, generally elongate, and narrowed toward the posterior end. There is a sharp abrading sculpture on the anterior end. They commonly gape at both ends. Distributed in all seas.

Genus *Barnea* Risso 1826

BARNEA SUBTRUNCATA (Sow.) **Pacific Piddock** Pl. 26
  Range: San Francisco to Baja California.
  Habitat: Shallow water; soft shaly mud.
  Description: A pure-white shell about 2½ in. long. Shape rather cylindrical; anterior end pointed and reflected, the posterior elongate and squarely rounded. Valves thin and brittle, and sculptured with concentric lines, sharp and distinct on anterior end and faint or lacking on posterior end. There is a delicate spoonlike appendage beneath the hinge. In addition to the 2 valves, there is a long triangular shelly piece extending above the ligament — so this mollusk is in a sense a trivalve rather than a bivalve.
  Remarks: Formerly known as *B. pacifica* Stearns and *B. spathulata* Desh.

Genus *Zirfaea* Gray 1847

ZIRFAEA PILSBRYI Lowe   **Pilsbry's Piddock**   Pl. 26

Range: Bering Sea to Baja California.

Habitat: Bores in claybanks.

Description: A large and rugged borer, capable of penetrating the stiffest of hard-packed clay. Shell pure white, and up to 4 in. long. Valves divided into 2 zones by an oblique fold: the posterior part bearing concentric lines of growth and the anterior part is decorated with sharp scales in addition to the concentric lines. It is this filelike end that enables the mollusk to do its boring.

Remarks: This species used to be called *Z. gabbi* Tryon. It is commonly known also as the Rough Piddock.

Genus *Parapholas* Conrad 1848

PARAPHOLAS CALIFORNICA (Con.)   Pl. 26
California Piddock

Range: Oregon to San Diego, California.

Habitat: Mud and claybanks.

Description: An unusual clam, cylindrical in shape and nearly 4 in. long. There are no less than 8 accessory plates, 2 along basal margin extending nearly whole length of shell. A diagonal line from the beaks divides the shell into 2 parts: anterior part, rounded and sculptured with very sharp ridges, and the elongate posterior part, with concentric lines. Posterior tip truncate. Color brownish white.

Genus *Penitella* Valenciennes 1846

PENITELLA GABBI (Tryon)   **Gabb's Piddock**   Pl. 26

Range: Alaska to San Pedro, California.

Habitat: Bores in shale.

Description: About 2 in. long, most specimens somewhat smaller. Color pure white. Posterior end long and bluntly rounded, decorated only with concentric lines. The short and abruptly sloping anterior end bears close-set concentric ridges and radiating lines. In dry cabinet specimens of this group the anterior portion gapes widely, but when the mollusk is alive this part of the shell is covered by a thin shelly structure known as the callum.

PENITELLA PENITA (Con.)   **Common Piddock**   Pl. 26

Range: Alaska to San Diego, California.

Habitat: Bores in wood and rocks.

Description: The common boring clam of the West Coast; usually 1 in. or so long, sometimes more. Anterior end rounded and bulbous, provided with a rough, rasplike sculpture. Posterior elongate, decorated with concentric lines only. Color grayish white. There is a small triangular plate over the hinge line.

Genus *Chaceia* Turner 1954

CHACEIA OVOIDEA (Gould)   **Oval Piddock**   Pl. 26
Range: Bering Sea to Gulf of California.
Habitat: Bores in soft rocks.
Description: A short and stubby borer, its length about 2 in. when fully grown. General shape oval, beaks close to anterior end. That end bears sharp radiating lines set with scales; the longer posterior end is marked only by growth lines. Periostracum often extends over and beyond the posterior end, forming a tubelike projection for the siphon. Color grayish white.

Genus *Nettastomella* Carpenter 1864

NETTASTOMELLA ROSTRATA (Val.)   Pl. 26
Beaked Piddock
Range: Puget Sound to San Diego, California.
Habitat: Bores in stone and dead shells.
Description: Thin and delicate, generally less than ½ in. long. Pure white. Anterior end rounded and swollen and widely gaping, the posterior prolonged into a tubelike affair that has been compared to the bill of a duck.

Family Teredinidae: Shipworms

THE shipworms are elongate mollusks that infest floating and submerged timbers. There is a tiny vestigial bivalve shell, but most of the animal lives in a shelly tube that may be several inches long. These mollusks are distributed in all seas.

Genus *Bankia* Gray 1842

BANKIA SETACEA (Tryon)   **Shipworm**   Pl. 26
Range: Bering Sea to Gulf of California.
Habitat: Wood.
Description: This is a free-swimming bivalve when very young, but at an early age it bores into a submerged log or timber and stays there for life, enlarging its burrow by lengthening it and keeping it about the same diam. Vestigial shell is only ½ in. long; however, the shelly tube that contains most of the animal may be several inches long. If many individuals are present, the timber may be a mass of small galleries. Color of shell white, sometimes tinged with pink.

Genus *Teredo* Linné 1758

TEREDO DIEGENSIS Bar. **San Diego Shipworm**   Pl. 26
   Range: San Francisco Bay to San Diego, California.
   Habitat: Wood.
   Description: This shell is quite small, perhaps slightly more than
   ¼ in. long. Color white. Like the others, it gapes widely;
   anterior end is very prettily sculptured. The clam burrows with
   the grain of the wood, and infected timbers may be so honey-
   combed by the elongate galleries that they eventually disinte-
   grate and crumble away.
   Remarks: The actual range of any of the shipworms is rather
   unpredictable, since they often live in floating and drifting
   timbers.

Family Lyonsiidae: Paper Shells

SHELLS small, inequivalve, and fragile. The hinge bears a narrow
ledge to which the ligament is attached. Interior pearly. These
mollusks are represented in both the Atlantic and Pacific Oceans,
living on mudflats close to shore.

Genus *Lyonsia* Turton 1822

LYONSIA ARENOSA (Möll.) **Sanded Lyonsia**   Pl. 27
   Range: Circumpolar; south to Vancouver I.
   Habitat: Shallow water.
   Description: About ½ in. long, pearly beneath a very thin
   olive-gray periostracum. Frail in substance, the valves are
   translucent; anterior end rounded and posterior broadly and
   squarely cut off. Surface of periostracum covered with radiating
   wrinkles; these are minutely fringed, so as to entangle grains of
   sand, with which the shell is often coated.

LYONSIA CALIFORNICA Con. **California Lyonsia**   Pl. 27
   Range: Alaska to Mexico.
   Habitat: Shallow water.
   Description: A thin and delicate shell, in length just under
   1 in. There is a thin olive periostracum that is easily lost,
   revealing a pearly-white shell more or less translucent. Anterior
   end rather inflated and rounded; posterior end elongate, narrowed, often crooked, and truncate at the tip.
   Remarks: This small bivalve may be found close to shore, nestling in little pits on the mudflats.

LYONSIA PUGETENSIS Dall **Puget Lyonsia**   Pl. 27
   Range: Alaska to Puget Sound.
   Habitat: Shallow water.

Description: About 1 in. long. A pearly-white shell beneath its thin grayish periostracum. Valves very fragile and slightly inequivalve. Anterior end short and rounded, posterior prolonged, narrowed, and somewhat truncate at tip. Usually a few sand grains are entrapped in the periostracum.

LYONSIA STRIATA (Mtg.)   **Striate Lyonsia**   Pl. 27
Range: Aleutian Is. to Strait of Juan de Fuca.
Habitat: Moderately shallow water.
Description: About ½ in. long, a rather blocky but fragile shell, thin and translucent. More oblong than *L. pugetensis* (above), and gray. Lower portion of shell almost invariably coated with grains of sand.

Genus *Entodesma* Philippi 1845

ENTODESMA SAXICOLA (Baird)   **Rock Entodesma**   Pl. 27
Range: Aleutian Is. to Baja California.
Habitat: Moderately shallow water; holes and crevices in rocks.
Description: A rather large shell, the length averaging 3 or 4 in. Lives in holes and crevices among the rocks, and usually grows to conform with its particular home. When not crowded, tends to assume a pear shape, the anterior end narrow and short and posterior swollen but abruptly truncate and gaping. Periostracum strong, rough, and brown.
Remarks: The valves, although not particularly thin, are weak and brittle, and cabinet specimens are often broken by shrinking of the periostracum.

Genus *Mytilimeria* Conrad 1837

MYTILIMERIA NUTTALLII Con.   **Sea Bottle**   Pl. 27
Range: Alaska to Mexico.
Habitat: Intertidal and offshore waters.
Description: Height about 1½ in., color pure white. There is a thin periostracum that is pale yellowish brown. Shell oval in shape, rather inflated, and very thin and delicate.
Remarks: This is an uncommon mollusk, not often seen in collections. Ascidians (*Amaroucium californicum*) cluster together to form sheetlike mats an inch or so deep, and this clam lives beneath the mats, its presence indicated by narrow slits where the tips of its valves protrude.

Family Pandoridae: Pandoras

SHELLS small, very thin and flat, with inconspicuous beaks. Color white, and interior pearly. These bivalves are distributed in all seas, generally living on stony or pebbly bottoms.

Genus *Pandora* Chemnitz 1795

PANDORA BILIRATA Con.   Pl. 27
    Range: Alaska to Baja California.
    Habitat: Moderately shallow water.
    Description: About ¾ in. long, the left valve is moderately inflated and the right one flat. Both valves thin and fragile, white. Shell is rather elongate, with a sharply truncate posterior end; a distinct angular ridge extends from base of truncate tip to the beaks. Interior very pearly, as with all of this group.

PANDORA FILOSA Carp.   **Western Pandora**   Pl. 27
    Range: Alaska to Baja California.
    Habitat: Moderately shallow water; gravelly bottoms.
    Description: About 1 in. long and pure white. Both the anterior and posterior dorsal margins are fairly straight, with entire basal margin gently rounded. Small beaks slightly closer to anterior end; posterior tip is somewhat upturned and squared off. Inside very pearly.

PANDORA GLACIALIS Leach   **Northern Pandora**   Pl. 27
    Range: Arctic Ocean to Strait of Juan de Fuca; also North Atlantic.
    Habitat: Moderately deep water.
    Description: About 1¼ in. long, the shell is short and broad, and somewhat fatter than many of its genus. Anterior end acutely rounded, posterior end somewhat lengthened, and bearing a slightly upturned tip. Color grayish white; pearly interior.
    Remarks: This species occurs virtually around the world in northern waters. The type locality is in Spitsbergen.

PANDORA PUNCTATA Con.   **Dotted Pandora**   Pl. 27
    Range: Vancouver I. to Mexico.
    Habitat: Moderately deep water.
    Description: A very thin pure-white shell about 2 in. long. Anterior end regularly rounded; posterior end expanded, acutely rostrate and truncate, with a deeply concave area between tip and beaks. Interior pearly, and features very minute scars like pinpricks.

Family Thraciidae: Thracias

RATHER large pelecypods, with shells that are quite inequivalve and more or less gaping. Beaks are prominent, and one of them is commonly perforated to receive the point of its mate. Occur in moderately deep water.

Genus *Thracia* Blainville 1824

THRACIA TRAPEZOIDES Con. **Pacific Thracia** Pl. 27
Range: Alaska to Redondo Beach, California.
Habitat: Moderately deep water.
Description: A sturdy shell nearly 2 in. long. Beaks about central and rather prominent, with one of them perforated by friction with the other. Right valve slightly larger than left, and both ends are regularly rounded, the posterior end somewhat flattened and partially truncate. Color brown; surface faintly marked with concentric lines.
Remarks: This species is common as a fossil in the Pleistocene deposits of San Pedro, California.

Genus *Cyathodonta* Conrad 1849

CYATHODONTA UNDULATA Con. **Wavy Thracia** Pl. 27
Range: Monterey, California, to Mexico.
Habitat: Moderately deep water.
Description: A pure-white shell, rather thin and fragile, its length about 1½ in. Sculptured with concentric undulations that are somewhat oblique. Internal ligament rests on a chondrophore in left valve. Posterior end of shell is rather abruptly truncate.

Family Periplomatidae: Spoon Shells

SHELLS mostly white, small, fragile, and slightly gaping. The common name spoon shells derives from the chondrophore, a low, spoon-shaped tooth in each valve. There is a small triangular process lying next to this tooth that is generally lost when the animal is removed from its shell.

Genus *Periploma* Schumacher 1817

PERIPLOMA DISCUS Stearns **Round Spoon Shell** Pl. 27
Range: Monterey, California, to Gulf of California.
Habitat: Moderately deep water.
Description: The outline of this species is nearly circular, with a corner developed at the upper posterior tip. About 1½ in. long. Valves white and very thin and brittle, with numerous exceedingly fine concentric lines. A prominent spoonlike tooth (chondrophore) under the beaks in each valve.
Remarks: This bivalve is not very common; in fact, it can be classed as a fairly rare shell on the West Coast.

PERIPLOMA PLANIUSCULUM Sow.   Pl. 27
Western Spoon Shell
   Range: Point Conception, California, to Peru.
   Habitat: Just below low-water level; mud.
   Description: From 2 to 3 in. long, a neat shell nicely formed; pure
   white. Anterior end short and rounded; posterior, long and
   evenly rounded, with beaks closer to the front end. Right valve
   inflated and left rather flattened. Inside, each valve bears a
   prominent spoonlike process (chondrophore) that projects into
   the beak cavity.

Family Cuspidariidae: Dipper Shells

SHELLS pear-shaped, inequivalve, thin, and commonly ribbed. All
are small, many tiny, and most are confined to deep water. The
common name dipper shells comes from their handle-like posterior
end.

Genus *Cuspidaria* Nardo 1840

CUSPIDARIA APODEMA Dall   **Smooth Dipper Shell**   Pl. 27
   Range: Alaska to Mexico.
   Habitat: Moderately deep water.
   Description: About ½ in. long, the valves swollen a little to
   present a well-inflated appearance. Anterior end regularly
   rounded, the longer posterior end terminating in a tubular
   rostrum. Surface quite smooth, with a few wrinkle-like lines on
   dorsal side of rostrum. Color white.
   Remarks: Perhaps the commonest member of its group on
   West Coast.

CUSPIDARIA GLACIALIS Sars   **Northern Dipper Shell**   Pl. 27
   Range: Circumpolar; south to B.C.
   Habitat: Moderately deep water.
   Description: Attaining a length of nearly ¾ in. Posterior end
   narrowed to form a definite "handle," but it is not as long or as
   pronounced as in some of the group, so that the clam appears
   to be rather squat. Beaks high; anterior end regularly rounded.
   Color pure white.

Genus *Cardiomya* A. Adams 1864

CARDIOMYA CALIFORNICA (Dall)   Pl. 27
California Dipper Shell
   Range: Puget Sound to San Diego, California.
   Habitat: Deep water.
   Description: A tiny shell, generally less than ¼ in. long. Bears

a number of distinct radiating ribs, or lines, usually about 20. Color is creamy white, with a very thin and delicate periostracum.

CARDIOMYA OLDROYDI (Dall) Pl. 27
Oldroyd's Dipper Shell

Range: Puget Sound to Catalina I., California.
Habitat: Deep water.
Description: Another tiny bivalve, its length seldom more than ¼ in. Color a soiled white. Shell short and inflated; anterior end swollen and rounded, posterior end produced to a small tube. Surface sculptured with sharp radiating lines, which are absent on the posterior tubular part.

CARDIOMYA PECTINATA (Carp.) Pl. 27
Ribbed Dipper Shell

Range: Puget Sound to Panama Bay.
Habitat: Deep water.
Description: About ½ in. long. Anterior end rounded and posterior end drawn out to a long, narrow, tip. Valves thin and brittle, and somewhat gaping. Surface ornamented with about 12 sharp radiating ridges. Color white.

II

West Coast Gastropods

Family Haliotidae: Abalones

SHELLS spiral, depressed, cup-shaped; spire small. The body whorl constitutes most of the shell. There is a row of round or oval holes along the left margin, those near the edge being open. Interior pearly and often multicolored. Animals live attached to rocks like the limpets. All are edible. Common in the Pacific and Indian Oceans, with perhaps the greatest variety occurring on our own West Coast.

Genus *Haliotis* Linné 1758

HALIOTIS ASSIMILIS Dall   **Threaded Abalone**   **Pl. 28**
  Range: Farallon Is. to San Francisco, California.
  Habitat: Rather deep water.
  Description: Shell relatively thin but strong and solid. Length averages about 4 in. Shape roundly oval, the outer surface decorated with numerous threadlike ridges. The spire is quite distinct, and there are about 5 open holes. Color brown; inner surface silvery, with tints of pink and green; there is no observable muscle scar.

HALIOTIS CORRUGATA Gray   **Corrugated Abalone**   **Pl. 29**
  Range: Monterey, California, to Baja California.
  Habitat: Moderately shallow water.
  Description: Shell rather circular and well arched, length about 8 in. Surface quite rough, with wavy corrugations; the 3 or 4 open holes are often large and bordered by sharply elevated rims. Color grayish brown; interior highly iridescent, generally tinged with bluish.

HALIOTIS CRACHERODII Leach   **Black Abalone**   **Pl. 29**
  Range: Oregon to Baja California.
  Habitat: Close to shore; rocks.
  Description: Shell rather plump, bluntly oval in outline, its adult length between 5 and 6 in. Outer surface smooth, greenish black, with only faint suggestions of spiral lines. Interior

silvery, with green and pink reflections. There are generally about 8 open holes.

Remarks: This is the most abundant species of abalone on our coast. A rare form is occasionally found with the holes lacking. This has been named subspecies *H. c. holzneri* Hemp., and *H. c. imperforata* Dall, but modern authors regard it as merely an individual variation, without subspecific value.

HALIOTIS FULGENS Phil.   **Green Abalone**   Pl. 29
Range: Monterey, California, to Baja California.
Habitat: Moderately deep water.
Description: A fine large shell from 6 to 8 in. long. The shape is almost round and flatly coiled, with such a flaring aperture that at first glance it looks like half of a bivalve mollusk. There are generally about 6 open holes at the margin, plus a notch at the edge. Outer surface decorated with rounded spiral ribs and is reddish brown in color, but the shell is usually overgrown with bryozoa and other marine growths. Interior brilliantly iridescent and beautifully polished. Principal shade bluish green; there is an area at the center, where the muscle was attached, that is especially deep-colored and shines with a prismatic luster.
Remarks: It is a commercial mollusk, the legal length 6¼ in.

HALIOTIS KAMTSCHATKANA Jonas   Pl. 28
Japanese Abalone
Range: Aleutian Is. to cent. California.
Habitat: Moderately deep water.
Description: Length about 5 in., shape rather elongate. Shell moderately thin, with a noticeable spire. There are about 5 open holes, with raised rims. Outer surface rough, mottled brown and gray; inner surface iridescent with pale greens and blues.
Remarks: In many books this species is listed as occurring from N. America to Japan, and it is commonly known as the Japanese Abalone. However, the Japanese shell is now regarded as specifically different, and has been named *H. hannai* Ino.

HALIOTIS RUFESCENS Swain.   **Red Abalone**   Pls. 3, 29
Range: Bodega Bay, California, to Mexico.
Habitat: Moderately deep water.
Description: One of the largest of our abalones. A large, thick, heavy species, attaining a length of some 10 in. General shape oval, not very convex, and the color dull reddish brown. The sculpture consists of rounded spiraling ribs and low radiating waves. Inside, the shell is highly polished, and variegated with hues of bluish, pink, and copper, the pink predominating. The outer rim projects over the pearly interior and forms a red edge. There are usually about 4 open holes at the margin.

Family Fissurellidae: Keyhole Limpets

SHELL conical, oval at base. Apex perforated, or there is a slit or notch, in the margin of the shell. The surface is usually strongly ribbed. Distributed in all but the coldest seas.

Genus *Fissurella* Bruguière 1798

FISSURELLA VOLCANO Reeve   **Volcano Limpet**   Pl. 30
Range: California to Panama.
Habitat: Shallow water; rocks.
Description: About 1 in. long. A conical shell, well elevated, with an oval base, somewhat narrower in front. At the summit there is an oblong perforation, situated somewhat in front of the center. Surface sculptured with unequal radiating ribs. Color ashy pink, with distinct brownish or reddish rays. The animal is gaily colored too, bearing red stripes and having a yellow foot.
Remarks: *F. v. crucifer* Dall is a color form, with 4 equidistant white rays. It occurs from Monterey, California, to Baja California.

Genus *Diodora* Gray 1821

DIODORA ASPERA (Esch.)   **Rough Keyhole Limpet**   Pl. 30
Range: Alaska to Baja California.
Habitat: Shallow water.
Description: A solid shell, in length averaging 1½ in. but in some cases growing to a full 2 in. Base oval, the apex moderately well elevated, with a small oval or nearly circular hole at the summit. Inside, the perforation is somewhat excavated at the rear (see Plate 30, No. 8). Surface ornamented by numerous radiating ribs, about every 4th one considerably enlarged. Margins finely crenulate. Color gray or white, often with purplish-brown rays; interior plain white.

Genus *Megathura* Pilsbry 1890

MEGATHURA CRENULATA (Sow.)   Pl. 30
Great Keyhole Limpet
Range: Monterey, California, to Mexico.
Habitat: Moderately deep water offshore.
Description: A real giant, attaining a length of 4 in. Shell oval and rather flat, with a large roundish opening at the top. Surface bears numerous strong radiating lines, and a few well-separated growth lines. Margins strongly crenulate, and there is a rim of heavy enamel around the orifice. Color grayish white; inside white and very smooth.

Remarks: The animal is larger than its shell, which is partially concealed by the brownish mantle.

Genus *Lucapinella* Pilsbry 1890

LUCAPINELLA CALLOMARGINATA (Dall) Pl. 30
Hard-edged Keyhole Limpet
> **Range:** Bodega Bay, California, to Nicaragua.
> **Habitat:** Shallow water; rocks.
> **Description:** About ¾ in. long, with an oval base that is some-what narrower at anterior end. Not very highly arched. Orifice large, usually shaped about the same as outline of whole shell. Margins finely crenulate; surface bears fine radiating lines. Color gray or white with dark rays; interior is white. There is usually a rim of paler color bordering the perforation at the summit.

Genus *Megatebennus* Pilsbry 1890

MEGATEBENNUS BIMACULATUS (Dall) Pl. 30
Two-spotted Keyhole Limpet
> **Range:** Alaska to Mexico.
> **Habitat:** Water's edge; under stones.
> **Description:** About ½ in. long. Shape oval and moderately flat, with both ends turned slightly upward. Perforation large and oval. Surface bears radiating ribs and fine concentric lines, imparting a cancellate sculpture. Color grayish; interior white.

Genus *Puncturella* Lowe 1827

PUNCTURELLA CUCULLATA (Gould) Pl. 30
Hooded Keyhole Limpet
> **Range:** Alaska to California.
> **Habitat:** Fairly deep water.
> **Description:** Fully an inch in height and almost the same in length, this shell is somewhat oval in outline, with narrower anterior and broader posterior ends. Apex acute, sometimes curving forward; the narrow perforation is just in front of the tip. Shell rugged and solid, decorated with some 25 robust ribs, with smaller ribs between them. Margins scalloped. Color greenish gray; interior white.
> **Remarks:** The similar species *P. galeata* (Gould), ranging from Alaska to California also, is the same size but is ornamented by fine lines rather than heavy ribs, and its margins are smooth.

PUNCTURELLA MULTISTRIATA Dall Pl. 30
Many-ribbed Puncturella
> **Range:** Aleutian Is. to California.
> **Habitat:** Fairly deep water.

Description: A distinctive shell, its length nearly ¾ in. Shape oval, the summit only moderately elevated. There is a very narrow slit at the anterior end. Surface decorated with numerous main radiating ribs, smaller lines separating them. Color white.

Family Acmaeidae: Limpets

SHELLS conical, oval, and open at base, with no opening at the apex. Not spiral at any stage of growth and never iridescent within. Herbaceous gastropods, living on stones and grasses at the shoreline, generally between the tide limits. Interior bears a muscle scar shaped like a horseshoe, open at the front. The genus *Acmaea* is abundant, both as to species and individuals, on West Coast.

Genus *Acmaea* Eschscholtz 1830

ACMAEA ASMI Midd.   **Black Limpet**   Pl. 31
    Range: Alaska to Mexico.
    Habitat: This species attaches itself to a shell of a snail, usually of the genus *Tegula*.
    Description: Our smallest limpet. Black, and only about ¼ in. long. Shell thin but strong, with the pointed apex well elevated. Surface dull and commonly eroded. Interior also black, or deep brown, sometimes with a paler border.

ACMAEA CONUS Test   **Test's Limpet**   Pl. 30
    Range: Point Conception, California, to Mexico.
    Habitat: Near low-water line; stones.
    Description: Another small limpet (less than 1 in. long) that can easily be confused with the larger *A. scabra*, and may eventually turn out to be a subspecies. Bears low radiating ribs and a scalloped margin. Color gray on outside; inside, the shell has a brown center that is smooth and glossy, not roughened as in *A. scabra*.

ACMAEA DIGITALIS Esch.   **Finger Limpet**   Pl. 31
    Range: Aleutian Is. to Mexico.
    Habitat: Close to and above high-water mark; rocks.
    Description: Slightly more than 1 in. long, oval in outline. Apex commonly overhangs anterior end, so that the shell between the tip and that margin is concave. Surface fairly smooth on short end, but posterior slope decorated with strong and rough radiating ridges. Color gray, with stripes and blotches of brown and white. Interior pale bluish, with a large brown patch at center and a narrow black or brown border at rim.
    Remarks: This is one of the most abundant limpets on the West Coast.

ACMAEA FENESTRATA Reeve   **Fenestrate Limpet**   **Pl. 30**
Range: Alaska to Mexico. *A. f. fenestrata*, Alaska to cent. California; *A. f. cribraria*, Point Conception, California, south.
Habitat: Stones and pebbles in loose sand.
Description: A rather solid shell, oval in outline and about 1 in. long. It is moderately arched, the apex slightly ahead of the middle. There are 2 subspecies. The typical form, *A. f. fenestrata* (Reeve), is grayish green with flecks of pale yellowish, the inside bluish white, with a narrow brown border. The northern form, the subspecies *A. f. cribraria* (Carp.), also on Plate 30, is darker within, almost a solid brown, its upper surface like the typical form. At a point where the two forms meet there are many intergrades.

ACMAEA INSESSA (Hinds)   **Seaweed Limpet**   **Pl. 31**
Range: Alaska to Baja California.
Habitat: Various sea plants and algae; attached to holdfast.
Description: A small caplike shell about ½ in. long. Apex bluntly rounded, the parallel sides quite steep. Color brown, both inside and outside; surface is smooth and shiny.

ACMAEA INSTABILIS (Gould)   **Unstable Limpet**   **Pl. 31**
Range: Alaska to San Diego, California.
Habitat: Stems of large seaweeds.
Description: Elongate-oval, with the sides straight and the ends rounded. Length about 1 in. Apex moderately elevated, and closer to anterior end. Surface bears fine radiating lines or ribs. Color is dark brown, sometimes nearly black. Interior bluish white, with a brown center; narrow border of brown at the rim.

ACMAEA LIMATULA Carp.   **File Limpet**   **Pl. 31**
Range: Puget Sound to Mexico.
Habitat: Rocks between tides.
Description: Roundish oval in outline, diam. about 1 in. and only moderately arched. Apex closer to anterior end. Color light brown to almost black, the surface bearing numerous closely set radiating lines or ridges that are scaly. Interior white or bluish white and very glossy, with a brown central spot and a solid black border at the rim.

ACMAEA MITRA Esch.   **White-capped Limpet**   **Pl. 31**
Range: Bering Sea to Baja California.
Habitat: Usually below the low-water line.
Description: A conical, caplike shell with a circular base about 1 in. long. Height usually less than 1 in. Occasionally larger specimens are found. Apex bluntly pointed and nearly central in position, being just a shade closer to the anterior margin. Color dull white, inside and out; some shells tinged with

pink or pale green, owing to the presence of algal growths.
Remarks: Although this snail prefers to live well beyond the
low-water mark as a rule, empty shells are not uncommon on
the beaches. It is one of the most steeply conical of its group.

ACMAEA PELTA Esch.   Shield Limpet   Pl. 31
Range: Alaska to Baja California.
Habitat: Shoreline; rocks.
Description: A strong and rugged shell, its length about 1½ in.
Apex pointed, well elevated, and located just off the center.
Color gray, often with black lines; surface sculptured with blunt
radiating ribs. Young specimens may be shiny black. Interior
white, with a small brown blotch at the center; there is a border,
of black more or less flecked with yellowish.

ACMAEA PERSONA Esch.   Mask Limpet   Pl. 31
Range: Aleutian Is. to Monterey, California.
Habitat: Well above high-tide mark; rocks.
Description: A rather oddly shaped limpet, average length 1 in.
Shell well arched, apex close to anterior end. From the apex to
that end there is a steep slope; but from apex to posterior end
the shell is gently curved. Color mottled gray and brown;
interior bluish white, with a central brownish patch.

ACMAEA SCABRA Gould   Rough Limpet   Pl. 31
Range: B.C. to Mexico.
Habitat: Often well above high-tide mark; rocks.
Description: Shell somewhat variable, but with most specimens
the apex is moderately elevated and placed nearer the anterior
end. Summit sharp, and from it radiate strong rounded ridges,
their ends making the margins of the shell scalloped. Length
about 1 in. Gray or mottled gray and black; interior is whitish,
with a brown center somewhat roughened.
Remarks: This species used to be listed as *A. spectrum* Nutt.

ACMAEA TESTUDINALIS SCUTUM Esch.   Pl. 31
Plate Limpet
Range: Alaska to Mexico; rare south of Oregon.
Habitat: Shoreline; rocks.
Description: An oval shell from 1 to 2 in. long. Rather flat,
with the blunt apex a little closer to anterior end. Color clouded
brown and gray, often with suggestions of radiating lines and
spots. Inside bluish white and glossy, with a patch of brown at
the center and a narrow border around the rim that is rich
brown checked with white.
Remarks: The typical *A. testudinalis* Müll. is an Atlantic species.
This Pacific subspecies also has been listed as *A. tessulata* Müll.
and *A. patina* Esch

Genus *Lottia* Sowerby 1833

LOTTIA GIGANTEA Sow.   **Owl Limpet**   **Pl. 28**
  Range: Crescent City, California, to Baja California.
  Habitat: Rocks between tides.
  Description: The largest unperforated limpet on our coast.
  Length 3 to 4 in. Shape oval, the apex right next to anterior
  end, the shell only slightly arched. Surface rough, mottled gray
  and black; interior brownish black, with a bluish owl-shaped
  patch at the center. Interior highly polished, and outer surface
  can also be given a mirrorlike finish with a little polishing.
  Remarks: The largest specimens come from the southern parts
  of its range.

Family Trochidae: Pearly Top Shells

HERBIVOROUS snails, widely distributed in warm seas, generally
among seaweeds in shallow water. A few members thrive in cold
waters. The shells are composed largely of iridescent nacre,
although the pearly layer may be hidden by a periostracum during
life. Varied in shape, but commonly pyramidal. Operculum thin
and corneous.

Genus *Margarites* Gray 1847

MARGARITES COSTALIS (Gould)   **Ridged Margarite**   **Pl. 32**
  Range: Circumpolar; south to B.C.
  Habitat: Seaweeds.
  Description: Nearly $\frac{1}{2}$ in. high and ashy gray, sometimes tinged
  with greenish. Shell thin and of a low pyramidal shape, with 5
  or 6 whorls rendered angular by prominent revolving ribs.
  Surface also bears very fine lines of growth. Umbilicus broad
  and deep, aperture circular, with a thin and sharp outer lip.
  Worn shells show considerable iridescence.

MARGARITES PUPILLUS (Gould)   **Puppet Margarite**   **Pl. 32**
  Range: Alaska to San Pedro, California.
  Habitat: Shallow water; weedy bottoms.
  Description: Generally less than $\frac{1}{2}$ in. high, with some specimens a little larger. There are 4 or 5 whorls, each decorated
  with a few revolving ribs. Apex rather blunt, and base of shell
  boasts a small umbilicus. Aperture nearly round. Color dull
  chalky gray, sometimes yellowish, with the aperture showing
  tinges of iridescence.

MARGARITES SUCCINCTUS (Carp.)   Pl. 32
Tucked Margarite
　　Range: Alaska to San Diego, California.
　　Habitat: Seaweeds.
　　Description: A tiny snail, generally less than ¼ in. high. There are 4 whorls and a rather low spire. Shell relatively solid, gray, banded with narrow lines of purplish brown. The sutures are deeply impressed. There is a small umbilicus.

Genus *Solariella* Wood 1842

SOLARIELLA PERAMABILIS Carp.   **Lovely Top**   Pl. 32
　　Range: Alaska to San Diego, California.
　　Habitat: Moderately deep water.
　　Description: Small and thin-shelled, the height about ½ in., composed of about 4 rounded whorls. Spire low, the apex sharp, and aperture circular. There is a prominent umbilicus. The volutions are sculptured with revolving ridges crossed by fine lines. Color pinkish gray; an iridescent layer on the inside.

SOLARIELLA VARICOSA (Mig. & C. B. Adams)   Pl. 32
Varicose Top
　　Range: Arctic Ocean to San Diego, California.
　　Habitat: Moderately deep water.
　　Description: A stout little shell composed of about 4 convex whorls. Spire low but sharp, umbilicus broad and deep, and aperture round. Height about ½ in. Whorls marked with oblique vertical ribs, as well as distinct revolving lines. Color yellowish white; aperture pearly.

Genus *Lischkeia* Fischer 1879

LISCHKEIA CIDARIS (Carp.)   **Spiny Top**   Pl. 32
　　Range: Alaska to Baja California.
　　Habitat: Moderately deep water.
　　Description: Nearly 1 in. high. A shell of 6 or 7 well-rounded whorls, tapering to a sharp apex. Sutures well defined. Sculpture consists of double row of small knobs on each volution, with base of the shell bearing strong revolving lines. Aperture round, and pearly within, the shell itself grayish white.

Genus *Calliostoma* Swainson 1840

CALLIOSTOMA ANNULATUM (Hum.)   **Ringed Top**   Pls. 4, 32
　　Range: Alaska to San Diego, California.
　　Habitat: Moderately deep water; weedy bottoms.
　　Description: Usually under 1 in. high and sharply conical in shape. About 8 rather flattened whorls, decorated with small

beaded ridges. Color yellowish brown, dotted with darker brown on the revolving bands of beads; apex pink, and there is more or less purplish pink showing at the sutures. Aperture shows iridescent hues of green and pink.

CALLIOSTOMA CANALICULATUM (Hum.) Pl. 32
Channeled Top

Range: Alaska to San Diego, California.
Habitat: Just off shore; seaweeds.
Description: About 1½ in. high. Shell thin but strong, and brown, ranging from fairly rich brown to light tan. There are 7 whorls, sculptured with revolving ridges paler in tone than the spaces between them. Ridges on upper portions of shell tend to become beaded. Interior pearly. Apex sharply pointed, the columella often bearing small patches of blue; there is no umbilicus.
Remarks: This species used to be listed as *C. canaliculatum* Mtyn., but Martyn's work has been rejected by the International Commission on Zoological Nomenclature. In many books this snail is listed as *C. doliarium* Hol.; however, there is an earlier validation of the name by Humphrey, so now we again know this attractive snail as *C. canaliculatum*.

CALLIOSTOMA GEMMULATUM Carp. Gem Top Pl. 32
Range: San Pedro, California, to Mexico.
Habitat: Seaweeds.
Description: Somewhat less than 1 in. high, its shape resembles a swollen top with a very sharp tip. There are about 7 whorls, the sutures distinctly marked. Sculpture consists of revolving rows of granules, 2 rows on each volution standing out more prominently than the others. Color greenish brown, with darker stripes radiating from the apex.

CALLIOSTOMA LIGATUM (Gould) Costate Top Pl. 32
Range: Alaska to San Diego, California.
Habitat: Close to shore; weeds.
Description: Averages about ¾ in. high. Color bluish brown, the blue a pearly layer just under the surface and often visible on worn shells. About 7 whorls that are rather rounded, each with numerous closely set revolving ridges. Apex sharply pointed. Whole shell is rather solid-appearing.

CALLIOSTOMA SPLENDENS Carp. Splendid Top Pl. 32
Range: Monterey, California, to Mexico.
Habitat: Moderately deep water.
Description: A rather uncommon species, only about ¼ in. high. Color yellowish brown, and there are 5 or 6 whorls, decorated with prominent revolving ridges, those at the shoulders strongly

beaded. The shell often shows an orange iridescence between the ridges.

CALLIOSTOMA SUPRAGRANOSUM Carp. Pl. 32
Granose Top

Range: Monterey, California, to Baja California.

Habitat: Rocks at low tide.

Description: Somewhat less than ½ in. high, this species is stoutly conical in shape. There are 6 whorls, sculptured with revolving lines, some of them weakly beaded near the sutures. Color pale brown, with a band of brown and white dots on each whorl.

Remarks: This species is not especially common.

CALLIOSTOMA TRICOLOR Gabb Three-colored Top Pl. 32

Range: S. California to Mexico.

Habitat: Moderately shallow water.

Description: Slightly more than ½ in. high and rather variable in shape. Strongly conical as a rule, with sloping whorls, and flattish at the base. Color yellowish brown, each whorl with beaded ridges, 3 of which are marked with alternate dashes of white and purple. Shell very pearly inside, as well as just under the surface, so that worn shells usually exhibit a generous area of pearl.

CALLIOSTOMA VARIEGATUM Carp. Variegated Top Pl. 32

Range: Alaska to California.

Habitat: Deep water.

Description: About 1 in. high, sometimes a little more, with about 6 somewhat concave whorls and indistinct sutures. Apex very sharp, the body whorl swollen. Volutions decorated with strongly beaded revolving lines. Color yellowish white.

Remarks: An uncommon species.

Genus *Norrisia* Bayle 1880

NORRISIA NORRISII (Sow.) Norris Top Pl. 33

Range: Cent. California to Mexico.

Habitat: Kelp.

Description: A rather heavy and solid shell, orbicular in outline, growing to a diam. of about 2 in. There are 3 or 4 whorls, the last one making up most of the shell; spire very low, almost flat. A well-defined umbilicus. Surface smooth; color yellowish brown. Edge of outer lip black, and area of the umbilicus tinged with green. The animal is pale red. The horny operculum is shaggy on the outside.

Remarks: Formerly very abundant, this snail is now quite rare, because of the disappearance of the kelp beds from large areas.

Genus *Tegula* Lesson 1832

TEGULA AUREOTINCTA For.   **Gilded Top**   Pl. 32
Range: S. California to Mexico.
Habitat: Close to shore; rocks.
Description: About 1 in. high, this species is black or dark gray,
strongly marked with bright yellow within the deep umbilicus,
which is bordered by a rim of pale blue. There are 5 whorls,
spirally ribbed on lower portion and marked with radiating folds
above. Apex commonly eroded, and many specimens will be
found that have much of the surface of the early whorls broken
away to reveal the pearly underlayer.

TEGULA BRUNNEA (Phil.)   **Brown Top**   Pl. 32
Range: Mendocina Co. to Santa Barbara Is., California
Habitat: Rocks at low tide.
Description: This shell grows to be nearly 2 in. high, but most
individuals are slightly smaller. There are 6 whorls, the shoul-
ders marked with diagonal folds, sometimes obscure. Color
yellowish brown; aperture white. There are 2 small knoblike
teeth at base of columella.
Remarks: As with many of this group, the pearly luster often
shows through in places where the surface has become worn.
This species is often found as a fossil in the Pliocene deposits of
San Pedro, California.

TEGULA FUNEBRALIS (A. Adams)   **Black Top**   Pl. 32
Range: B.C. to Baja California.
Habitat: Shoreline; rocks.
Description: A strong and robust shell, averaging about 1½ in.
high. Shell bluntly pyramidal, or top-shaped, and consists of 4
or 5 whorls faintly wrinkled at the sutures. There are 2 small
knobs at base of columella. Periostracum deep purplish black,
and just beneath the outer surface is a beautiful pearly layer.
The early volutions are frequently more or less eroded.

TEGULA GALLINA (For.)   **Speckled Top**   Pl. 32
Range: San Francisco to Baja California.
Habitat: Rocks between tides.
Description: Another solid shell, 1½ in. high. There are 5 or 6
whorls, and a rather blunt apex, the general outline top-shaped.
Color purplish black, vertically flecked with white. Apex commonly eroded, and tinged with orange. Outer lip bears a black
edge, and the shell is pearly within. As in all of this genus, the
operculum is small, thin, circular, and corneous.

TEGULA LIGULATA (Menke)   **Banded Top**   Pl. 32
Range: Monterey, California, to Baja California.
Habitat: Rocks between tides.

Description: A solid shell nearly 1 in. high. Shape rather variable, but it is generally about as broad as it is high. There are 4 or 5 rounded whorls, decorated with raised spiral lines often broken into elongate beads. There is a deep umbilicus. Color brownish tan.

TEGULA MONTEREYI (Kiener)   **Monterey Top**   Pl. 32
Range: Bolinas Bay, California, to Santa Barbara Is.
Habitat: Moderately deep water.
Description: About 1½ in. high and about the same in diam. Shape pyramidal, with a fairly sharp apex and very flat-sided whorls. Base flat and surface smooth, with only very weak spiral lines. Umbilicus deep and bordered by a slight ridge. Color brown, the base white.

TEGULA PULLIGO (Gmel.)   Pl. 32
Range: Alaska to Santa Barbara Is., California.
Habitat: Moderately deep water.
Description: About 1 in. high, with steep sides, the sutures weakly impressed. There are 5 or 6 whorls, the apex sharply pointed. Surface is relatively smooth. Color purplish gray. The base is flat, the umbilicus wide and deep.

TEGULA REGINA Stearns   **Queen Top**   Pls. 4, 32
Range: Catalina I. to Gulf of California.
Habitat: Deep water.
Description: A solid shell, steeply conical, some 2 in. high. There are about 7 whorls, decorated with slanting ribs, and the margins of each volution are crenulate and slightly overhang the whorl below. The base is marked with sharp curving lines. Color dark purplish gray, the umbilical region stained a bright golden orange.
Remarks: A rare shell, eagerly sought by collectors.

Family Turbinidae: Turbans

SHELLS generally heavy and solid, turbinate (top-shaped), and often brilliantly colored, with pearl beneath the outer layer. Surface may be smooth, rugose, or spiny. There is a heavy, calcareous operculum, and no umbilicus. These are herbivorous gastropods, and beautifully colored pearl buttons are cut from the shells of some species. The famous cat's eye of South Pacific jewelry is the colorful operculum of a member of this family (*Turbo petholatus* Linné).

Genus *Astraea* Röding 1798

ASTRAEA GIBBEROSA (Dill.)   **Red Turban**   Pl. 32
    Range: Vancouver I. to San Diego, California.
    Habitat: Moderately shallow water.
    Description: Height about 2 in. There are 6 or 7 steep-sided whorls, decorated with numerous vertical folds, and a weakly knobbed sutural band. Color dull reddish brown.
    Remarks: Formerly listed as *A. inaequalis* Mtyn.

ASTRAEA UNDOSA (Wood)   **Wavy Turban**   Pls. 4, 32
    Range: Ventura, California, to Baja California.
    Habitat: Moderately shallow water.
    Description: A large, solid, and heavy shell, attaining a height of fully 4 in. and a diam. about the same. There are 6 to 8 steeply sloping whorls, a sharp apex, and a rather flat base. Each volution is decorated with a series of wavy vertical ridges, and a prominent knobby band that resembles a twisted cord follows the suture line. Color pale brown under a darker brown periostracum, but the shell is so pearly that only on very fresh specimens is the iridescent sheen obscured. Operculum calcareous, and thickened by strong concentric grooves.

Genus *Homalopoma* Carpenter 1864

HOMALOPOMA CARPENTERI (Pils.)   **Dwarf Turban**   Pl. 32
    Range: Alaska to Mexico.
    Habitat: Shallow water.
    Description: A solid, globose minute shell, just about ¼ in. broad. The last whorl makes up most of the shell, and is decorated with a number of evenly spaced revolving lines. Color pinkish red, the interior pearly, and the columella bears 2 or 3 weak nodules. Aperture round, and closed by a solid, calcareous operculum.

Family Lacunidae: Chink Shells

THESE snails are stoutly conical and thin-shelled. The aperture is half-moon-shaped, and the distinguishing character is a lengthened groove, or chink, alongside the columella.

Genus *Lacuna* Turton 1827

LACUNA CARINATA (Gould)   **Carinate Chink Shell**   Pl. 33
    Range: Alaska to Monterey, California.
    Habitat: Moderately shallow water; kelp.
    Description: A squat shell, somewhat less than ½ in. high.

There are 4 or 5 whorls, the body whorl sloping and expanding to a large aperture. There is a wide chink at the umbilicus. forming a groove partway up the columella. Color yellowish brown, with a thin periostracum; the surface smooth.

Remarks: Formerly listed as *L. porrecta* Carp.

LACUNA VINCTA Turt.　**Northern Chink Shell**　Pl. 33
Range: Alaska to California; Labrador to New Jersey.
Habitat: Moderately shallow water; seaweeds.
Description: About ⅓ in. high and dingy white, sometimes weakly banded with purplish. Shell thin and conical, with about 5 rather stoutish whorls separated by moderately deep sutures. The surface bears minute lines of growth, and the aperture is moderately large. Inner lip flattened, and excavated by a smooth, elongate groove terminating in a tiny umbilicus.
Remarks: These small snails are easily recognized by the peculiar umbilicus, which forms a prominent groove beside the columella After storms, specimens can often be collected in quantities from seaweeds that have been cast ashore.

Family Littorinidae: Periwinkles

A LARGE family of shore-dwelling gastropods, found clinging to the rocks between the tidemarks, and sometimes well above the average high-tide limits. The shell is usually sturdy, has few whorls, and is without an umbilicus. Distribution worldwide.

Genus *Littorina* Férussac 1822

LITTORINA PLANAXIS Phil.　**Flat Periwinkle**　Pl. 33
Range: Puget Sound to Baja California.
Habitat: Rocks at the high-tide line.
Description: Slightly more than ½ in. high, a rather smooth shell of 3 or 4 whorls. Form moderately stout, apex bluntly pointed and more often than not eroded. Aperture large; outer lip sharp. The columella is flattened. Color pale chocolate, often speckled with white. Juveniles are sometimes banded with whitish.

LITTORINA SCUTULATA Gould　　　　　　　　Pl. 33
Checkered Periwinkle
Range: Alaska to Baja California.
Habitat: Rocks between tides.
Description: About ½ in. high, the color reddish brown, more or less checkered with white. Interior of aperture purplish. There are about 4 whorls, a moderately tall spire for this group, and a sharp apex. Surface smooth and shiny.

LITTORINA SITKANA Phil. **Sitka Periwinkle** Pl. 33
Range: Bering Sea to Puget Sound.
Habitat: Rocks between tides.
Description: This species grows to be nearly ¾ in. high, and is
fairly solid in appearance. The 4 or 5 whorls are quite stout, and
decorated with strong spiral ridges. Dark chocolate-brown; there
may be a rather broad paler band on the body whorl. Columella
whitish.

Family Turritellidae: Turret Shells

GREATLY elongated, many-whorled shells, generally turreted. A
large family, living chiefly in tropic seas. Many of the South
Pacific species are very colorful and much sought by collectors.

Genus *Turritella* Lamarck 1799

TURRITELLA COOPERI Carp. **Cooper's Turret** Pl. 33
Range: Monterey, California, to San Diego.
Habitat: Moderately shallow water; sandy bottoms.
Description: A slender, spikelike shell about 1½ in. high, con-
sisting of some 17 rather flattish whorls with distinct sutures.
Whorls decorated with a pair of revolving ridges and marked by
fine spiral lines. Aperture round, the outer lip thin and sharp.
Color yellowish, often with brown or chocolate streaks.
Remarks: Rather common as a fossil in the Pleistocene deposits
at San Pedro, California.

Genus *Turritellopsis* Sars 1878

TURRITELLOPSIS ACICULA STIMPSONI Dall Pl. 33
Stimpson's Turret
Range: B.C. to San Diego, California.
Habitat: Moderately deep water.
Description: A thin, brownish-white shell about ½ in. high.
There are about 10 well-rounded whorls, spirally ribbed, and with
weak vertical striations. Aperture round, the lip thin and sharp.
Remarks: The typical *T. acicula* Stim. is an Atlantic shell, and
is slightly more slender than the subspecies *T. a. stimpsoni*.

Genus *Tachyrhynchus* Mörch 1868

TACHYRHYNCHUS EROSUM (Couth.) Pl. 33
Eroded Turret
Range: Arctic Ocean to B.C.; also North Atlantic Coast.
Habitat: Moderately deep water.
Description: A pale to dark brown shell about 1 in. high. It is

elongate, high-spired, with about 10 flattish whorls, each deeply grooved with 5 blunt furrows that give the surface a spiral ornamentation. Aperture almost round, operculum horny. Apex commonly eroded or broken in the majority of shells found.

Remarks: Often taken from the stomachs of fishes.

Family Vermetidae: Worm Shells

SHELL tubular, extended, and irregular in growth. Generally spiraled when very young. The animal is wormlike, and the shells are usually erroneously called "worm tubes." They often grow on one another in a tangled mass. Ordinarily attached to stones, pilings, other shells, or corals. Confined to warm and temperate seas.

Genus *Serpulorbis* Sassi 1827

SERPULORBIS SQUAMIGERUS (Carp.)   Pl. 33
Scaled Worm Shell
  Range: California to Mexico.
  Habitat: Just below the low-water line.
  Description: Growing in twisted, sprawling masses, the individual tubes in diam. about ½ in. and may be several inches long. The sculpture consists of strong longitudinal lines that are somewhat scaly. Color pinkish gray.

Family Potamididae: Horn Shells

SMALL to medium-sized shells, usually brownish, living in muddy situations in bays and coves, frequently in brackish waters. The anterior canal is less strongly developed than in the next family, Cerithiidae.

Genus *Cerithidea* Swainson 1840

CERITHIDEA CALIFORNICA Hald.   Pl. 34
California Horn Shell
  Range: Bolinas Bay, California, to Baja California.
  Habitat: Mudflats.
  Description: This is a strong and stoutly spikelike shell about 1½ in. high. There are some 10 rounded whorls, sculptured with vertical ribs and revolving ridges. Aperture circular, and closed by a horny operculum. Color dark brown, sometimes with a narrow paler band on each whorl.

Family Cerithiidae: Horn Shells

A LARGE family of generally elongate, many-whorled snails, living in moderately shallow water, mostly on grasses and seaweeds, in tropical and semitropical seas. The aperture is small and oblique, and there is a short anterior canal, commonly more or less twisted.

Genus *Bittium* Gray 1847

BITTIUM ESCHRICHTI (Midd.)   **Eschricht's Bittium**   Pl. 34
 Range: Alaska to Crescent City, California.
 Habitat: Shallow water.
 Description: A small shell, about ¾ in. high. There are 9 or 10 whorls, producing a tall spire. Volutions sculptured with prominent revolving grooves. Aperture small and oval; outer lip thin and sharp, and wavy; inner lip partially reflected. Color grayish brown.

BITTIUM MUNITUM (Carp.)   **Beaded Bittium**   Pl. 34
 Range: Alaska to Oregon.
 Habitat: Shallow water; under stones.
 Description: About ¼ in. high, a slender shell of about 6 whorls. Sutures distinct and apex bluntly pointed. The sculpture consists of weak revolving lines that are faintly beaded, 3 to a volution. Color grayish white.

Genus *Cerithiopsis* Forbes & Hanley 1849

CERITHIOPSIS ALCIMA Bar.   **Flattish Horn Shell**   Pl. 34
 Range: San Pedro, California, south.
 Habitat: Moderately deep water.
 Description: A slender shell just under ½ in. high. There are about 11 whorls, each decorated with spiraling rows of tiny beads. Base quite flat, the aperture small. Color yellowish brown.

CERITHIOPSIS COSMIA Bar.   **Regular Horn Shell**   Pl. 34
 Range: California to Mexico.
 Habitat: Shallow water.
 Description: About ¼ in. high, the whorl count around 8. There are 3 rows of rounded beads encircling each volution, and the sutures are not very deeply impressed. Aperture small, with a short, straight canal. The color ranges from white to brownish.

CERITHIOPSIS GLORIOSA Bar.   **Glorious Horn Shell**   Pl. 34
 Range: S. California.
 Habitat: Moderately deep water.

Description: A neat little shell, slender and well formed, consisting of some 10 whorls and attaining a height of ½ in. Sutures plainly marked, and each volution bears 3 rows of small beads. Aperture small and oval; inner lip partially twisted and the outer lip thin and wavy. Color yellowish white.

Genus *Seila* A. Adams 1861

SEILA MONTEREYENSIS Bar. **Monterey Seila** Pl. 33
Range: Monterey, California, to Baja California.
Habitat: Moderately shallow water.
Description: An elongate brown shell of some 10 whorls, the height about ½ in. The whorls are ornamented with strong revolving lines, the grooves between them broadly rounded. Aperture relatively small; whole shell appears solid and substantial.

Family Triphoridae: Left-handed Snails

AN interesting family of small, elongate, left-handed (sinistral) snails. They are widely distributed in warm seas, bear numerous whorls, and the surface is usually beaded.

Genus *Triphora* Blainville 1828

TRIPHORA PEDROANA Bar. **San Pedro Triphora** Pl. 34
Range: San Pedro, California, to Mexico.
Habitat: Shallow water.
Description: About ¼ in. high, this is a slender shell of 8 or 9 whorls. The coiling is reversed from the normal, so that this is a sinistral, or "left-handed" gastropod. Each volution bears 3 rows of tiny rounded beads. Aperture small and narrow; color pale brown.

Family Epitoniidae: Wentletraps

THESE are predatory, carnivorous snails, occurring in all seas and popularly known as wentletraps and staircase shells. The shells are high-spired, usually white, and consist of many rounded, ribbed whorls. Outer lip considerably thickened by a reflected border, secreted during rest periods in shell growth, and this thickened lip becomes a new, riblike varix as the mollusk increases in size. Wentletraps are among the most delicately graceful of all marine gastropods, and are great favorites with shell collectors.

Genus *Opalia* H. & A. Adams 1853

OPALIA INSCULPTA (Carp.) **Sculptured Wentletrap** Pl. 33
Range: Monterey, California, to Mexico.
Habitat: Rocks at low tide.
Description: Height about ¾ in., whorl count about 8. Shell strong and solid, white. There are about a dozen varices on each volution, often indistinct on sides of whorls but stronger and more prominent at sutures. A slight keel just below the suture gives whorls a somewhat flattened appearance from above.
Remarks: Formerly listed as *Epitonium* or *Opalia crenimargina-tum* Dall.

OPALIA WROBLEWSKII (Mörch) Pl. 33
Wroblewski's Wentletrap
Range: Alaska to Puget Sound.
Habitat: Moderately shallow water.
Description: About 1 in. high and solid in appearance. There are 7 or 8 whorls that are only slightly rounded; each whorl bears from 6 to 8 blunt varices that are often indistinct, sometimes fading out at center of whorl. Outer lip thickened, aperture round. Color white or yellowish white.
Remarks: South of Puget Sound this species is replaced by a very similar snail, *O. chacei* Strong, which ranges to s. California.

Genus *Epitonium* Röding 1798

EPITONIUM BELLASTRIATUM (Carp.) Pl. 33
Striped Wentletrap
Range: Monterey, California, to San Pedro.
Habitat: Moderately shallow water.
Description: A bit more than ½ in. high, this is a squat shell, the spire not very tall and the body whorl quite large. Color white, sometimes with darker blotches on volutions. Varices quite numerous; sutures are deep. Fine spiral ridges discernible between the varices.

EPITONIUM GROENLANDICUM (Perry) Pl. 33
Greenland Wentletrap
Range: Alaska to B.C.; also Greenland to Rhode Island.
Habitat: Moderately deep water.
Description: A pale brownish to grayish shell about 1 in. high. There are 8 or 9 whorls, the elongate spire tapering to a sharp point. Whorls somewhat flattened, and barred with about 8 stout, flattish, oblique ribs (varices), the spaces between them sculptured with round ridges that follow the volutions of the shell. Aperture round, and bordered by a stoutly thickened outer lip that will in turn become another rib (varix).

EPITONIUM INDIANORUM (Carp.)   Pl. 33
Indian Wentletrap
  Range: Alaska to Baja California.
  Habitat: Moderately shallow water.
  Description: A slender, spikelike shell nearly 1 in. high, some-
  times slightly more. There are about 10 whorls, each with from
  12 to 15 distinct, sharp varices. Aperture round. This is a neat,
  pure-white shell; probably most abundant wentletrap on
  West Coast.

EPITONIUM TINCTUM (Carp.)   **Tinted Wentletrap**   Pl. 33
  Range: Monterey, California, to Baja California.
  Habitat: Just off shore; stones.
  Description: A delicate small shell, generally less than 1 in.
  high. Color white, sometimes with a purplish tinge on lower
  whorls, or on lower portions of the volutions. About 8 rounded
  whorls, each with approximately 12 sharp varices. As with the
  other wentletraps, aperture is circular and operculum horny.

Family Janthinidae: Violet Snails

THESE are pelagic, floating mollusks living miles from land. Very
delicate lavender or purplish shells, shaped much like land snails.
As a result of their mode of life they are widely distributed, and
occur in all of the warmer seas. They float about in huge colonies,
and occasionally currents and onshore winds combine to wash great
numbers onto the shore, where they may line the beach for miles.
The animal is capable of ejecting a purplish fluid when disturbed.

Genus *Janthina* Röding 1798

JANTHINA GLOBOSA Blain.   **Round Violet Snail**   Pl. 33
  Range: Worldwide in warm seas.
  Habitat: Pelagic.
  Description: Somewhat globular in shape, averaging about 1 in.
  long. Shell thin and fragile, with about 3 rounded whorls; color
  pale violet all over. The last volution is slightly constricted in
  the middle, giving the outer lip a prominent notch.
  Remarks: The commonest *Janthina* on the California coast,
  sometimes occurring in large numbers. See also Plates 8 and 66.

JANTHINA JANTHINA (Linné)   **Violet Snail**   Pl. 33
  Range: Worldwide in warm seas.
  Habitat: Pelagic.
  Description: A fragile, thin-shelled snail about 1½ in. long,
  sometimes slightly more. Shape flatly globular, with 3 or 4
  whorls. Two-toned, the upperpart pale lavender and the lower
  part rich purple.

Remarks: This is another pelagic gastropod; it lives in large colonies at sea. During the spawning season it hangs suspended from a bubble raft to which the eggs are attached. These snails are occasionally wafted ashore in huge numbers; but individual shells are now and then to be picked up along the California coast. See also Plate 66, No. 10.

Family Hipponicidae: Hoof Shells

SHELLS thick and obliquely conical, the apex hooked backward, but not spiral. The surface is generally rough and wrinkled, and grayish white. The animal secretes a shelly plate between itself and the object on which it lives. Since this plate was once believed to be a second valve, several species were described as bivalve mollusks.

Genus *Hipponix* Defrance 1819

HIPPONIX ANTIQUATUS (Linné)   **Hoof Shell**   **Pl. 34**
  Range: Crescent City, California, to Panama; also Atlantic Coast.
  Habitat: Moderately shallow water.
  Description: About ½ in. high and white or yellowish white. The shell is thick, conical, cap-shaped, and concave at the base. Apex bluntly pointed and not coiled. Surface variable, sometimes fairly smooth, but usually wrinkled by coarse laminations. There is a hairy periostracum during life.
  Remarks: This snail lives attached to some rock or dead shell, and grows to conform to its particular shape of seat, secreting a calcareous plate between itself and the object to which it adheres.

Family Trichotropidae: Hairy-keeled Shells

SMALL, stoutly conic shells with horny opercula and a hairy periostracum. The shoulders are keeled, and there is a small umbilicus. Natives of cold seas.

Genus *Trichotropis* Broderip & Sowerby 1829

TRICHOTROPIS BOREALIS Brod. & Sow.   **Pl. 34**
Northern Hairy Shell
  Range: Circumpolar; south to B.C.
  Habitat: Moderately deep water.
  Description: About ½ in. high, sometimes a bit larger, and brown. Shell rather well inflated, consisting of about 4 whorls,

with deeply channeled sutures. Body whorl relatively large, and encircled by 2 prominent rounded ribs, or keels, as well as 2 or 3 inconspicuous ones. There is a yellowish periostracum, which rises like a bristly fringe along the keels and growth lines. Aperture broad and rounded behind and somewhat narrowed and pointed in front, and there is a chinklike umbilicus.

TRICHOTROPIS CANCELLATA Hinds   Pl. 34
Cancellate Hairy Shell
   Range: Bering Sea to Oregon.
   Habitat: Moderately deep water.
   Description: Nearly 1 in. high, this is a rugged shell of 6 or 7 well rounded whorls, the sutures deeply impressed. Spire fairly well elevated, apex sharp, and aperture moderately large and truncate at its base. Sculpture consists of strong revolving ribs and vertical lines, so that the surface is plainly cancellate, although you have to remove the hairy periostracum in order to see it. Color yellowish white; the periostracum rusty yellow.

Family Calyptraeidae: Cup-and-Saucer Limpets and Slipper Shells

LIMPET-LIKE gastropods, with a cuplike process or diaphragm on the inner side of the shell, living attached to other shells or stones. Found in all seas, from shallow water to moderate depths.

Genus *Calyptraea* Lamarck 1799

CALYPTRAEA FASTIGIATA Gould   **Chinese Hat**   Pl. 34
   Range: Alaska to s. California.
   Habitat: Moderately deep water.
   Description: A small, polished, conical shell with a circular base about ¾ in. broad. Apex central in position and rather sharp. Inside there is a thin, curving diaphragm, extending about half a volution. Color white, sometimes darker toward the apex; shell rather thin and delicate.

Genus *Crucibulum* Schumacher 1817

CRUCIBULUM SPINOSUM (Sow.)   Pl. 34
Cup-and-Saucer Limpet
   Range: Monterey, California, to S. America.
   Habitat: Moderately shallow water.
   Description: Nearly circular in outline and about 1½ in. broad. Some specimens are well arched and others may be rather flat, with the apex near the center. Surface decorated with radiating

ridges that are fine and somewhat wrinkled, studded with short spines. Color yellowish white, often flecked with brown, both inside and outside. The interior bears a large, white, cuplike structure laterally compressed. See also Plate 67, No. 10.

Genus *Crepidula* Lamarck 1799

CREPIDULA ACULEATA (Gmel.) **Prickly Slipper Shell Pl. 34**
  Range: Santa Barbara, California, to S. America; also Atlantic Coast and Hawaii.
  Habitat: Shallow water.
  Description: From 1 to 1½ in. long, this is an oval, sometimes nearly circular slipper shell that is only moderately arched. The surface bears prominent radiating ridges set with small spines. The color may be yellowish or grayish brown, often with distinct color bands; interior usually brown, with a white diaphragm. See also Plate 67, No. 11.

CREPIDULA ADUNCA Sow. **Hooked Slipper Shell Pl. 34**
  Range: B.C. to Baja California.
  Habitat: Moderately shallow water.
  Description: This species is about 1 in. long. It is a well-arched shell with a sharp apex, or beak, that is curved and often hooked. Color brown, with interior platform white.

CREPIDULA EXCAVATA Brod. **Pl. 34**
Excavated Slipper Shell
  Range: Monterey, California, to Peru.
  Habitat: Shallow water.
  Description: Rather long and narrow, with parallel sides. The shell is quite thick, fairly well arched, and often somewhat twisted. Length about 1 in. Color whitish, the exterior commonly flecked with purplish brown.

CREPIDULA NUMMARIA Gould **White Slipper Shell Pl. 34**
  Range: Alaska to Panama.
  Habitat: Shallow water.
  Description: Moderately thick and heavy, and only weakly arched, some specimens being almost flat. It is oval and about 1½ in. long, sometimes a little more. Color white, pure and shining on the inside and dull and dingy on the outside. There may be a thin yellowish periostracum.
  Remarks: This rather flattish shell is usually found in the aperture of some old and wave-worn snail shell.

CREPIDULA ONYX Sow. **Onyx Slipper Shell Pl. 34**
  Range: Monterey, California, to Chile.
  Habitat: Shallow water.

Description: A fairly large shell, commonly 2 in. long. Shape cuplike, with an oval margin; the small apex is close to the margin and turned to one side. The inner cavity is partially divided by a horizontal platform, or diaphragm. Color of exterior grayish brown, often with dull reddish rays; interior rich dark brown. The diaphragm (deck) is pure white.

Remarks: Two species of slipper shell have been introduced in Pacific waters, presumably along with importations of the Atlantic oyster. One is a little fellow, scarcely ½ in. long. It is deep brown, highly arched, with a prominent, often hooked, apex. This is *C. convexa* Say (Convex Slipper Shell; see Plate 34, No. 17). The other is *C. fornicata* Linné (Atlantic Slipper Shell; see Plate 34, No. 14), a shell of some 2 in. or more when fully grown. It is obliquely oval in outline, with the apex prominent and turned to one side. Fairly well arched, but shape varies according to object on which it is seated. Color bluish gray, usually flecked with reddish brown.

Genus *Crepipatella* Lesson 1830

CREPIPATELLA LINGULATA (Gould)   Pl. 34
Half-slipper Shell
   Range: Bering Sea to Panama.
   Habitat: Moderately shallow water.
   Description: This is a somewhat circular shell, only moderately arched, with the apex rather inconspicuous. Diam. not quite 1 in. Shell thin and brittle, brownish gray; interior shiny white, often stained with pale brown. Diaphragm attached at only one side, and shows a distinct ridge at its center.
   Remarks: This species is usually found on other shells, chiefly scallops.

Family Lamellariidae: Wide-mouthed Snails

SHELLS mainly internal, very thin and fragile. The aperture is large and flaring and the spire low. There is no operculum.

Genus *Lamellaria* Montagu 1815

LAMELLARIA DIEGOENSIS Dall   Pl. 35
San Diego Ear Shell
   Range: S. California.
   Habitat: Moderately deep water.
   Description: A thin and fragile shell, semitransparent whitish color, the height about ½ in. The shell is chiefly internal and

consists of 3 whorls, the last one constituting most of the whole. Shape somewhat globose, with a large and flaring aperture.

Genus *Velutina* Fleming 1821

VELUTINA LAEVIGATA (Linné)   **Smooth Velvet Shell**   Pl. 35
Range: Circumpolar; south to Monterey, California.
Habitat: Moderately deep water.
Description: About ½ in. high, this is another thin and delicate shell. There are 3 whorls, with deeply impressed sutures. Aperture very large, and nearly circular. Color pinkish white, but the shell is covered with a soft brown velvety periostracum.

Family Atlantidae: Atlantas

SMALL, thin, glassy-shelled snails, pelagic in habits, living out their lives at sea. They can swim by means of a finlike foot, and can rest by attaching themselves to floating objects. Confined to warm seas.

Genus *Atlanta* Lesueur 1817

ATLANTA PERONI Les.   **Peron's Atlanta**   Pl. 34
Range: S. California; also Atlantic.
Habitat: Pelagic.
Description: A flatly coiled small snail, diam. about ½ in. There are about 3 whorls, which appear to have been squeezed flat, and there is a thin bladelike keel at the periphery. Shell extremely fragile, glassy-white color.
Remarks: Although this snail lives out in the ocean, empty shells are now and then washed ashore, but unless collected quicklv they soon break up.

Family Naticidae: Moon Shells

THESE are carnivorous snails found in all seas. The shell is globular, sometimes depressed, smooth, and frequently polished. The foot of the animal is very large, and often conceals the entire shell when the mollusk is extended.

Genus *Natica* Scopoli 1777

NATICA CLAUSA Brod. & Sow.   **Arctic Moon Shell**   Pl. 35
Range: Circumpolar; south to San Diego, California.
Habitat: Moderately shallow water.
Description: About 1 in. high and nearly the same in diam. A

globular bluish-white or grayish shell of 4 or 5 whorls. Spire only slightly elevated. Aperture oval; umbilicus usually closed by a shiny white callus. The operculum is calcareous and bluish white.

Genus *Polinices* Montfort 1810

POLINICES DRACONIS (Dall)   **Drake's Moon Shell**   **Pl. 35**
Range: Alaska to Mexico.
Habitat: Moderately deep water.
Description: This shell is much like the more abundant *P. lewisii* (below), but is less heavy in build and has a larger umbilicus. Its height is between 2 and 3 in. General shape globular, and there are about 4 whorls. Aperture large and semilunar, and there is a reflected callus on the columella. Color yellowish brown.

POLINICES LEWISII (Gould)   **Lewis' Moon Shell**   **Pl. 35**
Range: B.C. to Baja California.
Habitat: Shallow water; sandflats.
Description: A large globular shell, the largest of its genus. From 4 to 5 in. high. There are 4 or 5 whorls, the body whorl constituting most of the shell. Surface smooth, with an angle at shoulder of the last volution, where there sometimes are a few wrinkles. Umbilicus open, and there is a semilunar horny operculum. Color yellowish gray.
Remarks: Some modern authors place this moon shell in the genus *Lunatia* Gray.

POLINICES PALLIDA (Brod. & Sow.)   **Pl. 35**
Northern Moon Shell
Range: Alaska to California.
Habitat: Moderately deep water.
Description: This shell grows to a height of nearly 2 in., with a short spire, so that its shape is less globular than *P. lewisii* (above). There are 4 well-rounded whorls and a pointed apex. A noticeable callus is present on the inner lip, and there is a small umbilicus. Color white, but concealed during life by a yellowish periostracum.

Genus *Neverita* Risso 1826

NEVERITA RECLUSIANUS (Desh.)   **Pl. 35**
Récluz's Moon Shell
Range: Crescent City, California, to Mexico.
Habitat: Moderately shallow water.
Description: A strong and solid shell, generally about 2 in. high. There are 4 or 5 whorls, with the spire rising to a blunt point. The umbilicus is partially, sometimes completely, covered by a

lobe of shelly material, usually white. Color brownish or grayish, the young specimens pale bluish.

Genus *Sinum* Röding 1798

SINUM SCOPULOSUM (Con.) **Baby's Ear**   Pl. 35
  Range: Monterey, California, to Baja California.
  Habitat: Shallow water; mudflats.
  Description: This is a flat shell, looking somewhat like a *Polinices* that has been stepped on. It is about 1 in. long, and has only 2 or 3 whorls, no spire, and is practically all body whorl. Color white; surface delicately sculptured with finely incised revolving lines.
  Remarks: This species used to be listed as *S. californicum* Old.

Family Cypraeidae: Cowries

THE cowries are a large family of brightly colored and brilliantly polished shells that have always been great favorites with collectors. Shell more or less oval and well inflated, the spire covered by the body whorl in adults, and the aperture, lined with teeth on both lips, runs full length of underside. No operculum. This is a tropical family, with scores of richly colored representatives distributed all around the world. Only 1 species, however, gets as far north as s. California.

Genus *Cypraea* Linné 1758

CYPRAEA SPADICA Swain. **Chestnut Cowry**   Pls. 4, 35
  Range: Santa Barbara, California, to Cerros I., Baja California.
  Habitat: Reefs.
  Description: An oval, egg-shaped shell nearly 2 in. long. Surface smooth and glossy. A narrow toothed aperture extends the length of the underside, with a notch at each end visible from above. Color of lower side bluish white. Sides flesh-colored, the back (or top) has a brown central area edged with a band of richer, darker brown that follows the outline of the shell.
  Remarks: Many taxonomists consider the subgenera in this group as full genera, and would list this species as *Zonaria spadica* (Swain.). Only example of the colorful cowries to be found on our coast.

Family Eratoidae: Sea Buttons

SMALL cowry-like gastropods, the shell not polished. The upper surface usually bears a distinct median groove, or furrow, and strong radiating ridges that continue around to the underside and into the aperture. Chiefly in tropic seas.

Genus *Erato* Risso 1826

ERATO VITELLINA Hinds   **Apple Seed**   **Pl. 35**
   Range: Bodega Bay, California, to Mexico.
   Habitat: Seaweeds.
   Description: A small shell that is bulbous at one end, so its shape is somewhat pearlike. Length about ½ in. Aperture long and narrow, the outer lip thickened and provided with small teeth; the inner lip bears distinct pleats. Color dark reddish brown, the aperture white, the surface smooth but not polished.

Genus *Trivia* Broderip 1837

TRIVIA CALIFORNIANA (Gray)   **Coffee Bean**   **Pl. 35**
   Range: Crescent City, California, to Mexico.
   Habitat: Shallow water.
   Description: An oval shell, flat on the bottom and round on top. Length just under ½ in. Upper surface decorated with 12 radiating ridges and a whitish, sunken groove. The ridges, too, are whitish; the shell itself is deep purplish brown. The underside bears a long and narrow aperture bordered by inwardly rolled lips with numerous small riblike teeth.
   Remarks: The animal is bright scarlet.

TRIVIA SOLANDRI (Sow.)   **Sea Button**   **Pl. 35**
   Range: Catalina I., California, to Panama.
   Habitat: Shallow water.
   Description: This species resembles *T. californiana* (above), but is larger, about ¾ in. long. Color varies from reddish brown to light pink; upper surface sculptured with widely spaced paler ridges that radiate from the prominent dorsal groove. The ridges continue around the shell into the aperture. Base flattish, paler in tone, and bears the long and narrow aperture.
   Remarks: This species is uncommon in the north, abundant in the southern parts of its range.

Family Ovulidae: Simnias

SHELLS long and slender, and thin, with a straight aperture notched at each end. Occurring in warm seas, the mollusks live attached to sea fans.

Genus *Neosimnia* Fischer 1884

NEOSIMNIA AVENA (Sow.)   **Chubby Simnia**   Pl. 35
  Range: Monterey, California, to Panama.
  Habitat: Sea fans.
  Description: A short and stubby shell, its length about ½ in.
  Aperture wider at lower end, and columella bears a swollen
  twist. Surface shows fine spiral lines. The color varies from
  pale pink to purplish red, generally matching very closely the
  shade of the particular sea fan on which it is living.

Family Cymatiidae: Tritons

THESE are more or less decorative shells, rugged and strong, with
no more than 2 varices to a volution. The closely related Muricidae
have 3. The canal is prominent, and teeth are commonly present
on the lips. Distributed chiefly in warm and temperate seas.

Genus *Fusitriton* Cossmann 1903

FUSITRITON OREGONENSE (Red.)   **Hairy Triton**   Pl. 36
  Range: Pribilof Is. to Puget Sound; also Japan.
  Habitat: Moderately shallow water.
  Description: A large and sturdy shell, attaining a height of
  some 5 in. There are 5 or 6 rounded whorls, the apex rather
  blunt, and the whole shell may be described as stoutly elongate.
  Surface sculptured with prominent vertical ribs, about 20 to a
  volution, and with spiral ridges, producing a pattern of small
  squares. Aperture moderately large, the outer lip simple, and
  there is a short canal. Color yellowish white, with a shaggy
  brownish periostracum that clings persistently to the shell.
  Remarks: This species may be found in deep water as far south
  as San Diego, California.

Family Bursidae: Frog Shells

SHELLS ovate or oblong, more or less compressed laterally, with 2
rows of continuous varices, one on each side. Deep-water forms
have the varices thin and bladelike, whereas those living among
rocks and on coral reefs are more nodular. Inhabit warm seas.

Genus *Bursa* Röding 1798

BURSA CALIFORNICA (Hinds)   **California Frog Shell**   Pl. 36
  Range: Monterey, California, to Gulf of California.
  Habitat: Moderately shallow water.

Description: Average height about 3 in., but occasional specimens are found that are considerably larger. A stout and rugged shell, rather flattish in appearance because of presence of a thickened ridge on each side, running from canal to apex. These varices are very knobby, as is the surface between them, so that the whole shell has an angular and bulgy look. Aperture rather large, and white; shell mostly yellowish brown.

Family Muricidae: Rock Shells

SHELLS thick and solid, generally more or less spiny. These are active, carnivorous snails, preferring rocky or gravelly bottoms and moderately shallow water as a rule. They occur in all seas, but are most abundant in the tropics. Many of the snails of this group develop bizarre spines, nodes, or fronds on the outer lip, subsequently to become part of the varix. This produces perhaps the most decorative of all marine shells, and they have always been great favorites with collectors.

Genus *Forreria* Jousseaume 1880

FORRERIA BELCHERI (Hinds)   **Belcher's Chorus Shell**   **Pl. 36**
Range: Morro Bay, California, to Mexico.
Habitat: Mudflats.
Description: One of our largest gastropods, attaining a height of fully 6 in. It is pear-shaped, with 6 or 7 rather squarish whorls, the body whorl very large and the turreted spire rather short. Shoulders crowned with a series of hollow spines, about 8 to a volution, the spines continuing down sides of whorls as thickened varices. Surface quite smooth. Aperture large; outer lip thin, and sharp, with a toothlike projection at the lower part; inner lip strongly reflected, the moderately long canal curved and open. There is a small umbilicus, and the operculum is horny. Color yellowish white, more or less streaked with brown.

Genus *Trophon* Montfort 1810

TROPHON CERROSENSIS CATALINENSIS Old.   **Pls. 4, 36**
Catalina Trophon
Range: S. California.
Habitat: Deep water.
Description: A fairly large shell, from 3 to 4 in. high, but very light in weight. There are about 6 strongly turreted whorls, each with 6 or 7 extremely thin varices that extend into long, hollow, winglike spines at the shoulders. Aperture small; inner lip reflected; canal long and open. Color yellowish brown.
Remarks: The typical *T. cerrosensis* Dall is found at the southern

end of Baja California, and the form that occurs off the coast of California is a subspecies, *T. c. catalinensis*. Some authors have placed it in the genus *Forreria*. It is perhaps as eagerly sought by collectors as any West Coast mollusk.

Genus *Pterynotus* Swainson 1833

PTERYNOTUS CARPENTERI (Dall)   Pl. 36
Carpenter's Rock Shell
    Range: Monterey, California, to San Diego.
    Habitat: Moderately deep water; rocks.
    Description: Some 2 in. high, this shell closely resembles *P. rhyssus* (below). The thin bladelike varices are very conspicuous, especially the one bordering the lip. Aperture small; inner lip partially reflected; the tightly closed canal curves to the right. Color yellowish brown.
    Remarks: This species differs from *P. rhyssus* in lacking the vertical knobs between the varices, and also in having that area smooth instead of horizontally ribbed.

PTERYNOTUS RHYSSUS (Dall)   **St. Peter's Rock Shell**   Pl. 36
    Range: Santa Barbara, California, to Baja California.
    Habitat: Moderately deep water.
    Description: A highly ornate shell of 5 or 6 turreted whorls, its height a little more than 2 in. Each volution is decorated with 3 bladelike varices that are expanded at the shoulder to form frondlike projections. Between these varices the shell is finely ribbed horizontally, and there is a small varix. Aperture small; canal moderately long and tightly closed. Color yellowish brown.
    Remarks: This gastropod used to be called *P. petri* (Dall), which accounts for its common name.

PTERYNOTUS TRIALATUS (Sow.)   Pl. 36
Three-winged Rock Shell
    Range: California to Mexico.
    Habitat: Moderately shallow water.
    Description: Fully 3 in. high, composed of about 6 whorls. Sutures indistinct, and tops of shoulders slightly excavated. There are 3 large but thin varices, the spaces between them relatively smooth. Aperture small; canal rather short and tightly closed. The color varies from light to dark brown, with or without whitish bands.

Genus *Maxwellia* Baily 1950

MAXWELLIA GEMMA (Sow.)   **Gem Rock Shell**   Pls. 4, 36
    Range: Santa Barbara, California, to Baja California.
    Habitat: Moderately shallow water.

Description: A small snail, in height averaging just over 1 in. There are 4 or 5 whorls, deeply excavated at the sutures. Shell vertically ribbed by a series of thick and rounded varices, 6 on the body whorl. Aperture rather small; canal long and closed. Color gray or white, closely banded with narrow lines of reddish brown.

Genus *Jaton* Pusch 1837

JATON FESTIVUS (Hinds) **Festive Rock Shell** Pl. 36
  Range: Morro Bay, California, to Baja California.
  Habitat: Moderately shallow water.
  Description: From 1 to 2 in. high, with about 6 rounded whorls. A decorative shell with 3 prominent varices that are not thin and bladelike but thick and blunt. There is a strong vertical node between each varix, and the surface of the shell bears coarse revolving lines. Color yellowish brown, more or less banded with darker brown. Aperture relatively large, bordered by a very thick outer lip; the short canal is partially closed.

Genus *Ceratostoma* Herrmannsen 1846

CERATOSTOMA FOLIATUM (Gmel.) Pls. 4, 36
Leafy Hornmouth
  Range: Alaska to San Pedro, California.
  Habitat: Moderately shallow water.
  Description: A large species, attaining a height of more than 3 in. There are 6 or 7 whorls, each decorated with 3 large and thin varices, the spaces between rather strongly sculptured with revolving cordlike ridges. Aperture moderately large; outer lip toothed below but without the single slender tooth of *C. nuttalli* (below). Canal short and closed, and noticeably bent backward. This curved canal is retained in the last previous varix, so that the bottom of the shell is often forked. Color yellowish white, more or less banded with brown.

CERATOSTOMA NUTTALLI (Con.) Pl. 36
Nuttall's Hornmouth
  Range: Monterey, California, to Baja California.
  Habitat: Moderately deep water.
  Description: A 2-in. shell of about 5 whorls, the sutures indistinct. The 3 major varices are large, thin, bladelike, and decorative, and there is a smaller riblike node between each varix. Canal short and tightly closed; inner lip reflected on the body whorl; near base of outer lip there is a slender, spikelike tooth projecting outward. Color of shell mottled yellowish gray and brown, often banded.
  Remarks: Juvenile shells lack the projecting tooth.

Genus *Boreotrophon* Fischer 1884

BOREOTROPHON ALBOSPINOSUS (Will.) Pl. 36
Spiny Trophon
  Range: S. California.
  Habitat: Deep water.
  Description: This shell is slightly less than 1 in. high, and rather blocky in build. There are about 5 turreted whorls, each decorated with some 9 or 10 thin varices that form pointed projections at the shoulders. Canal moderately long, and open. Color white or dingy white.

BOREOTROPHON MULTICOSTATUS (Esch.) Pl. 36
Many-ribbed Trophon
  Range: Alaska to San Pedro, California.
  Habitat: Moderately deep water.
  Description: About 1 in. high, sometimes a bit more, with about 9 thin varices, the spaces between them showing fine revolving lines. Shoulders quite prominent. The aperture is large, the canal very short. Color gray; aperture reddish brown.

BOREOTROPHON PACIFICUS (Dall) Pacific Trophon Pl. 36
  Range: Alaska to Baja California.
  Habitat: Moderately deep water.
  Description: A spindle-shaped shell about 1 in. high. There are about 6 whorls, the shoulders not flattened to any degree, so that the spire is not noticeably turreted. About 12 thin varices on each volution, but they blend into the sutures and do not form spines at the shoulders. Canal moderately long and open. Color grayish or whitish.

BOREOTROPHON TRIANGULATUS (Carp.) Pl. 36
Triangular Trophon
  Range: Monterey, California, to San Pedro.
  Habitat: Deep water.
  Description: About 1 in. high, with 6 or 7 whorls. There is a prominent spire, and each volution bears distinct vertical ridges that produce hollow spines at the shoulders. Canal moderately short and open, the aperture large with the inner lip reflected on the body whorl. Color whitish.

Genus *Trophonopsis* Bucquoy et al. 1882

TROPHONOPSIS LASIUS (Dall) Sandpaper Trophon Pl. 37
  Range: Bering Sea to Baja California.
  Habitat: Moderately deep water.
  Description: A slender, spindle-shaped shell of about 6 whorls, the height about 1½ in. Surface sculptured with distinct revolv-

ing lines, and with vertical ribs, about 12 to a volution. There is a very slight angle at the shoulders, but the spire is not turreted. Aperture moderately large; canal open and slightly curved. Color gray; aperture shiny white.

Genus *Ocenebra* Gray 1847

OCENEBRA CIRCUMTEXTA (Stearns) Pl. 37
Circled Rock Shell
Range: Monterey, California, to San Diego.
Habitat: Shoreline; rocks.
Description: A stout shell of 4 or 5 rounded whorls, less than 1 in. high. Surface with deeply impressed revolving ridges that are wavy at intervals to produce vertical riblets. Aperture rather large; outer lip thickened, feebly toothed within. Canal short and open. Color grayish white, strongly banded with chocolate-brown.

OCENEBRA INTERFOSSA (Carp.) Pl. 37
Sculptured Rock Shell
Range: Alaska to California.
Habitat: Shoreline; rocks.
Description: A spindle-shaped shell about ¾ in. high. There are 5 whorls, producing a somewhat turreted spire and a sharp apex. Sculpture consists of revolving wavy lines of alternating sizes, plus rather strong vertical ridges, the whole surface rough and rasplike. Color grayish brown.

OCENEBRA JAPONICA Dun. Japan Rock Shell Pl. 37
Range: Puget Sound.
Habitat: Near shore; rocks.
Description: About 1½ in. high, with 5 whorls, the tops of the shoulders flattened and each whorl bearing about 8 riblike varices. There is 1 conspicuous ridge encircling each volution, with a weaker rib above and below. Outer lip considerably thickened, inner lip reflected. Canal moderately short and closed. Color grayish white.
Remarks: This is a Japanese mollusk, introduced some time ago in Puget Sound.

OCENEBRA LURIDA (Midd.) Lurid Rock Shell Pl. 37
Range: Alaska to California.
Habitat: Near shore; rocks.
Description: Slightly more than 1 in. high, with about 6 whorls. Marked with revolving cordlike ridges, sometimes wrinkled at the shoulders. Outer lip scalloped by edges of the ridges, and just inside bears several small teeth. Color grayish or brownish, sometimes banded.

OCENEBRA POULSONI Carp. **Poulson's Rock Shell** Pl. 37
Range: Santa Barbara, California, to Baja California.
Habitat: Near shore; rocks.
Description: A very common snail from 1 to 2 in. high, rugged and strong, with about 6 whorls. Each volution bears about 9 very knobby varices; the surface is sculptured with fine but sharp revolving lines. Inner lip reflected on last whorl, and there are 3 or 4 small teeth on the outer lip, well within the aperture. Color gray; aperture shiny white.

OCENEBRA SQUAMULIFERA Carp. **Scaly Rock Shell** Pl. 37
Range: Santa Barbara to San Pedro, California.
Habitat: Near shore; rocks.
Description: An ornate small shell, less than ½ in. high as a rule. There are 4 or 5 whorls, flat at the shoulders and bearing small pointer knobs at the shoulder angles. Aperture wide at top and narrowed at the short canal. Color gray; aperture bluish white.

Family Thaididae: Dye Shells

STOUT shells with a greatly enlarged body whorl, wide aperture, and usually a short spire. These are predatory gastropods, living close to shore in rocky situations. The common name dye shells derives from the fact that the body secretes a colored fluid that may be green, scarlet, or purple. The famous Tyrian purple of the ancients was a dye obtained by crushing the bodies of a Mediterranean snail of this group. They occur in all seas.

Genus *Thais* Röding 1798

THAIS CANALICULATA (Duc.) **Channeled Dogwinkle** Pl. 37
Range: Aleutian Is. to Monterey, California.
Habitat: Shallow water.
Description: Height about 1 in. There are 4 or 5 rounded whorls and a well-elevated spire terminating in a sharp apex. Surface decorated with strong revolving ribs, the spaces between them deep and vertically checked. Aperture large, canal short, the inner lip flattened and slightly twisted at the base. Color yellowish brown, often banded with a lighter shade; aperture stained bright yellow.

THAIS EMARGINATA Desh. **Emarginate Dogwinkle** Pl. 37
Range: Bering Sea to Baja California.
Habitat: Shallow water.
Description: A variable species — some individuals being short and stout, others taller and more elongate. Usually 5 whorls, the

body whorl making up most of the shell. Average height about 1 in. A sculpture of very strong revolving ridges, often a large ridge alternating with a smaller one. Color yellowish brown, with darker spiral bands; aperture reddish brown.

THAIS LAMELLOSA (Gmel.)   **Frilled Dogwinkle**   **Pls. 4, 37**
Range: Alaska to Santa Cruz, California.
Habitat: Moderately shallow water.
Description: This shell grows to be more than 4 in. high, but its average is between 2 and 3 in. Rugged and sturdy, and quite variable in form. Those from the north are decorated with numerous frilly varices, as many as 15 to a whorl; specimens from the southern parts of its range are apt to be relatively smooth. Canal short, and there is a small umbilicus. The color may be white, yellowish, or orange; many individuals are banded.

THAIS LIMA (Gmel.)   **File Dogwinkle**   **Pl. 37**
Range: Arctic Ocean to n. California; Japan.
Habitat: Shallow water.
Description: From 1 to 2 in. high, this shell is composed of about 5 whorls, the sutures rather indistinct. Sculpture consists of revolving lines or ridges of alternating sizes. Aperture rather large; outer lip thin and sharp, canal very short. Color white or grayish white.

Genus *Acanthina* Waldheim 1807

ACANTHINA LUGUBRIS (Sow.)   **Sad Unicorn**   **Pl. 37**
Range: San Diego, California, to Baja California.
Habitat: Moderately shallow water.
Description: A thick and heavy shell 1 in. high. There are only 3 or 4 whorls, the spire is short, and the snail appears squat. The surface bears revolving rows of bumpy knobs, with the sutures rather indistinct. Aperture large and flaring; outer lip with a series of wrinkle-like teeth well back from the edge; a single hornlike tooth near the canal that is characteristic of this genus, giving the group the common name of unicorn shells. Color mottled gray and white; aperture shiny brown.

ACANTHINA PAUCILIRATA (Stearns)   **Pl. 37**
Checkered Unicorn
Range: San Pedro, California, to Baja California.
Habitat: Rocks above high tide.
Description: About ½ in. high, a solid shell of 4 whorls, the sutures indistinct. Surface with weak revolving lines. Aperture rather narrow; outer lip thickened and toothed within. A single hornlike tooth near the canal that is characteristic of this genus,

giving the group the common name of unicorn shells. Color pale
yellowish white, with squares of black or brown.

ACANTHINA PUNCTULATA (Sow.) **Spotted Unicorn** Pl. 37
Range: Monterey, California, to Mexico.
Habitat: Moderately shallow water.
Description: A squat little shell almost as broad as it is high.
About ¾ in. tall, with 3 or 4 stout whorls, sutures very indistinct. Surface sculptured with numerous revolving rows of
elongate dots or beads which are dark gray on a pale gray background. Aperture bluish white and brown, with the single long
tooth projecting near base of outer lip; the tooth is characteristic
of this genus, giving the group the common name of unicorn
shells.

ACANTHINA SPIRATA (Blain.) **Angular Unicorn** Pl. 37
Range: Puget Sound to San Diego, California.
Habitat: Moderately shallow water; stones.
Description: About 1¼ in. high, a somewhat elongate shell of
5 or 6 whorls, sutures indistinct. Whorls sharply angled at
shoulders, producing a spire that is more or less turreted. A
single hornlike tooth near the canal that is characteristic of this
genus, giving the group the common name of unicorn shells.
Surface with numerous narrow revolving lines. Color dark gray,
aperture bluish gray.

Family Columbellidae: Dove Shells

SMALL, fusiform shells, with an outer lip commonly thickened at
the center. Shells sometimes quite colorful, and often shiny.
Normally to be found in warm seas.

Genus *Anachis* H. & A. Adams 1853

ANACHIS PENICILLATA Carp. **Penciled Dove Shell** Pl. 37
Range: San Pedro, California, south.
Habitat: Near shore; stones.
Description: A small fusiform shell, its height no more than ¼
in. There are from 4 to 6 whorls, all but the 1st decorated with
vertical grooves, and the sutures are quite distinct. Aperture
long and narrow; outer lip thin and sharp. Pale brown, with
darker spottings.

Genus *Mitrella* Risso 1826

MITRELLA CARINATA (Sow.) **Keeled Dove Shell** Pl. 37
Range: San Francisco to Baja California.
Habitat: Shallow water; roots and stones and marine plants.

Description: About ¼ in. high and pale brown; 5 whorls, the body whorl bearing a conspicuous keel at the shoulder. Aperture elongate; outer lip rather thickened.

MITRELLA GAUSAPATA (Gould)   Pl. 37
Range: Alaska to San Diego, California.
Habitat: Moderately shallow water.
Description: Attains a height of nearly ½ in. There are 6 whorls, the sutures plainly marked. Color yellowish white, more or less reticulated or spotted with brown. Surface usually well polished.

Genus *Amphissa* H. & A. Adams 1853

AMPHISSA BICOLOR Dall   Two-tinted Amphissa   Pl. 37
Range: Farallon Is., California, to San Diego.
Habitat: Moderately shallow water.
Description: Height about ½ in. There are 5 whorls, with vertical ribs, or folds, that are well separated. Aperture oval; outer lip thin and sharp, and there are no teeth within. Yellowish-tan color, commonly with a darker band near middle of shell.

AMPHISSA COLUMBIANA Dall   Columbian Amphissa   Pl. 37
Range: Alaska to San Pedro, California.
Habitat: Moderately shallow water.
Description: Nearly 1 in. high and composed of 5 whorls. Sculpture of distinct vertical folds and weaker revolving lines, the lower half of the body whorl showing only the revolving lines, and those very sharply. Aperture elongate, wider at bottom; inner lip reflected. Light yellowish-brown color.

AMPHISSA VERSICOLOR (Dall)   Pl. 37
Joseph's Coat Amphissa
Range: Oregon to Baja California.
Habitat: Shallow water.
Description: A stout shell of 4 or 5 whorls, its height about ½ in. Surface sculptured with vertical folds and spiral lines, with the sutures well delineated. Outer lip feebly toothed within. Color variable, ranging from pale yellow to reddish brown, often with faint mottlings of darker shade.

Family Nassariidae: Dog Whelks

GENERALLY small, carnivorous snails, found in all seas. The shells ordinarily are rather strongly built, with a pointed spire, a short notchlike canal, and commonly with a marked columellar callus.

Genus *Nassarius* Duméril 1805

NASSARIUS FOSSATUS (Gould)   **Pl. 37**
Channeled Dog Whelk
  Range: B.C. to Baja California.
  Habitat: Shallow water.
  Description: A fine showy shell, 1½ in. high, the largest member of its genus on the West Coast. There are about 7 whorls, a well-elevated spire, and a sharply pointed apex. Surface bears fine revolving lines, with small vertical folds encircling upper half of each whorl, the lower portion showing only the revolving lines. Aperture large; inner lip reflected and plastered on the columella in the form of a callus. Canal a deep notch at the aperture. Color yellowish tan; callus and interior bright orange; the whole shell commonly shiny.

NASSARIUS INSCULPTUS (Carp.)   **Smooth Dog Whelk**   **Pl. 37**
  Range: Point Arena, California, to Mexico.
  Habitat: Shallow water.
  Description: Somewhat more than ½ in. high, this is a sturdy shell of about 7 whorls, the sutures quite distinct. Sculpture consists of fine and closely spaced revolving lines, with a few vertical folds that are confined to the early whorls. The inner lip forms a small callus at base of shell, and there is a deep notch for the canal. Color yellowish white.

NASSARIUS MENDICUS (Gould)   **Lean Dog Whelk**   **Pl. 37**
  Range: Alaska to San Diego, California.
  Habitat: Moderately shallow water.
  Description: A rather slender shell, nearly 1 in. high, made up of about 8 whorls. Sculpture of strong revolving lines, and each whorl bears 8 rather prominent vertical ridges. Aperture rather small; the inner lip well reflected and outer lip thin and sharp. Color yellowish brown; aperture bluish white.
  Remarks: From Puget Sound south we find a form of this species, listed as *N. m. cooperi* (For.), Cooper's Dog Whelk, which is shorter and relatively stouter, and generally has fewer vertical ridges; see Plate 37, No. 22.

NASSARIUS OBSOLETUS (Say)   **Black Dog Whelk**   **Pl. 37**
  Range: California; also Atlantic Coast.
  Habitat: Mudflats.
  Description: Nearly 1 in. high, with about 6 whorls. Apex rather blunt, and commonly more or less eroded. The only sculpture consists of weak revolving lines, plus a few vertical folds on the early whorls. Inner lip deeply arched. Color deep purplish black.
  Remarks: This is an East Coast snail, probably introduced into Californian waters with young oysters. It is a scavenger; a dead

fish thrown into shallow water quickly calls together scores of these individuals.

NASSARIUS PERPINGUIS (Hinds)   **Fat Dog Whelk**   **Pl. 37**
Range: Puget Sound to Baja California.
Habitat: Moderately shallow water.
Description: An attractive shell 1 in. high and relatively stout. Shell rather thin in substance and sculptured with revolving lines and vertical ridges, so surface bears a close network pattern. Color grayish yellow.

NASSARIUS TEGULUS (Reeve)   **Mud Dog Whelk**   **Pl. 37**
Range: Cent. California south.
Habitat: Mudflats.
Description: About ¾ in. high, a stocky shell of 5 or 6 whorls with a sharply pointed apex. Sculpture of weak revolving lines and stronger vertical ridges. Color gray or brownish, sometimes faintly banded. Inner lip broadly expanded, outer lip thickened.

Family Buccinidae: Whelks

SHELLS generally large, with few whorls. The aperture is large, and usually notched at the base. These are carnivorous snails, occurring in northern seas for the most part. Some of them are used for food in other countries.

Genus *Buccinum* Linné 1758

BUCCINUM BAERI Midd.   **Baer's Whelk**   **Pl. 38**
Range: Alaska to B.C.
Habitat: Moderately shallow water.
Description: Thin and light in weight, with about 5 whorls. Height about 2 in. when fully grown. Spire fairly tall. Surface nearly smooth, with only a few suggestions of vertical folds. Color lavender-brown; aperture bright orange and shiny.

BUCCINUM ELATIUS Tryon   **Silky Whelk**   **Pl. 38**
Range: Circumpolar; south to Washington; also Atlantic Coast.
Habitat: Deep water.
Description: This shell is brownish yellow and about 3 in. high. Approximately 7 convex whorls, with deep sutures. The surface is decorated with numerous vertical folds and extremely fine spiral lines that impart a silky appearance. Aperture large; outer lip thin and sharp; canal little more than a notch. There is a horny operculum.

BUCCINUM EUGRAMMATUM Dall   **Ribbed Whelk**   Pl. 38
Range: Bering Sea to s. Alaska.
Habitat: Deep water.
Description: An uncommon species, not often seen in collections. It is a sturdy shell some 2 in. high, consisting of 5 or 6 whorls that are well rounded but decidedly flattened at the shoulders. There is a sculpture of strong, well-spaced encircling ribs, the one on the shoulder sometimes weakly beaded. Color yellowish brown.

BUCCINUM GLACIALE Linné   **Glacial Whelk**   Pl. 38
Range: Circumpolar; south to Strait of Juan de Fuca.
Habitat: Moderately deep water.
Description: From 1 to 2 in. high, this shell has about 6 whorls, each somewhat flattened at the side and bearing a keel at the shoulder and base. Sutures well defined; there are some revolving ridges on the body whorl, as well as vertical folds. Color dull yellowish gray; aperture white.

BUCCINUM PLECTRUM Stim.   **Lyre Whelk**   Pl. 38
Range: Arctic Ocean to Puget Sound.
Habitat: Moderately deep water.
Description: A rather elongate shell, large but thin, attaining a height of about 3 in. There are 7 or 8 rounded whorls, the sutures deeply impressed. Shell decorated with vertical folds, strongly on the early whorls and weaker on the last volution. Aperture somewhat squarish; outer lip simple and inner lip slightly reflected, and twisted at the base. Color yellowish brown.

Genus *Volutopsius* Mörch 1857

VOLUTOPSIUS HARPA Mörch   **Left-handed Whelk**   Pl. 39
Range: S. Alaska.
Habitat: Deep water.
Description: About 4 in. high, this is a sinistral snail, turning in the opposite direction from most gastropods. There are about 4 whorls, a low spire, and a large flaring aperture. Sculpture consists of revolving ridges, plus a few weak vertical folds. Color grayish brown, with a yellowish-brown periostracum.

VOLUTOPSIUS STEFANSSONI Dall   Pl. 38
Stefansson's Whelk
Range: S. Alaska.
Habitat: Deep water.
Description: A large and heavy shell reaching a height of about 7 in. There are 5 or 6 rapidly expanding whorls, the sutures indistinct. The volutions are inflated, and the surface is smooth, with sometimes a few obscure folds at the shoulders. Aperture

very large; outer lip thickened; canal short and wide. Color grayish white.

Genus *Colus* Röding 1798

COLUS HALLI Dall   **Hall's Colus**   Pl. 38
  Range: Bering Sea to California.
  Habitat: Deep water.
  Description: 1¾ in. high. A spindle-shaped shell of about 5 moderately convex whorls, sutures distinct. Apex rather blunt, canal open and slightly curved. Surface bears very fine revolving lines, but they are almost concealed by a tough yellowish-brown periostracum. Aperture, including a broad area on columella, pure white.

COLUS JORDANI Dall   **Jordan's Colus**   Pl. 38
  Range: Bering Sea to Monterey, California.
  Habitat: Deep water.
  Description: A 2-in. shell of about 7 moderately rounded whorls, the sutures fairly distinct. Surface bears weak revolving lines, and is whitish; there is a dark orange-brown periostracum that hides both the sculpture and color. Aperture white; canal short and wide.

COLUS SPITZBERGENSIS (Reeve)   **Spitsbergen Colus**   Pl. 38
  Range: Circumpolar; south to Vancouver; also Arctic Ocean south to Nova Scotia.
  Habitat: Deep water.
  Description: A rather large shell, less fusiform than many of its group. Height about 3 in., color yellowish brown. There are 7 or 8 rounded whorls, each decorated with small but prominent revolving ridges, about 20 to a volution. Aperture nearly circular; outer lip thin and sharp; canal quite short.
  Remarks: This species is well known in Europe and Japan.

Genus *Plicifusus* Dall 1902

PLICIFUSUS KROYERI (Möll.)   **Kroyer's Whelk**   Pl. 38
  Range: Circumpolar; south to B.C.
  Habitat: Deep water.
  Description: Height about 2 in., whorl count 6, the general shape rather plump. Early volutions sculptured with distinct vertical ribs; major part of shell smooth. Aperture large, outer lip thin and sharp, inner lip partially reflected. Short, open canal. Color yellowish white, with a dark brown periostracum.

Genus *Beringius* Dall 1886

BERINGIUS CREBRICOSTATA Dall   Pl. 39
Thick-ribbed Whelk
    Range: Alaska.
    Habitat: Deep water.
    Description: A large shell, attaining height of 5 in. There are 5 or 6 whorls, sculptured with very heavy revolving ribs that have deep channels between them. Spire tall, the aperture moderately large. Inner lip reflected on body whorl. Color white; thin grayish periostracum.
    Remarks: This gastropod (and *B. kennicotti*, below) will be found in some books listed under the generic name of *Jumula* Friele. However, *Jumula* is the Finnish word for God, and the International Commission on Zoological Nomenclature in recent years bars names that might give offense on religious or political grounds, so it seems best to adopt Dall's *Beringius* for this group.

BERINGIUS KENNICOTTI Dall   **Kennicott's Whelk**   Pl. 39
    Range: Alaska to Vancouver I.
    Habitat: Deep water.
    Description: A large and sturdy shell, some 5 in. high. There are 5 or 6 well-shouldered whorls, the sutures very distinct. Sculpture consists of revolving threadlike lines and prominent vertical folds, about 12 on the body whorl. Apex bulbous, aperture moderately large. Outer lip strongly arched, inner lip forms a thick white callus on columella. Color yellowish gray.
    Remarks: See Remarks for *B. crebricostata* (above).

Genus *Neptunea* Röding 1798

NEPTUNEA AMIANTA (Dall)   **Unspotted Whelk**   Pl. 39
    Range: Bering Sea to Monterey, California.
    Habitat: Deep water.
    Description: A pure white or yellowish-white shell, 5 in. or more in height. About 7 rounded whorls, terminating in a small bulbous nucleus at the apex. Surface bears fine revolving lines, and the early whorls may or may not be marked with vertical folds. Aperture large; canal moderately short, and open.

NEPTUNEA LYRATA (Gmel.)   **Ridged Whelk**   Pl. 39
    Range: Alaska to Point Pinos, California.
    Habitat: Moderately deep water.
    Description: A fine large shell, its height about 4 in. There are 5 robust whorls, each decorated with evenly spaced revolving ribs, the spaces between them concave. Spire partially turreted. Aperture large; outer lip sharp and made wavy by the ends of

ribs. Canal moderately long, and open. Color reddish brown, sometimes darker on the ribs.

NEPTUNEA PHOENICEA (Dall)   **Phoenician Whelk**   **Pl. 39**
   Range : Alaska to Oregon.
   Habitat : Deep water.
   Description : Another fine shell, with height about 4 in. There are 6 or 7 rounded whorls, the general shape fusiform. An ornamentation of revolving ribs, with smaller riblets between them. Color yellowish brown; aperture and columella usually brown. There is a horny operculum. Canal open and moderately long.

NEPTUNEA PRIBILOFFENSIS (Dall)   **Pribilof Whelk**   **Pl. 39**
   Range : Pribilof Is. to Queen Charlotte Is.
   Habitat : Moderately deep water.
   Description : Height about 5 in., whorl count about 6. Each volution bears 3 or 4 weak revolving ribs, the upper one forming a slight shoulder. Aperture large; inner lip partially reflected; canal short and open. Color yellowish white.

NEPTUNEA SMIRNIA (Dall)   **Chocolate Whelk**   **Pl. 39**
   Range : Nunivak I. to Puget Sound.
   Habitat : Moderately deep water.
   Description : A fine large shell of 5 or 6 rounded whorls, growing to a height of about 5 in. The early volutions are sculptured with low flat spiral cords, but the body whorl is relatively smooth. Sutures distinct. Aperture wide and oval; canal short, open, and somewhat recurved. Color rich chocolate-brown. Juvenile specimens have a thin grayish periostracum that is usually lacking on mature shells.

NEPTUNEA TABULATA (Baird)   **Tabled Whelk**   **Pl. 39**
   Range : B.C. to San Diego, California.
   Habitat : Moderately deep water.
   Description : A solid and sturdy shell about 4 in. high, composed of 7 or 8 whorls. Spire well elevated and strongly turreted. Surface marked with weak revolving lines, and the top of each whorl is flat, or concave, so that there is a winding concave channel ascending the spire. Aperture moderate; canal curved and open; and there is a tiny umbilicus. Color yellowish white.

Genus *Volutharpa* Fischer 1856

VOLUTHARPA AMPULLACEA (Midd.)   **Pl. 38**
Big-mouthed Whelk
   Range : Alaska to Vancouver I.
   Habitat : Moderately deep water.
   Description : About 1 in. high, this is a stout shell that is nearly

all body whorl. There are only about 3 volutions, and the flaring aperture is fully as large as the rest of the shell. Thin and fragile in substance, the shell bears a few wrinkled growth lines but no other ornamentation. Thin olive-brown periostracum, and the operculum is horny. Aperture, and the broad area over columella, dark chestnut-brown, rich and shiny.

Genus *Kelletia* Fischer 1884

KELLETIA KELLETI (For.)   **Kellet's Whelk**   Pl. 38
    Range: Santa Barbara, California, to Mexico.
    Habitat: Moderately shallow water.
    Description: A rugged and heavy shell nearly 6 in. high. Shoulders sloping, each volution bearing 8 or 9 very strong vertical folds that come to rounded points at the center of the whorl. There are numerous threadlike revolving lines as well. Aperture large; outer lip simple; canal moderately long and open. Color yellowish.
    Remarks: One of the largest gastropods found on the West Coast.

Genus *Searlesia* Harmer 1916

SEARLESIA DIRA (Reeve)   **Dire Whelk**   Pl. 37
    Range: Alaska to Monterey, California.
    Habitat: Moderately shallow water.
    Description: A solid shell of 5 or 6 whorls, the height about $1\frac{1}{2}$ in. Ornamentation of sharp revolving lines, narrow and crowded. Outer lip thick but simple; short canal open, with a slight fold at the base of the columella. Color dull purplish brown.

Genus *Macron* H. & A. Adams 1853

MACRON LIVIDUS A. Adams   **Livid Macron**   Pl. 38
    Range: Farallon Is., California, to Baja California.
    Habitat: Near shore; under stones.
    Description: About 1 in. high, this is an uninteresting shell of some 5 or 6 whorls. Spire short and bluntly pointed. The only sculpture is a series of closely spaced growth lines. Color pale bluish white, but shell covered with a thick brownish periostracum. Aperture white; columella polished and showing a strong revolving ridge at its upperpart.

Family Fusinidae: Spindle Shells

COMMONLY large, more or less spindle-shaped shells. Lip not thickened; umbilicus wanting. Operculum horny. The spire is long, acuminate, and many-whorled, and the canal is long and straight. Chiefly in warm seas.

Genus *Fusinus* Rafinesque 1815

FUSINUS KOBELTI Dall **Kobelt's Spindle** Pl. 40
Range: Monterey, California, to San Diego.
Habitat: Moderately deep water.
Description: This shell attains a height of about 2 in. There are 7 or 8 whorls, and the shape is fusiform. Sculpture sharp and prominent, consisting of vertical folds crossed by strong revolving lines. Canal quite long, with upper angle marking center of shell. Color grayish.

Genus *Aptyxis* Troschel 1868

APTYXIS LUTEOPICTA (Dall) **Painted Spindle** Pl. 40
Range: Monterey, California, to Baja California.
Habitat: Moderately deep water.
Description: About 1 in. high, with 6 or 7 whorls. Shape fusiform, sutures well defined, spire moderately tall. Volutions sculptured with distinct vertical folds, over which are impressed spiral lines. Aperture rather small; canal short, the inner lip somewhat reflected. Color brown, with a yellowish encircling band.
Remarks: Found as a Pleistocene fossil at San Pedro, California.

Family Olividae: Olive Shells

MEMBERS of this family are more or less cylindrical in shape, with a greatly enlarged body whorl that conceals most of the earlier volutions. Shells smooth and highly polished, often brightly colored. They are widely distributed in warm and tropical seas.

Genus *Olivella* Swainson 1840

OLIVELLA BAETICA Carp. **Beatic Olive** Pl. 40
Range: S. Alaska to Baja California.
Habitat: Shallow water; sandy bottoms.
Description: A small and slender shell, its height about ½ in. There are 4 or 5 whorls, a rather prominent spire, and an aperture about half the length of the whole shell. There is a tiny operculum, something that is lacking in the true olive shells of the genus *Oliva* Brug. 1789. This is a smooth, highly polished shell. Color bluish to brownish, with a paler band following the suture.

Remarks: This species ranges farther north than most of its group.

OLIVELLA BIPLICATA (Sow.) **Purple Olive** Pl. 40
Range: Vancouver I. to Baja California.
Habitat: Shallow water; sandflats.
Description: A very popular shell about 1 in. high. Generally there are 4 whorls, a short spire, and an enlarged body whorl. Aperture long, narrow at top and wide at bottom, where there is a distinct notch. Columella heavily plastered with enamel and bearing 2 small pleats at base. Surface smooth and polished, color showing considerable variation. Some individuals are nearly white and others very dark, but most are bluish gray, marked more or less with purple at the suture and canal.
Remarks: Generally living in colonies that quickly burrow under the sand when the tide goes out.

Family Mitridae: Miters

MEMBERS of this family on our shores are mostly small shells. In the South Pacific and Indian Oceans they are much larger, and in many cases extremely colorful. Shell spindle-shaped and usually thick and solid, with a sharply pointed spire. Aperture small and notched in front; and there are several distinct pleats on the columella. Confined to warm seas.

Genus *Mitra* Röding 1798

MITRA CATALINAE Dall **Catalina Miter** Pl. 40
Range: Crescent City, California, to San Diego.
Habitat: Moderately shallow water.
Description: A dark brown, almost black shell, the height about ¾ in. There are 4 or 5 whorls with no shoulders, so that the shell tapers regularly to a blunt apex. Sutures plainly marked. There are 3 strong pleats on the columella; the inside of the aperture is nearly as dark as exterior of shell.

MITRA IDAE Mel. **Ida's Miter** Pl. 40
Range: Farallon Is., California, to San Diego.
Habitat: Moderately deep water.
Description: An elongate shell nearly 2 in. high, consisting of about 6 cylinder-like whorls. Surface appears smooth but there are very fine revolving lines. Aperture long and narrow; outer lip somewhat thickened; columella bears 3 or 4 pleats. Color of shell pale brown, but most specimens are covered by a thick, coal-black periostracum. Aperture white.

Family Cancellariidae: Nutmegs

MOSTLY small but solid shells, usually with a striking cross-ribbed sculpture. The aperture is drawn out, with a short canal at the base. Inner lip strongly plicate, the outer lip ribbed within. There is no operculum. These snails are vegetarians, living chiefly in warm seas.

Genus *Cancellaria* Lamarck 1799

CANCELLARIA COOPERI Gabb   **Cooper's Nutmeg**   **Pl. 40**
   Range: Monterey, California, to Baja California.
   Habitat: Moderately deep water.
   Description: Averaging between 2 and 3 in., but said to reach a full 7 in. occasionally. There are 6 or 7 whorls, the shoulders angled so as to produce a turreted spire. About 15 ribs to each volution, rather weak on the sides but rising to small sharp spines at the shoulders, and there is a sculpture of spiral lines as well. Color yellowish brown, with narrow revolving lines of darker hue.
   Remarks: An uncommon shell, much sought by collectors.

Genus *Admete* Kröyer 1842

ADMETE COUTHOUYI (Jay)   **Couthouy's Nutmeg**   **Pl. 40**
   Range: Circumpolar; south to San Diego, California; also Atlantic Coast to Massachusetts.
   Habitat: Moderately deep water.
   Description: A stout shell nearly ½ in. high. About 5 well-rounded whorls, body whorl relatively large, the sutures well impressed. Sculpture consists of both revolving and vertical lines, giving the surface a more or less network pattern. Aperture large; outer lip thin and sharp. Color yellowish white, with a broad whitish area on the columella.
   Remarks: While most of this group prefer warm waters, this one ranges into the Arctic Ocean.

Family Marginellidae: Marginellas

THESE are small, porcelaneous, highly polished shells, found on sandy bottoms in warm seas. Spire short and body whorl large. Aperture narrow and long; outer lip somewhat thickened; columella plicate.

Genus *Marginella* Lamarck 1799

MARGINELLA CALIFORNICA Tom.   **Pl. 40**
California Marginella
    Range: Santa Monica, California, to Mexico.
    Habitat: Shallow water; sandy bottoms.
    Description: A moderately elongate, cylindrical shell just over
¼ in. high. There are about 4 whorls but the spire is very low.
Aperture narrow and long; 4 oblique pleats on the columella.
Surface smooth and polished, the color white, with 3 yellowish-
brown bands.

MARGINELLA JEWETTI Carp.   **Jewett's Marginella**   **Pl. 40**
    Range: Monterey, California, to San Diego.
    Habitat: Shallow water; sandy bottoms.
    Description: A pure-white shell that is nearly all body whorl, its
height no more than ¼ in., generally less. Spire very short and
glazed over. Aperture long and narrow; a few pleats on columella. Surface very glossy, lacking lines or sculpture of any kind.

MARGINELLA PYRIFORMIS Carp.   **Pl. 40**
Pear-shaped Marginella
    Range: Alaska to Mexico.
    Habitat: Mudflats.
    Description: A tiny shell, only about ⅛ in. high. It is pear-
shaped, and white or grayish white. Aperture long and narrow,
with 4 pleats on columella; the outer lip also bears a number of
teeth, microscopic in size.

Family Conidae: Cone Shells

THIS is a large family of many-whorled, cone-shaped snails noted
for their variety of color and pattern. They live among the rocks
and corals in tropic seas, only a single example being found along
the West Coast. This family is unusual among mollusks in that
some of its members possess poison glands. The venom passes
through a tiny duct to the teeth of the radula and serves to benumb
the gastropod's prey, chiefly small fishes and worms. Our small
representative of this great group seems harmless, but certain
South Pacific and Indian Ocean species are capable of inflicting
wounds that can be serious, and even fatal.

Genus *Conus* Linné 1758

CONUS CALIFORNICUS Hinds   **California Cone**   **Pl. 40**
    Range: Farallon Is., California, to Baja California.
    Habitat: Moderately shallow water; stones.

Description: Height about 1 in., whorl count 6 or 7. Spire but slightly elevated, and the general shape is certainly like an inverted cone. In life, shell covered with a reddish-brown periostracum; surface beneath, grayish white. Aperture shows tints of brownish.

Family Terebridae: Auger Shells

SLENDER, elongate, many-whorled shells, confined to warm and tropic seas. No pleats on columella, but the short canal bears a sharp twist. In the islands of the South Pacific we find many members of this group that are both large and colorful, in contrast to the rather somber aspects of the single representative that lives along our shores.

Genus *Terebra* Bruguière 1789

TEREBRA PEDROANA Dall San Pedro Auger Pl. 40
  Range: Redondo Beach, California, to Mexico.
  Habitat: Shallow water.
  Description: A slender, spikelike shell of 10 or 11 whorls, the taper very regular to a sharp apex. Height slightly more than 1 in. Each volution decorated with numerous weak vertical ridges and a few obscure revolving lines, and there is a series of closely spaced beads spiraling up the sutures. Aperture small; inner lip twisted at the notchlike canal. Color yellowish white, with irregular splashes of brown; some individuals nearly solid brown.

Family Turridae: Slit Shells
or Tower Shells

THIS is a very large family of marine gastropods, containing hundreds of genera and thousands of species. Many of them are small but highly ornate. The general shape is fusiform, and the outer lip commonly bears a slit, or notch. They are lovers of deep water as a rule, and occur in warm, temperate, and cold seas.

Genus *Elaeocyma* Dall 1918

ELAEOCYMA EMPYROSIA (Dall) Turret Tower Pl. 40
  Range: San Pedro, California, to San Diego.
  Habitat: Moderately deep water.
  Description: A solid shell roughly 1 in. high. About 9 whorls, each decorated with distinct revolving lines and by vertical folds that tend to pinch out at center of the whorl. Spire tall and apex sharp. Aperture relatively small; canal short and some-

what curved. Color yellowish white, often shading to brown on
the later volutions.

Genus *Ophiodermella* Bartsch 1944

OPHIODERMELLA INCISA (Carp.) **Incised Tower** Pl. 40
Range: Puget Sound to San Diego, California.
Habitat: Moderately deep water.
Description: A spikelike shell, its height about 1 in. There are
7 or 8 whorls, with only a slight constriction at the sutures.
Sculpture consists of weak revolving lines and stronger vertical
ridges closely spaced and peculiarly bent at the center. Aperture
small; outer lip thin; canal short. Color dove-gray, with pale
reddish bands.

Genus *Pseudomelatoma* Dall 1918

PSEUDOMELATOMA MOESTA (Carp.) Pl. 40
Doleful Tower
Range: Monterey, California, to Mexico.
Habitat: Moderately deep water.
Description: A fusiform shell, the height about ¾ in. There are
7 or 8 whorls and a tall spire that terminates in a sharp apex.
Aperture rather long and narrow; outer lip thin; canal short.
There are 9 or 10 somewhat curved vertical ridges on each
whorl, the spaces between smooth and polished; a faint row of
beads is present just below the suture line. Color greenish brown.

Genus *Burchia* Bartsch 1944

BURCHIA REDONDOENSIS (Burch) **Redondo Tower** Pl. 40
Range: Redondo Beach, California.
Habitat: Moderately deep water.
Description: A fine, graceful shell nearly 2 in. high. There are
about 8 whorls, the sutures rather distinct. The surface bears
curving vertical ridges, and revolving lines as well, with just a
suggestion of nodular beads at the suture. Aperture narrow;
inner lip partially reflected and the outer lip with a deep notch
at its upper end. Color deep brown to almost black; aperture
bluish white.

Genus *Oenopota* Mörch 1852

OENOPOTA ROSEA (Sars) **Rosy Oenopota** Pl. 40
Range: Alaska to Puget Sound.
Habitat: Deep water.
Description: Only ¼ in. high, a stout shell with about 6 whorls.
There is a slight shoulder to each volution, and the sutures are
well impressed. Surface with revolving lines and pronounced

vertical ridges. Aperture small; canal open and moderately short. Color pale reddish.

Genus *Granatoma* Bartsch 1941

GRANATOMA EXCURVATA (Carp.)   **Curved Tower**   Pl. 40
Range: Bering Sea to Puget Sound.
Habitat: Moderately deep water.
Description: Less than ½ in. high, a fusiform shell tapering to base and to apex. About 6 whorls, sutures well impressed. There is a series of curving vertical ridges on each whorl, and distinct revolving lines as well. Aperture elongate; outer lip thin and simple; there is a broad polished area on the columella. Color yellowish gray.

Genus *Mitromorpha* Carpenter 1865

MITROMORPHA FILOSA Carp.   **Filose Tower**   Pl. 40
Range: Monterey, California, to Mexico.
Habitat: Moderately shallow water.
Description: This tiny shell is only about ¼ in. high, generally slightly less, and extremely fusiform in shape. There are 5 or 6 whorls, the sutures rather indistinct. Shell quite solid, decorated with revolving lines that are more or less beaded. Color yellowish brown.

Genus *"Lora"* Gistel 1848

"LORA" HARPULARIA (Couth.)   **Harp Lora**   Pl. 40
Range: Arctic to Puget Sound; Arctic to Rhode Island.
Habitat: Moderately deep water.
Description: A buffy-white shell about ½ in. high. Stoutly elongate, with 6 to 8 angled whorls flattened somewhat above the angle, forming sloping shoulders. Each volution bears numerous oblique rounded ribs which are crossed by fine revolving lines. Ribs on body whorl fade toward basal margin. Aperture oval and narrow; inner lip smooth, white, and slightly arched.
Remarks: The generic status of this group is now uncertain. These shells were once listed under *Bela* Gray, and later under *Lora* Gistel. Many authorities believe that they belong in the genus *Oenopota* Mörch; but until more decisive work is done on them it seems best to leave them in *Lora*, and by placing that name in quotation marks show that it is uncertain.

"LORA" NOBILIS (Möll.)   **Noble Lora**   Pl. 40
Range: Circumpolar; south to Puget Sound and Rhode Island.
Habitat: Moderately deep water.
Description: Yellowish-white color, about ½ in. high. Shell

stoutly fusiform, with about 7 whorls, the shoulders flattened to produce a turreted spire. About 15 vertical ribs to a volution, crossed by prominent spiral lines. Aperture small and narrow; canal short.

Remarks: See Remarks for *"L."* *harpularia* (above).

"LORA" PRIBILOVA Dall   **Pribilof Lora**   Pl. 40
Range: Arctic Ocean to Estero Bay, California.
Habitat: Moderately deep water.
Description: Another small snail, its shell about ¼ in. high, and it has about 5 whorls. Shoulders flattened, the spire somewhat turreted. The vertical ribs are conspicuous and rather widely spaced, and the revolving lines are obscure. Aperture narrow, canal short. Color creamy white.
Remarks: See Remarks for *"L."* *harpularia* (above).

"LORA" RETICULATA (Brown)   **Reticulate Lora**   Pl. 40
Range: South to B.C.
Habitat: Moderately deep water.
Description: Height about ¼ in. There are 6 somewhat rounded whorls, with no shoulders to speak of but with well-impressed sutures. The vertical ribs are only slightly stronger than the revolving lines, so that the surface has a reticulate pattern. Aperture narrow and rather long, being half as long as the entire shell. Color yellowish white.
Remarks: See Remarks for *"L."* *harpularia* (above).

Family Eulimidae: Obelisk Shells

SMALL, high-spired shells, usually polished and commonly white. The spire is often slightly bent to one side. A very large family, living chiefly in warm seas. Many of the genera are parasitic on other forms of marine life. This family formerly known as Melanellidae.

Genus *Balcis* Gray 1847

BALCIS CATALINENSIS (Bar.)   **Catalina Balcis**   Pl. 33
Range: Santa Rosa I., California, to Mexico.
Habitat: Shallow water.
Description: Elongate and graceful, with just a slight bend to the right. The highly polished surface is bluish white. Height nearly ½ in., the whorl count 8 or 9. Volutions rather flattish, with indistinct sutures. Aperture small and oval.

BALCIS GRIPPI (Bar.)   **Gripp's Balcis**   Pl. 33
Range: San Pedro, California, to Baja California.
Habitat: Moderately shallow water.

Description: A strongly curved shell about ½ in. high. Approximately 12 whorls, separated by rather indistinct sutures. Aperture teardrop shape, bordered by a thickened lip. Color white, surface glossy.

BALCIS MICANS (Carp.)   **Shining Balcis**   Pl. 33
  Range: B.C. to Baja California.
  Habitat: Moderately shallow water.
  Description: A beautifully polished shell, white, sometimes shading to amber near apex. About 10 whorls; height just under ½ in. Apex very sharp, the shell presenting a spikelike appearance. Aperture small and elongate.

BALCIS OLDROYDI (Bar.)   **Oldroyd's Balcis**   Pl. 33
  Range: B.C. to Mexico.
  Habitat: Moderately deep water.
  Description: A slender, spikelike shell about ½ in. high. The apex is very sharp, and there are about 10 whorls, with no shoulders, so that the taper is very regular. Color bluish white. Aperture small and oval.

BALCIS RANDOLPHI (Van.)   **Randolph's Balcis**   Pl. 33
  Range: Aleutian Is. to Puget Sound.
  Habitat: Shallow water; under stones.
  Description: A small white shell, highly polished, its height about ¼ in. There are 7 or 8 whorls, with rather indistinct sutures. The form is quite slender, but the apex is moderately blunt. Aperture small and oval, with outer lip slightly thickened.

BALCIS RUTILA (Carp.)   **Starfish Balcis**   Pl. 33
  Range: Alaska to Baja California.
  Habitat: Parasitical on starfish and sea cucumbers.
  Description: A very slender shell only about ¼ in. high. There are 7 or 8 rather flattish whorls, the last one somewhat lengthened. Shell well polished; color rosy white.
  Remarks: Probably the most abundant member of this genus in California waters.

Family Pyramidellidae: Pyramid Shells

MANY workers are now placing this family and the last one, Eulimidae, with the Opistobranchiata, since they appear to be closely related to the bubble shells. They are small pyramidal or conical shells, usually white and polished, and many-whorled. They inhabit sandy bottoms of warm and tropic seas, many being parasitic. The number of species in this family runs into the hundreds, and many are so alike that even the experts are not in complete agreement. A few of the common forms are here discussed and illustrated.

Genus *Pyramidella* Lamarck 1799

PYRAMIDELLA ADAMSI Carp. **Adam's Pyramidella** Pl. 33
Range: Monterey, California, to Baja California.
Habitat: Moderately shallow water.
Description: Less than $\frac{1}{2}$ in. high, this is an elongate shell consisting of some 9 or 10 moderately rounded whorls. Base fairly long, and well rounded; aperture oval, with a thin outer lip. The inner lip bears a strong plication. Color white over most of shell, but later volutions may be clouded with brown.
Remarks: An uncommon species on Californian shores

Genus *Turbonilla* Risso 1826

TURBONILLA CASTANEA Keep **Chestnut Turbonilla** Pl. 33
Range: San Pedro to San Diego, California.
Habitat: Shallow water.
Description: About $\frac{1}{2}$ in. high and chestnut-brown. There are about 10 rather flattish whorls, with deeply impressed sutures. Each volution is decorated with numerous vertical folds, as many as 20 on the body whorl. Small aperture pear-shaped, outer lip thin and sharp.
Remarks: The genus *Turbonilla* is one of the largest of the snail groups, more than 100 different species having been described from the West Coast alone. All are small, and many so alike that it requires a specialist to separate them.

TURBONILLA REGINA Dall & Bar. **Queen Turbonilla** Pl. 33
Range: Santa Rosa to Catalina I., California.
Habitat: Moderately shallow water.
Description: About $\frac{1}{2}$ in. high, with a slender, spikelike appearance. There are about 12 whorls, separated by well-defined sutures and ornamented with numerous vertical folds, or grooves. Color yellowish brown, the surface commonly shiny.
Remarks: See Remarks for *T. castanea* (above).

TURBONILLA VALDEZI Dall & Bar. Pl. 33
Valdez Turbonilla
Range: Vancouver I. to Monterey, California.
Habitat: Moderately deep water.
Description: A rather stout little shell of 6 or 7 flattish whorls, the sutures well impressed. Height usually less than $\frac{1}{4}$ in. Sculpture consists of numerous vertical grooves; color is brownish white. Aperture small and oval; lip thin and sharp.
Remarks: As with the others of this genus, the 1st (nuclear)

whorl is coiled at right angles to the rest of the shell. An example for *T. regina* is shown enlarged on Plate 33, No. 9. Also see Remarks for *T. castanea* (above).

Genus *Odostomia* Fleming 1817

ODOSTOMIA HELGA Dall & Bar.   **Helga Odostome**   Pl. 33
Range: San Pedro to Coronado Is., California.
Habitat: Moderately shallow water.
Description: A tiny univalve, milk-white and only about 1/10 in. high. Stoutly conic, with 4 or 5 well-rounded whorls. The volutions are sculptured with rounded revolving bands, each separated by a moderately deep line. Aperture large and oval; lip thin and sharp.
Remarks: This is another large group, containing even more members than the last genus.

ODOSTOMIA LASTRA Dall & Bar.   Pl. 33
Cancellate Odostome
Range: Catalina I. to San Diego, California.
Habitat: Moderately shallow water.
Description: A larger shell than *O. helga* (above), nearly ½ in. high. About 7 whorls, the last one large and rounded, and the taper quite regular to the sharp apex. Sutures well impressed. Sculpture consists of strong revolving lines and weaker vertical lines, giving the surface a cancellate appearance. Aperture large and oval; outer lip thin and sharp. Color white.
Remarks: This is another large group, containing even more members than the last genus.

ODOSTOMIA TENUISCULPTA Carp.   Pl. 33
Weak Odostome
Range: Vancouver I. to Baja California.
Habitat: Shallow water.
Description: An elongate-oval shell of some 5 rounded whorls, the height about ⅛ in. Aperture relatively large, and oval; lip thin and sharp. The sutures are plainly delineated, and the surface is but weakly sculptured and appears rather smooth, and unpolished. Color white.
Remarks: This is another large group, containing even more members than the last genus.

Family Acteonidae: Small Bubble Shells

SMALL, solid shells, cylindrical, with a short sharp spire. The inner lip bears a single pleat. Surface usually spirally grooved, and the aperture is long and narrow.

Genus *Acteon* Montfort 1810

ACTEON PUNCTOCAELATUS Carp. **Barrel Shell** Pl. 40
Range: Monterey, California, to Mexico.
Habitat: Shallow water.
Description: An attractive small shell, consisting of 4 or 5 whorls, and attaining a height of about ½ in. Spire short and pointed, the body whorl making up most of the shell. Aperture long and narrow; outer lip crenulate within and the inner lip bearing a single fold, or pleat. There is a sculpture of very sharp revolving punctate grooves. Color white, with 2 black bands encircling the volutions. Surface well polished.

Family Acteocinidae: Glassy Bubble Shells

SMALL cylindrical shells as a rule. The spire usually short or completely concealed. Aperture long, widening at the base. Chiefly in cool waters.

Genus *Acteocina* Gray 1847

ACTEOCINA CULCITELLA (Gould) **Barrel Bubble** Pl. 40
Range: Kodiak I., Alaska, to California.
Habitat: Shallow water.
Description: About ½ in. high, this is a rather solid shell, oval-cylindrical in shape. There are 5 whorls, with a short, pointed spire, the sutures plainly marked. Color bluish white, with a straw-colored periostracum. Sculpture consists of fine revolving lines, most discernible when the periostracum is present.

Genus *Cylichna* Lovén 1846

CYLICHNA ALBA (Brown) **White Barrel Bubble** Pl. 40
Range: Circumpolar; south to San Diego, California; also North Carolina.
Habitat: Moderately shallow water.
Description: A fragile, tiny shell of 3 or 4 whorls, the height about ¼ in. Color white, with a thin rusty periostracum. The spire is sunken, with a shallow pit at the top of the shell. Shape cylindrical. Surface bears very delicate lines of growth, but the general appearance is smooth and often shiny.
Remarks: Empty shells frequently can be found by searching in the drift that marks the high-tide level.

Family Bullidae: True Bubble Shells

SMALL to fairly large shells, usually rolled up like a scroll. The shell is thin and light. These are carnivorous snails, burrowing in the sands and muds for their prey.

Genus *Bulla* Linné 1758

BULLA GOULDIANA Pils.   **Gould's Bubble**   Pl. 40
Range: Santa Barbara, California, to Mexico.
Habitat: Shallow water; mudflats.
Description: A fine large shell, one of the largest of the bubble shells to be found anywhere in the world. Height more than 1½ in. General shape roundly oval. The enlarged body whorl completely hides the earlier volutions, so that instead of a spire this snail has a depressed area, or pit, at the top of its shell. Aperture flaring, and longer than the rest of the shell; inner lip spreads over the body whorl in a layer of enamel. Whole shell rather thin and delicate. Color varies from pale to very dark brown, most specimens showing considerable mottling. Aperture white, but the shell is so thin that the mottling shows through on the inside.

Family Akeridae: Paper Bubble Shells

SMALL, glassy, and very fragile shells inhabiting muddy and brackish waters, chiefly in warm seas. The animal is too large for its shell, which is partially internal.

Genus *Haminoea* Turton & Kingston 1830

HAMINOEA VESICULA (Gould)   **Blister Paper Bubble**   Pl. 40
Range: Alaska to Gulf of California.
Habitat: Shallow water.
Description: Nearly 1 in. high, the body whorl concealing the earlier whorls, the lip extending high above the top of the shell. Shell thin and fragile, the color pale greenish yellow, with a thin brownish periostracum.

HAMINOEA VIRESCENS (Sow.)   **Green Paper Bubble**   Pl. 40
Range: Puget Sound to Mexico.
Habitat: Shallow water.
Description: Another fragile, semitransparent shell, its height about ½ in. The outer lip is very thin, and it extends well above the top of the shell. Aperture narrow at top and greatly expanded at bottom. Color pale greenish yellow.

Family Trimusculidae: Button Shells

THESE are air-breathing mollusks, living in the sea. They have a limpet-like shell, with a weak siphonal groove on the inside of the shell.

Genus *Trimusculus* Schmidt 1818

TRIMUSCULUS RETICULATUS (Sow.)   Pl. 40
Reticulate Button Shell
Range: Farallon Is., California, to Mexico.
Habitat: Shallow water.
Description: This white, solid shell is almost circular in outline, and bluntly conical in shape, but from the irregularities of its station in life many variations result. It lives attached to stones after the manner of a limpet, and there is a horseshoe-like muscle scar on the inside. The surface is sculptured with radiating riblets that are reticulated by coarse lines of growth.

Family Ellobiidae: Marsh Snails

THESE are salt-marsh snails, spending most of their time out of water. The shell is spiral, and covered with a horny periostracum. The aperture is elongate, with folds on the inner lip.

Genus *Melampus* Montfort 1810

MELAMPUS OLIVACEUS Carp.   **Salt-marsh Snail**   Pl. 40
Range: Monterey Bay, California, to Mexico.
Habitat: Salt marshes.
Description: This small shell probably does not belong in a book about marine mollusks, but it is very abundant in salt marshes and many empty shells are washed into the ocean, later to be found among the beach litter. Beginners in shell collecting often believe they have found young cone shells, since they do have the general shape of members of the *Conus* group — wide at the top and narrowing toward the bottom. Height about ½ in., the spire short and aperture long. Color greenish olive, more or less mottled, and there is a strong periostracum. Deep within the outer lip are several elevated white revolving ridges that do not reach the edge of the lip.
Remarks: This gastropod inhabits marshes that are occasionally flooded by the tide, and is never far from the high-tide mark. When the tide comes in these snails clamber up the tops of marsh grass, as if to avoid getting wet for as long as possible.

III

West Coast Amphineurans and Scaphopods

CLASS AMPHINEURA

THESE are the chitons, or "coat-of-mail" shells, mollusks that usually live in rocky situations close to shore. They are nocturnal in habits, feeding chiefly on decaying marine vegetation at night and spending the daytime clinging to the undersides of stones and dead shells, safely out of sight. They are not exclusively herbivorous, however, and most of them will feed on animal matter to some extent.

The chiton shell is composed of 8 separate but overlapping plates (valves). These form a sort of dorsal shield, which when empty and turned over suggests a small boat. The girdle is the leathery skin in which the plates are imbedded, and generally extends beyond the plates, all the way around, to form a thin border. This girdle may be smooth or granular, or it may be covered with scales or bristly tufts of hair. It frequently has the appearance of snakeskin.

The chiton crawls about on a muscular creeping organ, the foot, which is really the whole ventral surface of the animal. It can cling to a wave-washed rock with surprising tenacity, and removing a specimen without injuring the shell is not an easy task. Slipping a thin knifeblade under one is the best way to dislodge it. In death they commonly curl up like a pill-bug, but they can be relaxed by being soaked in water and spread out on a thin board, such as a lath, and secured by wrapping with strong thread. The tied-down chitons can be placed, board and all, in a container of some kind (2-quart fruit jars do nicely) and covered with either a 10 per cent solution of Formalin or a 50 per cent solution of alcohol. If a specimen is large you can dig out most of the fleshy part before fastening it to the board. After soaking for about two weeks, the chitons can be taken out and allowed to dry slowly in a shady place. Then they may be removed from the boards and they are now ready for the collection, although there will be some shrinkage of the girdle. There also will be some loss of color, so the chitons rarely make as attractive cabinet specimens as do the snails and clams.

Many collectors remove the 8 plates of the shell, and clean and reassemble them. The resulting specimens are things of beauty, exhibiting a surprising range of colors, from pure white to rich blue-green, including splashes and shadings of yellow, rose, and orange. It makes a most attractive collection to have a few of these calcareous plates cleaned and displayed in the same tray with the complete dried specimen.

To prepare them, simply boil the chiton for about 5 minutes, then remove the plates and place them in pure Clorox for one-half hour. This softens any adhering tissue so that its removal with a stiff brush is easy. After being dried on a paper towel the plates can be glued together in the proper sequence. When completely dry and set, they can be lightly wiped with mineral oil to which a small amount of neat's-foot oil has been added, and then they are ready for the cabinet.

Chitons are found from temperate to tropic seas, but are more numerous where the waters are warm, and these grow to an average larger size, even though the largest chiton known occurs on our Northwest coast. In the United States chitons are more abundant, both as to species and to individuals, on our Pacific shores.

Family Lepidochitonidae: Chitons

Genus *Tonicella* Carpenter 1873

TONICELLA LINEATA (Wood)   **Lined Chiton**   Pl. 41
Range: Aleutian Is. to San Diego, California.
Habitat: Near shore; under stones.
Description: One of the most colorful and attractive of the West Coast chitons, oval in shape and about 1 in. long, sometimes a bit longer. The plates are smooth and shiny, moderately arched at the center, and yellowish brown to orange. Sides of plates decorated with oblique wavy lines of dark reddish brown edged with white. On the end plates the lines are concentric. Girdle thin and smooth, alternating pale gray and brownish-gray color. Interior of plates white.
Remarks: Some of the plates are likely to be partially or completely unlined, so that the collector can find all sorts of combinations.

Genus *Cyanoplax* Gray 1821

CYANOPLAX HARTWEGI (Carp.)   **Hartweg's Chiton**   Pl. 41
Range: Puget Sound to Baja California.
Habitat: Moderately shallow water.
Description: Oval, somewhat flattened, the length about 1½ in. Color slaty or brownish gray, commonly speckled or spotted

with darker mottlings. The plates bear irregularly scattered granules, almost microscopic in size but easily seen by side-lighting, and are colored bluish green on the underside. Girdle narrow and very finely granulated.

Genus *Nuttallina* Dall 1879

NUTTALLINA CALIFORNICA (Reeve)   Pl. 41
California Nuttall Chiton
   Range: Vancouver I. to San Diego, California.
   Habitat: Rocks between tides.
   Description: An elongate species attaining a length of about 1½ in., colored olive-brown to dark brown. Plates irregularly mottled black and white (bluish inside) and sculptured with a weak furrow on each side, the surface very finely granular. The anterior plate bears weak radiating ridges. Girdle rather broad, dark brown, with a velvety appearance. The foot is pale red.

Family Mopaliidae: Chitons

Genus *Mopalia* Gray 1847

MOPALIA CILIATA (Sow.)   **Hairy Chiton**   Pl. 41
   Range: Alaska to Monterey, California.
   Habitat: Shallow water; under stones.
   Description: An oval species, its length about 1½ in. The plates are somewhat beaked, and bear coarsely granulated lateral areas. The center shows vertical riblets, and the two areas are separated by a raised line of beads. Color grayish green, with blotches of black and bright green. Girdle broad and yellowish brown, and covered with short hairs. Interior of plates greenish white.

MOPALIA LIGNOSA Gould   **Woody Chiton**   Pl. 41
   Range: Alaska to Baja California.
   Habitat: Moderately shallow water.
   Description: From 1 to 2½ in. long, the shape is oval. Central regions of the plates bear vertical ridges and the sides are pitted, the two areas separated by diagonal ridges. Colors variable, but commonly the plates are streaked with black and rich green. Sometimes they show splashes of bright yellow or orange. Interior may be bluish or pinkish. Girdle yellowish brown and quite hairy — although it lacks the stiff hairs and mossy look of *M. muscosa* (below).
   Remarks: A series of the plates o this species, cleaned and mounted, will astonish those who have never considered the chitons objects of beauty.

MOPALIA MUSCOSA Gould **Mossy Chiton**   Pl. 41
Range: Alaska to Baja California.
Habitat: Shallow water; rocks.
Description: A roundly oval chiton about 2 in. long. The color is usually olive or grayish brown, but living examples are apt to be covered with seaweeds and other marine growths. Plates strongly sculptured with vertical ridges on anterior parts and horizontal beaded ridges on posterior parts. The anterior plate bears radiating beaded ridges. Girdle moderately broad, and heavily adorned with stiff hairs, so that the creature does indeed have a mossy appearance.

Genus *Katharina* Gray 1847

KATHARINA TUNICATA Wood **Black Katy**   Pl. 41
Range: Aleutian Is. to California.
Habitat: Rocks between tides.
Description: Oblong-oval shape, rather well arched at the center. Length from 2 to 3 in. Color usually bluish white on the plates, both above and below. Each plate bears a deep diagonal groove along the sides, but in life this is concealed by the leathery girdle that covers about ⅔ of the shell area. This girdle is destitute of hairs or scales, and is coal-black and shiny. The foot is reddish.

Family Ischnochitonidae: Chitons

Genus *Ischnochiton* Gray 1847

ISCHNOCHITON ALBUS (Linné) **White Chiton**   Pl. 41
Range: Circumpolar; south to San Diego, California.
Habitat: Moderately deep water.
Description: Averaging about ½ in. long, this is a stoutly oval species, most abundant in cool waters. In life the color is bluish gray, but this rubs off easily, and most cabinet specimens vary from cream to nearly white. Plates weakly marked with growth lines; the narrow girdle is sandpapery.

ISCHNOCHITON CONSPICUUS Pils.   Pl. 41
Conspicuous Chiton
Range: San Miguel I., California, to Mexico.
Habitat: Under rocks between tides.
Description: A rather large species, attaining a length of 4 in., sometimes even more. It is elongate-oval, the back well arched. Central area of plates relatively smooth, lateral areas bearing coarse, wavy, horizontal ridges. Color grayish, with streaks of green, the plates pinkish underneath. Girdle narrow and grayish green, studded with short hairlike scales that give it a velvety feeling.

ISCHNOCHITON HEATHIANA Berry   **Heath's Chiton**   **Pl. 41**
Range : Coos Bay, Oregon, to Baja California.
Habitat: Shallow water.
Description: An elongate species of 2 or 3 in., the color dark greenish gray. Plates ornately sculptured with fine vertical grooves at the center and beaded horizontal ridges at the sides, the two separated by a raised diagonal ridge. Anterior plate bears fine radiating lines that are weakly beaded. Plates bluish on underside, each with a patch of white at the posterior. Girdle rather narrow, covered with minute scales, and colored with alternating bands of brown and yellowish green.

Family Cryptoplacidae: Chitons

Genus *Cryptochiton* Middendorff 1847

CRYPTOCHITON STELLERI Midd.   **Giant Chiton**   **Pl. 41**
Range : Alaska to California.
Habitat: Moderately deep water.
Description: A large, oblong, moderately flattened chiton reaching the almost unbelievable length of 12 in. Most individuals are between 6 and 8 in., but this species is recognized as the world's largest member of the group. Plates completely hidden under girdle, which covers entire top of animal. Girdle thick and leathery, and varies from yellowish brown to reddish brown, minutely dotted with white. The surface bears tiny spicules that impart a sandpapery feeling that has been described as gritty. The positions of the plates can be discerned through the skin, and when removed are seen to be pure white, rarely tinged with rose underneath.
Remarks: Although usually preferring several feet of water, this big chiton may be found in shallow water during the spawning season in May (Puget Sound). Some authorities place it in the genus *Amicula* Gray 1842.

CLASS SCAPHOPODA

AN external tubular shell, open at both ends and usually curved, covers the animal in this class of mollusks. The shape of the shell is responsible for the common names tusk shell and tooth shell that are generally applied to members of this class.

Found only in the sea, where they range from just below the low-tide mark to depths of several hundred fathoms, they show a preference for clean sand, but are sometimes found living on muddy bottoms. The typical shell is long and tapering, cylindrical, and usually pure white, although some tropical varieties may be pale green or pink. The surface may be smooth and glossy, dull and chalklike, or ribbed longitudinally. They live in the sand with the small end up, and from the larger end protrudes the foot, a tough elastic organ admirably adapted for burrowing. In fact, the name scaphopod means "plow-footed."

In primitive times the shells were used for money and for ornaments by various Indian tribes, particularly those from our Northwest, where the tubular shells were cut into short sections for beads.

Family Dentaliidae: Tusk Shells

Genus *Dentalium* Linné 1758

DENTALIUM PRETIOSUM Sow. **Indian Money Tusk** Pl. 41
   Range: Alaska to Baja California.
   Habitat: Moderately shallow water.
   Description: This shell grows to be nearly 2 in. long, but most individuals are somewhat smaller. It is slightly curved, and tapers gradually and regularly from the small upper end to the larger bottom end. It is a solid shell, ordinarily pure white (sometimes grayish) and with the texture of ivory, but occasionally highly polished.
   Remarks: The northwestern Indians used to string these shells together like beads for use as money.

IV

Gulf of California Pelecypods

Family Nuculidae: Nut Shells

(see p. 1)

Genus *Nucula* Lamarck 1799

NUCULA DECLIVIS Hinds   Pl. 42
  Range: Gulf of California to Panama.
  Habitat: Moderately shallow water.
  Description: Usually less than ¼ in. long. Shell obliquely oval, olive-green on the outside, with a thin periostracum; pearly within, the margins crenulate. A series of comblike teeth on each side of the beaks.

Family Nuculanidae: Nut Shells and Yoldias

(see p. 2)

Genus *Nuculana* Link 1807

NUCULANA ELENENSIS (Sow.)   Pl. 42
  Range: Gulf of California to Ecuador.
  Habitat: Moderately shallow water.
  Description: About 1½ in. long, this shell is rounded at the anterior end and drawn out to a blunt point at the posterior, the beaks nearly central. There are 2 series of hinge teeth, separated by a shallow pit for the ligament. Weak concentric lines decorate the surface. Color greenish brown; interior white. Inner margin not crenulate.

Genus *Adrana* H. & A. Adams 1858

ADRANA CULTRATA Keen   Pl. 42
  Range: Gulf of California to Ecuador.
  Habitat: Moderately deep water.
  Description: Long and narrow, this bivalve grows to almost 2 in. Beaks extremely low, situated at center of shell, with the dor-

sal margin nearly straight and the basal margin gently rounded. Both ends bluntly pointed. Valves thin and delicate, white.
Remarks: A southern species, but it has been taken from the southern end of the Gulf of California.

ADRANA PENASCOENSIS (Lowe) Pl. 42
Range: Northern end of Gulf of California.
Habitat: Moderately deep water.
Description: Another very thin and delicate shell; whitish, its length about 1¼ in. The shell is little more than ¼ in. high. Beaks closer to the anterior end, and that shorter end, as well as the long posterior end, is bluntly pointed. Surface bears very fine concentric lines.

Family Arcidae: Ark Shells

(see p. 5)

Genus *Arca* Linné 1758

ARCA MUTABILIS (Sow.) Pl. 42
Range: Gulf of California to Peru.
Habitat: Under rocks at low tide.
Description: Rather variable in shape but generally oblong, the beaks well separated and the length about 1½ in. There is a distinct posterior slope decorated with coarse ribs, the rest of the shell bearing finer radiating lines. Hinge line long and straight, well provided with comblike teeth. Color brown, under a coarse yellowish-brown periostracum. Interior chocolate-brown.

ARCA PACIFICA (Sow.) Pl. 42
Range: Gulf of California to Peru.
Habitat: Intertidal; rocks.
Description: A rugged and rough shell attaining a length of about 5 in. It, like *A. mutabilis* (above), is variable in outline, with a broad flat area on top that keeps the beaks well separated. The valves gape at the basal margin. Color gray. Sculpture of strong radiating ribs, but they are likely to be concealed by a shaggy brown periostracum. Young specimens decorated with violet-brown streaks.

Genus *Barbatia* Gray 1847

BARBATIA ALTERNATA (Sow.) Pl. 42
Range: Northern end of Gulf of California to Ecuador.
Habitat: Moderately deep water.

Description: A rather attractively shaped shell, thin and brittle, somewhat more than 1 in. long. Beaks moderately low, the anterior end rounded and the posterior with a pronounced slope. Weak radiating lines rather widely spaced cover most of the shell, with several strong ridges at the posterior end, rendering that margin scalloped. Color grayish white.

BARBATIA GRADATA (Brod. & Sow.)   Pl. 42
Range: Gulf of California to Peru.
Habitat: Shallow water; rocky shores.
Description: A rather narrow shell, the anterior end shortest and the posterior with a sharp slope. Length about 1 in. The sculpture consists of coarse radiating lines and sharp concentric lines, producing a cancellate surface. Color yellowish white.

BARBATIA ILLOTA (Sow.)   Pl. 42
Range: Gulf of California to Peru.
Habitat: Intertidal; rocks.
Description: Rather well inflated and 1½ in. long. Beaks well rounded. The shell is thin in substance and decorated with numerous fine, threadlike lines. Color whitish; periostracum brown.

BARBATIA LURIDA (Sow.)   Pl. 42
Range: Gulf of California to Peru.
Habitat: Intertidal; rocks.
Description: Rather shaggy, with its brown periostracum; when cleaned it shows a sculpture of fine radiating lines, with a few coarser ones at the posterior end. Hinge line not long, the strong teeth somewhat oblique. Interior purplish brown. Length about 1½ in.

BARBATIA REEVEANA (Orb.)   Pl. 42
Range: Gulf of California to Peru.
Habitat: Intertidal; rocks.
Description: Length about 3 in., color white, with a grayish periostracum. Valves but little inflated, marked with fine but sharp radiating lines and weaker concentric lines.
Remarks: One of the commonest of the ark shells in the Gulf. The valves are often distorted, owing to the mollusk's preference for living attached between rocks.

Genus *Arcopsis* Koenen 1885

ARCOPSIS SOLIDA (Sow.)   Pl. 42
Range: Gulf of California to Peru.
Habitat: Intertidal; rocks.
Description: About 1 in. long, a plump little shell with the

anterior end rounded and the posterior sloping slightly. Surface with fine radiating lines. Color yellowish white.

Remarks: This species is quickly recognized by its triangular black ligament just under the beaks.

Genus *Anadara* Deshayes 1830

ANADARA FORMOSA (Sow.)   Pl. 42
    Range: Gulf of California to Peru.
    Habitat: Moderately shallow water.
    Description: Attains a length of 5 in. Shell strong and solid, moderately inflated, decorated with flattish radiating ribs. Anterior end short and rounded, posterior long, sloping back to the dorsal margin. Hinge teeth small but numerous. White, with a somewhat hairy black periostracum.

ANADARA GRANDIS (Brod. & Sow.)   Pl. 42
    Range: Gulf of California to Peru.
    Habitat: Sandbars at low tide.
    Description: A large and heavy clam, the largest ark shell to be found in this area. Length may be as much as 6 in., and it is nearly as high as it is long. Valves thick and well inflated, hinge teeth very sturdy. Sculpture consists of broad radiating ribs, the spaces between them narrower. Color white, with a dark brown to black periostracum.

ANADARA NUX (Sow.)   Pl. 42
    Range: Cent. Gulf of California to Peru.
    Habitat: Shallow water.
    Description: *A. grandis* (above) is the largest ark shell from this region and this is one of the smallest. Only about ½ in. long, this solid shell is decorated with radiating ribs, some of them weakly checked. Color white.

ANADARA PERLABIATA (Grant & Gale)   Pl. 42
    Range: Gulf of California to Peru.
    Habitat: Sandbars at low tide.
    Description: Just over 1 in. long and about the same in height. Beaks swollen, posterior end only slightly longer than anterior. Basal margin curved up as it approaches the posterior tip. Sculpture consists of radiating ribs marked by horizontal checks. Color white.

ANADARA TUBERCULOSA (Sow.)   Pl. 42
    Range: Gulf of California to Peru.
    Habitat: Mangrove swamps.
    Description: A large boxlike shell, length about 3 in. There are approximately 35 strong radiating ribs, some of them bearing

rounded tubercles, especially those toward the anterior end.
Color white, with a dark, almost black, periostracum.

Genus *Noetia* Gray 1857

NOETIA REVERSA (Sow.)   Pl. 42
Range: Cent. Gulf of California to Peru.
Habitat: Shallow water; muddy bottoms.
Description: Beaks closer to anterior end and curve backward.
Shell solid and moderately inflated, the anterior end well rounded
and the shorter posterior end considerably flattened. Radiating
ribs cover the exterior, the grooves between them crossed by
tiny transverse lines. Length about 1½ in. Color white.

Family Glycymeridae: Bittersweet Shells

(see p. 6)

Genus *Glycymeris* Da Costa 1778

GLYCYMERIS GIGANTEA (Reeve)   Pls. 5, 43
Range: Gulf of California to Acapulco, Mexico.
Habitat: Shallow water.
Description: Some 3 or 4 in. long, this is one of the largest members of its genus. Shape nearly round, the dorsal margin flattened
a little. Beaks central and prominent, the valves solid in substance and fairly well inflated. Surface smooth, but there are
fine radiating lines. Hinge teeth in a curving row and smallest
at the center, larger toward the two ends. Color creamy white,
mottled with reddish brown, often in a zigzag pattern.

GLYCYMERIS INAEQUALIS (Sow.)   Pl. 43
Range: Gulf of California to Peru.
Habitat: Shallow water; muddy bottoms.
Description: A solid shell 1½ in. long, decorated with 6 or 7
broad rounded ribs that radiate from the beaks, the ribs marked
by very fine lines. Hinge teeth very robust, and the beaks are
inclined to turn forward a little. Color gray, with broad wavy
bands of chocolate-brown.

GLYCYMERIS MULTICOSTATA (Sow.)   Pl. 43
Range: Gulf of California to Ecuador.
Habitat: Moderately shallow water.
Description: There are numerous radiating ribs on this shell, as
its specific name implies. The bivalve is round in outline, and
grows to be nearly 2 in. long. The hinge teeth are strong and
rugged, numbering about 20. Color reddish brown and white.

Plate 1

WEST COAST PELECYPODS

All shells approximately ⅓ natural size

1. **Gari californica** SUNSET SHELL   p. 37
   Oval, thick-shelled; pinkish rays.

2. **Tivela stultorum** PISMO CLAM   p. 26
   Large, triangular; thick and heavy; radiating rays.

3. **Pteria sterna** WINGED OYSTER   p. 13
   Long or moderately short posterior wing; deep purplish brown;
   interior pearly.

4. **Trachycardium quadragenarium**   p. 23
   GIANT PACIFIC COCKLE
   Large, inflated; strong ribs with scales.

5. **Siliqua patula** PACIFIC RAZOR CLAM   p. 39
   Large, elongate-oval; vertical rib under beaks.

6. **Modiolus capax** FAT HORSE MUSSEL   p. 8
   Large, swollen; brown to pinkish red.

Plate 2

WEST COAST PELECYPODS

All shells approximately ⅓ natural size

Plate 3

WEST COAST GASTROPODS
Shells approximately ⅛ natural size

1. **Haliotis rufescens**   RED ABALONE   p. 53
   Interior iridescent, verging on pink.

2. **Haliotis rufescens** polished

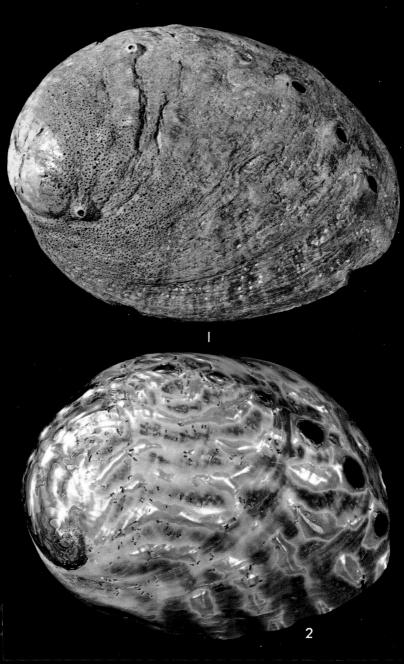

1

2

Plate 4

WEST COAST GASTROPODS

All shells approximately ⅛ natural size

1. **Maxwellia gemma** GEM ROCK SHELL   p. 83
   Vertical ribs; small aperture; tightly closed canal.

2. **Calliostoma annulatum** RINGED TOP   p. 60
   Flattened whorls; beaded ridges.

3. **Cypraea spadica** CHESTNUT COWRY   p. 79
   Egg-shaped; highly polished.

4. **Tegula regina** QUEEN TOP   p. 64
   Base strongly ridged; umbilicus orange.

5. **Thais lamellosa** FRILLED DOGWINKLE   p. 88
   Frilly vertical ridges.

6. **Astraea undosa** WAVY TURBAN   p. 65
   Large, pearly; wavy band at suture; calcareous operculum.

7. **Trophon cerrosensis catalinensis**   p. 82
   CATALINA TROPHON
   Large but light; long spines at shoulders.

8. **Ceratostoma foliatum** LEAFY HORNMOUTH   p. 84
   Large and thin varices; cordlike ridges; canal closed.

Plate 5

GULF OF CALIFORNIA PELECYPODS
All shells approximately ⅓ natural size

Plate 6

GULF OF CALIFORNIA GASTROPODS

All shells approximately ⅓ natural size

1. **Hexaplex erythrostomus**   p. 175
   Rugged; white or pinkish white; rosy-pink aperture.

2. **Terebra strigata**   p. 201
   Spikelike; vertical streaks.

3. **Conus princeps**   PRINCELY CONE   p. 199
   Irregular vertical streaks.

4. **Hexaplex brassica**   p. 175
   Large, rugged; aperture pinkish.

5. **Hexaplex regius**   p. 175
   Rugged; spiny varices; brown stain on columella.

6. **Oliva porphyria**   TENT OLIVE   p. 191
   Zigzag brown lines, white triangles; highly polished.

Plate 7

HAWAIIAN GASTROPODS

All shells approximately ⅛ natural size

1. **Architectonica perspectiva** SUNDIAL   p. 223
   Round, flattish; umbilicus deep and crenulate.

2. **Terebra dimidiata** DIVIDED AUGER   p. 251
   Impressed spiral line below suture; whitish streaks.

3. **Cymatium nicobaricum**   p. 235
   ORANGE-MOUTHED TRITON
   Rugged; thick varices; orange aperture.

4. **Terebra crenulata** CRENULATE AUGER   p. 251
   Wrinkles at shoulders; encircling dots.

5. **Conus pennaceus** PEARLED CONE   p. 249
   Moderate spire; orange-brown, with paler triangles.

6. **Cypraea tessellata** TESSELLATE COWRY   p. 232
   Globose; pair of squarish spots on each side; polished.

7. **Trochus intextus** HAWAIIAN TOP   p. 220
   Sloping sides; beaded lines.

8. **Harpa conoidalis** HARP SHELL   p. 246
   Flaring aperture; thin varices; spines at shoulders.

9. **Distorsio anus** WARPED SHELL   p. 237
   Constricted aperture; granular area on columella.

Plate 8

HAWAIIAN GASTROPODS
All shells approximately natural size

1. **Morula uva** GRAPE MORULA   p. 241
   Fusiform, solid; squarish black nodes.

2. **Cypraea semiplota** LITTLE SPOTTED COWRY   p. 232
   Small, polished; pale brown, with whitish spots.

3. **Pustularia cicercula** CHICK PEA COWRY   p. 233
   Inflated; pinched out at ends.

4. **Torinia variegata** VARIEGATED SUNDIAL   p. 223
   Round, flattish; deep umbilicus.

5. **Drupa grossularia** FINGER DRUPE   p. 240
   Orange aperture; lip with projections.

6. **Trochus intextus** HAWAIIAN TOP   p. 220
   Top-shaped; sloping sides; beaded lines.

7. **Pyramidella sulcata** SULCATE PYRAMIDELLA   p. 254
   Rounded whorls; distinct sutures; plicate inner lip.

8. **Terebra strigilata** PAINTED AUGER   p. 252
   Narrow, spikelike; twisted inner lip.

9. **Mitra auriculoides** BANDED MITER   p. 244
   Fusiform, smooth; plicate inner lip.

10. **Janthina globosa** ROUND VIOLET SNAIL   p. 226
    Globular, thin.

11. **Hydatina amplustre** PINK BUBBLE   p. 255
    No spire; thin and fragile.

12. **Nassarius hirtus** ROUGH DOG WHELK   p. 242
    Vertical lines at shoulders; notch at base.

13. **Strombus maculatus** SPOTTED STROMB   p. 227
    Small; wide outer lip.

14. **Nerita polita** POLISHED NERITE   p. 221
    Flattish, polished; brightly hued.

15. Group of **Achatinella** sp. HAWAIIAN TREE SNAILS   p. 257
    See text.

Plate 9

NUT AND ARK SHELLS, YOLDIAS, AND OTHERS

Plate 10

MUSSELS, PEARL OYSTERS, AND OTHERS

1. **Musculus substriata** ×1 NESTLING MUSSEL p. 10
   Broadly oval; yellowish brown.

2. **Pteria sterna** ×1 WINGED OYSTER p. 13
   Long or moderately short posterior wing; purplish brown;
   interior pearly.

3. **Musculus discors** ×½ p. 9
   Small, oval; ridged posterior; nearly black.

4. **Musculus niger** ×1 LITTLE BLACK MUSSEL p. 10
   Brownish black; radiating lines at ends, smooth at center.

5. **Isognomon chemnitziana** ×1 PURSE SHELL p. 12
   Vertical grooves at hinge; purplish black; pearly within.

6. **Pododesmus cepio** ×½ PEARLY MONIA p. 18
   Large, heavy; large perforation; interior pearly, with
   green and purple at hinge.

7. **Hormomya adamsiana** ×1 STEARNS' MUSSEL p. 8
   Purplish brown; strongly ribbed.

8. **Anomia peruviana** ×1 JINGLE SHELL p. 18
   Thin, waxy, yellowish green; 1 valve perforated.

9. **Septifer bifurcatus** ×1 PLATFORM MUSSEL p. 8
   Small deck under beaks; dark bluish black.

10. **Mytilus californianus** ×½ CALIFORNIA MUSSEL p. 7
    Large, elongate; coarsely ribbed; bluish black.

11. **Philobrya setosa** ×8 p. 7
    Very small, plump; see text.

12. **Mytilus edulis** ×1 BAY MUSSEL p. 7
    Smooth; blue to bluish black.

Plate 12

SCALLOPS

Pecten caurinus ×½ WEATHERVANE SCALLOP   p. 14
Large; valves equally inflated; mottled purplish red.

Plate 11

MUSSELS, DATE SHELLS, ASTARTES, AND OTHERS

1. **Lithophaga aristata** ×1
   Small processes that cross at tips; pale brown. p. 11

2. **Modiolus capax** ×⅔   FAT HORSE MUSSEL
   Large, swollen; brown to pinkish red. p. 8

3. **Modiolus rectus** ×1   STRAIGHT HORSE MUSSEL
   Long and narrow; brownish. p. 9

4. **Modiolus modiolus** ×⅔   HORSE MUSSEL
   Large, broad; brownish to purplish black. p. 9

5. **Limatula subauriculata** ×2
   Tiny, white; oval-elongate. p. 17

6. **Crenella decussata** ×3   NETTED CRENELLA
   Small, oval; fine lines; brown. p. 10

7. **Lima hemphilli** ×2   HEMPHILL'S FILE
   Thin radiating lines; white. p. 16

8. **Adula californiensis** ×1   CALIFORNIA PEA-POD SHELL
   Elongate, curved; brownish black. p. 11

9. **Lithophaga plumula** ×1   ROCK BORER
   Cylindrical; tufts at tips; rusty brown. p. 12

10. **Adula falcata** ×1   PEA-POD SHELL
    Elongate; surface strongly wrinkled; brownish periostracum. p. 11

11. **Astarte alaskensis** ×1   ALASKA ASTARTE
    Broad concentric furrows; brown. p. 18

12. **Modiolus demissus** ×1   RIBBED MUSSEL
    Strong radiating ribs; yellowish green; silvery white within. p. 8

13. **Axinopsida sericata** ×5   SILKY AXINOPSIDA
    Tiny, brownish. p. 21

14. **Cardita carpenteri** ×2   CARPENTER'S CARDITA
    Small; strong radiating ridges; brownish gray. p. 19

15. **Thyasira gouldii** ×1   GOULD'S THYASIRA
    Small, whitish; fold on posterior. p. 21

16. **Astarte fabula** ×1
    Thin concentric lines; dark brown. p. 19

17. **Astarte esquimalti** ×2   ESQUIMALT ASTARTE
    Small, rich brown; irregular ribs. p. 19

18. **Cardita redondoensis** ×2   REDONDO CARDITA
    See Remarks under *C. ventricosa* text. p. 20

19. **Astarte borealis** ×1   NORTHERN ASTARTE
    Large; weak concentric lines; deep brown. p. 19

20. **Cardita ventricosa** ×2   STOUT CARDITA
    Roundish, solid, inflated; radiating ribs; whitish. p. 20

21. **Thyasira bisecta** ×½   CLEFT THYASIRA
    Large; fold from beaks to posterior tip; grayish white. p. 20

Plate 13

SCALLOPS

Pecten diegensis ×⅔   SAN DIEGO SCALLOP   p. 14
  Large; upper valve flat, lower cupped; flat valve rosy brown, often
  mottled; cupped valve unspotted, often white or yellowish.

Plate 14

SCALLOPS

1. **Delectopecten vancouverensis** ×2   p. 15
   TRANSPARENT SCALLOP
   Tiny, thin; valves semitransparent, with hinge of yellowish gray.

2. **Chlamys hericius** ×1   PINK SCALLOP   p. 14
   Broadly rayed with pink or lavender.

3. **Chlamys hastatus** ×1   SPEAR SCALLOP   p. 14
   Radiating ribs set with spines; red to purple to yellow.

4. **Chlamys islandicus** ×½   ICELAND SCALLOP   p. 15
   Closely set radiating ribs; pale to dark reddish brown.

Plate 15

SCALLOPS AND MUSSELS

1. **Leptopecten latiauratus** ×1 p. 15
   KELP-WEED SCALLOP
   Small, thin; white markings on dark ground.

2. **Musculus senhousia** ×2 JAPANESE MUSSEL p. 10
   Thin, semitransparent; brownish scrawls on interior.

3. **Propeamussium alaskense** ×1 p. 16
   Small, silvery gray; ribs on interior.

4. **Chlamys rubidus** ×1 HINDS' SCALLOP p. 15
   Posterior wing expanded; many ribs; pink to white.

5. **Hinnites multirugosus** ×½ p. 16
   GIANT ROCK SCALLOP
   Large, heavy; rough exterior; gray; purple at interior of hinge.

Plate 16

JEWEL BOXES, LUCINES, AND COCKLES

1. **Chama pellucida** ×1   AGATE JEWEL BOX   p. 22
   Strong, thick, solid; very inequivalve; white or cream, with rosy rays.

2. **Lucina approximata** ×2   p. 21
   Small, white; sharp radiating lines.

3. **Lucina tenuisculpta** ×1   FINE-LINED LUCINA   p. 22
   Small, roundish; faint lines; whitish.

4. **Pseudochama exogyra** ×1   p. 23
   REVERSED JEWEL BOX
   Beaks with sinistral twist; white.

5. **Nemocardium centifilosum** ×1   p. 24
   HUNDRED-LINED COCKLE
   Small, white; fine ribs; concentric lines at one end.

6. **Epilucina californica** ×1   CALIFORNIA LUCINA   p. 22
   Roundish, pure white; fine concentric lines.

7. **Lucina nuttalli** ×1   NUTTALL'S LUCINA   p. 22
   Round, thin; sharp sculpture; pure white.

8. **Clinocardium fucanum** ×1   FUCAN COCKLE   p. 24
   Small, plump; many ribs; grayish-brown periostracum.

9. **Lucina annulata** ×1   RINGED LUCINA   p. 21
   Flattish; strong concentric rings; white.

10. **Clinocardium nuttallii** ×1   NUTTALL'S COCKLE   p. 24
    Large, inflated; beaks high; squarish ribs; white or yellowish white.

11. **Clinocardium ciliatum** ×1   ICELAND COCKLE   p. 24
    Large, inflated; numerous ribs; white; interior pale yellow.

Plate 17

COCKLES AND OTHERS

1. **Diplodonta orbella** ×1   ORB DIPLODONTA   p. 20
   Roundish, smooth; white.

2. **Trigoniocardia biangulata** ×1   p. 25
   STRAWBERRY COCKLE
   Angled at posterior slope; yellowish white.

3. **Laevicardium elatum** ×½   GIANT EGG COCKLE   p. 25
   Large, inflated; weak ribs; yellow.

4. **Trachycardium quadragenarium** ×½   p. 23
   GIANT PACIFIC COCKLE
   Large, inflated; strong ribs with scales; yellowish-brown
   patches; interior orange-brown.

5. **Kellia laperousii** ×1   KELLY SHELL   p. 23
   Bluntly oval, smooth; shiny pale brown.

6. **Laevicardium substriatum** ×1   p. 25
   LITTLE EGG COCKLE
   Small, thin-shelled; yellowish brown; interior mottled purplish.

7. **Compsomyax subdiaphana** ×1   MILKY VENUS   p. 29
   Smooth, inflated; semitransparent; white or pale gray.

8. **Miodontiscus prolongatus** ×2   p. 20
   Small, solid; rounded margins; white.

9. **Serripes groenlandicus** ×1   GREENLAND COCKLE   p. 25
   Large, inflated, thin-shelled; posterior gaping; drab gray.

10. **Tivela stultorum** ×½   PISMO CLAM   p. 26
    Large, thick, and heavy; triangular; often with radiating
    brown rays; grayish.

Plate 18

HARD-SHELLED CLAMS

1. **Prototheca staminea** ×1   PACIFIC LITTLENECK   p. 28
   Large, oval; surface heavily streaked; creamy white to brown.

2. **Chione fluctifraga** ×1   p. 27
   SMOOTH CALIFORNIA VENUS
   Roundish oval; weak ribs at ends; yellowish white, often with
   darker bands.

3. **Prototheca tenerrima** ×1   p. 28
   THIN-SHELLED LITTLENECK
   Oval; concentric lines; grayish brown.

4. **Irus lamellifera** ×1   RIBBED VENUS   p. 29
   Bladelike concentric ribs; white.

5. **Cooperella subdiaphana** ×1   p. 30
   Plump, thin-shelled; shiny tan.

6. **Prototheca laciniata** ×1   FOLDED LITTLENECK   p. 28
   Large, oval; radiating and concentric lines; yellowish gray to
   reddish brown.

Plate 19

HARD-SHELLED CLAMS

1. **Humilaria kennerleyi** ×1   KENNERLEY'S VENUS   p. 29
     Large, roundish, thick-shelled; white.

2. **Chione undatella** ×1   p. 28
     FRILLED CALIFORNIA VENUS
     Solid; sculpture scaly; mottled grayish white.

3. **Chione californiensis** ×1   CALIFORNIA VENUS   p. 27
     Solid; sharp concentric bands; dull grayish.

4. **Tapes japonica** ×½   JAPANESE LITTLENECK   p. 29
     Yellowish gray; fine radiating lines.

5. **Saxidomus nuttalli** ×1   WASHINGTON CLAM   p. 27
     Oval and large; regular concentric lines; grayish white.

6. **Ventricolaria fordi** ×1   FORD'S VENUS   p. 26
     Heavy, thick-shelled; large beaks; yellowish brown.

Plate 20

SURF CLAMS

1. **Spisula planulata** ×1   FLAT SURF CLAM   p. 32
   Small, flattish; triangular; grayish white.

2. **Mactra californica** ×1   CALIFORNIA SURF CLAM   p. 31
   Oval, thin; furrows on umbones; whitish.

3. **Spisula falcata** ×1   HOOKED SURF CLAM   p. 31
   Thin, yellowish brown; anterior slightly concave.

4. Hinge of *Mactra* ×2

5. Hinge of *Spisula* ×2

6. **Spisula alaskana** ×⅔   ALASKA SURF CLAM   p. 31
   Large, solid; grayish white.

7. **Spisula dolabriformis** ×1   MATTOCK SURF CLAM   p. 31
   Oval; weak posterior ridge; white.

8. **Mactra nasuta** ×1   PACIFIC SURF CLAM   p. 31
   Oval, yellowish white; brittle.

9. **Spisula hemphilli** ×1   HEMPHILL'S SURF CLAM   p. 32
   Large, swollen; large ligament pit; yellowish white.

Plate 21

TELLINS AND MACOMAS

1. **Tellina carpenteri** ×2 CARPENTER'S TELLIN   p. 33
   Small; valves compressed; glossy pink to pinkish white.

2. **Tellina lutea** ×½ GREAT ALASKAN TELLIN   p. 33
   Large, thick-shelled; chalky white to pinkish.

3. **Tellina idae** ×1 IDA'S TELLIN   p. 33
   Large, thin; concentric lines; white.

4. **Tellina salmonea** ×2 SALMON TELLIN   p. 33
   Small, creamy white, roundish; concentric zones of color.

5. **Tellina modesta** ×1 MODEST TELLIN   p. 33
   Valves compressed; shiny white.

6. **Tellina bodegensis** ×1 BODEGA TELLIN   p. 33
   Elongate, thin; yellowish white, shiny.

7. **Macoma yoldiformis** ×1   p. 36
   Oval, shiny white.

8. **Macoma calcarea** ×1 CHALKY MACOMA   p. 34
   Oval, thin; chalky white.

9. **Macoma inconspicua** ×1   p. 35
   INCONSPICUOUS MACOMA
   Small, roundish, thin; white or pinkish white.

10. **Macoma incongrua** ×1 INCONGRUOUS MACOMA   p. 34
    Small, roundish; shiny white.

11. **Macoma irus** ×1 IRUS MACOMA   p. 35
    Posterior slope; grayish white.

12. **Macoma balthica** ×1 BALTIC MACOMA   p. 34
    Roundish; dull pinkish white.

13. **Cumingia californica** ×1   p. 38
    CALIFORNIA CUMING SHELL
    Small, somewhat triangular; concentric lines; dingy white.

14. **Macoma planiuscula** ×1   p. 35
    Posterior slope; yellowish-gray periostracum.

15. **Macoma carlottensis** ×1   p. 34
    QUEEN CHARLOTTE MACOMA
    Elongate, thin-shelled; grayish white.

16. **Macoma brota** ×1   p. 34
    Oval; large anterior end; grayish white.

17. **Macoma nasuta** ×1 BENT-NOSED MACOMA   p. 35
    Thin, egg-shaped; posterior tip bent; grayish white.

18. **Macoma secta** ×1 WHITE SAND MACOMA   p. 35
    Large, thin; polished white.

Plate 22

SEMELES, BEAN CLAMS, AND OTHERS

1. **Semele decisa** ×1   BARK SEMELE   p. 38
   Large, circular; brownish white; deep pallial sinus; concentric furrows.

2. **Semele rupicola** ×1   ROCK-DWELLING SEMELE   p. 38
   Small, circular; grayish.

3. **Semele rubropicta** ×1   ROSE-PETAL SEMELE   p. 38
   Thin-shelled, faintly rayed; grayish white.

4. **Heterodonax bimaculata** ×1   FALSE DONAX   p. 37
   Roundish, thin; rays showing on inside; bluish white.

5. **Petricola carditoides** ×1   p. 30
   HEART ROCK DWELLER
   Oblong, smooth; chalky white.

6. **Petricola pholadiformis** ×1   FALSE ANGEL WING   p. 30
   From Atlantic; see Remarks under *P. carditoides* text.

7. **Donax californica** ×1   CALIFORNIA BEAN CLAM   p. 36
   Elongate, pointed at both ends; yellowish white.

8. **Donax gouldii** ×1   LITTLE BEAN CLAM   p. 36
   Posterior end lengthened; white to purple.

9. **Amiantis callosa** ×1   WHITE VENUS   p. 26
   Large, thick-shelled, white; concentric furrows.

Plate 23

RAZOR AND BASKET CLAMS AND OTHERS

1. **Sanguinolaria nuttallii** ×1   PURPLE CLAM   p. 37
   Large, thin; strong brownish periostracum, purplish beneath.

2. **Solen rosaceus** ×1   ROSY RAZOR CLAM   p. 39
   Elongate; pinkish white.

3. **Ensis myrae** ×1   MYRA'S RAZOR CLAM   p. 40
   Elongate, thin, curved; greenish.

4. **Solen sicarius** ×1   BLUNT RAZOR CLAM   p. 40
   Elongate; abruptly truncate; white.

5. **Corbula luteola** ×2   BASKET CLAM   p. 43
   Small, solid; posterior ridge; usually yellow, but may be pink
   or rose.

6. **Siliqua lucida** ×1   TRANSPARENT RAZOR CLAM   p. 39
   Elongate-oval; interior rib under beaks; greenish-brown
   periostracum.

7. **Siliqua patula** ×1   PACIFIC RAZOR CLAM   p. 39
   Large, elongate-oval; vertical rib under beaks; shiny brown.

Plate 24

GIANT CLAMS

Plate 25

SOFT-SHELLED CLAMS AND OTHERS

1. **Mya arenaria** ×1   SOFT-SHELLED CLAM   p. 41
   Pallial sinus present; dull gray or chalky white.

2. **Mya truncata** ×1   TRUNCATED MYA   p. 42
   Oval, wrinkled; anterior truncate; dingy white.

3. **Hiatella arctica** ×1   ARCTIC ROCK BORER   p. 40
   Bluntly oval, coarsely wrinkled; white, with dingy yellowish
   periostracum.

4. **Hiatella pholadis** ×1   p. 40
   Elongate, wrinkled; chalky white.

5. **Tagelus californianus** ×½   JACKKNIFE CLAM   p. 37
   Elongate-oval; weak concentric lines; dull white, yellowish
   periostracum.

6. **Platyodon cancellatus** ×1   CHUBBY MYA   p. 42
   Oval; short anterior; inflated; concentric lines; gray.

7. **Modiolus flabellatus** ×⅓   p. 9
   FAN-SHAPED HORSE MUSSEL
   Large; broad posterior end; whitish lavender; periostracum
   glossy brown.

8. **Cryptomya californica** ×1   p. 42
   CALIFORNIA SOFT-SHELLED CLAM
   Small; pallial line entire, no sinus; ashy gray.

9. **Panomya ampla** ×1   AMPLE PANOMYA   p. 41
   Squarish, heavy; chalky white.

Plate 26

BORING CLAMS

1. **Penitella penita** ×1   COMMON PIDDOCK   p. 44
   Elongate; sharp sculpture at anterior; grayish white.

2. **Penitella gabbi** ×1   GABB'S PIDDOCK   p. 44
   Oval, white; sharp sculpture on anterior, posterior fairly
   smooth.

3. **Penitella penita** ×1, showing callum

4. **Barnea subtruncata** ×1   PACIFIC PIDDOCK   p. 43
   Posterior truncate; abrading sculpture; pure white.

5. **Parapholas californica** ×½   p. 44
   CALIFORNIA PIDDOCK
   Large; anterior rounded, posterior elongate; brownish white.

6. Apophysis of *Zirfaea pilsbryi* ×2

7. **Chaceia ovoidea** ×1   OVAL PIDDOCK   p. 45
   Anterior sharply truncate; grayish white.

8. **Zirfaea pilsbryi** ×½   PILSBRY'S PIDDOCK   p. 44
   Large, white; large "spoon" under beaks.

9. **Zirfaea pilsbryi** ×½, showing anterior gape

10. **Nettastomella rostrata** ×1   BEAKED PIDDOCK   p. 45
    Small, short; flaring posterior tip; pure white.

11. Shipworms in wood

12. **Bankia setacea** ×5   SHIPWORM   p. 45
    Diminutive, white; see text.

13. **Teredo diegensis** ×5   SAN DIEGO SHIPWORM   p. 46
    Diminutive, white; see text.

14. **Teredo diegensis** ×5, showing animal

Plate 27

PANDORAS, DIPPERS, PAPER SHELLS, SPOON SHELLS, AND OTHERS

1. **Lyonsia californica** ×1   CALIFORNIA LYONSIA   p. 46
   Elongate, thin; pearly white, semitransparent.
2. **Lyonsia arenosa** ×2   SANDED LYONSIA   p. 46
   Thin, fragile; whitish; olive-gray periostracum.
3. **Lyonsia striata** ×1   STRIATE LYONSIA   p. 47
   Squarish, thin; gray, iridescent.
4. Sand entangled at margin of *Lyonsia pugetensis* ×10
5. **Lyonsia pugetensis** ×1   PUGET LYONSIA   p. 46
   Small, thin; white.
6. **Pandora glacialis** ×1   NORTHERN PANDORA   p. 48
   Squarish, thin; grayish white; pearly within.
7. **Pandora bilirata** ×1   p. 48
   Thin, elongate; white; pearly within.
8. **Pandora filosa** ×1   WESTERN PANDORA   p. 48
   Thin, elongate; white; pearly within; long posterior.
9. **Cardiomya oldroydi** ×2   p. 51
   OLDROYD'S DIPPER SHELL
   Tiny, whitish; coarse ribs.
10. **Cuspidaria apodema** ×1   SMOOTH DIPPER SHELL   p. 50
    Smooth, white; pronounced rostrum.
11. **Cardiomya pectinata** ×2   RIBBED DIPPER SHELL   p. 51
    Tiny, white; radially ribbed; long rostrum.
12. **Cardiomya californica** ×3   p. 50
    CALIFORNIA DIPPER SHELL
    Thin, creamy white; radially ribbed.
13. **Cuspidaria glacialis** ×1   p. 50
    NORTHERN DIPPER SHELL
    Larger than No. 12; smooth, white.
14. **Mytilimeria nuttallii** ×1   SEA BOTTLE   p. 47
    Inflated; white; periostracum pale yellowish brown.
15. **Pandora punctata** ×1   DOTTED PANDORA   p. 48
    Large, thin; white; interior with tiny pinpricks.
16. **Cyathodonta undulata** ×1   WAVY THRACIA   p. 49
    Thin-shelled; undulating ribs; white.
17. **Periploma discus** ×1   ROUND SPOON SHELL   p. 49
    Orbicular, thin; "spoon" at hinge; white.
18. **Periploma planiusculum** ×1   p. 50
    WESTERN SPOON SHELL
    Oval, white; "spoon" at hinge.
19. **Entodesma saxicola** ×1   ROCK ENTODESMA   p. 47
    Large, thick; heavy brown periostracum.
20. **Thracia trapezoides** ×1   PACIFIC THRACIA   p. 49
    Large, inequivalve; brown.

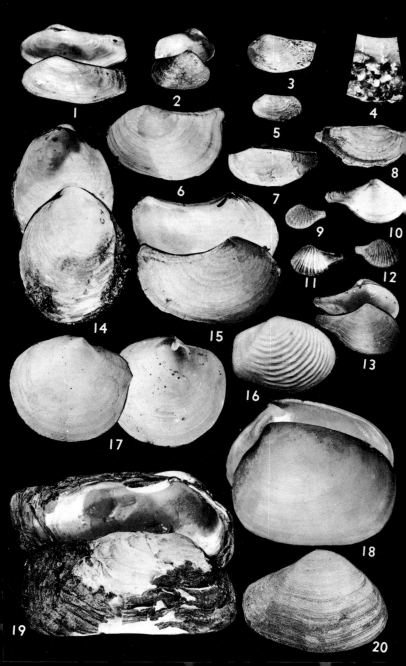

Plate 28

OWL LIMPETS AND ABALONES

1. **Lottia gigantea** ×1   OWL LIMPET   p. 59
   Large, oval; apex at one end; polished interior very dark;
   exterior mottled.

2. **Haliotis kamtschatkana** ×¼   JAPANESE ABALONE   p. 53
   Oval, thinner-shelled than No. 3; spire noticeable; mottled
   brown and gray.

3. **Haliotis assimilis** ×¼   THREADED ABALONE   p. 52
   Surface with threadlike lines; color brown; interior silvery.

Plate 29

ABALONES

1. **Haliotis fulgens** $\times \frac{1}{4}$ GREEN ABALONE   p. 53
   Interior deep bluish green; exterior reddish brown.

2. **Haliotis cracherodii** $\times \frac{1}{3}$ BLACK ABALONE   p. 52
   Surface relatively smooth; deep greenish black.

3. **Haliotis corrugata** $\times \frac{1}{4}$ CORRUGATED ABALONE   p. 52
   Surface with wavy corrugations; interior bluish; exterior grayish brown.

4. **Haliotis rufescens** $\times \frac{1}{4}$ RED ABALONE   p. 53
   Interior iridescent, verging on pink; exterior dull reddish brown.

Plate 30

LIMPETS AND KEYHOLE LIMPETS

1. **Acmaea fenestrata fenestrata** ×1   p. 57
   FENESTRATE LIMPET
   Typical form. Oval, moderately arched; interior light; grayish green, with yellowish flecks.

2. **Acmaea conus** ×1   TEST'S LIMPET   p. 56
   Small; scalloped margin; gray; interior glossy.

3. **Acmaea fenestrata cribraria** ×1   p. 57
   FENESTRATE LIMPET
   Oval, moderately arched; interior dark; exterior same as *A. f. fenestrata*.

4. **Fissurella volcano** ×1   VOLCANO LIMPET   p. 54
   Oval, radiating lines; oval perforation; ashy pink.

5. **Diodora aspera** ×1   ROUGH KEYHOLE LIMPET   p. 54
   Large, apex closer to one end; perforation nearly round; gray or white.

6. **Puncturella cucullata** ×1   p. 55
   HOODED KEYHOLE LIMPET
   Highly elevated; strong ridges; narrow slitlike perforation; greenish gray.

7. Perforation of *Fissurella* ×2, interior view

8. Perforation of *Diodora* ×2, interior view

9. **Megatebennus bimaculatus** ×1   p. 55
   TWO-SPOTTED KEYHOLE LIMPET
   Oval with parallel sides, rather flat; large perforation; grayish.

10. **Lucapinella callomarginata** ×1   p. 55
    HARD-EDGED KEYHOLE LIMPET
    Oval, rather flat; elongate perforation; gray or white with dark rays.

11. **Megathura crenulata** ×1   p. 54
    GREAT KEYHOLE LIMPET
    Very large, flattish; perforation large; margins crenulate; grayish white.

12. **Puncturella multistriata** ×1   p. 55
    MANY-RIBBED PUNCTURELLA
    Small; numerous ribs; perforation narrow; white.

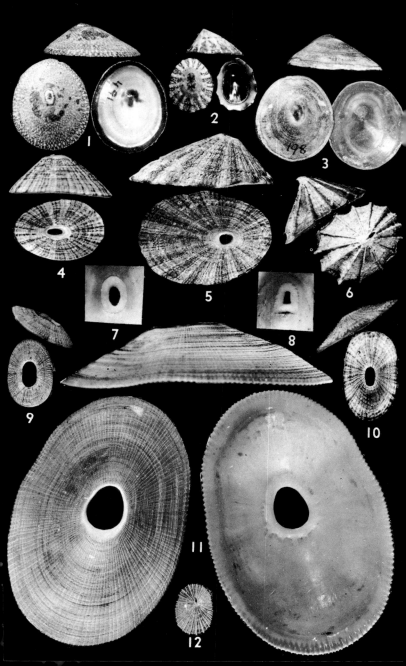

Plate 31

LIMPETS

1. **Acmaea scabra** ×1 ROUGH LIMPET   p. 58
   Large; rough exterior; scalloped margin; gray or gray-black.

2. **Acmaea pelta** ×1 SHIELD LIMPET   p. 58
   Roundish; radiating rays; exterior gray; interior white.

3. **Acmaea mitra** ×1 WHITE-CAPPED LIMPET   p. 57
   Round, pointed; dull white.

4. **Acmaea limatula** ×1 FILE LIMPET   p. 57
   Apex closer to anterior end; flattish; scaly lines; light brown
   to black.

5. **Acmaea instabilis** ×1 UNSTABLE LIMPET   p. 57
   Elongate; parallel sides; brown.

6. **Acmaea insessa** ×1 SEAWEED LIMPET   p. 57
   Small, high; parallel sides; brown.

7. **Acmaea asmi** ×1 BLACK LIMPET   p. 56
   Tiny, high; brownish black.

8. **Acmaea persona** ×1 MASK LIMPET   p. 58
   Well arched; apex close to anterior end; mottled gray and
   brown.

9. **Acmaea testudinalis scutum** ×1 PLATE LIMPET   p. 58
   Large, rather flat; spotted border at rim; brown and gray.

10. **Acmaea digitalis** ×1 FINGER LIMPET   p. 56
    Apex at anterior end; radiating ridges; gray, with brown and
    white stripes and blotches.

Plate 32

TOPS AND TURBANS

1. **Calliostoma annulatum** ×1   RINGED TOP   p. 60
   Flattened whorls; beaded ridges; sutures purplish; yellowish brown.
2. **Calliostoma gemmulatum** ×1   GEM TOP   p. 61
   Slight shoulders; revolving beads; greenish brown.
3. **Calliostoma canaliculatum** ×1   CHANNELED TOP   p. 61
   Sharply pointed; revolving ridges; brown to tan.
4. **Calliostoma tricolor** ×1   THREE-COLORED TOP   p. 62
   Sharply conical; white, purple dashes; brownish.
5. **Calliostoma variegatum** ×1   VARIEGATED TOP   p. 62
   Rounded whorls; revolving beads; apex sharp; whitish.
6. **Calliostoma ligatum** ×1   COSTATE TOP   p. 61
   Rounded whorls; revolving lines; brown; pearly within.
7. **Calliostoma splendens** ×1   SPLENDID TOP   p. 61
   Small; revolving lines; yellowish brown.
8. **Calliostoma supragranosum** ×1   GRANOSE TOP   p. 62
   Rounded whorls; weak spiral ridges; pale brown.
9. **Solariella peramabilis** ×1   LOVELY TOP   p. 60
   Squat; deep umbilicus; pinkish gray.
10. **Margarites costalis** ×1   RIDGED MARGARITE   p. 59
    Weak revolving growth lines; aperture iridescent; ashy gray.
11. **Margarites pupillus** ×1   PUPPET MARGARITE   p. 59
    Rounded whorls; deep sutures; gray; pearly within.
12. **Margarites succinctus** ×1   TUCKED MARGARITE   p. 60
    Small; gray; purplish-brown spiral lines.
13. **Solariella varicosa** ×2   VARICOSE TOP   p. 60
    Flattish; oblique ribs; yellowish white; aperture pearly.
14. **Lischkeia cidaris** ×1   SPINY TOP   p. 60
    Pointed; distinct revolving ridges; whitish.
15. **Homalopoma carpenteri** ×2   DWARF TURBAN   p. 65
    Small, solid; pinkish red; calcareous operculum.
16. **Tegula ligulata** ×1   BANDED TOP   p. 63
    Solid; revolving broken ridges; tan; interior pearly.
17. **Tegula gallina** ×1   SPECKLED TOP   p. 63
    Blunt apex; vertically flecked with white.
18. **Tegula pulligo** ×1   p. 64
    Flat-sided; sharp apex; lacks umbilical ridge; grayish.
19. **Tegula montereyi** ×1   MONTEREY TOP   p. 64
    Flat-sided; sharp apex; ridge around umbilicus; brown.
20. **Tegula regina** ×½   QUEEN TOP   p. 64
    Large; base strongly ridged; gray; umbilicus orange.
21. **Tegula funebralis** ×1   BLACK TOP   p. 63
    Heavy and rugged; strong black periostracum.
22. **Tegula brunnea** ×1   BROWN TOP   p. 63
    Brownish; white aperture; diagonal folds at shoulder.
23. **Tegula aureotincta** ×1   GILDED TOP   p. 63
    Low-spired; very pearly within and on eroded surfaces.
24. **Astraea gibberosa** ×½   RED TURBAN   p. 65
    Sloping whorls; vertical grooves; dull reddish brown.
25. **Astraea undosa** ×½   WAVY TURBAN   p. 65
    Large, pearly; wavy band at suture; operculum calcareous.
26. Operculum of *Astraea undosa* ×½

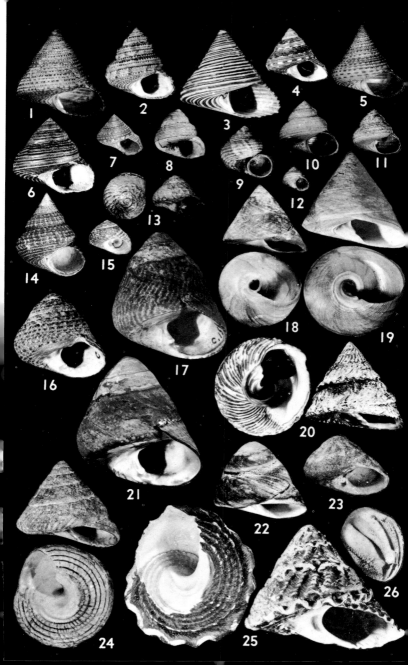

Plate 33

WENTLETRAPS, PERIWINKLES, AND OTHERS

Plate 34

SLIPPER SHELLS, HORN SHELLS, AND OTHERS

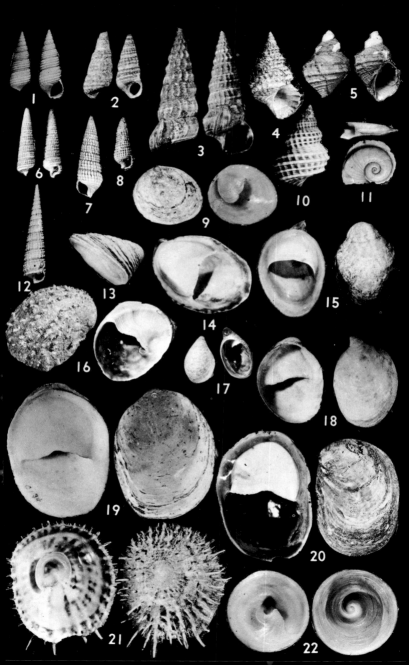

Plate *35*

COWRIES, MOON SHELLS, AND OTHERS

1. **Erato vitellina** ×1   APPLE SEED   p. 80
   Smooth, reddish-brown top; toothed aperture.

2. **Trivia californiana** ×1   COFFEE BEAN   p. 80
   Transverse ribs; deep purplish brown.

3. **Trivia solandri** ×1   SEA BUTTON   p. 80
   Median groove; transverse ribs; reddish brown to light pink.

4. **Neosimnia avena** ×2   CHUBBY SIMNIA   p. 81
   Lip thickened; weak encircling lines; pale pink to purplish red.

5. **Neosimnia avena** on *Gorgonia* (coral) ×2

6. **Cypraea spadica** ×1   CHESTNUT COWRY   p. 79
   Top brown; sides flesh-colored; polished.

7. **Natica clausa** ×1   ARCTIC MOON SHELL   p. 77
   Globular; shelly operculum; bluish white or grayish.

8. **Lamellaria diegoensis** ×1   SAN DIEGO EAR SHELL   p. 76
   Thin, glassy; wide aperture; whitish.

9. **Sinum scopulosum** ×1   BABY'S EAR   p. 79
   Flat; low spire; large aperture; white.

10. **Polinices pallida** ×1   NORTHERN MOON SHELL   p. 78
    Short spire; callus on columella; operculum horny;
    white, with yellowish periostracum.

11. **Neverita reclusianus** ×1   RECLUZ'S MOON SHELL   p. 78
    Sturdy; shelly lobe over umbilicus; brownish or grayish.

12. **Velutina laevigata** ×2   SMOOTH VELVET SHELL   p. 77
    Thin, fragile; flaring aperture; velvety periostracum, pinkish
    white.

13. **Polinices draconis** ×1   DRAKE'S MOON SHELL   p. 78
    Globular; deep umbilicus; yellowish brown.

14. **Polinices lewisii** ×½   LEWIS' MOON SHELL   p. 78
    Large, swollen; wrinkles at shoulders; yellowish gray.

Plate 36

ROCK SHELLS

1. **Trophon cerrosensis catalinensis** ×1   p. 82
   CATALINA TROPHON
    Large but light; long spines at shoulders; yellowish tan.

2. **Maxwellia gemma** ×1 GEM ROCK SHELL p. 83
    Vertical ribs; small aperture; closed canal; gray or white.

3. **Pterynotus trialatus** ×1   p. 83
   THREE-WINGED ROCK SHELL
    Strong, thin varices; revolving ridges; light to dark brown.

4. **Pterynotus rhyssus** ×1   p. 83
   ST. PETER'S ROCK SHELL
    Frilly varices; small aperture; yellowish brown.

5. **Pterynotus carpenteri** ×1   p. 83
   CARPENTER'S ROCK SHELL
    Broad, frilly varices; small aperture; yellowish brown.

6. **Boreotrophon pacificus** ×2 PACIFIC TROPHON p. 85
    Fusiform; weak vertical lines; open canal; grayish or whitish.

7. **Boreotrophon multicostatus** ×1   p. 85
   MANY-RIBBED TROPHON
    Many thin varices; shorter canal than No. 6; gray.

8. **Boreotrophon albospinosus** ×1 SPINY TROPHON p. 85
    Sharp ridges at shoulders; long canal; white.

9. **Boreotrophon triangulatus** ×1   p. 85
   TRIANGULAR TROPHON
    Stoutly fusiform; hollow spines at shoulders; whitish.

10. **Ceratostoma foliatum** ×1 LEAFY HORNMOUTH p. 84
     Large and thin varices; cordlike ridges; yellowish white.

11. **Jaton festivus** ×1 FESTIVE ROCK SHELL p. 84
     Thick outer lip; strong varices; thin encircling lines; yellowish
    white.

12. **Ceratostoma nuttalli** ×1   p. 84
    NUTTALL'S HORNMOUTH
     Rugged; large aperture; slender horn at base; mottled yellowish
    gray and brown.

13. Apertural tooth of *Ceratostoma nuttalli* ×5

14. **Fusitriton oregonense** ×⅔ HAIRY TRITON p. 81
     Large; rounded whorls; hairy periostracum; yellowish white.

15. **Bursa californica** ×½   p. 81
    CALIFORNIA FROG SHELL
     Large, solid; strong varices; large aperture; yellowish brown.

16. **Forreria belcheri** ×½   p. 82
    BELCHER'S CHORUS SHELL
     Large, smooth; spines at shoulders; yellowish white, streaked.

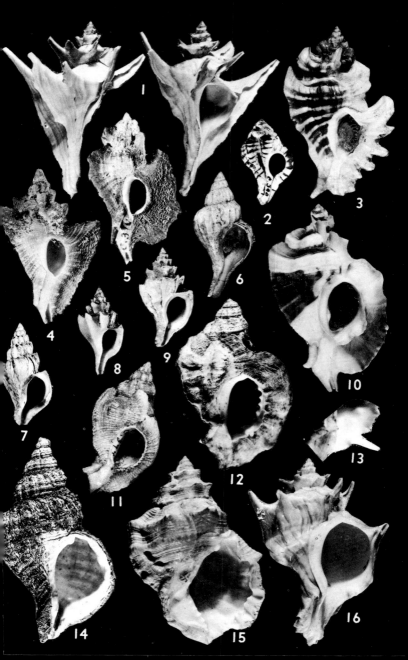

Plate 37

ROCK SHELLS AND OTHERS

1. **Acanthina paucilirata** ×1   CHECKERED UNICORN   p. 88
   Stoutly fusiform; outer lip toothed within; yellowish white.
2. **Acanthina lugubris** ×1   SAD UNICORN   p. 88
   Squat and rough; revolving wrinkle-like ridges; mottled gray.
3. **Acanthina punctulata** ×1   SPOTTED UNICORN   p. 89
   Stoutly fusiform; revolving dots; dark gray.
4. **Acanthina spirata** ×1   ANGULAR UNICORN   p. 89
   Sloping shoulders; revolving lines; dark gray.
5. **Trophonopsis lasius** ×1   SANDPAPER TROPHON   p. 85
   Slender, fusiform; sloping shoulders; gray.
6. **Ocenebra squamulifera** ×1   SCALY ROCK SHELL   p. 87
   Long aperture; triangular knobs at shoulders; gray.
7. **Ocenebra lurida** ×1   LURID ROCK SHELL   p. 86
   Folds on upper whorls; body whorl with encircling lines; grayish or brownish.
8. **Ocenebra circumtexta** ×1   CIRCLED ROCK SHELL   p. 86
   Teeth in outer lip; grayish white, broadly banded.
9. **Ocenebra interfossa** ×1   SCULPTURED ROCK SHELL   p. 86
   Fusiform; network sculpture; grayish brown.
10. **Ocenebra poulsoni** ×1   POULSON'S ROCK SHELL   p. 87
    Rounded vertical ribs; encircling lines; gray.
11. **Amphissa bicolor** ×1   TWO-TINTED AMPHISSA   p. 90
    Darker central band; vertical ridges; yellowish tan.
12. **Anachis penicillata** ×2   PENCILED DOVE SHELL   p. 89
    Small, longitudinal ridges; pale brown, spotted.
13. **Ocenebra japonica** ×1   JAPAN ROCK SHELL   p. 86
    Shouldered whorls; thick outer lip; grayish white.
14. **Amphissa versicolor** ×1   JOSEPH'S COAT AMPHISSA   p. 90
    Rather stout; vertical folds; aperture long; variable color.
15. **Amphissa columbiana** ×1   COLUMBIAN AMPHISSA   p. 90
    Distinct vertical folds; yellowish brown.
16. **Mitrella gausapata** ×2   p. 90
    See text.
17. **Mitrella carinata** ×3   KEELED DOVE SHELL   p. 89
    Shoulders keeled; long aperture; pale brown.
18. **Thais lima** ×1   FILE DOGWINKLE   p. 88
    Fusiform; prominent spiral ridges; white or grayish white.
19. **Thais emarginata** ×1   EMARGINATE DOGWINKLE   p. 87
    Variable in stoutness; large aperture; yellowish brown.
20. **Nassarius tegulus** ×1   MUD DOG WHELK   p. 92
    Stocky; vertical ridges; gray or brownish.
21. **Nassarius mendicus** ×1   LEAN DOG WHELK   p. 91
    High-spired; revolving ribs and knobs; yellowish brown.
22. **Nassarius mendicus cooperi** ×1   COOPER'S DOG WHELK   p. 91
    See Remarks under *N. mendicus* text.
23. **Thais lamellosa** ×1   FRILLED DOGWINKLE   p. 88
    Variable; usually with frilly ridges; color variable.
24. **Thais canaliculata** ×1   CHANNELED DOGWINKLE   p. 87
    Strong and sharp revolving ridges; yellowish brown.
25. **Nassarius fossatus** ×1   CHANNELED DOG WHELK   p. 91
    Large, sharply pointed; vertical ridges; yellowish tan.
26. **Nassarius obsoletus** ×1   BLACK DOG WHELK   p. 91
    Atlantic; deep purplish black; apex eroded; see text.
27. **Nassarius perpinguis** ×1   FAT DOG WHELK   p. 92
    Beaded ridges; sturdy; grayish yellow.
28. **Nassarius insculptus** ×1   SMOOTH DOG WHELK   p. 91
    Surface smoother than No. 27; early whorls ridged.
29. **Searlesia dira** ×1   DIRE WHELK   p. 97
    Fusiform; revolving lines; purplish brown.

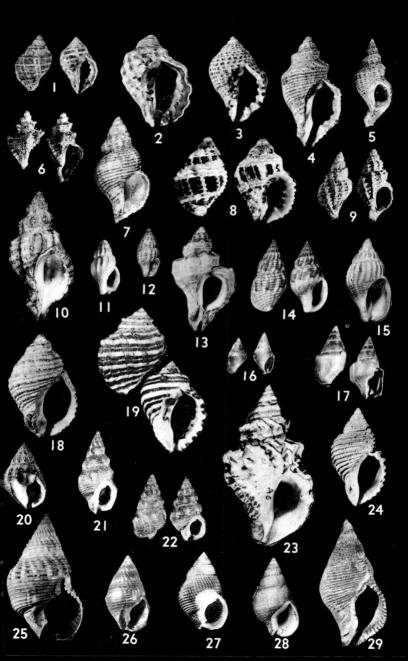

Plate 38

WHELKS

1. **Buccinum elatius** ×½ SILKY WHELK   p. 92
   Thin-shelled; large aperture; weak ridges; brownish yellow.

2. **Buccinum baeri** ×1 BAER'S WHELK   p. 92
   Smooth; large aperture; lavender-brown.

3. **Buccinum glaciale** ×1 GLACIAL WHELK   p. 93
   Encircling lines; wavy vertical folds; yellowish gray.

4. **Buccinum plectrum** ×⅔ LYRE WHELK   p. 93
   Inflated whorls; curving vertical ridges; yellowish brown.

5. **Buccinum eugrammatum** ×1 RIBBED WHELK   p. 93
   Shorter, sturdy; encircling ridges; yellowish brown.

6. **Colus halli** ×1 HALL'S COLUS   p. 94
   Fusiform, smooth; strong brownish periostracum.

7. **Volutharpa ampullacea** ×1   p. 96
   BIG-MOUTHED WHELK
   Large flaring aperture; short spire; olive-brown periostracum.

8. **Macron lividus** ×1 LIVID MACRON   p. 97
   Small, fusiform; brownish periostracum.

9. **Plicifusus kroyeri** ×⅔ KROYER'S WHELK   p. 94
   Aperture large; heavy periostracum; yellowish white.

10. **Colus jordani** ×1 JORDAN'S COLUS   p. 94
    Short canal; orange-brown periostracum.

11. **Colus spitzbergensis** ×⅔ SPITSBERGEN COLUS   p. 94
    Deep sutures; rounded whorls; spiral ridges; yellowish brown.

12. **Volutopsius stefanssoni** ×½   p. 93
    STEFANSSON'S WHELK
    Large, inflated; inner lip reflected.

13. **Kelletia kelleti** ×½ KELLET'S WHELK   p. 97
    Fusiform; well-spaced vertical folds; yellowish.

Plate 39

WHELKS

1. **Neptunea phoenicea** $\times \frac{1}{2}$ PHOENICIAN WHELK   p. 96
   Rounded whorls; encircling lines; yellowish brown.

2. **Beringius kennicotti** $\times \frac{2}{3}$ KENNICOTT'S WHELK   p. 95
   Large; slender spire; strongly fluted; yellowish gray.

3. **Neptunea smirnia** $\times \frac{1}{2}$ CHOCOLATE WHELK   p. 96
   Large, smooth; chocolate-brown.

4. **Neptunea tabulata** $\times \frac{1}{2}$ TABLED WHELK   p. 96
   Deep shelflike channel at suture; yellowish white.

5. **Volutopsius harpa** $\times \frac{1}{2}$ p. 93
   LEFT-HANDED WHELK (from Dall)
   Large; short spire; large aperture; left-handed; grayish brown.

6. **Beringius crebricostata** $\times \frac{1}{2}$ p. 95
   THICK-RIBBED WHELK (from Dall)
   Elongate; strong revolving ridges; white.

7. **Neptunea lyrata** $\times \frac{1}{2}$ RIDGED WHELK   p. 95
   Flattish shoulders; prominent revolving ridges; reddish brown.

8. **Neptunea pribiloffensis** $\times \frac{1}{2}$ PRIBILOF WHELK   p. 96
   Stout; large aperture; weak revolving ridges; yellowish white.

9. **Neptunea amianta** $\times \frac{1}{2}$ p. 95
   UNSPOTTED WHELK (from Dall)
   Shouldered whorls; weak revolving and vertical lines; white or
   yellowish white.

Plate 40

MISCELLANEOUS SNAILS

1. **Mitra idae** ×1   IDA'S MITER   p. 99
   Elongate; small aperture; plicate lip; dark periostracum.
2. **Mitra catalinae** ×1   CATALINA MITER   p. 99
   Smooth, fusiform; plicate lip; dark brown.
3. **Fusinus kobelti** ×1   KOBELT'S SPINDLE   p. 98
   Shouldered whorls; vertical knobs; revolving lines; grayish.
4. **"Lora" harpularia** ×2   HARP LORA   p. 104
   See text.
5. **"Lora" nobilis** ×2   NOBLE LORA   p. 104
   See text.
6. **"Lora" reticulata** ×2   RETICULATE LORA   p. 105
   See text.
7. **"Lora" pribilova** ×2   PRIBILOF LORA   p. 105
   See text.
8. **Conus californicus** ×1   CALIFORNIA CONE   p. 101
   Rounded spire; reddish-brown periostracum.
9. **Terebra pedroana** ×1   SAN PEDRO AUGER   p. 102
   Slender, many-whorled; twisted columella; yellowish white.
10. **Aptyxis luteopicta** ×1   PAINTED SPINDLE   p. 98
    Shouldered whorls; vertical ridges; brown; central band.
11. **Burchia redondoensis** ×1   REDONDO TOWER   p. 103
    Flat-sided; weak folds; partly reflected inner lip; dark brown.
12. **Ophiodermella incisa** ×1   INCISED TOWER   p. 103
    Slender; incised line below suture; dove-gray.
13. **Granatoma excurvata** ×2   CURVED TOWER   p. 104
    Fusiform; deep sutures; vertical ridges; yellowish gray.
14. **Oenopota rosea** ×2   ROSY OENOPOTA   p. 103
    Fusiform; vertical ridges; pale reddish.
15. **Mitromorpha filosa** ×2   FILOSE TOWER   p. 104
    Small, fusiform; narrow aperture; yellowish brown.
16. **Pseudomelatoma moesta** ×1   DOLEFUL TOWER   p. 103
    Moderately stout; folds at shoulders; greenish brown.
17. **Elaeocyma empyrosia** ×1   TURRET TOWER   p. 102
    Turreted spire; vertical folds; yellowish white.
18. **Admete couthouyi** ×1   COUTHOUY'S NUTMEG   p. 100
    Stout; cancellate sculpture; thin outer lip; yellowish white.
19. **Olivella biplicata** ×1   PURPLE OLIVE   p. 99
    Stout; short spire; narrow aperture; polished; color varies.
20. **Olivella baetica** ×1   BEATIC OLIVE   p. 98
    Slender; narrow aperture; polished; bluish to brownish.
21. **Cancellaria cooperi** ×1   COOPER'S NUTMEG   p. 100
    Solid, rugged; strong shoulders; yellowish brown, dark enciriclng bands.
22. **Marginella jewetti** ×3   JEWETT'S MARGINELLA   p. 101
    Small, flat-topped; lip plicate; polished; white.
23. **Marginella pyriformis** ×4   PEAR-SHAPED MARGINELLA   p. 101
    Tiny, polished; white or grayish white.
24. **Marginella californica** ×3   CALIFORNIA MARGINELLA   p. 101
    Elongate; short spire; polished; white, yellowish-brown bands.
25. **Melampus olivaceus** ×1   SALT-MARSH SNAIL   p. 111
    Thin-shelled; cone-shaped; olive-green periostracum.
26. **Acteon punctocaelatus** ×2   BARREL SHELL   p. 109
    Fusiform; thin revolving lines; white, strongly banded.
27. **Acteocina culcitella** ×3   BARREL BUBBLE   p. 109
    Cylindrical; short spire; narrow aperture; bluish white.
28. **Cylichna alba** ×4   WHITE BARREL BUBBLE   p. 109
    Cylindrical; sunken spire; white.
29. **Haminoea virescens** ×1   GREEN PAPER BUBBLE   p. 110
    Globular; thin and fragile; greenish yellow; smaller than No. 30.
30. **Haminoea vesicula** ×1   BLISTER PAPER BUBBLE   p. 110
    Globular; thin and fragile; greenish yellow.
31. **Bulla gouldiana** ×1   GOULD'S BUBBLE   p. 110
    Large; mottled; white inner lip.
32. **Trimusculus reticulatus** ×1   p. 111
    RETICULATE BUTTON SHELL
    Round, cap-shaped; solid; white.

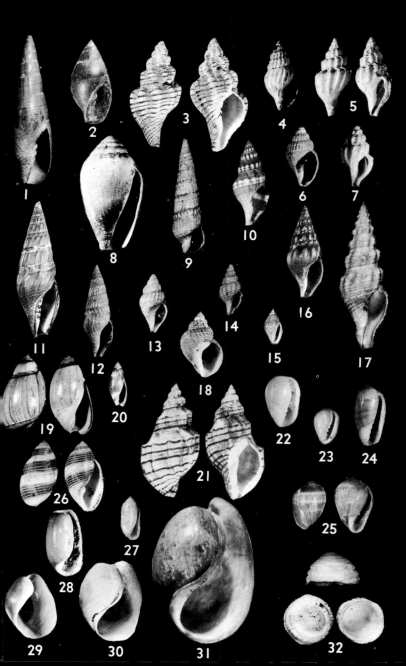

Plate 41

CHITONS AND TUSK SHELLS

1. **Mopalia lignosa** ×1 WOODY CHITON p. 114
   Showing animal. Plates streaked with green and black.

2. **Tonicella lineata** ×1 LINED CHITON p. 113
   Yellowish brown to orange; white lines.

3. **Mopalia muscosa** ×1 MOSSY CHITON p. 115
   Girdle bristly; olive or grayish brown.

4. **Ischnochiton conspicuus** ×½ p. 115
   CONSPICUOUS CHITON
   Horizontal ridges on sides; back arched; grayish green.

5. **Nuttallina californica** ×1 p. 114
   CALIFORNIA NUTTALL CHITON
   Plates mottled; girdle velvety; olive-brown to dark brown.

6. **Katharina tunicata** ×1 BLACK KATY p. 115
   Girdle shiny black; plates partially concealed; bluish white.

7. **Mopalia ciliata** ×1 HAIRY CHITON p. 114
   Oval; plates beaked; girdle hairy; grayish green, blotched.

8. **Dentalium pretiosum** ×1 INDIAN MONEY TUSK p. 117
   Tubular; polished; white.

9. **Ischnochiton albus** ×1 WHITE CHITON p. 115
   Small; grayish white, variable.

10. **Cyanoplax hartwegi** ×1 HARTWEG'S CHITON p. 113
    Oval, flattened; girdle narrow; slaty or brownish gray.

11. **Ischnochiton heathiana** ×⅔ HEATH'S CHITON p. 116
    Girdle scaly; greenish gray.

12. **Cryptochiton stelleri** ×½ GIANT CHITON p. 116
    Upper surface. Girdle covers back; yellowish brown to gray.

13. **Cryptochiton stelleri** ×½
    Plates removed and mounted.

14. **Cryptochiton stelleri** ×½
    Underside, animal removed.

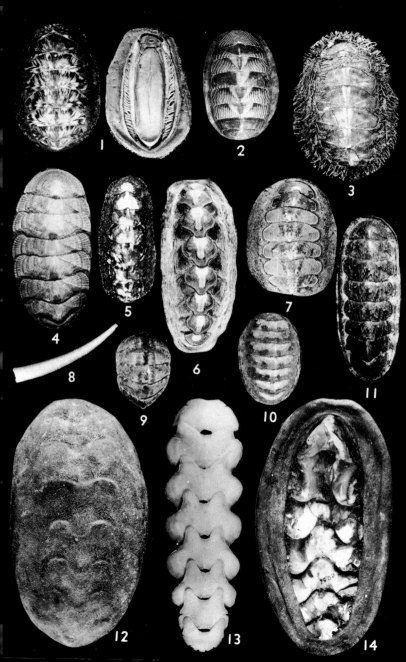

Plate 42

GULF OF CALIFORNIA NUT AND ARK SHELLS

1. **Nucula declivis** ×1 p. 118
    Small, oval; shiny; pearly interior; olive-green.

2. **Nuculana elenensis** ×1 p. 118
    Pointed posterior; pit between rows of teeth; greenish brown.

3. **Adrana cultrata** ×1 p. 118
    Elongate, beaks central; dorsal line straight; white.

4. **Adrana penascoensis** ×1 p. 119
    Posterior end lengthened; fine concentric lines; whitish.

5. **Arca mutabilis** ×½ p. 119
    Squarish, inflated; posterior slope; interior brown.

6. **Arca pacifica** ×½ p. 119
    Ponderous; gaping at base; gray, shaggy brown periostracum.

7. **Barbatia alternata** ×1 p. 119
    Posterior slope, margin scalloped; grayish white.

8. **Anadara nux** ×1 p. 121
    Small, squarish; ribs weakly checked; white.

9. **Anadara formosa** ×⅔ p. 121
    Large, inflated; flattened ribs; shaggy periostracum; white.

10. **Barbatia reeveana** ×⅔ p. 120
    Thin; fine ribs; white.

11. **Barbatia lurida** ×1 p. 120
    Teeth larger at ends; interior purplish brown.

12. **Barbatia gradata** ×1 p. 120
    Beaks full; cancellate surface; yellowish white.

13. **Barbatia illota** ×1 p. 120
    Well inflated; fine ribs; whitish.

14. **Anadara tuberculosa** ×⅔ p. 121
    Broad ribs; narrow interspaces; white.

15. **Anadara perlabiata** ×1 p. 121
    Shell high; posterior slope; ribs checked; white.

16. **Noetia reversa** ×1 p. 122
    Flattened posterior slope; white.

17. **Arcopsis solida** ×⅔ p. 120
    Small, squarish; fine ribs; yellowish white.

18. **Anadara grandis** ×½ p. 121
    Massive; broad ribs; full beaks; white.

Plate 43

GULF OF CALIFORNIA BITTERSWEETS, SCALLOPS, AND OTHERS

1. **Glycymeris inaequalis** ×1   p. 122
   Fine lines and broad folds; curving hinge teeth; gray, with brown bands.

2. **Glycymeris gigantea** ×½   p. 122
   Round, solid; well inflated; curving teeth; white, mottled.

3. **Glycymeris multicostata** ×1   p. 122
   Roundish; ribs broader than interspaces; reddish brown and white.

4. **Aequipecten circularis** ×½   p. 127
   Well inflated; wings nearly equal; heavily mottled.

5. **Lyropecten subnodosus** ×⅓   p. 128
   Large, heavy; radiating folds; somewhat knobby; pinkish white to reddish purple.

6. **Aequipecten tumbezensis** ×1   p. 127
   Small, thin; wings unequal; gray to nearly black.

7. **Pecten vogdesi** ×½   p. 127
   Upper valve flat, lower cupped; upper buffy yellow.

8. **Lima pacifica** ×1   p. 128
   Elongate; short hinge; inflated; thin lines; white.

9. **Anomia adamas** ×½   p. 130
   Thin; wavy surface; waxy luster; yellowish brown to orange.

10. **Lima tetrica** ×½   p. 128
    Thin, solid; strong scaly ribs; white.

11. **Placunanomia cumingii** ×½   p. 130
    Sharply folded; broad ridges and deep valleys; gray.

Plate 44

GULF OF CALIFORNIA PEN SHELLS
AND OYSTERS

1. Interior of *Pinna* $\times \frac{1}{2}$

2. Interior of *Atrina* $\times \frac{1}{2}$

3. **Pinna rugosa** $\times \frac{1}{5}$
   Thin and light; ribs with large hollow spines; yellowish brown
   to black.

4. **Atrina tuberculosa** $\times \frac{1}{4}$
   Thin and light; rows of tubercular spines; dark brown.

5. **Atrina maura** $\times \frac{1}{4}$
   Curved margins; dark brown to black.

6. **Ostrea megodon** $\times \frac{1}{2}$
   Elongate, curved; wavy margins; grayish.

Plate 45

GULF OF CALIFORNIA PEARL AND OTHER OYSTERS

1. **Pinctada mazatlanica** $\times \frac{1}{2}$ PEARL OYSTER   p. 126
   Valves flattened; scaly concentric ridges; greenish brown.

2. **Spondylus calcifer** $\times \frac{1}{3}$ p. 129
   Heavy, solid; interlocking hinge; interior white, reddish purple border.

3. **Ostrea fisheri** $\times \frac{1}{3}$ FISHER'S OYSTER   p. 129
   Ponderous, irregular; single muscle scar; gray.

4. **Ostrea palmula** $\times 1$ p. 130
   Irregular in growth; lower valve usually deep; margins scalloped; purplish gray.

5. **Spondylus princeps** $\times \frac{1}{2}$ p. 129
   Massive; rows of brown spines; white to orange or reddish.

6. Interlocking hinge of *Spondylus princeps* $\times \frac{2}{3}$

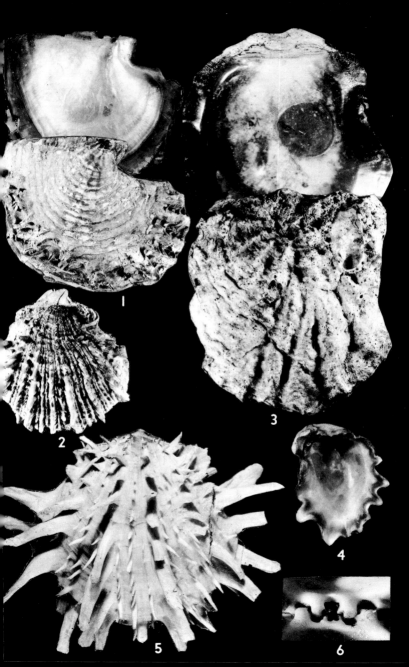

Plate 46

GULF OF CALIFORNIA MUSSELS, JEWEL BOXES, AND OTHERS

1. **Lithophaga attenuata** $\times \frac{2}{3}$ DATE SHELL p. 125
   Elongate, thin; short anterior; brown periostracum.

2. **Mytella guyanensis** $\times \frac{2}{3}$ p. 125
   Broad posterior; concentric lines; green to almost black.

3. **Choromytilus palliopunctatus** $\times \frac{2}{3}$ p. 125
   Broadly elongate; small beaks; purplish blue.

4. **Cardita megastropha** $\times \frac{1}{2}$ p. 131
   Solid; beaks recurved; strong hinge; pinkish red.

5. **Mytella speciosa** $\times \frac{2}{3}$ p. 125
   Thin-shelled; short anterior, broad posterior; greenish yellow.

6. **Cardita crassicostata** $\times \frac{2}{3}$ p. 131
   Broad ribs, strongly checked; hinge rugged; orange-red, blotched.

7. **Cardita affinis californica** $\times 1$ p. 131
   Elongate; broad ribs; wavy on posterior slope; yellowish brown.

8. **Septifer zeteki** $\times 2$ PLATFORM MUSSEL p. 125
   Small, elongate; platform under beaks; greenish gray.

9. **Cardita laticostata** $\times 1$ p. 131
   Short anterior; broad ribs; mottled brown and white.

10. **Chama echinata** $\times 1$ SPINY JEWEL BOX p. 133
    Spiny surface; interior purple.

11. **Chama buddiana** $\times \frac{1}{2}$ p. 133
    Thick, heavy; small spines; interior white, margins sometimes reddish.

12. **Crassatella gibbosa** $\times \frac{1}{2}$ p. 130
    Pinched-out posterior; hinge sturdy; buffy yellow; dark brown periostracum.

13. **Chama frondosa** $\times 1$, juvenile

14. **Chama frondosa** $\times \frac{1}{2}$ FRONDOSE JEWEL BOX p. 133
    Broad frondlike spines on some; interior white, purple border.

Plate 47

GULF OF CALIFORNIA COCKLES, LUCINES, AND DISK SHELLS

Plate 48

GULF OF CALIFORNIA HARD-SHELLED CLAMS

1. **Periglypta multicostata** $\times\frac{1}{2}$ p. 135
    Roundish, inflated; concentric ribs and radiating lines; yellowish white.

2. **Ventricolaria isocardia** $\times\frac{1}{2}$ p. 135
    Roundish; strong concentric ribs; pinkish gray.

3. **Chione pulicaria** $\times\frac{1}{2}$ p. 138
    Chiefly concentric ridges; mottled; buffy yellow.

4. **Tivela planulata** $\times 1$ p. 135
    Triangular; surface smooth; radiating lines of brown.

5. **Pitar lupanaria** $\times 1$ p. 136
    Concentric ribs; spines on posterior ridge; white to lavender.

6. **Tivela byronensis** $\times\frac{2}{3}$ p. 135
    Triangular, smooth; beaks full; color variable.

7. **Pitar concinnus** $\times\frac{2}{3}$ p. 136
    Concentric lines; radiating bands of purplish.

8. **Pitar alternatus** $\times\frac{2}{3}$ p. 136
    Concentric lines alternating in size; brownish to white.

9. **Pitar vulneratus** $\times\frac{2}{3}$ p. 136
    Roundish, plump; smooth; concentric bands of purple.

10. **Chione amathusia** $\times\frac{1}{2}$ p. 137
    Radiating and concentric ribs; yellowish gray.

11. **Chione gnidia** $\times\frac{1}{2}$ p. 137
    Concentric ribs with frilly edges; yellowish white.

12. **Megapitaria squalida** $\times\frac{1}{3}$ p. 137
    Solid; surface smooth; grayish periostracum.

13. **Megapitaria aurantiaca** $\times\frac{1}{3}$ p. 136
    Solid; surface smooth; orange to brown periostracum.

Plate 49

GULF OF CALIFORNIA HARD-SHELLED CLAMS, SURF CLAMS, AND OTHERS

1. **Anomalocardia subimbricata tumens** ×1   p. 138
   Stout; swollen concentric ribs; see Remarks under *A. subimbricata* text.

2. **Protothaca asperrima** ×1   p. 138
   Fine radiating, scaly lines; yellowish gray.

3. **Anomalocardia subimbricata** ×1   p. 138
   Thick and sturdy; purple spot at anterior tip.

4. **Anomalocardia subrugosa** ×1   p. 138
   Rounded concentric ribs; shiny; pinkish gray.

5. **Petricola robusta** ×1   p. 139
   Stubby; thin radiating lines; white.

6. **Harvella elegans'** ×½   p. 140
   Thin and delicate; wide concentric grooves; white.

7. **Protothaca grata** ×1   p. 139
   Plump; yellowish gray, blotched with brown or black.

8. **Protothaca columbiensis** ×½   p. 139
   Rounded radiating ribs; gray, mottled with brown and white.

9. **Anatina undulata** ×½   p. 140
   Thin and light, well inflated; concentric grooves; white.

10. **Mactrellona clisia** ×½   p. 141
    Large, thin-shelled; thin ridge at posterior; yellowish white.

11. **Petricola parallela·** ×1   p. 139
    Elongate, thin-shelled; radiating lines; white.

12. **Mulinia coloradoensis** ×⅔   p. 140
    Triangular, posterior flattened; whitish; periostracum yellowish brown.

13. **Mactra velata** ×⅔   p. 140
    Heavy, robust; pit under beaks; yellowish gray.

Plate 50

GULF OF CALIFORNIA BEAN CLAMS, TELLINS, AND OTHERS

Plate 51

GULF OF CALIFORNIA SEMELES, BORERS, AND OTHERS

1. **Semele bicolor** ×2   p. 146
   Roundish, moderately inflated; whitish, purplish at beaks.

2. **Gari regularis** ×⅔   p. 145
   Broadly oval; shiny surface; mottled.

3. **Gari maxima** ×⅔   p. 145
   Broadly oval; weak rays; yellowish gray.

4. **Semele quentinensis** ×1   p. 147
   Thin, little inflated; whitish; interior purple at beaks.

5. **Semele junonia** ×½   p. 147
   Anterior larger than posterior; concentric lines; interior rosy.

6. **Semele flavescens** ×⅔   p. 146
   Valves flattish; beaks nearly central; pallial sinus deep; yellowish.

7. **Semele formosa** ×1   p. 146
   Both ends rounded; concentric lines; broken purplish bands.

8. **Corbula nasuta** ×2   p. 148
   Posterior pointed, anterior rounded; whitish.

9. **Corbula ovulata** ×1   p. 148
   See text.

10. **Corbula bicarinata** ×1   p. 148
    Stubby; beaks full; inequivalve; white.

11. **Gastrochaena ovata** ×1   p. 148
    Oval, widely gaping; yellowish gray.

12. **Iphigenia altior** ×1   p. 144
    Triangular, sturdy; strong greenish periostracum.

13. **Ensis californicus** ×1   p. 147
    Slender, elongate; slightly curved; yellowish green.

14. **Tagelus politus** ×1   p. 146
    Elongate; ends rounded; reinforcing internal rib; violet.

15. **Tagelus affinis** ×1   p. 145
    Elongate, ends gaping; yellowish-tan periostracum.

16. **Tagelus violascens** ×1   p. 146
    Elongate; no reinforcing internal rib; pale violet.

17. **Parapholas acuminata** ×1   p. 149
    Bulbous anterior, pointed posterior; grayish white.

18. **Pholas chiloensis** ×1   p. 149
    Elongate; short anterior; shelly hood over beaks; white.

19. **Cyrtopleura crucigera** ×1   p. 149
    Short, thin, and brittle; anterior gaping; white.

Plate 52

GULF OF CALIFORNIA LIMPETS AND KEYHOLE LIMPETS

Plate 53

GULF OF CALIFORNIA TOP SHELLS, TURBANS, NERITES, AND OTHERS

1. **Calliostoma palmeri** ×1 PALMER'S TOP p. 153
Shouldered whorls; encircling dots; pale ivory.
2. **Calliostoma eximium** ×1 p. 152
Pyramidal; base flattish; black, white, and red checks.
3. **Calliostoma leanum** ×1 LEA'S TOP p. 153
Spire elevated; dull reddish brown.
4. **Calliostoma lima** ×1 FILE TOP p. 153
Conical; encircling beaded lines; yellowish, spotted.
5. **Tegula byroniana** ×1 RETICULATE TOP p. 153
Revolving rows of beads; greenish spot on columella.
6. **Tegula rubroflammulata** ×1 p. 154
Revolving knobby ridges; brown, streaked with pinkish.
7. **Tegula globulus** ×1 GLOBULAR TOP p. 153
Low, blunt spire; small umbilicus; mottled.
8. **Tegula mariana** ×1 p. 154
Small, flattish; reddish-brown dots.
9. **Tegula rugosa** ×1 ROUGH TOP p. 154
Solid, sturdy; rounded whorls; aperture pearly.
10. **Turbo fluctuosus** ×1 p. 154
Angled shoulders; aperture iridescent; shelly operculum.
11. **Turbo saxosus** ×1 (showing interior of operculum) p. 155
Sharp vertical growth lines; shelly operculum.
12. **Astraea buschii** ×1 BUSCH'S TURBAN p. 155
Pyramidal; base flat; green, blotched.
13. **Astraea unguis** ×1 p. 155
Vertical ridges; scalloped margin; brown or gray.
14. **Astraea olivacea** ×1 OLIVE TURBAN p. 155
(with operculum)
Rugged, pyramidal; umbilical area orange-red.
15. **Epitonium phanium** ×1 p. 163
See text.
16. **Epitonium wurtsbaughi** ×1 p. 163
See text.
17. **Planaxis planicostatus** ×1 p. 160
Coarse revolving ribs; aperture notched above and below; brown.
18. **Planaxis obsoletus** ×1 p. 160
Fine revolving lines; aperture notched; reddish brown.
19. **Littorina fasciata** ×1 p. 157
Sturdy; revolving lines; inner lip brown.
20. **Littorina conspersa** ×1 p. 157
Revolving ribs; aperture light brown.
21. **Littorina aspera** ×1 p. 157
Sharp apex; blotched with gray and brown.
22. **Nerita funiculata** ×1 p. 156
Flat-topped; large body whorl; columellar area pustulate; black.
23. **Nerita scabricosta** ×1 (with operculum) p. 156
Solid; inner lip toothed; gray to whitish, banded or blotched.
24. **Neritina luteofasciata** ×1 p. 156
Low-spired; polished; columellar area rich brown.

Plate 54

GULF OF CALIFORNIA HORN AND WORM SHELLS, TURRETS, AND OTHERS

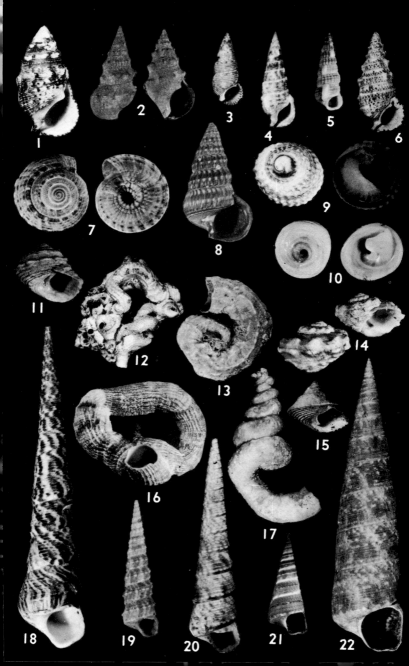

Plate 55

GULF OF CALIFORNIA MOON SHELLS, COWRIES, AND OTHERS

1. **Crucibulum scutellatum** ×1   p. 165
   Strong radiating ridges; scalloped margins; cup within; brownish.
2. **Cheilea cepacea** ×1   p. 164
   Fine radiating lines; horseshoe-shaped plate within; gray or white.
3. **Hipponix pilosus** ×1   HOOF SHELL   p. 164
   Thick, cap-shaped; hairy periostracum; white.
4. **Crepidula striolata** ×1   p. 165
   Oval, whitish; shelly platform within.
5. **Natica broderipiana** ×1 (with operculum)   p. 166
   Globular, smooth; encircling chocolate bars; shelly operculum.
6. **Natica elenae** ×1   p. 167
   Wavy vertical streaks; deep umbilicus; shelly operculum; ivory.
7. **Natica grayi** ×1   p. 167
   3 rows of small dots; deep umbilicus; shelly operculum; ivory.
8. **Polinices bifasciata** ×1 (with operculum)   p. 167
   Whitish bands; umbilical area deep brown; horny operculum.
9. **Polinices uber** ×1   p. 167
   Shiny white; callus over small umbilicus; horny operculum.
10. **Natica chemnitzi** ×1   p. 166
    Grayish, blotched at shoulders; deep umbilicus; shelly operculum.
11. **Parametaria dupontii** ×1   FALSE CONE   p. 183
    Cone-shaped; long aperture; pale blotches on spire.
12. **Northia northiae** ×½   p. 187
    High-spired; shiny; notch at top of aperture; olive-brown.
13. **Cyphoma emarginatum** ×1   p. 169
    White; hump across middle; outer lip rolled in.
14. **Jenneria pustulata** ×1   p. 169
    Orange pustules on bluish-gray background.
15. **Trivia sanguinea** ×1   p. 169
    Ridged exterior; no median groove; mahogany-brown.
16. **Trivia radians** ×1   p. 169
    Ridged exterior; distinct median groove; purplish gray.
17. **Cypraea annettae** ×1   ANNETTE'S COWRY   p. 168
    Bluish white, heavily dotted with brown.
18. **Cypraea arabicula** ×1   LITTLE ARABIAN COWRY   p. 168
    Broad band of violet at margins, spotted with black.
19. **Cypraea albuginosa** ×1   p. 168
    WHITE-SPOTTED COWRY
    Round chestnut spots; lilac border at margins and base.
20. **Cypraea cervinetta** ×⅔   LITTLE DEER COWRY   p. 168
    Large; round whitish spots; lower sides violet-brown.

Plate 56

GULF OF CALIFORNIA STROMBS, HELMETS, AND OTHERS

1. **Strombus gracilior** $\times \frac{2}{3}$ p. 166
   Solid; knobby shoulders; yellowish brown.

2. **Strombus galeatus** $\times \frac{1}{5}$ p. 165
   Massive; low spire; reddish brown.

3. **Strombus granulatus** $\times \frac{2}{3}$ p. 166
   Tall spire; knobby shoulders; ivory.

4. Operculum of *Cassis* $\times \frac{2}{3}$

5. Operculum of *Strombus* $\times 1$

6. **Cassis tenuis** $\times \frac{2}{3}$ p. 170
   Light in weight; low spire; lips toothed; orange-brown.

7. **Cassis centiquadrata** $\times \frac{2}{3}$ p. 170
   Stout; wide aperture; squarish spots of orange.

8. **Cassis coarctata** $\times 1$ p. 170
   Solid; toothed lips; mottled with reddish brown.

9. **Cymatium lignarium** $\times 1$ p. 171
   Stocky; cancellate sculpture; lips stained orange.

10. **Malea ringens** $\times \frac{1}{2}$ p. 173
    Large, rounded; gash in inner lip; yellowish white.

11. **Colubraria soverbii** $\times 1$ p. 173
    Varices staggered on spire; yellowish gray.

12. **Morum tuberculosum** $\times 1$ p. 171
    Flat-topped; long aperture; warty surface; white, mottled.

13. **Distorsio constrictus** $\times \frac{2}{3}$ p. 172
    Constricted aperture; revolving knobs; white.

14. **Ficus ventricosa** $\times \frac{1}{2}$ p. 174
    Thin and light; encircling ridges; yellowish gray.

15. **Bursa nana** $\times 1$ p. 173
    Knobs at shoulders; aperture notched above; purplish brown.

16. **Bursa caelata** $\times 1$ p. 172
    Inner lip plicate; strong varices on each side; brownish.

17. **Cymatium gibbosum** $\times 1$ p. 171
    Shouldered whorls; thickened lip; moderate canal; yellowish, mottled.

18. **Cymatium wiegmanni** $\times 1$ p. 172
    Shoulders sloping; aperture wide; yellowish brown.

Plate 57

GULF OF CALIFORNIA ROCK SHELLS
AND OTHERS

1. **Hexaplex regius** $\times \frac{1}{2}$ p. 175
   Rugged; spiny varices; brown stain on pink columella.

2. **Murex elenensis** $\times \frac{2}{3}$ p. 174
   Globular, long canal; 3 spiny varices; buffy or ivory-white.

3. **Hexaplex erythrostomus** $\times \frac{1}{2}$ p. 175
   Rugged; white or pinkish white; rosy-pink aperture.

4. Operculum of *Hexaplex erythrostomus* $\times \frac{1}{2}$, showing both sides

5. **Murex recurvirostris** $\times 1$ p. 174
   Long, closed canal; thickened lip; grayish.

6. **Eupleura nitida** $\times 1$ p. 178
   Flattish; broad varices; purplish gray to dark gray.

7. **Eupleura muriciformis** $\times 1$ p. 177
   Aperture small; moderate canal, nearly closed; gray.

8. **Trophon beebei** $\times 1$ p. 177
   Whorls loosely coiled and flat-topped; pale brown.

9. **Trophon cerrosensis** $\times 1$ p. 177
   Thin, bladelike varices; short open canal; pale yellowish.

10. **Muricopsis zeteki** $\times 1$ p. 176
    Fusiform; fold at base of columella; aperture whitish.

11. **Coralliophila madreporarum** $\times 2$ p. 178
    Aperture flaring; purplish inside.

12. **Muricopsis armatus** $\times 1$ p. 176
    Elongate-fusiform; small aperture; yellowish white.

13. **Coralliophila costata** $\times 1$ p. 178
    Small, rugged; rounded folds; aperture purple.

14. **Muricanthus nigritus** $\times \frac{1}{2}$ p. 175
    Rugged and solid; varices with hollow spines; whitish.

15. **Vitularia salebrosa** $\times 1$ p. 177
    Solid, rather slender; small knobs at shoulder; brownish olive.

16. **Muricanthus princeps** $\times \frac{1}{2}$ p. 176
    Hollow fronds on varices; canal broad, closed; whitish.

17. **Muricanthus oxyacantha** $\times \frac{2}{3}$ p. 176
    Short closed canal; spiny lip; yellowish brown.

18. **Hexaplex brassica** $\times \frac{1}{2}$ p. 175
    Large, rugged; aperture pinkish.

Plate 58

GULF OF CALIFORNIA DOVE AND DYE SHELLS AND OTHERS

1. **Pyrene major** ×1   p. 182
   Solid; lip thickened, toothed within; chestnut-brown.
2. **Pyrene strombiformis** ×1   p. 182
   Lip thickened and toothed; white dots on chestnut-brown.
3. **Pyrene haemastoma** ×1   p. 182
   Taller spire than No. 2; splashes of white, orange.
4. **Pyrene fuscata** ×1   p. 182
   Stout, smooth; whitish patches at suture.
5. **Morula ferruginosa** ×1   p. 180
   Revolving knobs; gray; aperture bluish.
6. **Anachis nigricans** ×2   p. 181
   Weak vertical lines; aperture narrow; brown to blackish.
7. **Anachis scalarina** ×1   p. 181
   Fusiform; vertical ridges; aperture narrow, toothed within.
8. **Anachis pygmaea** ×3   p. 181
   Small, fusiform; vertical ridges; white, spotted.
9. **Anachis varia** ×1   p. 182
   Strong vertical ribs; pale band on body whorl.
10. **Anachis coronata** ×1   p. 181
    Fusiform; weak vertical ridges; smooth surface; yellowish white.
11. **Mazatlania fulgurata** ×1   p. 183
    Slender; whorls flattened; aperture narrow; yellowish gray.
12. **Cantharus elegans** ×1   p. 186
    Sturdy; whorls shouldered; fold at base; yellowish brown.
13. **Cantharus sanguinolentus** ×1   p. 186
    Stocky; lips red, with white dots.
14. **Cantharus ringens** ×1   p. 186
    Stocky; aperture notched above; yellowish brown.
15. **Engina pulchra** ×1   p. 187
    Fusiform; narrow aperture; brownish or yellowish.
16. **Acanthina brevidentata** ×1   p. 180
    Stocky; lip toothed; white spots on dark surface.
17. **Cantharus gemmatus** ×1   p. 186
    Rugged, fusiform; weak revolving lines; dark brown.
18. **Engina maura** ×1   p. 187
    Stoutly fusiform; thickened lip; dark chocolate.
19. **Thais speciosa** ×½   p. 180
    Triangular; revolving knobs; wide aperture; whitish.
20. **Purpura patula pansa** ×½   p. 178
    Wide aperture; flattened columella; brown.
21. **Thais kiosquiformis** ×⅔   p. 179
    Turreted spire; spines at shoulders; grayish brown.
22. **Thais planospira** ×⅔   p. 179
    Moderate-sized aperture; lips with reddish lines.
23. **Acanthina muricata** ×1   p. 180
    Heavy, solid; rounded revolving ribs; aperture white.
24. **Thais biserialis** ×⅔   p. 179
    Rugged; wide aperture, notched at both ends; grayish.
25. **Acanthina tuberculata** ×1   p. 180
    Pointed spire; pronounced spines; fold at base; yellowish gray.

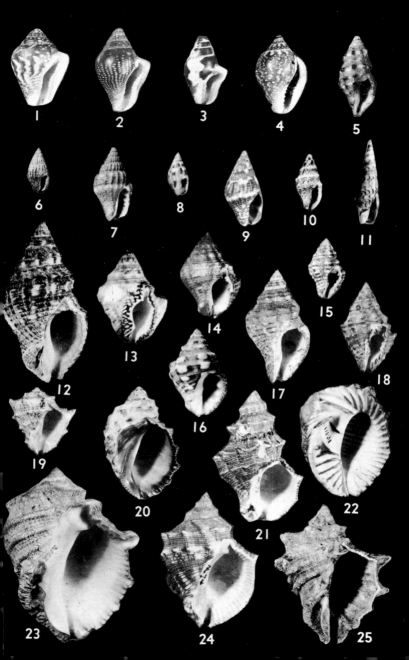

Plate 59

GULF OF CALIFORNIA DOG WHELKS, TULIP AND SPINDLE SHELLS, AND OTHERS

1. **Nassarius corpulentus** ×1   p. 185
   Short, stocky; lips thickened; whitish, banded.
2. **Nassarius versicolor** ×1   p. 185
   Yellowish white with brown bands.
3. **Nassarius pagodus** ×1   p. 185
   Rugged; shouldered whorls; yellowish white with brown bands.
4. **Nassarius complanatus** ×1   p. 185
   Stubby; encircling rows of beads; brownish.
5. **Nassarius angulicostis** ×1   p. 184
   Vertical ribs, angled at shoulder; yellowish.
6. **Nassarius luteostoma** ×1   p. 185
   Broad layer of enamel over body whorl; aperture with yellow callus.
7. **Mitrella ocellata** ×1½   p. 183
   See text.
8. **Mitrella millepunctata** ×3   p. 183
   See text.
9. **Strombina gibberula** ×1   p. 184
   Swollen base; sharp apex; gray.
10. **Strombina maculosa** ×1   p. 184
    High-spired; knobby shoulders; blotched with brown.
11. **Strombina recurva** ×1   p. 184
    Knobby shoulders; ridge within lip; yellowish brown.
12. **Latirus ceratus** ×½   p. 188
    Elongate, fusiform; blunt knobs at shoulders; brown.
13. **Latirus mediamericanus** ×⅔   p. 189
    Sturdy; vertical folds, revolving lines.
14. **Lyria cumingi** ×1   p. 195
    Stout; pointed apex; inner lip plicate; pinkish gray.
15. **Melongena patula** ×⅓   p. 188
    Large, heavy; wide aperture; strong periostracum; brown.
16. **Harpa crenata** ×1   p. 194
    Aperture flaring; pinkish with squarish spots of purplish brown; polished.
17. **Fusinus felipensis** ×1   p. 190
    Spindle-shaped; weak vertical folds; grayish brown.
18. **Fusinus ambustus** ×1   p. 189
    Whorls slightly shouldered; vertical folds; yellowish brown.
19. **Fusinus cinereus** ×1   p. 189
    Squarish vertical folds; canal short; dull grayish.
20. **Pleuroploca princeps** ×¼ (with operculum)   p. 188
    Massive; strong periostracum; tough, leathery operculum; brown.
21. **Fusinus dupetitthouarsi** ×1   p. 190
    Tall spire, long canal; whorls angled at periphery; yellowish brown.

Plate 60

GULF OF CALIFORNIA OLIVE SHELLS, MITERS, AND OTHERS

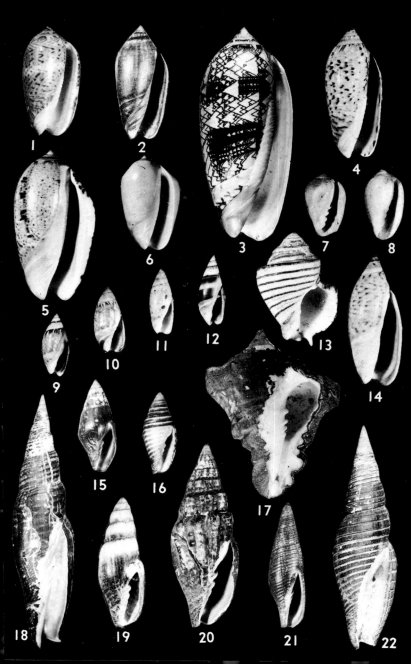

Plate 61

GULF OF CALIFORNIA NUTMEGS, SLIT SHELLS, AND AUGERS

1. **Cancellaria urceolata** ×1   p. 196
   Solid; cancellate sculpture; creamy white to pale brown.
2. **Cancellaria cassidiformis** ×1   p. 195
   Low spire; cancellate sculpture; pale yellow.
3. **Cancellaria obesa** ×1   p. 196
   Heavy; inner lip reflected; yellowish white.
4. **Cancellaria pulchra** ×1   p. 196
   Stubby, solid; wavy revolving lines; yellowish orange.
5. **Cancellaria clavatula** ×1   p. 196
   High-spired; cancellate sculpture; yellowish brown.
6. **Clavus aeolius** ×2   p. 202
   Small, shiny; impressed sutures; pale brown.
7. **Crassispira nymphia** ×1   p. 203
   Slender; brown with spiral of white beads.
8. **Crassispira aterrima** ×1   p. 202
   Small; revolving flattish ribs; lip deeply notched; brown.
9. **Crassispira collaris** ×2   p. 203
   Fusiform; revolving elongate beads; dark brown.
10. **Trigonostoma bullatum** ×1   p. 197
    Loosely coiled; flat-topped whorls; yellowish brown.
11. **Hormospira maculosa** ×1   p. 203
    Elongate; knobs at periphery; blotched with chestnut-brown.
12. **Crassispira martinensis** ×1   p. 203
    Fusiform; strong revolving lines; brownish.
13. **Pseudomelatoma pencillata** ×1   p. 204
    Strong vertical ribs; beads at suture; brown.
14. **Crassispira bottae** ×⅔   p. 202
    Sturdy; spiral ridge at suture; aperture notched above; brown.
15. **Knefastia funiculata** ×1   p. 202
    Slit in lip, smooth within; brown to yellowish brown.
16. **Knefastia dalli** ×1   p. 201
    Solid; slit in lip; yellowish brown.
17. Slit in outer lip of *Knefastia* ×3
18. **Pleuroliria picta** ×1   p. 203
    High-spired; slit in lip; canal long; white, spotted.
19. **Terebra strigata** ×1   p. 201
    Spikelike; vertical streaks of chestnut-brown.
20. **Terebra hindsi** ×1   HINDS' AUGER   p. 200
    Small knobs at shoulder; twisted inner lip; gray.
21. **Terebra variegata** ×1   VARIEGATED AUGER   p. 201
    Beads at suture; vertical brown lines below; inner lip strongly twisted.
22. **Hastula luctuosa** ×1   p. 201
    Slender, shiny; weak sutures; purplish brown.
23. **Terebra robusta** ×1   ROBUST AUGER   p. 200
    Broken vertical streaks; sutures distinct; yellowish brown.

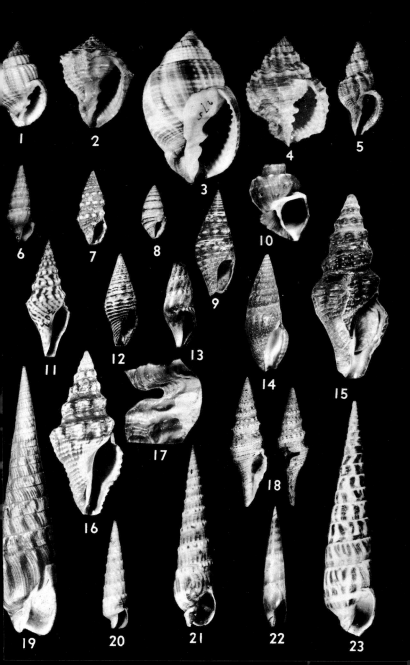

Plate 62

GULF OF CALIFORNIA CONES AND OTHERS

1. **Conus princeps** ×1   PRINCELY CONE   p. 199
   Irregular vertical lines on yellowish-brown background.

2. **Conus princeps lineolatus** ×1   p. 199
   See Remarks under *C. princeps* text.

3. **Conus dalli** ×⅔   DALL'S CONE   p. 198
   Elevated spire; zigzag markings enclose white triangles.

4. **Conus regularis** ×⅔   REGULAR CONE   p. 199
   Pointed apex; moderately slender; orange-brown blotches.

5. **Conus lucidus** ×½   SPIDERWEB CONE   p. 198
   Pale lavender, with hairlike lines.

6. **Conus vittatus** ×½   RIBBONED CONE   p. 200
   Low spire; pointed apex; central band of brown and white.

7. **Conus virgatus** ×⅔   p. 199
   Slender; pointed apex; wavy, vertical brown bands.

8. **Conus nux** ×1   NUT CONE   p. 198
   Small, flat-topped; variously mottled.

9. **Conus gladiator** ×1   GLADIATOR CONE   p. 198
   Sturdy; low spire; white band on body whorl.

10. **Conus ximenes** ×1   INTERRUPTED CONE   p. 200
    Spire elevated; encircling rows of purplish dots.

11. **Conus ximenes mahogani** ×1   p. 200
    See Remarks under *C. ximenes* text.

12. **Conus perplexus** ×1   PUZZLING CONE   p. 199
    Small, sturdy; tiny revolving dots; gray or pinkish.

13. **Conus brunneus** ×⅔   BROWN CONE   p. 197
    Sturdy; low spire; brown, spire blotched with white.

14. **Conus purpurascens** ×1   PURPLE CONE   p. 199
    (with operculum)
    Sturdy; violet-gray, clouded with darker.

15. **Conus patricius** ×½   PATRICIAN CONE   p. 198
    Large, flat-topped; heavy periostracum; immature are yellowish to orange; adults white.

16. **Bulla punctulata** ×1   p. 204
    Aperture flaring at base; surface pinkish gray, mottled.

17. **Dolabella californica** ×⅔   p. 205
    See text.

18. **Siphonaria maura** ×1   p. 204
    Limpet-like; radiating ridges; gray, mottled.

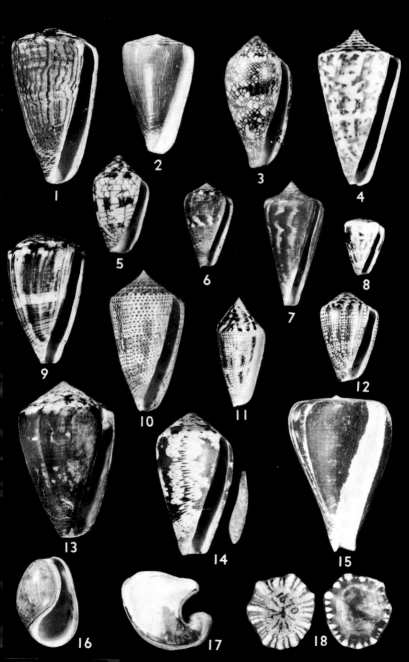

Plate 63

HAWAIIAN ARK SHELLS, MUSSELS, AND OTHERS

1. **Acar hawaiensis** ×1   RETICULATE ARK   p. 206
   Elongate-squarish; cross-barred pattern; yellowish white.

2. **Arca ventricosa** ×½   VENTRICOSE ARK   p. 206
   Elongate; broad hinge area; gaping base; yellowish brown.

3. **Arca kauaia** ×1   p. 206
   Small, thin; indented posterior end; yellowish gray.

4. **Barbatia hawaia** ×1   p. 207
   Oval, inflated; surface cancellate; white.

5. **Glycymeris diomedea** ×1   BUTTON SHELL   p. 207
   Radiating grooves; curving row of teeth; yellowish white,
   blotched.

6. **Barbatia oahua** ×1   p. 207
   Oval, compressed; beaks low; white.

7. **Musculus aviarius** ×2   p. 208
   Radiating lines on ends; yellowish-brown periostracum.

8. **Modiolus matris** ×½   SMOOTH MUSSEL   p. 208
   Short anterior end; small beaks; yellowish brown.

9. **Septifer rudis** ×1   PLATFORM MUSSEL   p. 207
   Wrinkled radiating lines; platform under beaks; almost black.

10. **Brachidontes crebristriatus** ×1   STRIATE MUSSEL   p. 208
    Bent appearance; fine radiating lines; purplish gray.

11. **Spondylus sparsispinosus** ×⅓   p. 211
    WEAK-SPINY OYSTER
    Roundish; equal wings; a few spines; reddish brown.

12. **Pinna semicostata** ×⅓   COSTATE PEN   p. 210
    Thin, elongate; weak folds; yellowish tan.

13. **Atrina nuttalli** ×¼   BENT PEN   p. 210
    Stout and somewhat twisted; weak folds; yellowish tan.

14. **Spondylus hawaiensis** ×⅓   p. 211
    HAWAIIAN SPINY OYSTER
    Ponderous, porcelaneous; interlocking hinge; whitish.

Plate 64

HAWAIIAN SCALLOPS, JEWEL BOXES, AND OTHERS

1. **Isognomon incisum** $\times\frac{1}{2}$ p. 209
   Thin, pearly inside; vertical grooves in hinge; purplish brown.

2. **Isognomon costellatum** $\times\frac{1}{2}$ p. 208
   COSTELLATE PURSE SHELL
   Radiating lines; vertical grooves in hinge; yellowish gray.

3. **Pteria nebulosa** $\times\frac{1}{2}$ LITTLE PEARL OYSTER   p. 209
   Thin, with radiating bands; pearly within.

4. **Anomia nobilis** $\times\frac{1}{2}$ JINGLE SHELL   p. 212
   Waxy luster; lower valve perforated; golden yellow.

5. **Nodipecten langfordi** $\times\frac{1}{2}$ LANGFORD'S SCALLOP   p. 211
   Broad ribs, knobby; usually reddish.

6. **Haumea juddi** $\times 1$ JUDD'S SCALLOP   p. 210
   Round; small wings; coarse ribs; white, mottled.

7. **Rocellaria hawaiensis** $\times 1$ p. 218
   Oval; widely gaping; thin-shelled; yellowish white.

8. **Chlamys cookei** $\times 1$ COOKE'S SCALLOP   p. 210
   Wings unequal; fine ribs; yellowish to orange.

9. **Ostrea sandwichensis** $\times 1$ HAWAIIAN OYSTER   p. 212
   Irregular, wavy surface; yellowish gray.

10. **Chama hendersoni** $\times 1$ p. 214
    HENDERSON'S JEWEL BOX
    Small, often twisted; scaly ribs; whitish.

11. **Chama iostoma** $\times 1$ p. 214
    VIOLET-MOUTHED JEWEL BOX
    Valves solid, unequal; interior with violet border.

12. **Crassostrea gigas** $\times\frac{1}{3}$ JAPANESE OYSTER   p. 212
    Irregular in growth, commonly elongate; gray.

13. **Pinctada galtsoffi** $\times\frac{1}{3}$ p. 209
    BLACK-LIPPED PEARL OYSTER
    Heavy and solid; pearly interior; large muscle scar.

Plate 65

HAWAIIAN COCKLES, TELLINS, AND OTHERS

1. **Arcinella thaanumi** ×2   THAANUM'S ARCINELLA   p. 213
   Short anterior; swollen posterior; radiating ribs; yellowish gray.

2. **Fragum thurstoni** ×1   BLUNT COCKLE   p. 215
   Small; posterior truncate; yellowish white.

3. **Trachycardium hawaiensis** ×½   p. 214
   HAWAIIAN COCKLE
   Oval; radiating ribs, thorny on posterior; yellowish white.

4. **Codakia thaanumi** ×1   RIBBED SAUCER SHELL   p. 213
   Orbicular; well-spaced radiating grooves; white.

5. **Anodontia hawaiensis** ×2   p. 213
   Roundish, inflated; smooth; white or yellowish white.

6. **Ctena bella** ×1   RETICULATE SAUCER SHELL   p. 213
   Orbicular; sharp radiating and concentric lines; white or yellowish.

7. **Meretrix meretrix** ×1   p. 216
   Triangular, swollen; smooth and polished; yellowish gray.

8. **Periglypta edmondsoni** ×1   RETICULATE VENUS   p. 215
   Strong and solid; wavy reticulate pattern; yellowish gray.

9. **Lioconcha hieroglyphica** ×1   p. 216
   HIEROGLYPHIC VENUS
   Inflated; white, with brown scrawls.

10. **Trapezium californicum** ×⅔   p. 215
    Elongate; very short anterior; weak posterior ridge; yellowish white.

11. **Tellina obliquilineata** ×1   p. 217
    Short anterior; smooth and polished; white, with rose rays.

12. **Tellina dispar** ×1   WHITE TELLIN   p. 217
    Oval, thin; shiny white.

13. **Tapes japonica** ×1   JAPANESE LITTLENECK   p. 216
    Strong and solid; broad spotted bands; yellowish gray.

14. **Tellina crassiplicata** ×1   SUNSET TELLIN   p. 216
    Yellowish, with pink radiating rays.

15. **Tellina palatam** ×1   ROUGH TELLIN   p. 217
    Rounded anterior, pointed posterior; wrinkled concentric lines; yellowish white.

16. **Tellina venusta** ×1   LONG TELLIN   p. 217
    Elongate; strong posterior ridge; polished; white.

17. **Tellina elizabethae** ×1   RASP TELLIN   p. 217
    Scaly surface; moderately solid; pale yellow.

Plate 66

HAWAIIAN LIMPETS, NERITES, AND OTHERS

1. **Cellana exarata** ×1   BLACK LIMPET   p. 219
   Black; strong radiating grooves.
2. **Diodora granifera** ×1   p. 219
   LITTLE KEYHOLE LIMPET
   Small, well arched; perforation at summit; whitish.
3. **Cellana argentata** ×1   KNEECAP SHELL   p. 219
   Large, roundish; slightly arched; shiny within; brown.
4. **Turbo intercostalis** ×1   GREEN TURBAN   p. 220
   Sturdy; round aperture; shelly operculum; greenish gray.
5. **Operculum of** *Turbo intercostalis* ×1
6. **Trochus intextus** ×1   HAWAIIAN TOP   p. 220
   Sloping sides; beaded lines; pinkish white.
7. **Nerita picea** ×1   COMMON NERITE   p. 221
   Inner lip weakly toothed; fine revolving lines; black flecked.
8. **Nerita plicata** ×1   PLICATE NERITE   p. 221
   Strong revolving ribs; toothed inner lip; yellowish white.
9. **Nerita polita** ×1   POLISHED NERITE   p. 221
   Color variable; polished.
10. **Janthina janthina** ×½   VIOLET SNAIL   p. 226
    Pale violet above, purple below.
11. **Janthina globosa** ×½   ROUND VIOLET SNAIL   p. 226
    Globose, thin; pale lavender.
12. **Epitonium lamellosum** ×1   p. 225
    BANDED WENTLETRAP
    Graceful, polished; prominent thin varices; white.
13. **Balcis aciculata** ×3   NEEDLE BALCIS   p. 253
    Sloping sides; sutures indistinct; polished white.
14. **Balcis peasei** ×3   PEASE'S BALCIS   p. 253
    Spire curved; sutures weak; polished; white.
15. **Balcis cumingi** ×2   CUMING'S BALCIS   p. 253
    Larger than No. 14; sutures better defined; polished; white.
16. **Eulima metcalfi** ×2   MOTTLED EULIMA   p. 253
    Buffy yellow or gray, streaked with brown; polished.
17. **Neritina tahitensis** ×1   TAHITIAN NERITE   p. 222
    Thin white plate under beak; moderate wings.
18. **Hipponix pilosus** ×1   HOOF SHELL   p. 226
    Cap-shaped; white; fibrous periostracum.
19. **Pyramidella terebellum** ×1   p. 254
    RINGED PYRAMIDELLA
    Yellowish white; ringed with chocolate; polished.
20. **Pyramidella sulcata** ×1   p. 254
    SULCATE PYRAMIDELLA
    Impressed sutures; mottled, polished; white.
21. **Neritina cariosa** ×1   WINGED NERITE   p. 221
    Black or dark brown, white inside; winged at each end of beak area.
22. **Neritina granosa** ×1   BLACK NERITE   p. 222
    Surface tuberculate; black exterior; *freshwater*.

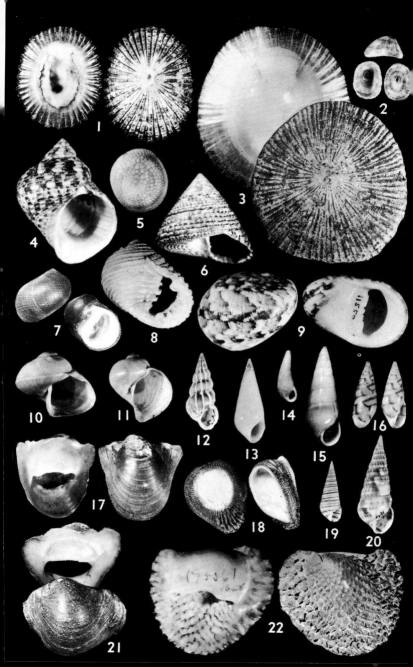

Plate 67

HAWAIIAN MOON SHELLS, STROMBS, AND OTHERS

1. **Natica marochiensis** ×1   MOON SHELL   p. 228
   Bulbous; banded; shelly operculum; color variable.
2. **Polinices melanostoma** ×1   p. 228
   BLACK-MOUTHED MOON SHELL
   Thin-shelled; brown stain at umbilicus; horny operculum.
3. **Polinices pyriformis** ×1   WHITE MOON SHELL   p. 228
   Solid; large callus over umbilicus; polished white.
4. **Modulus tectum** ×1   KNOBBY SNAIL   p. 223
   Rugged; large aperture; folds at shoulder; whitish.
5. **Littorina picta** ×1   PAINTED PERIWINKLE   p. 222
   Spotted or marbled with white; aperture purplish.
6. **Littorina pintado** ×1   DOTTED PERIWINKLE   p. 222
   Smooth; weak sutures; brown-dotted surface.
7. **Architectonica perspectiva** ×1   SUNDIAL   p. 223
   Round, flattish; umbilicus large and crenulate; yellowish gray.
8. **Littorina scabra** ×1   VARIEGATED PERIWINKLE   p. 222
   Thin-shelled; mottled surface; varied color.
9. **Torinia variegata** ×1   VARIEGATED SUNDIAL   p. 223
   Round, flattish; deep umbilicus; mottled.
10. **Crucibulum spinosum** ×½   CUP-AND-SAUCER LIMPET   p. 226
    Cuplike structure within; yellowish white, flecked with brown.
11. **Crepidula aculeata** ×½   PRICKLY SLIPPER SHELL   p. 226
    Flattish; exterior prickly; yellowish or grayish brown.
12. **Triphora incisus** ×3   p. 225
    Revolving lines; left-handed; yellowish, mottled.
13. **Triphora pallidus** ×3   p. 225
    Beaded lines; left-handed; white.
14. **Cerithium nesioticum** ×1   ISLAND HORN SHELL   p. 224
    Whorls flattish; sutures weak; whitish.
15. **Cerithium baeticum** ×1   BANDED HORN SHELL   p. 224
    Banded with chocolate-brown; beaded surface.
16. **Cerithium nassoides** ×2   SPOTTED HORN SHELL   p. 224
    Sutures weak; clouded or spotted with brown.
17. **Cerithium obeliscus** ×1   OBELISK HORN SHELL   p. 224
    Beaded shoulders; twisted canal; yellowish white, spotted.
18. **Cerithium thaanumi** ×2   THAANUM'S HORN SHELL   p. 225
    Sutures indented; beaded surface; whitish.
19. **Cerithium columna** ×1   COLUMNAR HORN SHELL   p. 224
    Knobby whorls; small aperture; grayish white.
20. **Thais intermedia** ×1   INTERMEDIATE THAIS   p. 239
    Large aperture; blunt encircling nodes; yellowish white, mottled.
21. **Thais aperta** ×1   WIDE-MOUTHED THAIS   p. 239
    Flat spire; wide aperture; broad inner lip; white.
22. **Thais harpa** ×1   HARP THAIS   p. 239
    Small; aperture stained brown.
23. **Strombus dentatus** ×1   TOOTHED STROMB   p. 227
    Outer lip with teeth at base; yellowish.
24. **Strombus maculatus** ×1   SPOTTED STROMB   p. 227
    Small, spotted; short spire; creamy white.
25. **Strombus helli** ×1   HELL'S STROMB   p. 227
    Small but solid; vertical ridges; surface smooth; yellowish.
26. **Strombus fragilis** ×1   FRAGILE STROMB   p. 227
    Thin-shelled; aperture narrow; surface smooth; yellowish.
27. **Strombus hawaiensis** ×½   HAWAIIAN STROMB   p. 227
    Large and solid; outer lip expanded and thickened; yellowish white.

Plate 68

HAWAIIAN COWRIES AND SEA BUTTONS

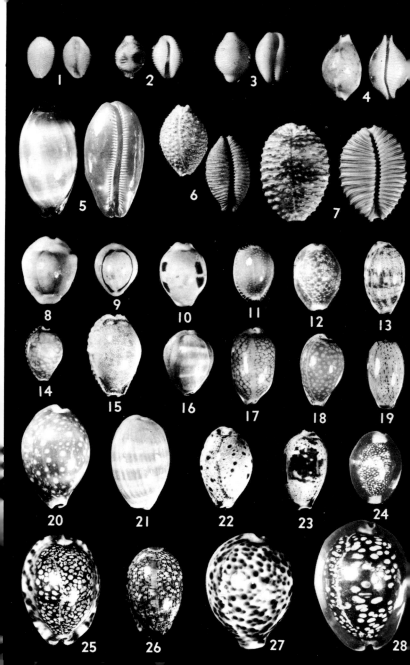

Plate 69

HAWAIIAN TRITONS, HELMETS, AND OTHERS

1. **Bursa affinis** ×1 FROG SHELL   p. 236
   Revolving beaded lines; notched aperture; yellowish brown.
2. **Cymatium nicobaricum** ×½   p. 235
   ORANGE-MOUTHED TRITON
   Rugged; thick varices; orange aperture.
3. **Cymatium muricinum** ×1   p. 235
   WHITE-MOUTHED TRITON
   Toothed outer lip; closed canal; white aperture.
4. **Bursa siphonata** ×1 SPOUTED TRITON   p. 237
   Stubby, solid; toothed aperture; whitish.
5. **Bursa bufonia** ×½ TOAD SHELL   p. 237
   Strong varices; notch at top of aperture; grayish white.
6. **Colubraria distorta** ×½ CROOKED SHELL   p. 237
   Varices in continuous line; spire curved; yellowish brown.
7. **Charonia tritonis** ×¼ TRUMPET SHELL   p. 236
   Large; weaker varices than No. 6; last whorl swollen; variegated color.
8. **Cymatium gemmatum** ×1 GEM TRITON   p. 235
   Outer lip thickened; both lips toothed; yellowish white.
9. **Cymatium pileare** ×½ HAIRY TRITON   p. 236
   Rugged; strong varices; shaggy periostracum; yellowish white,
   barred.
10. **Coralliophila madreporarum** ×1   p. 239
    Large flaring aperture; purple within.
11. **Distorsio anus** ×½ WARPED SHELL   p. 237
    Constricted aperture; granular area on columella; yellowish
    white, banded.
12. **Coralliophila neritoidea** ×1   p. 239
    Large aperture; purple within.
13. **Cymatium rubeculum** ×1 RED TRITON   p. 236
    Varices banded; aperture toothed; yellow to orange-red.
14. **Tonna olearium** ×⅓ TUN SHELL   p. 238
    Globose, thin-shelled; weak revolving lines; yellowish brown.
15. **Coralliophila deformis** ×1   p. 238
    Stout, rugged; deep umbilicus; chalky white.
16. **Phalium fortisulcata** ×½ GROOVED HELMET   p. 234
    Inner lip strongly reflected; revolving ribs; creamy white.
17. **Malea pomum** ×½ APPLE TUN SHELL   p. 238
    Solid; strong revolving ribs; excavation at base; creamy white.
18. **Phalium vibex** ×½ WHITE HELMET   p. 235
    Smooth, polished; dark brown checks on back of outer lip.
19. **Cassis cornuta** ×¼ HORNED HELMET   p. 234
    Ponderous; blunt spines; polished yellowish-orange base.
20. **Tonna perdix** ×⅓ PARTRIDGE SHELL   p. 238
    Wide aperture, short spire; heavily mottled; pale to rich
    brown.

Plate 70

HAWAIIAN DRUPES, MITERS, AND OTHERS

Plate 71

HAWAIIAN CONES

1. **Conus catus** ×⅔ CAT CONE   p. 247
   Small; revolving grooves; bluish gray, with brown patches.
2. **Conus lithoglyphus** ×⅔ PEBBLE CARVED CONE p. 248
   Checkered shoulders and central band; olive-brown.
3. **Conus flavidus** ×½ YELLOW-TINGED CONE   p. 247
   Pale bluish-gray central band; smooth spire.
4. **Conus sponsalis** ×½   p. 250
   Small but solid; shoulders tuberculated; bluish white.
5. **Conus pennaceus** ×⅓ PEARLED CONE   p. 249
   Moderate spire; orange-brown, with paler triangles.
6. **Conus obscurus** ×1 OBSCURE CONE   p. 249
   Thin-shelled; aperture wide at base; yellowish brown.
7. **Conus abbreviatus** ×1 ABBREVIATED CONE   p. 246
   Short and squat; revolving dots; bluish gray.
8. **Conus chaldeus** ×⅔ WORM CONE   p. 247
   Surface with vertical grooves; chiefly black.
9. **Conus pulicarius** ×½ FLEA-BITTEN CONE   p. 249
   Heavily spotted; knobby shoulders; white.
10. **Conus lividus** ×½ SPITEFUL CONE   p. 248
    Spire low; shoulders knobby; olive-tan.
11. **Conus miles** ×⅓ SOLDIER CONE   p. 248
    Large and heavy; thin vertical lines; yellowish brown.
12. **Conus rattus** ×½ RAT CONE   p. 250
    Smooth shoulders; flattish top; yellowish brown.
13. **Conus vexillum** ×¼ FLAG CONE   p. 250
    Heavy; blotched at shoulders and center of body whorl;
    chestnut-brown.
14. **Conus quercinus** ×¼ OAK CONE   p. 249
    Smooth, lemon-yellow to white; pointed spire.
15. **Conus distans** ×¼ KNOBBY-TOP CONE   p. 247
    Shoulders with small knobs; yellowish gray.
16. **Conus tessulatus** ×½ TESSULATE CONE   p. 250
    Encircling orange spots.
17. **Conus vitulinus** ×½ CALF CONE   p. 251
    Low spire; encircling band; olive-tan.
18. **Conus textile** ×⅓ CLOTH-OF-GOLD CONE   p. 250
    Well-developed spire; weblike markings; yellowish brown.
19. **Conus ebraeus** ×1 HEBREW CONE   p. 247
    Banded with heavy black blotches.
20. **Conus marmoreus** ×⅓ MARBLED CONE   p. 248
    Low spire; dark brown, with whitish or pinkish triangles.
21. **Conus imperialis** ×⅓ IMPERIAL CONE   p. 248
    Knobby shoulders, low spire; light brownish bands.
22. **Conus nussatella** ×⅔ SLENDER CONE   p. 249
    Cylindrical; moderate spire; yellowish white.
23. **Conus leopardus** ×¼ MANY-SPOTTED CONE   p. 248
    Large, heavy; flat-topped; revolving spots; creamy white.
24. **Conus striatus** ×⅓ STRIATE CONE   p. 250
    Large, heavy; weak striations; pinkish white.

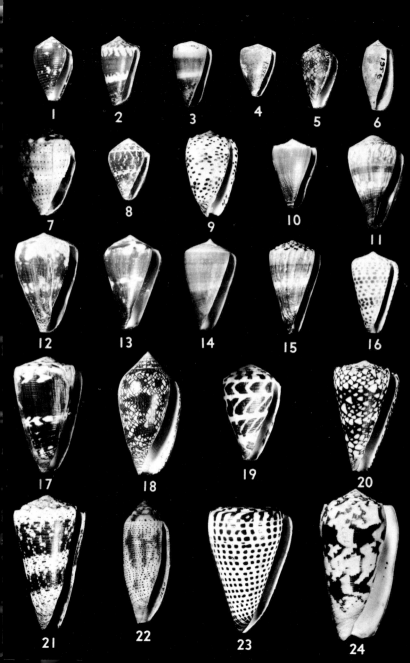

Plate 72

HAWAIIAN AUGERS, BUBBLE SHELLS, AND OTHERS

1. **Terebra crenulata** ×⅔ CRENULATE AUGER   p. 251
   Wrinkles at shoulders; encircling dots; cream-colored.

2. **Terebra dimidiata** ×⅔ DIVIDED AUGER   p. 251
   Impressed spiral line below suture; white streaks.

3. **Terebra felina** ×1 TIGER AUGER   p. 251
   Stout, smooth; encircling dots; pale gray or white.

4. **Terebra nitida** ×1 SHINING AUGER   p. 252
   Slender; vertical folds; yellowish gray.

5. **Terebra strigilata** ×1 PAINTED AUGER   p. 252
   Weak vertical grooves; yellowish gray, spotted band at suture.

6. **Terebra guttata** ×⅔ EYED AUGER   p. 252
   Large white spots on orange-brown background.

7. **Terebra maculata** ×½ BIG AUGER   p. 252
   Heavy, porcelaneous; vertical purplish streaks.

8. **Terebra gouldi** ×1 GOULD'S AUGER   p. 251
   Narrow vertical ribs; distinct sutures; yellowish white.

9. **Terebra subulata** ×⅔ SPOTTED AUGER   p. 252
   Slender; large chocolate spots.

10. **Bulla peasiana** ×1 BUBBLE SHELL   p. 254
    Cylindrical; mottled; white lips.

11. **Atys semistriata** ×2 STRIATE BUBBLE   p. 255
    Small; yellowish white; aperture longer than shell.

12. **Haminoea crocata** ×2 PAPER BUBBLE   p. 255
    Small, oval; translucent.

13. **Hydatina albocincta** ×1 CLOWN BUBBLE   p. 255
    Broad tan and white bands.

14. **Hydatina amplustre** ×1 PINK BUBBLE   p. 255
    Pink; brown and white bands.

15. **Melampus semiplicata** ×1   p. 257
    Dull brown; inner lip plicate.

16. **Hydatina physis** ×1 STRIPED BUBBLE   p. 256
    Wide aperture; revolving thin lines; yellowish gray.

17. **Umbraculum sinicum** ×1 UMBRELLA SHELL   p. 256
    Oval, flat; white; interior with dark brown center.

18. **Siphonaria normalis** ×1 FALSE LIMPET   p. 256
    Limpet-like; radiating ribs; marginal groove; dark gray.

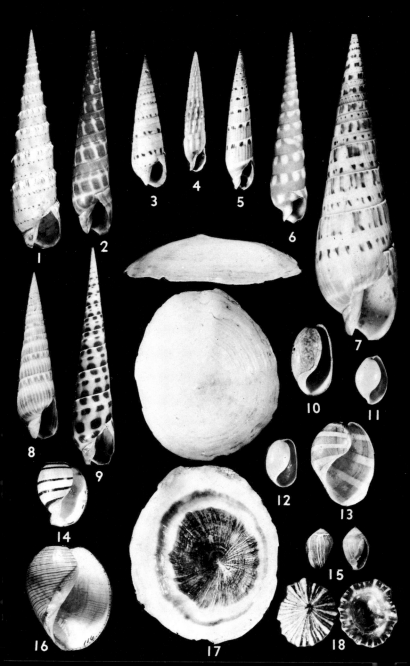

Family Mytilidae: Mussels

(see p. 7)

Genus *Choromytilus* Soot-Ryen 1952

CHOROMYTILUS PALLIOPUNCTATUS (Carp.)   Pl. 46
Range: Baja California to Panama.
Habitat: Shallow water.
Description: A fair-sized mussel some 3 in. long. Beaks at the
apex of a long triangle. Anterior margin more or less straight,
posterior margin rounded. Surface smooth, purplish blue, with
a shiny periostracum. Inside, the shell is deep purple with a
series of tiny dimples along the ventral side.

Genus *Mytella* Soot-Ryen 1955

MYTELLA GUYANENSIS (Lam.)   Pl. 46
Range: Southern end of Gulf of California south.
Habitat: Shallow water.
Description: A neat shell some 2 in. long. Anterior end rounded
and short, the posterior long and very broadly rounded. Beaks
rather low. The sculpture consists of prominent concentric lines.
The color varies from green to nearly black. Interior white.

MYTELLA SPECIOSA (Reeve)   Pl. 46
Range: Baja California to Ecuador.
Habitat: Shallow water.
Description: A thinner, more elongate shell than *M. guyanensis*
(above), its length about 2 in. A rather weak ridge extends from
the beaks to the posterior tip, producing a slight slope at that
end. Color greenish yellow.

Genus *Septifer* Récluz 1848

SEPTIFER ZETEKI Hert. & Strong   **Platform Mussel**   Pl. 46
Range: Baja California to Ecuador.
Habitat: Shallow water.
Description: Small and triangular, the shell nearly all posterior
end. Length about $\frac{1}{2}$ in. Surface with fine radiating lines.
Color greenish gray. Inside purplish brown, the dorsal margin
with a toothlike edge, and there is a small platform under
the beaks.

Genus *Lithophaga* Röding 1798

LITHOPHAGA ATTENUATA (Desh.)   **Date Shell**   Pl. 46
Range: Gulf of California.
Habitat: Moderately shallow water; bores in rocks.

Description: This shell attains a length of about 2½ in. Shell thin, elongate, cylindrical, and brownish. It does bear a striking resemblance to the seed of a date. Beaks low and insignificant, the hinge without teeth.

Remarks: These bivalves bore into rocks and masses of coral.

Family Pteriidae: Pearl Oysters
(see p. 12)

Genus *Pinctada* Röding 1798

PINCTADA MAZATLANICA (Han.)   **Pearl Oyster**   **Pl. 45**
   Range: Gulf of California to Peru.
   Habitat: Moderately shallow water.
   Description: A disklike shell of about 6-in. diam. The valves are flattened and nearly equal in size, and there is a byssal notch in the lower valve. Exterior bears scaly concentric ridges, sometimes very rough near the margins. Color greenish brown. Interior very pearly, with a gray to black border at the margins.
   Remarks: This is one of the valuable "pearl oysters," and in the past it was gathered extensively for the trade.

Family Pinnidae: Pen Shells
(see p. 13)

Genus *Pinna* Linné 1758

PINNA RUGOSA Sow.   **Pl. 44**
   Range: Gulf of California to Panama.
   Habitat: Mudflats.
   Description: A large specimen of this pen shell measures in length close to 20 in. Shell elongate-triangular, thin and brittle, and semitransparent when young. Adults are yellowish brown to nearly black. Valves bear radiating folds adorned with large hollow spines toward the margin.
   Remarks: In the genus *Pinna* there is a narrow groove down the center on the inside, separating the iridescent portion into 2 lobes. In the genus *Atrina* (below), this groove is absent, and the iridescent part is undivided.

Genus *Atrina* Gray 1847

ATRINA MAURA (Sow.)   **Pl. 44**
   Range: Gulf of California to Peru.
   Habitat: Mudflats.
   Description: Somewhat curved, growing to a length of about

12 in. There are several rows of broad but sharp spines, with the upper portion of the shell smooth. Color varies from dark brown to black.

ATRINA TUBERCULOSA (Sow.) **Pl. 44**
 Range: Gulf of California to Panama.
 Habitat: Mudflats.
 Description: Some 8 to 10 in. long. Dorsal margin straight, ventral margin rounded, and the posterior margin gapes. Valves decorated with about 12 rounded ribs that fade near the beaks; highly elevated tubular spines are present on the ribs, particularly near the margins. Color dark brown.
 Remarks: Occasional black pearls — of little value — are found under the mantle of this and other pen shells.

Family Pectinidae: Scallops

(see p. 13)

Genus *Pecten* Müller 1776

PECTEN VOGDESI Arn. **Pl. 43**
 Range: Gulf of California to Peru.
 Habitat: Shallow water.
 Description: About 3 in. long, the height about the same. Lower valve deeply cupped and sculptured with strong, rounded, radiating ribs; upper valve flat, sometimes a little concave, decorated with flat ribs, the wide spaces between them checked by fine lines. Arched valve buffy yellow, flat one reddish brown.
 Remarks: This scallop has been listed under several different names, including *P. cataractes* Dall, *P. dentatus* Sow., and *P. excavatus* Turt.

Genus *Aequipecten* Fischer 1886

AEQUIPECTEN CIRCULARIS (Sow.) **Pl. 43**
 Range: Gulf of California to Peru.
 Habitat: Shallow water.
 Description: This scallop is considerably inflated and presents a globose appearance. There are about 20 strong but smooth ribs, and the wings (ears) are nearly equal in size. Colors variable, but in general this bivalve is very brightly hued. Various shades of white and cream are overlain with blotches and mottlings of rich purples and browns, and sometimes orange or yellow.

AEQUIPECTEN TUMBEZENSIS (Orb.) **Pl. 43**
 Range: Gulf of California to Peru.
 Habitat: Moderately shallow water.
 Description: A neat shell, the length just over 1 in. There are

about 15 rounded ribs, the spaces between them rather wide. Valves moderately inflated, the ears unequal. Color gray to nearly black, more or less mottled, and covered with tiny whitish dots; upper valve lighter in tone.

Genus *Lyropecten* Conrad 1862

LYROPECTEN SUBNODOSUS (Sow.)   Pl. 43
  Range: Gulf of California to Ecuador.
  Habitat: Moderately deep water.
  Description: A large and sturdy shell, the largest scallop of the region; length about 6 in. There are approximately 12 broadly rounded ribs, some of them bearing large knobs, and the ribs as well as the grooves between them are marked by sharp lines. Color varies from pinkish white to reddish purple, usually with fine purple lines radiating from the beaks.

Family Limidae: File Shells
(see p. 16)

Genus *Lima* Bruguière 1797

LIMA PACIFICA Orb.   Pl. 43
  Range: Gulf of California to Peru.
  Habitat: Moderately shallow water.
  Description: Rather high and narrow, moderately inflated, about 1 in. long. Surface with fine and crowded radiating lines, the hinge short, with a deep triangular pit for the ligament. Color white.

LIMA TETRICA Gould   Pl. 43
  Range: Gulf of California to S. America.
  Habitat: Moderately shallow water.
  Description: A larger and sturdier shell than *L. pacifica* (above), and much coarser in appearance. Its height is about 2 in. and, like most of this group, the color is white. There are a number of strong ribs, with deep channels between them; the ribs become scaly toward the margins.

Family Spondylidae: Spiny Oysters

THESE bivalves are attached to some object by their right valves. The surface is ribbed or spiny, and the hinge consists of 2 interlocking teeth in each valve. Many specimens are brightly colored. They are confined to warm seas.

Genus *Spondylus* Linné 1758

SPONDYLUS CALCIFER Carp.   **Pl. 45**
Range: Gulf of California to Ecuador.
Habitat: Moderately deep water.
Description: A heavy, ponderous, roundly oval shell 6 or 7 in.
long. The valves are thick and sturdy, well inflated, joined at
the hinge by interlocking teeth, and are so well secured that in
most cases it is impossible to separate the valves without break-
ing the teeth. Surface with radiating lines set with short spines,
but in old individuals there is little sculpture to be seen. Color
pinkish red, young specimens showing paler radiating bands;
inside white, with a wide border of reddish purple.

SPONDYLUS PRINCEPS Brod.   **Pls. 5, 45**
Range: Gulf of California to Ecuador.
Habitat: Moderately deep water.
Description: Diam. about 6 in. This shell is built like *S. calcifer*
(above) but is usually decorated with long curving spines. Colors
range from pure white to orange or red, making this a most
attractive shell in collections. Interior white, with a red border.
Remarks: This has been called *S. crassisquama* Lam. and *S.
pictorum* Chem. Its counterpart in the Gulf of Mexico is *S.
americanus* Lam. These clams live attached to corals and rocks.

Family Ostreidae: Oysters

(see p. 17)

Genus *Ostrea* Linné 1758

OSTREA FISHERI Dall   Fisher's Oyster   **Pl. 45**
Range: Gulf of California to Peru.
Habitat: Shallow water.
Description: Large and heavy, some 6 to 8 in. long. Shape oval,
hinge line rather short. Surface rough and irregular, usually a
few folds showing at the margin. Color gray, interior brownish
purple, occasionally white.

OSTREA MEGODON Han.   **Pl. 44**
Range: Gulf of California to Peru.
Habitat: Shallow water.
Description: An oddly shaped bivalve, elongate and curved,
length 3 or 4 in. Margins of valves deeply folded, usually with
about 4 folds, which fit neatly into plications in the opposing
valve. Color grayish; interior soiled white, tinged with greenish
along the margins.

OSTREA PALMULA Carp.   Pl. 45
   Range: Gulf of California to Peru.
   Habitat: Shallow water.
   Description: Lower valve cupped, upper rather flat. Length
   usually less than 3 in. Both valves with plicate margins, sometimes deeply scalloped. Shape variable but generally more or
   less oval. Color purplish gray, sometimes tinged with greenish;
   interior white, with a deep muscle scar.

Family Anomiidae: Jingle Shells
(see p. 17)

Genus *Anomia* Linné 1758

ANOMIA ADAMAS Gray   Pl. 43
   Range: Gulf of California to Cent. America.
   Habitat: Shallow water.
   Description: Thin, yellowish brown to orange, with a waxy
   luster; commonly circular in shape, diam. about 1½ in. Lower
   valve small and flat, with a perforation for the passage of a
   muscular byssus. Upper valve arched, and sculptured with
   radiating lines and occasional concentric ridges

Genus *Placunanomia* Broderip 1832

PLACUNANOMIA CUMINGII Brod.   Pl. 43
   Range: Gulf of California to Ecuador.
   Habitat: Shallow water.
   Description: This oddly shaped bivalve is about 3 in. long. The
   shell is sharply folded, with 3 blunt ridges and 2 deep valley-like
   hollows. When viewed from the end, the margins of the valves
   make a perfect W. Color gray; interior white.

Family Crassatellidae: Crassatellas

THICK, heavy shells, the anterior rounded and the posterior rostrate.
The hinge structure is massive. The ligament is internal, and there
is no pallial sinus. Distributed in warm seas chiefly. There are
many fossil forms.

Genus *Crassatella* Lamarck 1799

CRASSATELLA GIBBOSA Sow.   Pl. 46
   Range: Gulf of California to S. America.
   Habitat: Moderately deep water; muddy bottoms.
   Description: A thick and heavy shell, growing to a length of

about 2 in. Shell regularly rounded at anterior end and well inflated, the posterior end truncate and distinctly sloping. Hinge exceptionally thick and strong. Color buffy yellow, with a dark brown periostracum.

Family Carditidae: Carditas
(see p. 19)

Genus *Cardita* Bruguière 1792

CARDITA AFFINIS CALIFORNICA Desh.   Pl. 46
Range: Gulf of California.
Habitat: Shallow water.
Description: An elongate shell, strong and sturdy, its length about 3 in. Anterior end rounded and short; posterior end long and broadly rounded. Surface with strong, rounded, scaly, radiating ribs, most pronounced on the posterior part. Color yellowish brown.
Remarks: The typical *affinis* Sow. is a smaller shell with a more southerly range.

CARDITA CRASSICOSTATA (Sow.)   Pl. 46
Range: Gulf of California to Peru.
Habitat: Moderately shallow water.
Description: Short and plump, rather squarish in outline, with high beaks and a more or less truncate posterior end. About 15 broad radiating ribs, the spaces between them mere slits. The ribs are marked by heavy scales. A colorful species, usually orange-red, with blotches of brown and white.

CARDITA LATICOSTATA Sow.   Pl. 46
Range: Gulf of California to Peru.
Habitat: Shallow water.
Description: Shape somewhat triangular, the posterior end sloping gradually to the tip and the anterior end short and rounded. Beaks full. There are about 25 squarish ribs, the spaces between them narrow. Margins of valves scalloped. Color mottled brown and white.

CARDITA MEGASTROPHA (Gray)   Pl. 46
Range: Gulf of California to Ecuador.
Habitat: Moderately shallow water.
Description: About 2 in. long, shell strong and solid, hinge structure especially rugged. About 12 low, rounded ribs, inner margin of valves deeply crenulate. Color pinkish red, more or less dotted with whitish.
Remarks: Formerly listed as *C. flammea* Mich.

Family Lucinidae: Lucines

(see p. 21)

Genus *Lucina* Bruguière 1797

LUCINA LAMPRA (Dall)   Pl. 47
  Range: Gulf of California.
  Habitat: Moderately shallow water.
  Description: A small round shell, rather compressed, the length
  just over ½ in. Beaks pointed, anterior and posterior ends about
  equal in size, with the posterior slightly flattened at the tip.
  Surface smooth, with very fine concentric lines, color varying
  from yellowish white to pale pink.

LUCINA LINGUALIS Carp.   Pl. 47
  Range: Gulf of California.
  Habitat: Moderately shallow water.
  Description: This shell is quite like *L. lampra* (above), but it may
  be slightly larger, and its outline is more round, its height about
  the same as its length. Surface smooth, color white. Interior
  often pale orange.

LUCINA UNDATOIDES Hert. & Strong   Pl. 47
  Range: Gulf of California.
  Habitat: Moderately shallow water.
  Description: About ½ in. long, a solid little shell featuring about
  5 very broad folds radiating from its beaks. In addition there
  are numerous concentric lines. Color white.

Genus *Anodontia* Link 1807

ANODONTIA EDENTULOIDES (Ver.)   Pl. 47
  Range: Gulf of California.
  Habitat: Moderately deep water.
  Description: Round and plump, this bivalve is the Pacific
  counterpart of the very common buttercup of the Atlantic
  Coast, *A. alba* Link. It is much more uncommon than the
  Atlantic bivalve. Length about 1½ in. Color white, with a
  more or less chalky surface.
  Remarks: The specimen shown on Plate 47 is the one used by
  Verrill when he first described this species in 1870.

Genus *Codakia* Scopoli 1777

CODAKIA DISTINGUENDA (Tryon)   Pl. 47
  Range: Baja California to Panama.
  Habitat: Shallow water.
  Description: A handsome and showy shell, much prized by col-

lectors. The length is about 4 in., and the color white. Shell solid, quite orbicular in outline and but little inflated. Beaks sharp and prominent, the hinge teeth large and sturdy. Surface sculptured with many narrow radiating lines, crossed by occasional elevated growth lines. On the inside each valve has a yellow center and a rosy-pink border.

Family Chamidae: Jewel Boxes
(see p. 22)

Genus *Chama* Linné 1758

CHAMA BUDDIANA C. B. Adams   **Pl. 46**
  Range: Gulf of California to Panama.
  Habitat: Moderately deep water.
  Description: About 2 in. long, the shell is round, thick, and heavy, and fastened to some object by its deep left valve. Right valve smaller, flatter, and fitting tightly to its mate. Surface rough, reddish brown, and more or less spiny, the spines usually small and white. Interior white, the crenulate margin sometimes marked with reddish.

CHAMA ECHINATA Brod.   **Spiny Jewel Box**   **Pl. 46**
  Range: Gulf of California to Peru.
  Habitat: Moderately shallow water; rocks.
  Description: About 2 in. long and boxlike in shape. Surface very spiny, although the spines are not long. Color brown; interior purple. Hinge area stained bright pink.

CHAMA FRONDOSA Brod.   **Frondose Jewel Box**   **Pl. 46**
  Range: Southern end of Gulf of California to Ecuador.
  Habitat: Moderately shallow water; rocks.
  Description: Some specimens of this shell display great beauty, with long and broad frondlike spines, and others, particularly old individuals, simply have rough, corrugated exteriors, often riddled by marine borers. Length about 4 in. Color yellowish gray; interior white, with a purple border.

Family Cardiidae: Cockles
(see p. 23)

Genus *Trachycardium* Mörch 1853

TRACHYCARDIUM CONSORS (Sow.)   **Pls. 5, 47**
Scaly Cockle
  Range: Gulf of California to Ecuador.
  Habitat: Moderately shallow water.

Description: Elongate-oval, the valves well inflated and rather substantial in substance. Surface sculptured with deeply chiseled radiating ribs that are studded with overlapping scales, usually most pronounced on the two ends. Length about 2½ in. Color yellowish brown; interior flushed with rose.

TRACHYCARDIUM PANAMENSE (Sow.)   Gulf Cockle   Pl. 47
Range: Gulf of California to Cent. America.
Habitat: Shallow water; mud.
Description: A neat and clean shell some 3 in. long, well inflated. About 20 radiating ribs, triangular in section, and on the posterior end their sharp ends produce a sawtooth effect. Color whitish, with a greenish periostracum somewhat spotted near the beaks.
Remarks: Some authors regard this cockle as a subspecies of the smaller *T. procerum* (Sow.) of more southern waters.

TRACHYCARDIUM PRISTIPLEURA (Dall)   Pl. 47
Range: Southern end of Gulf of California to Ecuador.
Habitat: Moderately shallow water.
Description: Length nearly 3 in., outline oval. A fairly solid shell, with flattened radiating ribs, the interspaces narrow. Color pale yellowish, with pinkish or purplish-brown blotches, often arranged in a more or less concentric fashion.

TRACHYCARDIUM SENTICOSUM (Sow.)   Pl. 47
Range: Throughout Gulf of California to Peru.
Habitat: Moderately shallow water.
Description: Well inflated, roundish in outline, length about 1½ in. There are numerous radiating ribs, those toward the two ends bearing sharp spines. Color whitish, with lilac blotches, or bands, and the interior is white.

Genus *Papyridea* Swainson 1840

PAPYRIDEA ASPERSA (Sow.)   Pl. 47
Range: Throughout Gulf of California to Peru.
Habitat: Shallow water.
Description: Somewhat elongate and attaining a length of about 2 in. Anterior end short and regularly rounded, posterior longer and bluntly rounded. Valves rather thin in substance, and gaping at posterior end. There is a sculpture of close radiating ribs that bear spines toward the margins. Color whitish, heavily mottled or blotched with reddish purple.

Genus *Trigoniocardia* Dall 1900

TRIGONIOCARDIA GRANIFERA (Brod. & Sow.)   Pl. 47
Range: Baja California to Peru.
Habitat: Moderately shallow water.

Description: A small white shell decorated with from 10 to 12 rather wide ribs, those on the anterior end bearing small nodules. Length about ½ in. Valves moderately inflated, and there is a distinct posterior slope.

Family Veneridae: Venus Clams
(see p. 26)

Genus *Periglypta* Jukes-Browne 1914

PERIGLYPTA MULTICOSTATA (Sow.)   Pl. 48
Range: Gulf of California to Peru.
Habitat: Moderately shallow water.
Description: Large and heavy, length nearly 5 in. Outline oval, the longer posterior end more broadly rounded than the anterior. Hinge structure rugged, pallial sinus well developed. Sculpture consists of closely set ridgelike concentric ribs, and weaker radiating lines, the surface having a filelike texture. Color yellowish white.

Genus *Ventricolaria* Keen 1954

VENTRICOLARIA ISOCARDIA (Ver.)   Pl. 48
Range: Gulf of California to S. America.
Habitat: Moderately shallow water.
Description: An almost globular shell nearly 4 in. long. Beaks full, the hinge teeth very strong. Pallial sinus short. Surface decorated with very regular concentric ribs, no radiating lines. Valves thick and solid. Color yellowish brown, sometimes blotched with darker shades, especially in juveniles. Interior white, pinkish near the beaks.
Remarks: The example shown on Plate 48 is one of the type specimens used by Verrill when he described this species in 1870.

Genus *Tivela* Link 1807

TIVELA BYRONENSIS (Gray)   Pl. 48
Range: Throughout the Gulf of California to Ecuador.
Habitat: Shallow water.
Description: Triangular in outline and fairly well inflated. Length about 2 in. Color rather variable, but usually yellowish brown, with a thin periostracum, and it may be decorated with wavy bands of dull red, particularly on the umbones. Surface smooth.

TIVELA PLANULATA (Brod. & Sow.)   Pl. 48
Range: Gulf of California to Ecuador.
Habitat: Shallow water.
Description: About 2 in. long, this bivalve is shaped like *T.*

byronensis (above), triangular with a rounded bottom. Color yellowish gray, with irregular radiating bands of brown or reddish brown. There is a very thin periostracum that is commonly missing over much of the surface.

Genus *Pitar* Römer 1857

PITAR ALTERNATUS (Brod.)   Pl. 48
   Range: Gulf of California to Peru.
   Habitat: Moderately shallow water.
   Description: A solid shell about 1½ in. long. Beaks full and situated a little closer to anterior end. Both ends are gracefully rounded. Surface ornamented by distinct concentric ribs, a smaller rib alternating with a larger one. Color pale brownish to white.

PITAR CONCINNUS (Sow.)   Pl. 48
   Range: Gulf of California to Peru.
   Habitat: Moderately shallow water.
   Description: About the size of *P. alternatus* (above) and not unlike it in shape. The sculpture consists of sharp concentric ribs, all of the same size, and the color is pale brownish, with broad radiating bands of purplish.

PITAR LUPANARIA (Less.)   Pls. 5, 48
   Range: Throughout Gulf of California to Peru.
   Habitat: Moderately shallow water.
   Description: A real beauty, much prized by collectors. Shell about 2 in. long, gracefully formed and decorated with distinct concentric lines. In addition there is a row of long spines on the posterior slope. Color ranges from white to pale lavender, usually with richer coloring at base of spines.
   Remarks: The Atlantic counterpart is *P. dione* (Linné) of the West Indies.

PITAR VULNERATUS (Brod.)   Pl. 48
   Range: Throughout Gulf of California to Panama.
   Habitat: Moderately shallow water.
   Description: Plump and smooth, the only sculpture weak concentric lines. Length about 1½ in. Shell pale yellowish gray, with concentric bands of purple. Color bands usually widely spaced. Interior white, flushed with lavender at the edges.

Genus *Megapitaria* Grant & Gale 1931

MEGAPITARIA AURANTIACA (Sow.)   Pl. 48
   Range: Gulf of California to Ecuador.
   Habitat: Moderately shallow water.
   Description: About 4 in. long, strong and solid. Anterior end

short and evenly rounded, posterior longer and more abruptly rounded. Surface smooth and pinkish gray, covered by an orange to brown periostracum. The interior is white, sometimes purplish around the hinge teeth.

MEGAPITARIA SQUALIDA (Sow.)   Pl. 48
Range: Throughout Gulf of California to Peru.
Habitat: Moderately shallow water.
Description: Another solid shell of about 4 in. There is a faint posterior ridge, producing a weak slope at that end. Color gray or whitish, with a shiny grayish periostracum. Interior white, sometimes flushed with pinkish.

Genus *Dosinia* Scopoli 1777

DOSINIA DUNKERI (Phil.)   Pl. 47
Range: Gulf of California to Peru.
Habitat: Moderately shallow water.
Description: A disklike shell, orbicular in outline, about 2 in. long. Beaks prominent. Surface sculptured with closely spaced and even concentric lines. Color pure white. Surface often appears polished.

DOSINIA PONDEROSA (Gray)   Pl. 47
Range: Gulf of California to Peru.
Habitat: Moderately shallow water.
Description: A flattish, orbicular shell that may attain a diam. of nearly 6 in. The sculpture on young shells is coarser than in the case of *D. dunkeri* (above), but on old individuals the surface is likely to be rather smooth. Hinge structure especially heavy. The shell sports a thin yellowish periostracum and is pure white in color, inside and outside.

Genus *Chione* Mühlfeld 1811

CHIONE AMATHUSIA (Phil.)   Pl. 48
Range: Gulf of California to Peru.
Habitat: Shallow water.
Description: Length 1½ in. Anterior end short and rounded, posterior longer and sloping to a blunt tip, the basal margin deeply rounded. Surface with strong radiating ribs that are crossed at regular intervals by sharp concentric ridges. Color yellowish gray.

CHIONE GNIDIA (Brod. & Sow.)   Pl. 48
Range: Throughout Gulf of California to Peru.
Habitat: Moderately shallow water.
Description: The largest member of its genus, it may reach a

length of 4 in. Solid in build, the anterior end rounded and the posterior presenting a curving downward slope to a blunt tip. The sculpture consists of regular radiating ribs and concentric ridges that often develop thin, scalloped, frilly edges. Color yellowish white.

CHIONE PULICARIA (Brod.) — Pl. 48

Range: Gulf of California to Colombia.
Habitat: Moderately shallow water.
Description: Nearly 2 in. long, this shell has the same outline as the two preceding species, but its ornamentation consists chiefly of concentric ridges, with little evidence of radiating lines. Color buffy yellow, more or less mottled with brown, often in the form of wavy bands.

Genus *Anomalocardia* Schumacher 1817

ANOMALOCARDIA SUBIMBRICATA (Sow.) — Pl. 49

Range: Gulf of California to Peru.
Habitat: Moderately shallow water.
Description: A thick and sturdy shell 1 in. long, the beaks well developed and the general outline roundish. Posterior end sloping and a little longer than the anterior. Surface bears rounded concentric ribs and weaker radiating lines. Color pale brown, with irregular darker markings, often wavy or zigzag in form. Interior white, with a purple stain at posterior tip.
Remarks: Throughout much of the Gulf there is a subspecies, *A. s. tumens* (Ver.), that is extremely stout, sculptured with just 4 or 5 very broadly rounded ribs. An example is illustrated on Plate 49 (No. 1).

ANOMALOCARDIA SUBRUGOSA (Wood) — Pl. 49

Range: Gulf of California to Peru.
Habitat: Moderately shallow water.
Description: Slightly larger than *A. subimbricata* (above), the shell has the same outline, and is decorated with concentric ribs that are strongest at the two ends. Surface generally quite shiny. Color pinkish gray, with radiating bands of purplish brown; there may be narrow vertical streaks of the same shade in the paler rays. Interior white, stained with purple around the beaks and at posterior tip.

Genus *Protot   haca* Dall 1902

PROTOTHACA ASPERRIMA (Sow.) — Pl. 49

Range: Throughout Gulf of California to Peru.
Habitat: Moderately shallow water.
Description: A yellowish-gray shell, sometimes lightly rayed

with violet. It is a roundish clam, the posterior only somewhat longer than the anterior. Length about 2 in. Valves covered with fine radiating lines composed of tiny scales, so that the surface is rough and filelike.

PROTOTHACA COLUMBIENSIS (Sow.) Pl. 49
Range: Mazatlán, Mexico, to Peru.
Habitat: Moderately shallow water.
Description: About 2 in. long and moderately inflated. Surface decorated with rather broad rounded radiating ribs, the spaces between them mere slits. Growth stages leave periodic ridges on the valves. Color gray, more or less mottled with brown and white.

PROTOTHACA GRATA (Say) Pl. 49
Range: Throughout Gulf of California to Chile.
Habitat: Shallow water.
Description: Slightly more elongate than *P. asperrima* and *P. columbiensis* (above), averages in length about 1½ in. Rather plump and sculptured with fine radiating lines. Color patterns almost infinite. Large areas are blotched with brown or black on a yellowish-gray background; it is unusual to find two examples marked alike. Even matching valves do not always agree.

Family Petricolidae: Rock Dwellers

(see p. 30)

Genus *Petricola* Lamarck 1801

PETRICOLA PARALLELA Pils. & Lowe Pl. 49
Range: Gulf of California to Nicaragua.
Habitat: Burrowings in claybanks.
Description: Elongate and thin, anterior end very short and posterior end very long. Valves sculptured with radiating lines, those on the anterior end rough and scaly. Length about 1 in. Color white.
Remarks: This bivalve reminds one of the Angel Wing, a burrowing species of an entirely different family.

PETRICOLA ROBUSTA (Sow.) Pl. 49
Range: Gulf of California to Ecuador.
Habitat: Burrowings in claybanks.
Description: One in. long, this is a stubby shell. Color white. Anterior end short and regularly rounded, the posterior longer and bluntly pointed. The ornamentation consists of fine radiating lines.

Family Mactridae: Surf Clams

(see p. 30)

Genus *Mactra* Linné 1767

MACTRA VELATA Phil.   Pl. 49
   Range: Gulf of California to Peru.
   Habitat: Moderately shallow water.
   Description: Large and heavy, reaching a length of 4 in. Valves thick but brittle, the beaks nearly central in position. There is a deep pit for the ligament under the beaks. Surface smooth, yellowish gray, with a brownish periostracum.

Genus *Mulinia* Gray 1837

MULINIA COLORADOENSIS Dall   Pl. 49
   Range: Gulf of California.
   Habitat: Shallow water.
   Description: About 2 in. long, broadly triangular in shape. Beaks full and central in position. Posterior slope flattened. Color whitish, under a pale yellowish-brown periostracum.

Genus *Anatina* Schumacher 1817

ANATINA UNDULATA (Gould)   Pl. 49
   Range: Gulf of California to Peru.
   Habitat: Moderately shallow water.
   Description: Thin and light, and well inflated, the length is about 3 in. Color pure white. The shell is oval and gaping, rather fragile, sculptured with evenly spaced, rounded, concentric grooves. Inside, on the hinge line, is a noticeable spoonlike cavity.
   Remarks: This is the Pacific counterpart of the well-known *A. plicatella* (Lam.), Channeled Duck, of the Atlantic.

Genus *Harvella* Gray 1853

HARVELLA ELEGANS (Sow.)   Pl. 49
   Range: Gulf of California to Peru.
   Habitat: Moderately deep water.
   Description: A most attractive pure-white shell, about 2 in. long. Valves thin and delicate, considerably inflated, marked with wide concentric grooves. The posterior slope bears a ridge, and beyond that the shell is smooth.

Genus *Mactrellona* Marks 1951

MACTRELLONA CLISIA (Dall)   Pl. 49
Range: Gulf of California to Ecuador.
Habitat: Moderately shallow water.
Description: A large and thin shell, the anterior end sloping and rounded, the posterior end abruptly slanting and sporting a thin ridge that may produce a finlike line down the slope. Surface smooth, color yellowish white. This is a showy shell, reaching a length of nearly 4 in.

Family Tellinidae: Tellins
(see p. 32)

Genus *Tellina* Linné 1758

TELLINA CRISTALLINA Speng.   **Crystal Tellin**   Pl. 50
Range: Gulf of California to Ecuador.
Habitat: Moderately shallow water.
Description: In this shell the beaks are central, the anterior end rounded, and the posterior with a straight slope down to a slightly upturned tip that is square. Valves thin and light and well inflated. Length 1 in. The surface is shiny, and features well-spaced concentric lines. Color white.

TELLINA CUMINGII Han.   **Cuming's Tellin**   Pl. 50
Range: Gulf of California to Colombia.
Habitat: Shallow water.
Description: About 2 in. long and not very high; the anterior end is longer and deeply rounded, the posterior end sloping and square at the tip. Surface bears distinct concentric lines, and posterior slope is decorated with wavy ridges. Color yellowish gray, with broken rays of brown or purple.
Remarks: A very similar tellin in the West Indies is *T. listeri* Röd.

TELLINA FELIX Han.   Pl. 50
Range: Mazatlán, Mexico, to Peru.
Habitat: Moderately shallow water.
Description: About ½ in. long and moderately compressed. Anterior end broadly rounded, posterior with a distinct slope. The surface is smooth and shiny, the color rosy pink.

TELLINA RECLUSA Dall   Pl. 50
Range: Baja California to Panama.
Habitat: Moderately shallow water.
Description: A small tellin, its length about ¾ in. Beaks closer

to posterior end, which is abruptly pointed and somewhat flattened. Surface with very fine concentric lines, the color white.

TELLINA RUBESCENS Han.   Pl. 50
   Range: S. Gulf of California to Peru.
   Habitat: Shallow water.
   Description: A deep rosy-red shell averaging in length about 1¼ in. The beaks are nearly central, with the posterior end sloping to a slight degree. Surface bears concentric lines but is usually quite shiny.

TELLINA SIMULANS C. B. Adams   Pl. 50
   Range: Gulf of California to Peru.
   Habitat: Shallow water.
   Description: This species is often confused with *T. rubescens* (above). It is much the commoner of the two, has the same color and outline, and is only slightly larger. The identifying character is the pallial sinus, which in this tellin does not touch the anterior muscle scar; in *T. rubescens* it runs squarely into the scar.

TELLINA VIRGO Han.   Pl. 50
   Range: Baja California to Peru.
   Habitat: Moderately shallow water.
   Description: Less than 1 in. long and white, sometimes flushed with pinkish. A well-polished shell. Over much of the surface, excluding the posterior slope, there is a sculpture of very fine lines that are more or less oblique, but one needs a hand lens to see them clearly.

TELLINA VIRIDOTINCTA (Carp.)   Pl. 50
   Range: Gulf of California to Peru.
   Habitat: Moderately shallow water.
   Description: One of the larger tellins of the area, reaching a length of 2½ in. It is fairly high, with the beaks about central, the anterior end regularly rounded and the posterior end bluntly pointed. Color white, and the ornamentation very fine concentric lines. Surface not shiny.

Genus *Apolymetis* Salisbury 1929

APOLYMETIS COGNATA CLARKI Dur.   Pl. 50
   Range: Gulf of California to Acapulco, Mexico.
   Habitat: Moderately deep water.
   Description: A rather large but thin shell about 3 in. long. Anterior end broadly rounded, the shorter posterior end with a flattened fold on the right valve, so that the shell has an oddly twisted appearance at that end. The valves are well inflated, and chalky white.

Remarks: *A. c. cognata* (Pils. & Van.) occurs from Mazatlán to the Galápagos Is.

Genus *Strigilla* Turton 1822

STRIGILLA COSTULIFERA (Mörch)   Pl. 50
Range: Baja California to Ecuado .
Habitat: Moderately shallow water.
Description: Not quite 1 in. long, thiʒ is a roundish clam with well-inflated valves. Surface sculptured with fine but distinct oblique lines that render the shell most attractive when viewed with a low-power lens. The color varies from white to pinkish, with the interior usually more brightly hued than the outside.

Genus *Tellidora* H. & A. Adams 1856

TELLIDORA BURNETI (Brod. & Sow.)   Pl. 50
Range: Gulf of California to Ecuador.
Habitat: Moderately shallow water.
Description: An odd little bivalve about 1 in. long, sometimes a bit larger. The shell is compressed, the left valve flatter than the right, and the outline is somewhat triangular, the beaks about central. Posterior end slants to a folded tip; anterior margin is concave. Basal margin rounded. The surface bears concentric lines that form teeth on the lateral margins, giving the top of the clam a saw-toothed appearance. Color white.
Remarks: In Florida and the West Indies we find a very similar bivalve, *T. cristata* (Réc.).

Family Donacidae: Bean Clams

(see p. 36)

Genus *Donax* Linné 1758

DONAX ASSIMILIS Han.   Pl. 50
Range: Mazatlán, Mexico, to Ecuador.
Habitat: Shallow water; sandy bottoms.
Description: A large shell for the genus, 1½ in. or more long and rather deep in build. Valves thick and solid; the anterior end long and acutely rounded, the posterior shorter and showing a pronounced slope. Surface bears radiating lines. Color grayish purple.

DONAX CARINATUS Han.   Pl. 50
Range: S. Gulf of California to S. America.
Habitat: Shallow water.
Description: Anterior end long and acutely rounded, posterior short and sloping so sharply that the back of the shell is nearly

concave. Length slightly over 1 in. Surface decorated with distinct radiating lines. Color grayish purple; interior bright purple.

DONAX NAVICULA Han.   Pl. 50
Range: Gulf of California to Panama.
Habitat: Shallow water.
Description: A smaller shell than *D. carinatus* (above), with a polished surface. Shape rather long and narrow, the length under 1 in. Both ends rounded, the posterior only a little shorter than the anterior. Color yellowish brown; interior purplish; inner margins crenulate.

DONAX PUNCTATOSTRIATUS Han.   Pl. 50
Range: Gulf of California to Peru.
Habitat: Shallow water.
Description: Strong and solid, rather high in build, the length is just over 1 in. Beaks full, with the posterior end sloping rather more sharply than the anterior. Surface bears fine radiating lines, the spaces between them pitted. Color brownish gray; interior purplish.

DONAX TRANSVERSUS Sow.   Pl. 50
Range: Mazatlán, Mexico, to Nicaragua.
Habitat: Shallow water.
Description: A slim and shiny species, its length about 1 in. Posterior end very short, the slope so pronounced that a small keel is present. Anterior end long and rounded at tip. Surface smooth. Color yellowish gray, with broad purplish rays.
Remarks: Formerly listed as *D. scalpellum* Gray and *D. elongatum* Mawe.

Genus *Iphigenia* Schumacher 1817

IPHIGENIA ALTIOR (Sow.)   Pl. 51
Range: Gulf of California to Peru.
Habitat: Shallow water.
Description: A fair-sized shell, the length about 2½ in. Valves sturdy, somewhat triangular in outline, with both ends sloping to a rounded basal margin. Beaks nearly central. Surface bears no sculpture other than growth lines. The color is grayish purple, under a heavy greenish periostracum.

Family Sanguinolariidae: Gari Shells

(see p. 36)

Genus *Sanguinolaria* Lamarck 1799

SANGUINOLARIA BERTINI Pils. & Lowe   **Pls. 5, 50**
Range: Throughout Gulf of California to Peru.
Habitat: Moderately shallow water.
Description: Attaining a length of more than 3 in., this has an elongate-oval outline, the beaks nearly central. Anterior end rounded; posterior end slightly pointed. Valves but little inflated, the left one flatter than the right. Color dark red in zones, generally darker toward the beaks.

SANGUINOLARIA TELLINOIDES A. Adams   **Pl. 50**
Range: Cent. Gulf of California to S. America.
Habitat: Moderately shallow water.
Description: Shorter than *S. bertini* (above), reaching a length of about 2½ in. Posterior end a little longer than anterior, both ends rounded, the posterior one less broadly. Color pinkish red on the outside, deep red on the inside.

Genus *Gari* Schumacher 1817

GARI MAXIMA (Desh.)   **Pl. 51**
Range: Gulf of California to Colombia.
Habitat: Moderately shallow water.
Description: A broadly oval shell about 2 in. long. Valves moderately solid, the anterior end rounded and the posterior presenting a somewhat squarish appearance. Color pale yellowish gray, with pink and lilac rays.

GARI REGULARIS (Carp.)   **Pl. 51**
Range: Throughout Gulf of California.
Habitat: Moderately shallow water.
Description: This species is about the same size as *G. maxima* (above), and has the same general outline. The surface is smooth, sometimes almost shiny, and instead of rays of color the shell is decorated with a mottling of grays and purples.

Genus *Tagelus* Gray 1847

TAGELUS AFFINIS (C. B. Adams)   **Pl. 51**
Range: Gulf of California to Panama.
Habitat: Shallow water.
Description: An elongate shell, only slightly inflated, averaging

in length about 2 in. Beaks nearly central, both ends bluntly rounded and gaping. Color whitish, with a yellowish-tan periostracum that is usually worn off on upperpart of shell.

TAGELUS POLITUS (Carp.)   Pl. 51
  Range: Throughout Gulf of California.
  Habitat: Shallow water.
  Description: An elongate shell, the dorsal margin sloping slightly at each end. Length about 1½ in. Surface shiny, the color pale violet, often rayed. On the interior of each valve is a slanting rib.

TAGELUS VIOLASCENS (Carp.)   Pl. 51
  Range: Gulf of California to Costa Rica.
  Habitat: Shallow water.
  Description: A larger species than *T. politus* (above), attaining a length of some 3 in. Pale violet color beneath a grayish periostracum, generally unrayed.
  Remarks: This species can easily be confused with *T. politus*, but it lacks the reinforcing internal rib.

Family Semelidae: Semeles
(see p. 38)

Genus *Semele* Schumacher 1817

SEMELE BICOLOR (C. B. Adams)   Pl. 51
  Range: Gulf of California to Panama.
  Habitat: Moderately shallow water.
  Description: Roundish and moderately inflated, the beaks about central. Posterior end flattened slightly. Length about ¾ in. Surface appears smooth, but there are extremely fine radiating lines. Color whitish, flushed with purple over the umbones.

SEMELE FLAVESCENS (Gould)   Pl. 51
  Range: S. California to Peru.
  Habitat: Moderately shallow water.
  Description: A moderately large shell, attaining a length of more than 2 in. Valves rather flat, roundish in outline, beaks nearly central. Pallial sinus very deep. Surface sculptured with growth lines only. Color yellowish, usually darker within. There is a grayish-green periostracum.

SEMELE FORMOSA (Sow.)   Pl. 51
  Range: Gulf of California to Ecuador.
  Habitat: Moderately deep water.

Description: A handsome shell, probably the most colorful of its genus in this region, but unfortunately not very common. Length about 2 in., both ends rounded, the long posterior broadly, the shorter anterior more bluntly. Surface bears distinct concentric lines. Color pale yellowish, with weak radiating bands of pinkish and broken bands of rich purple.

SEMELE JUNONIA (Ver.)   Pls. 5, 51
Range: S. Gulf of California.
Habitat: Moderately deep water.
Description: Another colorful shell, this one quite rare. The shape is much the same as *S. formosa* (above), with a slight slope on the shorter anterior end. Surface with distinct concentric lines, length about 3 in. Upper portion of the shell deep orange in fresh specimens, grading to pale orange at margins; interior a beautiful pinkish rose.

SEMELE QUENTINENSIS Dall   Pl. 51
Range: Gulf of California to Costa Rica.
Habitat: Moderately deep water.
Description: Length about 1 in. Valves thin and but little inflated. Posterior end regularly rounded, anterior a bit shorter and displaying a slight slope. Color whitish; interior usually with purple at the beaks.

Family Solenidae: Razor Clams
(see p. 39)

Genus *Ensis* Schumacher 1817

ENSIS CALIFORNICUS Dall   Pl. 51
Range: Gulf of California to s. Mexico.
Habitat: Shallow water; sandy bottoms.
Description: Slender and elongate, reaching a length of about 2 in. The shell is somewhat cylindrical, very gently curved, and gapes at both ends. Surface has a glossy periostracum with a long, triangular space marked by concentric lines of growth. Color yellowish green.
Remarks: The common razor clam of California sand and mud-flats, *E. myrae* Berry, was once believed to be this species and is listed in many older books as *E. californicus*.

Family Corbulidae: Basket Clams
(see p. 43)

Genus *Corbula* Bruguière 1797

CORBULA BICARINATA Sow.   Pl. 51
   Range: Gulf of California to Ecuador.
   Habitat: Moderately shallow water.
   Description: A stubby shell less than ½ in. long. Beaks full,
   anterior end rounded and posterior sharply truncate. The shell
   is thick and solid for its diminutive size, and is more or less inequivalve, one valve commonly overlapping its mate. Sculpture
   limited to fine concentric lines. Color white.

CORBULA NASUTA Sow.   Pl. 51
   Range: Gulf of California to Peru.
   Habitat: Moderately shallow water.
   Description: About ½ in. long, the anterior end is rounded and
   the posterior end is abruptly sloping, terminating in a handle-
   like tip. The valves are sturdy and solid, fairly well inflated.
   Color whitish.

CORBULA OVULATA Sow.   Pl. 51
   Range: S. Gulf of California to Peru.
   Habitat: Moderately shallow water.
   Description: About 1 in. long, this species is large for the genus.
   The outlines are much the same as the last species, *C. nasuta*,
   the anterior end rounded and the posterior sloping and ending
   in a snoutlike tip. Surface bears weak concentric lines. The
   color is whitish, flushed with lavender near the beaks.

Family Gastrochaenidae: Gaping Clams

BURROWING or boring mollusks, living in coral, limestone, or dead
shells of other mollusks. The shells are equivalve and gape considerably along the anterior and basal margins.

Genus *Gastrochaena* Spengler 1783

GASTROCHAENA OVATA Sow.   Pl. 51
   Range: San Diego, California, to Ecuador; also in Atlantic.
   Habitat: In coral or dead shells.
   Description: Small and oddly shaped, a boring clam about 1 in.

long. The oval shell gapes widely, and is somewhat twisted in appearance. The beaks are set close to the anterior end, and that end slopes sharply back to the basal margin. Color yellowish gray, the surface bearing fine concentric lines.

Family Pholadidae: Piddocks
(see p. 43)

Genus *Pholas* Linné 1758

PHOLAS CHILOENSIS Mol.   Pl. 51
Range: N. Gulf of California to Chile.
Habitat: Burrowings in soft limestone.
Description: Snowy white and about 5 in. long, this is one of the "angel wing" type of bivalve. The shell is elongate, thin, and brittle, the anterior end short and the posterior very long. Both ends gape. The surface is sculptured with radiating ridges that are nodular toward the margins, and on the anterior end they are closely packed and spiny. There is a shelly hood over the beaks that is reinforced with thin vertical plates, and inside the shell, under the beaks, is a curving, toothlike structure called the apophysis.

Genus *Cyrtopleura* Tryon 1862

CYRTOPLEURA CRUCIGERA (Sow.)   Pl. 51
Range: Guaymas, Mexico, to Chile.
Habitat: Burrowings in clay and mud.
Description: A smaller boring clam than *P. chiloensis* (above), the length seldom exceeding 1½ in. Anterior end short and somewhat pointed, posterior long and acutely rounded. The dorsal margin is rolled back over the shell, and the valves are decorated with sharp radiating ridges, those on the anterior half bearing close-set scales. Color pure white.

Genus *Parapholas* Conrad 1848

PARAPHOLAS ACUMINATA (Sow.)   Pl. 51
Range: Baja California to Peru.
Habitat: Bores in rocks.
Description: Its length about 2 in., this borer has a short, rounded, almost bulbous anterior end, and a long and rather pointed posterior end. Valves divided into 3 distinct areas: the anterior 3rd is decorated with fine radiating lines, the posterior 3rd with coarse, transverse, ridgelike lines, and the area between merely with lines of growth. Anterior end gapes widely but is covered by a thin, globose callum. Color grayish white.

V

Gulf of California Gastropods

Family Fissurellidae: Keyhole Limpets
(see p. 54)

Genus *Fissurella* Bruguière 1798

FISSURELLA GEMMATA Menke   Pl. 52
White Keyhole Limpet
   Range: S. Gulf of California.
   Habitat: Shallow water.
   Description: Slightly more than 1 in. long and well elevated, usually with the front end narrower than the back. Perforation oblong, commonly constricted somewhat in the middle. Surface with radiating ribs and riblets of varying sizes, a few of them sometimes nodular. Color white or pale gray, sometimes a little mottled; interior white. There is a rather thick callus surrounding the perforation, and this is bordered by a narrow rim of black.
   Remarks: Formerly listed as *F. alba* Carp.

FISSURELLA VIRESCENS Sow.   Pl. 52
Green Keyhole Limpet
   Range: Mazatlán to Panama.
   Habitat: Shallow water.
   Description: A roundish oval limpet, the summit well arched. Length about 1½ in. A solid and sturdy shell, sculptured with alternating larger and smaller radiating ribs. Color greenish gray; inside greenish white, with a flattish white callus around the perforation. Inner margin crenulate.

Genus *Diodora* Gray 1821

DIODORA INAEQUALIS (Sow.)   Pl. 52
Rocking Keyhole Limpet
   Range: Gulf of California to the Galápagos Is.
   Habitat: Shallow water.
   Description: An elongate shell, the anterior end narrower and more pointed than the posterior, and with sides nearly parallel. The sides are slightly arched, so that on a level surface the shell

rests on the two ends. The elevation is only moderate, and the apex is close to the front end. Perforation long and narrow, commonly notched at sides. The sculpture consists of fine radiating lines and still finer concentric threadlike lines. Color grayish or yellowish, sometimes with darker rays; interior white.

Family Patellidae: Limpets

APEX of shell nearly central. Texture more or less fibrous, interior often iridescent or metallic. Generally lacking a distinct internal border. Worldwide in distribution, but most numerous in Africa.

Genus *Patella* Linné 1758

PATELLA MEXICANA Brod. & Sow.   **Giant Limpet**   Pl. 52
   Range: Gulf of California to Peru.
   Habitat: Shoreline; rocks.
   Description: A real giant, the largest of all limpets, some individuals attaining a length of 10 in. Shell thick, heavy, and oval in outline. It is moderately arched, and the surface is almost always badly eroded or incrusted, but one can make out several low radiating ridges. Color dull white; the interior with a muscle scar bordered by pale brownish.
   Remarks: Said to be used sometimes as a washbasin by the coastal Indians.

Family Acmaeidae: Limpets
(see p. 56)

Genus *Acmaea* Eschscholtz 1830

ACMAEA ATRATA Carp.   Pl. 52
   Range: Throughout Gulf of California.
   Habitat: Shoreline; rocks.
   Description: A solid roundish shell, the apex a little closer to anterior end. The surface has radiating ribs unequal in size, with narrow grooves between them. Color gray, the ribs usually darker in tone. Length 1½ in. Interior white; there is a border of yellowish gray with square black dots, the central area bluish white, often with a narrow encircling line of brown.

ACMAEA DISCORS (Phil.)   Pl. 52
   Range: Mazatlán to Panama.
   Habitat: Shoreline; rocks.
   Description: This oval limpet is rather flat, only slightly arched with the apex nearly central. Growing to a length of about 1 in.,

it has the upper surface rather smooth, with indistinct radiating lines, commonly worn or eroded. At the apex there may be coarse wrinkles. Color mottled grayish; interior white, with a greenish-gray muscle scar and a narrow marginal border of the same hue.

ACMAEA PEDICULUS (Phil.)   Pl. 52
   Range: Gulf of California.
   Habitat: Shoreline; rocks.
   Description: A flattish species 1 in. long, usually not very common. The surface bears about 10 rounded radiating ribs, the spaces between them relatively smooth. The ribs produce noticeable points at the margins, so that the outline of the shell is scalloped. Color yellowish gray; interior white, with a brown center and a very pale brown marginal band.

Genus *Nomaeopelta* Berry 1958

NOMAEOPELTA DALLIANA (Pils.)   **Dall's Limpet**   Pl. 52
   Range: N. Gulf of California.
   Habitat: Shallow water; rocks.
   Description: A larger species than *N. stanfordiana* (below), its length almost 2 in. Shell flattish, the apex close to the front end, and it is sculptured with numerous fine, sometimes weakly beaded, lines. Color grayish brown, with staggered flecks of white; interior bluish white.

NOMAEOPELTA STANFORDIANA Berry   Pl. 52
Stanford's Limpet
   Range: Sonoran coast of Mexico.
   Habitat: Shallow water; rocks.
   Description: Roundly oval and only moderately arched, the length is usually just under 1 in., with the apex situated close to one end. Color mottled gray and black, commonly darker near the margins, where there are staggered bars of paler shades Interior rich bluish green.

Family Trochidae: Pearly Top Shells
(see p. 59)

Genus *Calliostoma* Swainson 1840

CALLIOSTOMA EXIMIUM (Reeve)   Pl. 53
   Range: Gulf of California to Ecuador.
   Habitat: Moderately shallow water.
   Description: An attractive shell, not quite 1 in. high. The shape is pyramidal, the base rather flattish, and there are about 6

shouldered whorls. No umbilicus. Color pale yellowish gray, the small encircling ribs checked with black, white, and red.

CALLIOSTOMA LEANUM (C. B. Adams)   **Lea's Top**   Pl. 53
Range: Guaymas to Panama.
Habitat: Moderately shallow water.
Description: About ¾ in. high. There are 6 or 7 whorls, each with revolving lines that are minutely beaded, and the sutures are moderately well impressed. Spire rather tall for this group, and sharply pointed. Color dull reddish brown.

CALLIOSTOMA LIMA (Phil.)   **File Top**   Pl. 53
Range: Mazatlán to Panama.
Habitat: Moderately shallow water.
Description: Composed of 8 or 9 whorls, this shell is about ¾ in. high Outline sharply conical, the whorls sloping regularly to a rounded periphery. Surface ornamented by encircling beaded lines of two sizes, generally a larger one alternating with a smaller one. Base rather flat, and beautifully decorated with spiraling beaded lines. Color yellowish, clouded and spotted with bluish gray. The columellar area and the interior are iridescent.

CALLIOSTOMA PALMERI Dall   **Palmer's Top**   Pl. 53
Range: Gulf of California.
Habitat: Moderately shallow water.
Description: Nearly 1 in. high and roughly the same in diam. There are about 6 whorls, each with a marked shoulder, so that the spire is somewhat turreted. The sculpture consists of encircling lines. Color pale ivory, with revolving rows of minute chestnut dots. The umbilicus is closed, but there is a small pit there that is pale violet in hue.

Genus *Tegula* Lesson 1832

TEGULA BYRONIANA (Wood)   **Reticulate Top**   Pl. 53
Range: Mazatlán to Panama.
Habitat: Moderately shallow water.
Description: An ornate shell of about 5 whorls, the sutures indistinct. Diam. ¾ in., height about ½ in. Surface decorated with encircling rows of tiny beads. No umbilicus. Color mottled purplish brown and gray, with a greenish spot on columella. There is a notch at the base of the inner lip; the aperture is silvery.
Remarks: Formerly listed as *T. reticulata* (Wood).

TEGULA GLOBULUS Carp.   **Globular Top**   Pl. 53
Range: Gulf of California.
Habitat: Moderately shallow water.

Description: A roundish little snail, its height about ½ in. There is a low spire, and only 5 rounded whorls, the sutures indistinct. The sculpture consists of revolving lines, weakly beaded. Color mottled greenish black and gray. There is a small umbilicus; the aperture is small and nearly round.

TEGULA MARIANA Dall   Pl. 53
Range: Gulf of California to Peru.
Habitat: Moderately shallow water.
Description: A small, flattish shell, diam. about ½ in., and less than that in height. There are 4 or 5 whorls, decorated with fine revolving lines, two of which are weakly nodular. Color gray, with minute reddish-brown dots. There is a deep umbilicus.

TEGULA RUBROFLAMMULATA (Koch)   Pl. 53
Range: Gulf of California to Panama.
Habitat: Moderately shallow water.
Description: About ¾ in. high, this is a solid little shell of 4 or 5 whorls, the sutures deeply channeled. Surface decorated with revolving knobby ridges, and there are a few revolving lines on the base. Small umbilicus; base of inner lip notched. Color brown, splashed and streaked with pinkish brown.

TEGULA RUGOSA (A. Adams)   Rough Top   Pl. 53
Range: Gulf of California.
Habitat: Moderately shallow water.
Description: Diam. about ¾ in. and height the same. Another solid shell of 4 or 5 rounded whorls, the sutures only lightly impressed. The surface bears weak revolving lines. Color mottled gray and pinkish, frequently with the pink arranged in oblique bars. Occasional specimens have blackish bars on a pinkish background. The umbilicus is small, the aperture pearly, and the inner lip is notched at its base.

Family Turbinidae: Turbans

(see p. 64)

Genus *Turbo* Linné 1758

TURBO FLUCTUOSUS Wood   Pl. 53
Range: Gulf of California to Peru.
Habitat: Moderately shallow water.
Description: A fairly large shell, attaining a height of more than 2 in. There are about 5 whorls, well angled at the shoulders. The sculpture consists of revolving lines, some of them nodular. This is a very variable gastropod; some specimens are quite

rough and others are relatively smooth. Aperture large and round, iridescent within, with the columella broadened to form a large pearly area. Color olive-green to brown, more or less mottled. The thick operculum has a central bulge that is granular, bordered by a deep and narrow concentric groove.

TURBO SAXOSUS Wood   Pl. 53
Range: Gulf of California to Peru.
Habitat: Moderately shallow water.
Description: A smaller shell than *T. fluctuosus* (above), the height about 1½ in. In other respects much like it, but with closely packed, sharp vertical growth lines. Sutures somewhat channeled. Operculum thick and heavy, brown on the inside and white on the outside, where there is a deep central pit bordered by a concentric furrow.

Genus *Astraea* Röding 1798

ASTRAEA BUSCHII (Phil.)   **Busch's Turban**   Pl. 53
Range: Gulf of California to Peru.
Habitat: Moderately shallow water.
Description: About 1½ in. high and the shape is conic and the whorl count 7. The surface bears revolving rows of rather sharp tubercles, usually a row at the base and at the shoulder, with 2 smaller rows between them. Base flat, with the columella showing a broad and deep excavation, but there is no umbilicus. Color greenish, blotched with black. Aperture pearly white.

ASTRAEA OLIVACEA (Wood)   **Olive Turban**   Pl. 53
Range: Gulf of California to Panama.
Habitat: Moderately shallow water.
Description: A conic shell, rugged and strong, some 2½ in. high and about the same in diam. There are 6 or 7 whorls noticeably swollen at the base. The sculpture consists of close diagonal ridges. Base concave, the aperture oblique, with a broad and deep excavation at side of columella. Color greenish olive; aperture pearly white, the umbilical area stained a bright orange-red, with a black center.

ASTRAEA UNGUIS (Wood)   Pl. 53
Range: Gulf of California to Peru.
Habitat: Moderately shallow water.
Description: A pyramidal, or top-shaped shell, generally somewhat wider than it is tall, its height about 1½ in. There are 5 or 6 sloping whorls, the sutures moderately impressed. Surface sculptured with fine vertical lines and heavy, rounded, knoblike ribs that render margin at the base scalloped. Color brown or gray, but beach specimens quickly bleach to pure white.

Family Neritidae: Nerites

CHIEFLY small, often brightly colored snails, mostly globular in shape. Shells strong and solid in general. There is no umbilicus, and the aperture frequently is toothed, on both the inner and outer lips. Operculum shelly. These mollusks inhabit warm seas, where they are often found abundantly in shallow water close to shore, in brackish water, and even in freshwater. All are herbivorous.

Genus *Nerita* Linné 1758

NERITA FUNICULATA Menke   Pl. 53
    Range: Guaymas to Peru.
    Habitat: Shallow water.
    Description: A flat-topped shell with practically no spire, the shell being nearly all body whorl. Approximately 3 volutions, the diam. about 1 in. Surface decorated with narrow, rounded, encircling ribs that are closely checked by vertical lines. Color black, with wavy bands of white. Broad columellar area glistening white, strongly marked with small pustules.

NERITA SCABRICOSTA Lam.   Pl. 53
    Range: Gulf of California to Ecuador.
    Habitat: Shallow water.
    Description: A globular shell, heavy and solid, attaining a diam. of 1¾ in. There are 4 whorls, rising to a sharply pointed apex. Sculpture consists of rounded revolving ribs. Color gray to whitish, strongly banded or blotched with black. The black-bordered lip bears 1 large and a whole row of smaller teeth well within the aperture; the inner lip is armed with 3 or 4 robust teeth. The broad columellar area is carved with numerous wrinkle-like grooves.

Genus *Neritina* Lamarck 1816

NERITINA LUTEOFASCIATA Mill.   Pl. 53
    Range: Gulf of California to Panama.
    Habitat: Shallow water.
    Description: A smooth, low-spired shell of about 4 whorls, somewhat less than ½ in. long. Color yellowish or greenish gray, spirally streaked with bluish white and black. The slightly flattened columellar area is distinctly marked with chestnut-brown.

Family Littorinidae: Periwinkles
(see p. 66)

Genus *Littorina* Férussac 1822

LITTORINA ASPERA Phil.   Pl. 53
Range: Mazatlán to Panama.
Habitat: Shoreline; rocks.
Description: About 1 in. high, composed of 5 or 6 whorls, the apex sharp. Volutions marked with revolving lines. Color whitish, with blotches of gray and brown. Inner lip chocolate-brown.

LITTORINA CONSPERSA Phil.   Pl. 53
Range: Gulf of California to Ecuador.
Habitat: Shoreline; rocks.
Description: A solid little shell, somewhat less than 1 in. high. The rounded whorls number 5, and are sculptured with sharp revolving lines. Color gray, sometimes dotted with purplish brown; aperture light brown.

LITTORINA FASCIATA Gray   Pl. 53
Range: Gulf of California to Ecuador.
Habitat: Shallow water.
Description: A larger shell than *L. conspersa* (above), attaining a height of about 1¼ in. There are around 5 whorls, a sharp apex, and an expanded body whorl, so that the snail appears more squat. Color yellowish brown, irregularly marked with darker brown.

Family Turritellidae: Turret Shells
(see p. 67)

Genus *Turritella* Lamarck 1799

TURRITELLA ANACTOR Berry   Pl. 54
Range: Upper Gulf of California.
Habitat: Moderately deep water.
Description: Nearly 5 in. high, this slender shell has about 15 whorls. The volutions have a slight keel just above the suture line, and their sides are somewhat concave. Color grayish, streaked and blotched with purplish brown.

TURRITELLA BANKSI Reeve   **Banks' Turret**   Pl. 54
Range: Guaymas to Panama.
Habitat: Moderately deep water.

Description: One of the smaller turrets, in height seldom exceeding 2½ in. It is rather broad at the base, tapering quite rapidly to the apex. Whorls moderately flat, sutures indistinct, each volution bearing prominent revolving lines. Color whitish, flecked with pale yellowish brown, and commonly well-defined bands of darker brown.

TURRITELLA GONOSTOMA Val.   Pl. 54
   Range: Gulf of California to Peru.
   Habitat: Moderately shallow water.
   Description: A strong and rugged shell fully 6 in. high, this is the largest and heaviest of western American turrets. There are about 20 rather flat whorls, the sutures not impressed. The early volutions have a noticeable ridge at the periphery, but this fades with age, and most of the shell is rather smooth. The sculpture consists of very fine spiral lines. Color bluish gray, thickly speckled and mottled with chocolate-brown.

TURRITELLA LEUCOSTOMA Val.   Tiger Turret   Pl. 54
   Range: Gulf of California to Panama.
   Habitat: Moderately deep water.
   Description: A strong shell, its height about 4 in. There are from 18 to 20 whorls that are swollen at the base and slope to the suture, so that the outline of the shell is more or less angular. Sutures deep. From 8 to 10 encircling riblets on each volution. Color grayish white, obliquely streaked with brown or chestnut.
   Remarks: Formerly listed as *T. tigrina* Kiener.

TURRITELLA NODULOSA King & Brod.   Pl. 54
Nodular Turret
   Range: S. Gulf of California to Ecuador.
   Habitat: Moderately deep water.
   Description: Averaging some 2 in. high, this shell has about 15 whorls, each with a strong circle of beads, or nodes, at the periphery. Smaller lines are present on each side of the peripheral band, and the sutures are quite distinct. Color pale yellowish brown, vertically streaked with chestnut.

Genus *Vermicularia* Lamarck 1799

VERMICULARIA EBURNEA (Reeve)   Pl. 54
   Range: Gulf of California to Panama.
   Habitat: Shallow water.
   Description: A yellowish-brown to whitish shell from 3 to 6 in. long. In its youthful stages the shell is tightly coiled and looks like a small *Turritella*, but as it grows older it becomes free and wanders off in an irregular and seemingly aimless fashion. The tubelike shell is closed by a circular, horny operculum. Several

individuals are generally found growing together in a tangled mass.

Remarks: This gastropod was formerly placed in the Family Vermetidae, but is now regarded as belonging to the Turritellidae. In S. America there is a species, *V. pellucida* Brod. & Sow., of which *V. eburnea* may be only a subspecies.

Family Vermetidae: Worm Shells
(see p. 68)

Genus *Petaloconchus* Lea 1843

PETALOCONCHUS FLAVESCENS (Carp.)   Pl. 54
   Range: S. Gulf of California.
   Habitat: Close to shore.
   Description: This worm shell builds dense colonies, many individuals growing together in a tangled mass. The shell is only about ⅛ in. in diam., and within the colony may grow in a tightly coiled fashion. Shell marked with beaded ridges. Color brown.

Genus *Serpulorbis* Sassi 1827

SERPULORBIS ERUCIFORMIS (Mörch)   Pl. 54
   Range: Gulf of California.
   Habitat: Shallow water.
   Description: Slightly smaller in size, and with a smoother shell, this species is very much like *S. margaritaceus* (below). The longitudinal ribs are fewer in number and more widely spaced. Color brownish.

SERPULORBIS MARGARITACEUS (Chenu)   Pl. 54
   Range: S. Gulf of California.
   Habitat: Shallow water.
   Description: This is a solitary snail as a rule, generally found attached to some rock or dead shell. It grows in a regular flat spiral coil by preference, always tightly attached, but when crowded may straighten the tube or twist about irregularly. The shell is about ¾ in. in diam. at the aperture, and is marked with strong longitudinal ridges. Color grayish brown.

Family Architectonicidae: Sundials

SHELLS solid, circular, conical, and but little elevated. The umbilicus is very broad and deep, bordered by a knobby keel. They are confined to warm seas.

Genus *Architectonica* Röding 1798

ARCHITECTONICA NOBILIS Röd.   **Sundial**   Pl. 54
  Range: Gulf of California to Peru; also Atlantic.
  Habitat: Moderately shallow water.
  Description: From 1 to 1½ in. in diam., this is a circular shell
  rising to a low cone, the base flat. Color grayish white, spotted
  and marbled with brown and purple. The surface is finely
  checked by crossing spiral lines and radiating ridges, producing
  a pattern of raised granules. The umbilicus is wide, deep, and
  strongly crenulate. Aperture round; lip thin and sharp.
  Remarks: This gastropod was named *A. granulatum* by Lamarck,
  but Röding's name has priority by 16 years.

Family Planaxidae: Grooved Snails

GENERALLY small brownish shells, living under stones in shallow
water and characterized by a spirally grooved sculpture. The
aperture is oval, well notched at both ends. Common in warm seas.

Genus *Planaxis* Lamarck 1822

PLANAXIS OBSOLETUS Menke   Pl. 53
  Range: Mazatlán to Panama.
  Habitat: Shallow water; stony bottoms.
  Description: About ½ in. high, composed of 5 or 6 whorls with
  indistinct sutures. There is a pointed spire and an aperture
  notched at both ends. The sculpture consists of very fine
  revolving lines. Color reddish brown.

PLANAXIS PLANICOSTATUS Sow.   Pl. 53
  Range: Mazatlán to Peru.
  Habitat: Shallow water; stony bottoms.
  Description: Fully 1 in. high, composed of 5 or 6 whorls with
  indistinct sutures. Surface decorated with flat revolving ribs,
  about 11 on the body whorl, each separated by a shallow groove.
  Aperture oval, strongly notched above and below; lip somewhat
  thickened; the grooves show plainly on the inside. There is a
  rather thick velvety-brown periostracum.

Family Modulidae: Modulus

FLATTISH, top-shaped shells, the whorls grooved and tuberculated.
There is a small, narrow umbilicus. The columella ends below in a
sharp tooth. Found in warm seas.

Genus *Modulus* Potiez & Michaud 1838

MODULUS CATENULATUS (Phil.)   Pl. 54
   Range: Gulf of California.
   Habitat: Shallow water.
   Description: A rather smooth little shell, diam. about ½ in.
Spire fairly low but sharply pointed. About 4 whorls, the body
whorl large, with sloping shoulders. There is a strong beaded
keel, at the periphery, with the rest of the volution bearing
revolving lines, especially prominent on the base. Small umbilicus, and a toothlike process at base of columella. Color whitish,
dotted with reddish brown.

MODULUS CERODES (A. Adams)   Pl. 54
   Range: Gulf of California to Panama.
   Habitat: Shallow water.
   Description: This shell is about the same size as *M. catenulatus*
(above), but much more knobby. The whorl count is 4, and the
spire is very low, with coarse sculpture. Instead of a beaded keel
this shell has a series of rounded knobs at the shoulder. Color
yellowish white, with a purplish-brown stain on the inner lip.

MODULUS DISCULUS (Phil.)   Pl. 54
   Range: Gulf of California to Panama.
   Habitat: Shallow water.
   Description: Diam. about ½ in., with a spire that is a bit more
elevated than *M. cerodes* (above), the shoulders more sloping.
There are about 4 whorls, the periphery sharply angled, with a
knobby ridge at the angle. The columella terminates in a toothlike process, as in the others of this group. Yellowish-white color,
the inner lip is usually violet-tinted.

Family Potamididae: Horn Shells

(see p. 68)

Genus *Cerithidea* Swainson 1840

CERITHIDEA ALBONODOSA Gould & Carp.   Pl. 54
   Range: Gulf of California.
   Habitat: Shallow water.
   Description: Approximately 1 in. high and composed of about
8 whorls. Outer lip greatly thickened, and rest periods during
shell growth leave a strong white varix on each volution, generally staggered up the spire. The ornamentation consists of
prominent vertical ribs which are cut by faint revolving lines.
Color whitish, clouded with purplish gray and pale brown.

CERITHIDEA MONTAGNEI Orb.   Pl. 54

Range: Gulf of California to Ecuador.
Habitat: Moderately shallow water.
Description: A stout shell of about 9 rounded whorls, the height about 1½ in. Sutures well indented. Aperture very large, the outer lip flaring at its edge, but this rim is resorbed during growth so that no varix is formed. No canal. The whorls bear very sharp oblique ribs; the base is spirally grooved. Color chocolate-brown, generally with a pair of narrow paler bands on each volution. Surface usually shiny.

Family Cerithiidae: Horn Shells

(see p. 69)

Genus *Cerithium* Bruguière 1789

CERITHIUM ADUSTUM Kiener   Pl. 54

Range: Mazatlán to Ecuador.
Habitat: Moderately shallow water.
Description: A sturdy shell, attaining a height of nearly 2 in. There are from 8 to 10 whorls, each decorated with a row of nodes near the shoulder, with 2 rows of smaller knobs between them. Small riblets encircle the volutions, and the sutures are not distinct. There is a marked callus at the base of the columella. The aperture is strongly notched at both ends; the canal bends sharply backward. Color whitish, heavily clouded with gray and purplish brown.

CERITHIUM GEMMATUM Hinds   Pl. 54

Range: Gulf of California to Ecuador.
Habitat: Shallow water.
Description: About 1 in. high and ruggedly built, this horn shell has about 10 whorls, the sutures quite distinct. Sculpture consists of revolving lines and tiny beads, those at the shoulders most prominent. Color creamy white, more or less clouded and spotted with brown.

CERITHIUM MACULOSUM Kiener   Pl. 54

Range: Gulf of California.
Habitat: Shallow water.
Description: About 2 in. high, with 9 or 10 well-shouldered whorls. A strong and rugged shell, but not as massive as *C. adustum* (above). The whorls are fairly smooth, with nodes at the shoulders. Color grayish, rather thickly dotted with reddish brown.

CERITHIUM SCULPTUM Sow. **Pl. 54**
  Range: Guaymas to Panama.
  Habitat: Shallow water.
  Description: A slender spikelike shell of 9 or 10 whorls, the height usually under 1 in. It is sculptured with spiral lines, and is gray, with 2 lines at the top of each volution checked with black and white. Aperture quite small. Surface of shell generally shiny.

CERITHIUM STERCUSMUSCARUM Val. **Pl. 54**
  Range: Gulf of California to Peru.
  Habitat: Shallow water.
  Description: About 1½ in. high, this is a rugged shell of 9 or 10 whorls, the sutures scarcely discernible. At the periphery of each volution there is a row of distinct pointed knobs, about 9 to a whorl. Small riblets encircle the shell between these knobby ridges. Aperture rather small, the lip thin and sharp, the canal slightly twisted. Color gray to brownish, thickly dotted with white.

Family Epitoniidae: Wentletraps
(see also p. 70)

THESE are ornate shells, high-spired and many-whorled, and great favorites with collectors. There are many species living in the Gulf of California, and their precise identification is a job for the experts. Just two examples will be illustrated here.

Genus *Epitonium* Röding 1798

EPITONIUM PHANIUM Dall **Pl. 53**
  Range: Gulf of California to Panama.
  Habitat: Moderately deep water.
  Description: This species is about ¾ in. high, and is typical for the group. There are 8 or 9 rounded whorls, each decorated with 7 or 8 thin, bladelike varices. Aperture round and bordered by a thickened lip that will in turn become another varix. Color pure white.

EPITONIUM WURTSBAUGHI Strong & Hert. **Pl. 53**
  Range: Gulf of California to S. America.
  Habitat: Moderately deep water.
  Description: This wentletrap is about ½ in. high, but it expands more abruptly than *E. phanium* (above), so that it is a stouter shell toward the base, and the varices are more widely spaced. Color white, as with most of the wentletraps; surface generally shiny.

Family Hipponicidae: Hoof Shells
(see p. 73)

Genus *Hipponix* Defrance 1819

HIPPONIX PILOSUS (Desh.)   **Hoof Shell**   Pl. 55
Range: Gulf of California to Ecuador; also Hawaii.
Habitat: Moderately shallow water; rocks.
Description: A small but solid shell, oval in outline and limpet-like in form. Apex moderately elevated and blunt. Surface with fine radiating lines. There is a heavy and hairy periostracum that overhangs the edge of the shell like a fringe. White; periostracum rusty yellow.
Remarks: Formerly called *H. barbatus* Sow.

Family Calyptraeidae: Cup-and-Saucer Limpets and Slipper Shells
(see p. 74)

Genus *Calyptraea* Lamarck 1799

CALYPTRAEA MAMILLARIS Brod.   Pl. 54
Range: Gulf of California to S. America.
Habitat: Shallow water.
Description: Round and conical, rather thin in substance, smooth, and white, becoming brownish toward apex. Diam. about 1 in. Interior glossy white, with a cuplike diaphragm that stands out at the center like a thickened inner lip and terminates in a thin edge near the margin of shell.

CALYPTRAEA SPIRATA (For.)   Pl. 54
Range: Gulf of California.
Habitat: Shallow water.
Description: A larger and sturdier shell than *C. mamillaris* (above), attaining a diam. of about 2 in. It is cap-shaped like *C. mamillaris*, but the surface is decorated with rather strong radiating ridges (deep furrows between them) and the margins are scalloped. Inside, there is a thin platelike shelf extending from the center to the margin. Color grayish white, more or less streaked with brownish; the interior, including the shelf, is brown.

Genus *Cheilea* Modeer 1793

CHEILEA CEPACEA (Brod.)   Pl. 55
Range: Gulf of California to Chile.
Habitat: Moderately shallow water.

Description: About 1 in. long and pale gray or white. The shell is almost orbicular in outline at the base, and rises to a blunt apex situated somewhat posterior in position. Exterior strongly rayed with fine but distinct ridges, and the edge of the shell is lightly crenulated. Inside the shell is a sturdy, horseshoe-shaped plate.

Genus *Crucibulum* Schumacher 1817

CRUCIBULUM SCUTELLATUM (Wood)   Pl. 55
Range: Gulf of California to Peru.
Habitat: Shallow water.
Description: A strong and solid brownish shell, diam. from 1 to 2¾ in. The shape is variable, usually oval and cap-shaped, but the apex may be high or moderately low, and commonly twisted to one side. Surface decorated with coarse radiating ribs and deep grooves, as well as smaller concentric ribs. Margins deeply scalloped. Interior bluish white, more or less stained with brown, and there is a cuplike septum closer to one end.

Genus *Crepidula* Lamarck 1799

CREPIDULA STRIOLATA Menke   Pl. 55
Range: Gulf of California to Panama.
Habitat: Shallow water.
Description: This slipper shell is oval, only moderately arched, and about 1½ in. long. It generally has a smooth surface and is whitish, with a yellowish-brown periostracum during life. The interior is shiny white, including the platform, which takes up nearly ½ of the inside.

Family Strombidae: Strombs

AN interesting family of very active gastropods, widely distributed in warm seas. The shells are thick and solid, with a greatly enlarged body whorl. Aperture long and narrow ordinarily, with a notch at each end; in adults the outer lip is usually thickened and expanded. The operculum is clawlike and does not close the aperture.

Genus *Strombus* Linné 1758

STROMBUS GALEATUS Swain.   Pl. 56
Range: Gulf of California to Ecuador.
Habitat: Moderately shallow water.
Description: A large and massive shell, possibly the heaviest of any shell to be found in w. N. America. The height may be as much as 9 in. Spire short and blunt, the shell nearly all body whorl. Surface with rounded encircling ribs but in old specimens

is more often than not badly eroded. Aperture large; outer lip thickened and flaring and plastered to shell up near the apex. Color dull reddish brown, with a brownish periostracum. Interior white in young specimens, dull orange in adults.

STROMBUS GRACILIOR Sow.   Pl. 56
   Range: Gulf of California to Peru.
   Habitat: Shallow water.
   Description: About 3 in. high, a robust shell of 6 or 7 whorls. Body whorl large, but there is a well-developed spire. Prominent blunt knobs at the shoulder, about 14 to a whorl, and above them the shell slopes gently to the suture. Aperture long and rather narrow; outer lip thickened at edge and expanded, distinctly notched below. Color yellowish brown, commonly with a paler band encircling the last whorl. The operculum is claw-like, used by the mollusk in crawling.

STROMBUS GRANULATUS Swain.   Pl. 56
   Range: Gulf of California to Ecuador.
   Habitat: Shallow water.
   Description: A shell of about 7 whorls, attaining a height of 3½ in. It is a rugged shell but graceful in shape, with a tall spire. Sculpture of a single row of prominent knobs on shoulders, with 3 or 4 rows of smaller knobs on body whorl. The outer lip bears a strong notch at its base and is granulated just inside the edge. Color ivory-white, with interrupted zigzag markings of chestnut-brown.

Family Naticidae: Moon Shells

(see p. 77)

Genus *Natica* Scopoli 1777

NATICA BRODERIPIANA Réc.   Pl. 55
   Range: Gulf of California to Peru.
   Habitat: Shallow water.
   Description: About 1 in. high, this is a sturdy little shell of 3 or 4 whorls, the spire short but sharply pointed. Aperture moderately large; and there is a groovelike umbilicus. Surface bears sharp, deeply impressed growth lines. The color is yellowish brown, with 2 or 3 evenly spaced bands of white, each boldly marked with squarish chocolate spots.

NATICA CHEMNITZI Pfr.   Pl. 55
   Range: Gulf of California to Peru.
   Habitat: Shallow water; sandbars.
   Description: This strong shell is globular in shape and 1½ in.

high. There are about 4 whorls, a short spire, and a pointed apex. Aperture quite large, semilunar in shape; there is an umbilicus partially blocked by a white callus. The surface is smooth. Color pale bluish gray, lighter on the base, with clouded bands of darker shade checked with white on the upper portions. Operculum shelly, as with all of this genus.

NATICA ELENAE Réc.   **Pl. 55**
    Range: Gulf of California to Ecuador.
    Habitat: Shallow water.
    Description: A stout shell with a blunt apex and about 4 whorls. Height around 1 in. Aperture relatively large; umbilicus deep. Surface smooth, often polished. Color pale ivory, with narrow stripes of tan that are often wavy. There is a spiral of darker V-shaped marks at the shoulder.

NATICA GRAYI Phil.   **Pl. 55**
    Range: Gulf of California to Ecuador.
    Habitat: Shallow water.
    Description: Slightly less than 1 in. high as a rule, this is a rather delicate shell of about 3 whorls. There is a very short spire; the shell is mainly body whorl. Large aperture semilunar; umbilicus choked by a thick callus. Surface smooth and polished. Color ivory, with 3 encircling bands of orange-brown dots. The tops of the volutions bear rather strong vertical lines.
    Remarks: Formerly listed as *N. catenata* Phil.

Genus *Polinices* Montfort 1810

POLINICES BIFASCIATA (Gray)   **Pl. 55**
    Range: Gulf of California to Panama.
    Habitat: Shallow water.
    Description: A semiglobular shell with a pointed apex. About 4 whorls, the height some 1½ in. Aperture large; operculum horny; small umbilicus partly covered by a lobelike callus. Color pale yellowish brown, with 2 well-separated and narrow whitish bands encircling the body whorl. Callus and umbilical region rich dark brown.

POLINICES UBER (Val.)   **Pl. 55**
    Range: Gulf of California to S. America.
    Habitat: Mudflats.
    Description: Attaining a height of nearly 2 in., this is a solid shell of about 4 whorls, the apex sharply pointed. Color polished white all over. There is a small umbilicus; and the inner lip is reflected on the body whorl as a heavy patch of enamel, covering the upperpart of the umbilicus. During life there is a pale brownish periostracum.

Family Cypraeidae: Cowries
(see p. 79)

Genus *Cypraea* Linné 1758

CYPRAEA ALBUGINOSA Gray   **White-spotted Cowry**   Pl. 55
Range: Gulf of California to Mazatlán.
Habitat: Moderately shallow water.
Description: In length averaging about 1 in., this is a pretty little cowry, oval in shape and plump in build. Color pale bluish white, dotted with round chestnut spots, some of them with white centers. The base is white, and there is a distinct lilac border all around the base of the shell.

CYPRAEA ANNETTAE Dall   **Annette's Cowry**   Pl. 55
Range: Gulf of California to Mazatlán.
Habitat: Moderately shallow water.
Description: Nearly 2 in. long, the outline is somewhat pear-shaped. Upper surface bluish white, very heavily spotted and marbled with chestnut-brown. Lower surface rich pinkish brown, more or less spotted with black toward sides.
Remarks: Formerly listed as *C. sowerbyi* Kiener.

CYPRAEA ARABICULA Lam.   **Little Arabian Cowry**   Pl. 55
Range: Gulf of California to Peru.
Habitat: Shallow water.
Description: A solid, oval shell, flattish on the base and regularly domed above. Length about 1¼ in. There is a curved elongate aperture, heavily toothed and deeply notched at each end. Surface highly polished, as is usual with the cowries. Color of upper surface mottled yellowish brown on a gray background, around the margins there being a rather broad border of violet, heavily spotted with black. Lower surface pinkish.

CYPRAEA CERVINETTA Kiener   **Little Deer Cowry**   Pl. 55
Range: S. Gulf of California to S. America.
Habitat: Moderately deep water.
Description: This is the largest species of cowry to be found in w. N. America, growing to a length of nearly 4 in. It is rather elongate, and colored yellowish brown above, commonly (but not always) with 3 or 4 broad bands of purplish brown and over all a series of round whitish spots, those along the sides of shell sometimes forming rings. Young specimens generally without spots. Aperture strongly toothed. Lower side violet-brown; inside of shell silvery purple.

Family Eratoidae: Sea Buttons
(see p. 79)

Genus *Trivia* Broderip 1837

TRIVIA RADIANS (Lam.)   **Pl. 55**
Range: Gulf of California to Ecuador.
Habitat: Intertidal.
Description: A strong and solid shell, growing to a length of about ¾ in. It is cowry-like in appearance, the base flat and heavily scored with transverse ridges, some of which may fork. Upper surface bears a deep median groove, with sharp ridges extending to margins. Some of these ridges swell into bumps as they reach the top of the shell. Color purplish gray.
Remarks: Members of the genus *Trivia* are popularly known as button shells.

TRIVIA SANGUINEA (Sow.)   **Pl. 55**
Range: Gulf of California to Ecuador.
Habitat: Intertidal.
Description: In length under ½ in., this is a neat, small shell, deep mahogany-brown in color. The median groove is lacking; sharp ridges cover the upper surface and continue around to the base.
Remarks: Members of the genus *Trivia* are popularly known as button shells.

Genus *Jenneria* Jousseaume 1884

JENNERIA PUSTULATA (Sol.)   **Pl. 55**
Range: S. Gulf of California to Ecuador.
Habitat: Shallow water.
Description: An oddly decorative shell, shaped like a cowry but with strong transverse teeth, or ridges, running all the way across the base. Upper surface covered with round, wartlike orange pustules; rest of shell bluish gray. The length is about ¾ in.
Remarks: This distinctive gastropod is the sole member of the genus.

Family Ovulidae: Simnias
(see p. 80)

Genus *Cyphoma* Röding 1798

CYPHOMA EMARGINATUM (Sowerby)   **Pl. 55**
Range: Gulf of California to Ecuador.
Habitat: Moderately shallow water.

Description: A shiny white or creamy-white shell, its length about ¾ in. It is long and narrow, solid and durable, with a dorsal ridge, or hump, near the center of the shell and extending squarely across it. Aperture narrow and runs length of lower side; it is strongly notched at each end; the lip is rolled in and thickened.

Remarks: The Atlantic counterpart of this species is *C. gibbosum* (Linné).

Family Cassididae: Helmets

THIS family contains the large and heavy helmet shells, many of them used for cutting cameos. The aperture is long, terminating in front in a recurved canal. Outer lip generally thickened. These are active, predatory mollusks, living on sandy bottoms in warm seas.

Genus *Cassis* Scopoli 1777

CASSIS CENTIQUADRATA (Val.)   Pl. 56
　　Range: Gulf of California to Ecuador.
　　Habitat: Moderately shallow water.
　　Description: Subglobular with a short pointed spire, the whorl count 5. Height about 3 in. There is a groove at the shoulders, and on each side of the groove is a nodular ridge producing a somewhat turreted spire. The rest of the shell bears revolving lines, regularly spaced. Aperture large; outer lip toothed within and considerably thickened. Inner lip folded over the twisted canal in a platelike fashion and it is strongly pustulate. Color ivory-white, with squarish bars of pale orange arranged in encircling bands.

CASSIS COARCTATA Sow.   Pl. 56
　　Range: S. Gulf of California to Ecuador.
　　Habitat: Moderately shallow water.
　　Description: About 2 in. high, a rugged shell of 4 or 5 tightly coiled whorls, the sutures indistinct and the last volution constituting most of the shell. The sculpture consists of 4 rows of obtuse tubercles and weak spiral ridges that are often granular. Short folded canal at base. Aperture, toothed on both lips, is constricted at top and widened below. Color yellowish white, heavily mottled with reddish brown.

CASSIS TENUIS Wood   Pl. 56
　　Range: S. Gulf of California to Ecuador.
　　Habitat: Moderately shallow water.
　　Description: Rather thin and light, attaining a height of 5 in.

About 5 whorls, with a short pointed spire; most of shell made up of the last volution. Shoulders knobby, and smaller rounded knobs encircle the body whorl in 2 rows. Surface scored by widely spaced spiral grooves, generally arranged in pairs. Aperture long; outer lip strongly reflected and toothed, with only a few groovelike teeth at the base of the inner lip. Color orange-brown, thickly studded with whitish vertical streaks.

Genus *Morum* Röding 1798

MORUM TUBERCULOSUM (Reeve)   Pl. 56
Range: Gulf of California to Peru.
Habitat: Moderately shallow water.
Description: This warty shell, solid and sturdy, grows to be about 1½ in. high. There is no spire, the top of the shell being perfectly flat. Surface with 4 or 5 rows of bumpy knobs, plus very weak revolving lines. Aperture long and narrow; outer lip thickened and toothed within. Inner lip smooth, and there is no twisted canal. Color white, heavily mottled and splashed with chocolate-brown and black.

Family Cymatiidae: Tritons

(see p. 81)

Genus *Cymatium* Röding 1798

CYMATIUM GIBBOSUM (Brod.)   Pl. 56
Range: Gulf of California to Ecuador.
Habitat: Moderately deep water.
Description: A knobby little shell, its height 1½ in. and whorl count about 7. Lip greatly expanded and thickened; varices left as the shell increases in size give the outline a bizarre appearance. There are distinct revolving ribs and threadlike vertical lines; at the shoulders are series of rounded, prominent knobs. Aperture small, with a moderate, nearly closed canal. Operculum horny. Mottled yellowish.

CYMATIUM LIGNARIUM (Brod.)   Pl. 56
Range: Gulf of California to Ecuador.
Habitat: Moderately deep water.
Description: Small but solid, the height about 1 in. There are 4 whorls, a rather small aperture, and a short canal. Sculpture consists of revolving lines and stout vertical folds. Outer lip greatly thickened, and both lips are strongly toothed. Color yellowish white, often banded with darker; both lips stained bright orange.

CYMATIUM WIEGMANNI (Anton)   Pl. 56
   Range: Gulf of California to Peru.
   Habitat: Moderately deep water.
   Description: A stout shell of about 6 whorls, its height nearly
3 in. There is a weakly beaded ridge at the shoulder, from which
the shell slopes gently up to the suture, so that the spire is somewhat turreted. Surface decorated with rounded revolving ribs,
alternating in size. Color yellowish brown, the spaces between
the ribs darker in tone. Aperture large; outer lip strongly
grooved within. Inner lip plastered on the columella. There is
a short canal.

Genus *Distorsio* Röding 1798

DISTORSIO CONSTRICTUS (Brod.)   Pl. 56
   Range: Gulf of California to Ecuador.
   Habitat: Moderately deep water.
   Description: Nearly 3 in. high, this is an odd shell of about 8
uneven whorls. The sutures are not distinct, and each volution
seems to bulge at one side, resulting in an unsymmetrical spire.
Surface ornamented with weak vertical ribs that are swollen at
intervals to produce revolving rows of knobs, with a double row
at the periphery. Aperture small and constricted, with a deep
notchlike groove well up on inner lip; the strongly toothed outer
lip is provided with a long projection leading into this notch.
Outer lip reflected, inner lip forming a thin bladelike patch over
the columella. There is a short canal, bending backward. White,
more or less tinged with orange-yellow.

Family Bursidae: Frog Shells
(see p. 81)

Genus *Bursa* Röding 1798

BURSA CAELATA (Brod.)   Pl. 56
   Range: Gulf of California to Peru.
   Habitat: Moderately deep water.
   Description: About 2 in. high, this is a solid shell of some 5 whorls.
The volutions are ornamented with rows of small knobs, and
there are 2 prominent varices on each whorl, directly opposite
each other, so that there is a more or less continuous ridge run-
ning up each side of the shell to the blunt apex. Aperture oval;
outer lip thickened and toothed within, the inner lip plicate.
There is a short anterior canal and a strong notch at the upper
angle of the aperture. Color brownish; aperture white.
   Remarks: The frog shells formerly were assigned to the genus
Ranella.

BURSA NANA (Brod. & Sow.)   Pl. 56
  Range: Mazatlán to Panama.
  Habitat: Moderately deep water.
  Description: A slightly smaller shell than *B. caelata* (above), but shaped much like it. Height usually no more than 1½ in. There is a band of prominent knobs at the shoulder of each volution, but most of the shell surface is relatively smooth. Color purplish brown, generally with a narrow whitish band on each whorl.
  Remarks: The frog shells formerly were assigned to the genus *Ranella*.

Family Colubrariidae: Curved Shells

FUSIFORM shells, with high spires and long apertures and short, recurved canals. The varices are usually irregularly placed. Distributed in warm and temperate seas.

Genus *Colubraria* Schumachei 1817

COLUBRARIA SOVERBII (Reeve)   Pl. 56
  Range: Cape San Lucas to S. America.
  Habitat: Moderately deep water.
  Description: About 7 whorls, the height ¾ in. Surface marked with a weak cancellate sculpture, each whorl with a strong rounded varix, staggered rather than aligned along the sides, as in the frog shells. Aperture small; outer lip thickened; short canal. Yellowish gray, more or less streaked with darker shades.

Family Tonnidae: Tun Shells

A small group of large or medium-sized gastropods, chiefly of the tropics. The shell is relatively thin and globular, usually with a greatly swollen body whorl. They also are called cask shells or wine jars.

Genus *Malea* Valenciennes 1832

MALEA RINGENS (Swain.)   Pl. 56
  Range: Mazatlán to Peru.
  Habitat: Moderately deep water.
  Description: Large and strong but quite light for its size. Growing to a height of 7 or 8 in., this shell has 5 whorls, the sutures indistinct. Body whorl large and swollen, the surface bearing broad flattened revolving ribs with wide spaces between. Outer lip reflected and strongly toothed. There is a short twisted canal, and midway of the inner lip there is a deep gougelike groove. Color yellowish white.

Family Ficidae: Fig Shells

THESE are graceful and gently curving shells, found in warm and tropical seas. There is no operculum. Usually sculptured with fine spiral and concentric lines. General shape much like that of a large fig.

Genus *Ficus* Röding 1798

FICUS VENTRICOSA (Sow.)   Pl. 56
   Range: Gulf of California to Ecuador.
   Habitat: Moderately shallow water.
   Description: From 3 to 4 in. high, this is a rather light shell with a short, flat spire and only 4 or 5 whorls. Aperture large-at top and narrowed to a long, gently curved canal at bottom. The sculpture consists of revolving cordlike lines and thinner vertical lines, so a network pattern is produced. Color yellowish gray, with reddish-brown spots on some of the larger riblets.

Family Muricidae: Rock Shells
(see p. 82)

Genus *Murex* Linné 1758

MUREX ELENENSIS Dall   Pl. 57
   Range: Gulf of California to Ecuador.
   Habitat: Moderately shallow water.
   Description: Some 3 in. high and composed of about 6 whorls. Shell globular with a short pointed spire and a long and slender canal almost closed throughout its length. Aperture oval; outer lip greatly thickened and decorated with spines that continue on down the canal. Shell growth leaves 3 of these "old lips" as varices on each whorl, so that the shell is armed with 3 rows of spines. The surface bears revolving lines that are raised into humps as they cross the vertical folds. Color buffy or ivory-white.

MUREX RECURVIROSTRIS Brod.   Pl. 57
   Range: S. Gulf of California to Ecuador.
   Habitat: Moderately shallow water.
   Description: About 2 in. high when fully grown, this is a shell of 4 or 5 rounded whorls, a short spire, and a long, slender canal. There are 3 thick and solid varices to a volution, each with a short spine at the shoulder. Shell sculptured further by vertical folds and thin encircling lines. Aperture not large; inner lip reflected on columella; the long canal is nearly closed, with a few short spines scattered along the edges. Color grayish, often with brown bands.

Genus *Hexaplex* Perry 1811

HEXAPLEX BRASSICA (Lam.)   **Pls. 6, 57**

   Range: Mazatlán to Peru.
   Habitat: Moderately shallow water.
   Description: This is our largest member of the genus, reaching a height of 8 in. The shell has about 8 whorls, each with several rather flattish varices, serrated at the edges and developing into frondlike spines at the shoulders. Color whitish or yellowish, sometimes pinkish, with 3 brown bands. Aperture pinkish.

HEXAPLEX ERYTHROSTOMUS (Swain.)   **Pls. 6, 57**

   Range: Guaymas to Peru.
   Habitat: Moderately shallow water.
   Description: This is a handsome shell, not uncommon but eagerly sought by collectors. The height is from 3 to 6 in., the whorl count 6. Sutures indistinct, general appearance rugged and sturdy. The surface has a number of spiny vertical folds and ridges, and very fine encircling lines. Aperture large and round; outer lip thickened at its edge and armed with hollow folded spines that will add another varix as the shell increases in size. There is a columellar callus reflected over the body whorl. Canal broad, closed, and bends backward. Color white, sometimes pinkish white; the polished aperture is a beautiful rosy pink.
   Remarks: This species was long known as *Murex bicolor* Val.

HEXAPLEX REGIUS (Swain.)   **Pls. 6, 57**

   Range: Gulf of California to Peru.
   Habitat: Moderately shallow water.
   Description: This shell is much like *H. erythrostomus* (above) in shape and appearance. Growing to a height of 5 or 6 in., the body whorl bears from 6 to 8 varices, each one a double row of serrated spines, with revolving ridges between them, and the canal is broad and closed. Color brown, more or less mottled; aperture bright pink, darkening into deep brown at upperpart of columella.

Genus *Muricanthus* Swainson 1840

MURICANTHUS NIGRITUS (Phil.)   **Pl. 57**

   Range: Gulf of California.
   Habitat: Moderately shallow water.
   Description: Another rugged and solid shell, attaining a height of 6 in. Spire short and pointed, sutures indistinct, with 6 whorls. Surface sculptured with broad revolving ribs, and by varices composed of hollow spines, 8 to 10 on the body whorl. The aperture is moderate in size; inner lip polished; the canal is straight, broad, and partially closed. Color whitish, with encircling ribs and spines of black.

MURICANTHUS OXYACANTHA (Brod.)   Pl. 57
    Range: S. Mexico.
    Habitat: Moderately shallow water.
    Description: A smaller shell than *M. nigritus* (above), seldom
more than 2 in. high. There are 7 or 8 whorls, with about 8
varices, each studded with long spines. The surface is also
decorated with stout encircling ribs, a small rib alternating with
a larger one. Aperture small and nearly round, the canal broad
and closed. Color yellowish brown, the spines darker in tone.
    Remarks: There is some question as to this species occurring as
far north as the Gulf of California.

MURICANTHUS PRINCEPS (Sow.)   Pl. 57
    Range: S. Gulf of California to Peru.
    Habitat: Moderately shallow water.
    Description: A very spiny shell, its height about 4 in. and the
whorl count 6 or 7. Edge of lip not thickened, but armed with
long, hollow, frondlike spines. Around the body whorl are 4 or 5
varices composed of decorative spines. The inner lip forms a
polished callus over the parietal wall; the curved canal is broad,
closed, and spiny. Color whitish, with the encircling bands dark
brown or black.

Genus *Muricopsis* Bucquoy, Dautzenberg, & Dollfus 1892

MURICOPSIS ARMATUS (A. Adams)   Pl. 57
    Range: Gulf of California.
    Habitat: Moderately shallow water.
    Description: About 1 in. high, with 5 whorls that produce a well-
elevated spire. Sutures rather indistinct. The vertical folds are
very prominent and are spinose, particularly at the shoulder.
Aperture small, the partially closed canal moderately long.
Color yellowish white.
    Remarks: Formerly listed as *Muricidea squamulata* Carp.

MURICOPSIS ZETEKI Hert. & Strong   Pl. 57
    Range: Mazatlán to Panama.
    Habitat: Moderately shallow water.
    Description: A small fusiform shell, its height about 1 in., fre-
quently less. There are 5 or 6 whorls, the sutures indistinct.
The surface bears revolving ribs which rise into short spines as
they cross vertical folds. Aperture narrow; outer lip thin and
serrated. There is a fold at the base of the columella. Color
grayish white.

Genus *Vitularia* Swainson 1840

VITULARIA SALEBROSA (King & Brod.)   Pl. 57
Range: Cedros I., Baja California, to Panama.
Habitat: Moderately shallow water.
Description: A solid, rather slender shell from 2 to 3 in. high.
There are about 5 whorls, the sutures plainly marked. A single
row of small knobs at the shoulder; rest of the surface roughened
like sandpaper by minute dimples and wartlike dots. Color
brownish olive; aperture white. The outer lip may be either thin
or greatly thickened and toothed within, and there may be an
occasional varix on some individuals.

Genus *Trophon* Montfort 1810

TROPHON BEEBEI Hert. & Strong   Pl. 57
Range: S. Gulf of California.
Habitat: Deep water.
Description: This species grows to be slightly more than 2 in.
high and has about 6 loosely coiled whorls. Each volution has
a circle of short spines at the shoulder, then the volution flattens
out to produce a turreted spire. The canal is long and open.
Color pale brown.

TROPHON CERROSENSIS Dall   Pl. 57
Range: S. Gulf of California.
Habitat: Deep water.
Description: This is a fancy shell — a real collector's item. The
height is about 2 in., the whorl count 6 or 7, and there is a moder-
ate spire. There are some 10 thin, bladelike varices to a volution.
Aperture oval, and there is a short canal. Color pale yellowish.
Remarks: The subspecies *T. c. catalinensis* Old. (Plate 4, No. 7,
and Plate 36, No. 1), found farther north, is a larger shell.

Genus *Eupleura* H. & A. Adams 1853

EUPLEURA MURICIFORMIS (Brod.)   Pl. 57
Range: Gulf of California to S. America.
Habitat: Shallow water.
Description: An easily recognized shell, 1¼ in. high, with about
5 whorls. The outer lip is considerably thickened, and there is
a single varix directly opposite, so that the shell has a flattish
look. Surface sculptured with prominent revolving ribs and by
vertical folds, about 8 to a whorl. Aperture relatively small; lip
slightly toothed within; the canal is moderately long and nearly
closed. The color is gray.

EUPLEURA NITIDA (Brod.)   **Pl. 57**
  Range: Mazatlán to Panama.
  Habitat: Shallow water.
  Description: Small and solid, the height no more than 1 in.,
  generally less. There are about 5 whorls, each with a broad
  varix on each side, so that the whole shell appears to be somewhat flattened. Aperture small, the canal short and almost
  closed. Color purplish gray to dark gray, sometimes marked
  with white.

Family Magilidae: Coral Snails

THESE are gastropods that feed upon corals, and spend all their
lives in coral colonies. Some South Pacific species become attached
to the coral and grow with it, producing almost tubular shells.
Any of them may be more or less distorted, owing to their manner
of life.

Genus *Coralliophila* H. & A. Adams 1853

CORALLIOPHILA COSTATA (Blain.)   **Pl. 57**
  Range: Gulf of California to Panama.
  Habitat: On coral.
  Description: A sturdy shell of some 5 whorls, its height about
  1 in. The sutures are indistinct. There are rather weak spiral
  lines, and strong rounded vertical folds, and the shell rather
  bulges at the periphery. Aperture elongate; outer lip somewhat
  thickened. Color gray; aperture purple.

CORALLIOPHILA MADREPORARUM (Sow.)   **Pl. 57**
  Range: S. Gulf of California to Panama; also Hawaii and
  Micronesia.
  Habitat: On coral.
  Description: This shell appears to be all aperture. There is a
  short and tiny apex, but most of the shell is body whorl. Slightly
  more than ½ in. high, the shell is pale gray; aperture purplish.
  Remarks: This is an Indo-Pacific snail that has become adapted
  to our shores. See also Plate 69, No. 10.

Family Thaididae: Dye Shells
(see p. 87)

Genus *Purpura* Bruguière 1789

PURPURA PATULA PANSA Gould   **Pl. 58**
  Range: S. Gulf of California to S. America.
  Habitat: Shoreline; rocks.

Description: Attaining a height of 4 in., the shell is rough and solid, the body whorl greatly enlarged. It is dull grayish green, the interior often salmon-pink. The surface bears revolving lines and numerous nodules, very pronounced in partly grown specimens but often worn and indistinct in old individuals. Aperture very large; outer lip thin and sharp; a polished area on the parietal wall. There is a small horny operculum, too small to close the aperture.

Remarks: The typical *P. patula* (Linné) is a Caribbean species, and the West Coast *P. p. pansa* is regarded as a subspecies of the Atlantic snail.

Genus *Thais* Röding 1798

THAIS BISERIALIS (Blain.)   Pl. 58

Range: Gulf of California to Chile.
Habitat: Near shore; rocks.
Description: Some 2 in. high and grayish, more or less clouded with brown. Shell strong and rugged, with a large body whorl, a sharply pointed apex, a moderate spire, and composed of about 6 whorls. Sutures distinct. The shoulders are sloping, and the surface is decorated with strong revolving lines. There is a double row of tubercles on each volution. Outer lip thick, crenulate within; aperture pinkish orange.

THAIS KIOSQUIFORMIS (Duc.)   Pl. 58

Range: Magdalena Bay to Peru.
Habitat: Shallow water.
Description: An ornate shell of 5 or 6 turreted whorls, height 2½ in. There are 2 rows of encircling spines on each volution, the upper row larger, and the rest of the shell bears distinct revolving lines, deeply impressed. Growth laminae pass over the sutures and touch the volutions, a characteristic of this mollusk. Aperture large; lip plain; short, twisted canal. Color grayish brown, revolving lines paler in tone.

THAIS PLANOSPIRA (Lam.)   Pl. 58

Range: Cape San Lucas to Peru.
Habitat: Shallow water.
Description: A solid shell about 2 in. high, with only about 3 whorls, the last one making up practically all of the shell. The top is flat, or concave, with a tiny spire at the center, and the surface is sculptured with revolving ribs that are coarser at the shoulders. In front the shell is all aperture, almost like an abalone. The outer lip and the very broad inner lip bear longitudinal ribs that are reddish on a white ground, and midway of the columella there is a large excavation crossed by an oblique black rib. Back of shell yellowish brown.

THAIS SPECIOSA (Val.)   Pl. 58
    Range : Gulf of California to Peru.
    Habitat : Shallow water.
    Description : Triangular shape, 1½ in. high, the shoulders wide
    and the shell tapering rapidly to the base. There is a short spire;
    the whorl count is 4, the sutures indistinct. There are 4 rows of
    pointed knobs on the body whorl, the largest row at the shoulder.
    Aperture moderate in size; lip thin and plain. Color whitish,
    with encircling bands of brown; aperture yellow.

Genus *Acanthina* Waldheim 1807

ACANTHINA BREVIDENTATA (Wood)   Pl. 58
    Range : Mazatlán to Panama.
    Habitat : Shallow water.
    Description : About 1¼ in. high, this is a chunky little shell of
    about 5 whorls, the sutures rather indistinct. There is a broad
    aperture; the outer lip is thickened and toothed within, and the
    inner lip bears a polished white area. The ornamentation con-
    sists of well-spaced nodules that are white, and the rest of the
    shell is grayish black.

ACANTHINA MURICATA (Brod.)   Pl. 58
    Range : Mazatlán to Ecuador.
    Habitat : Moderately shallow water.
    Description : A somewhat variable shell, heavy and solid, its
    height up to 3 in. There are 3 or 4 whorls, and a low spire that
    is sometimes almost flat. Surface bears about 4 revolving ribs
    that are large, thick, and rounded, and they are crossed by
    numerous thin, platelike lamellae. Aperture large; outer lip
    more or less scalloped by the ribs; the inner lip forming a broad
    polished area over the parietal wall, with a groovelike excavation
    at the base. Color yellowish gray.

ACANTHINA TUBERCULATA (Sow.)   Pl. 58
    Range : San Felipe to Cape San Lucas.
    Habitat : Moderately shallow water.
    Description : This snail is usually smaller than *A. muricata*
    (above), the height seldom exceeding 2 in. Spire higher than in
    A. muricata, and the revolving ribs are broken into a series of
    stout knobs on the upperpart of the whorls. Finer revolving
    lines encircle the body whorl, and the coarse lamellae of *A.
    muricata* are lacking. Color yellowish gray.

Genus *Morula* Schumacher 1817

MORULA FERRUGINOSA (Reeve)   Pl. 58
    Range : Gulf of California.
    Habitat : Moderately shallow water.

Description: About 1 in. high, this is a rather slender shell of some 5 whorls. The sculpture consists of obscure folds, plus 3 or 4 rows of rounded knobs, the knobs placed precisely on the upper angles of the folds. Aperture long and narrow; canal short and open. Color gray, the knobs black, sometimes with a paler band between them. Aperture bluish.

Family Columbellidae: Dove Shells

(see p. 89)

Genus *Anachis* H. & A. Adams 1853

ANACHIS CORONATA (Sow.)   Pl. 58
Range: Guaymas to Panama.
Habitat: Shallow water.
Description: A small shell of 6 whorls, its height ½ in. There is a double row of small tubercles on each volution (the upper row largest), with riblike ridges connecting the 2 rows. Spiral lines are present on the base, but in general the surface is quite smooth and shiny. Aperture narrow; outer lip sharp but weakly toothed within. Color yellowish white, flecked with brown.

ANACHIS NIGRICANS (Sow.)   Pl. 58
Range: Gulf of California to Panama.
Habitat: Shallow water.
Description: Fusiform in shape and just over ¼ in. high; composed of 5 whorls. The surface bears both revolving and vertical lines, the latter stronger; at the suture is a row of minute beads. Color brown to nearly black.

ANACHIS PYGMAEA (Sow.)   Pl. 58
Range: Gulf of California to Panama.
Habitat: Shallow water; under stones.
Description: Less than ¼ in. high, this is really a tiny shell, made up of 5 or 6 whorls. There are several prominent vertical ribs on each volution. Color white, with 2 or 3 rows of brownish spots to a whorl.

ANACHIS SCALARINA (Sow.)   Pl. 58
Range: Gulf of California to Panama.
Habitat: Shallow water.
Description: A stout shell of 6 whorls, the height just under 1 in. There are about 15 sharp vertical ribs to a volution, along with fine revolving lines. Aperture long and narrow; outer lip thick and toothed within. Color brownish, with a pair of whitish bands on the body whorl.

ANACHIS VARIA (Sow.)   **Pl. 58**
   Range: San Felipe to Panama.
   Habitat: Shallow water.
   Description: About ¾ in. high, a fusiform shell of 6 or 7 whorls. Sculpture consists of strong vertical ribs, crowded on the spire but becoming more widely spaced on the last volution. Spiral lines are also present, particularly toward the base. Aperture small and narrow; outer lip thin and sharp. Color dark brown or black, usually with a paler band below the center of the shell.

Genus *Pyrene* Röding 1798

PYRENE FUSCATA (Sow.)   **Pl. 58**
   Range: Gulf of California to Peru.
   Habitat: Shallow water.
   Description: A smooth, shining, inflated shell, tapering regularly to the apex and the base, the height ¾ in. There are about 5 whorls, the sutures plainly marked. Aperture long and narrow; outer lip thickened at the center and toothed within. Inner lip also toothed. Surface plum-colored, with numerous scattered dots of white, and at the suture there is a ring of whitish patches.

PYRENE HAEMASTOMA (Sow.)   **Pl. 58**
   Range: Gulf of California to Ecuador.
   Habitat: Shallow water.
   Description: Nearly 1 in. high, this is a smooth and solid shell of 5 whorls, the sutures sharply delineated. Spire well elevated, aperture long, narrow, and curved. The outer lip flares at the upper angle and is toothed within. Color chocolate-brown and white and orange, the colors arranged in broad splashes and streaks; scarcely any two shells are marked the same. Aperture bright orange.

PYRENE MAJOR (Sow.)   **Pl. 58**
   Range: Gulf of California to Peru.
   Habitat: Shallow water.
   Description: About 1 in. high, a solid shell of 6 stout whorls, the sutures well impressed. The shoulders are rounded, and the general outline of the shell is fusiform. Aperture long and narrow; outer lip thickened at the center and angled a little at the top. Inner margin of lip strongly toothed. Color chestnut-brown, with vertical streaks of white and numerous whitish dots.

PYRENE STROMBIFORMIS (Lam.)   **Pl. 58**
   Range: Gulf of California to Peru.
   Habitat: Shallow water.
   Description: This shell is shaped very much like *P. major* (above), but is somewhat larger and has a taller spire. The outer lip flares somewhat at the top like a *Strombus*, hence the specific name. Aperture narrow; the thickened lip strongly toothed

within. Surface smooth and shiny. Color chestnut-brown, with elongate dots of white encircling the shell.

Genus *Mazatlania* Dall 1900

MAZATLANIA FULGURATA (Phil.)   **Pl. 58**
Range: Mazatlán to Nicaragua.
Habitat: Moderately shallow water.
Description: A slender, spikelike shell about ¾ in. high, with 8 or 9 flattish whorls, the sutures fairly plain. Aperture narrow, the outer lip thin and sharp. Surface bears vertical ribs with rather wide concave spaces between them, and the finish of the shell is generally quite shiny. The inner lip forms a platelike layer of enamel on the body whorl. Color yellowish gray, somewhat streaked with brown.
Remarks: This snail was originally named by Philippi as a *Terebra*.

Genus *Mitrella* Risso 1826

MITRELLA MILLEPUNCTATA (Carp.)   **Pl. 59**
Range: S. Gulf of California.
Habitat: Moderately shallow water.
Description: Only ¼ in. high, this diminutive shell has 6 or 7 rather rounded whorls, the sutures well indented. Surface smooth, and grayish brown in tone, but so minutely punctate with orange dots that one usually needs a hand lens to see them. Outer lip thickened and toothed within.

MITRELLA OCELLATA (Gmel.)   **Pl. 59**
Range: Gulf of California.
Habitat: Moderately shallow water.
Description: A smooth, highly polished shell of 7 or 8 whorls, the height no more than ½ in. Apex commonly truncated. The aperture is long and narrow, the outer lip moderately thin. Color whitish, heavily reticulated with chocolate-brown; a series of white spots follows the suture line.

Genus *Parametaria* Dall 1916

PARAMETARIA DUPONTII (Kiener)   **False Cone**   **Pl. 55**
Range: Gulf of California.
Habitat: Moderately shallow water.
Description: This shell is broad at the top, tapering regularly to a small bottom, the narrow aperture runs the full length of the body whorl. Lower 3rd of shell bears sharp spiral lines. Color an irregular and blotched combination of white, brown, and orange.
Remarks: The uninitiated beachcomber would almost certainly

regard this snail as a member of the *Conus* group, since it bears a strong resemblance to that genus. It is sometimes called the False Cone.

Genus *Strombina* Mörch 1852

STROMBINA GIBBERULA (Sow.)   Pl. 59
Range: Gulf of California to Peru.
Habitat: Moderately shallow water.
Description: A fusiform shell with a swollen body whorl and a slender, sharply pointed spire, the height about ½ in. The last volution bears elongate humps on the back and sides. Aperture narrow; the lip thickened but sharp at the edge, and weakly toothed within. Color gray; "humps" usually whitish; aperture whitish too.

STROMBINA MACULOSA (Sow.)   Pl. 59
Range: Gulf of California to Panama.
Habitat: Moderately shallow water.
Description: A slender, high-spired shell of about 8 whorls, the height 1 in. There is a single row of prominent knobs at the shoulders, and a few spiral lines at the base; rest of shell smooth and usually quite well polished. Aperture narrow; outer lip with a few weak teeth well within, and the inner lip forms a ridge where it is cemented to the body whorl. Color creamy white, with blotches and faint tracings of chocolate.

STROMBINA RECURVA (Sow.)   Pl. 59
Range: Gulf of California.
Habitat: Moderately shallow water.
Description: A neat little shell just over 1 in. high, with 9 whorls producing a tall, sharply pointed spire. At the shoulder there is a circle of rounded knobs, which form a spiral up the spire, the earliest volutions bearing vertical folds. A few weak encircling lines are present at the shoulders, and several strong spiral lines adorn the base of the body whorl. Aperture long and narrow, somewhat constricted in the middle by a ridge just inside the outer lip. The inner lip is plastered on the columella, and there is a short open canal. Color yellowish brown.

Family Nassariidae: Dog Whelks
(see p. 90)

Genus *Nassarius* Duméril 1805

NASSARIUS ANGULICOSTIS (Pils. & Lowe)   Pl. 59
Range: Gulf of California to Panama.
Habitat: Shallow water.
Description: A strong little shell of 5 or 6 whorls, the height

½ in. Surface sculptured with stout vertical ribs, about 10 on the body whorl. Ribs angled at the shoulder, producing a slope that gives the spire a somewhat turreted appearance. Aperture small; outer lip thick and toothed within, the inner lip forming a callus on the parietal wall. There is a short twisted canal. Yellowish, commonly banded with brown.

NASSARIUS COMPLANATUS (Powys)   Pl. 59
Range: Gulf of California to Panama.
Habitat: Shallow water.
Description: A stubby shell, the height ½ in. and whorl count 6. The vertical ridges are rather obscure, but each volution bears encircling rows of small beads. Aperture relatively small, notched at each end; the outer lip is considerably thickened. Color brownish, more or less marked with white.

NASSARIUS CORPULENTUS (C. B. Adams)   Pl. 59
Range: Gulf of California to Ecuador.
Habitat: Shallow water.
Description: A stout shell, rather blocky in appearance, just over ½ in. high. There are about 6 whorls, each marked with strong revolving lines and vertical ridges. Both lips are thickened, and toothed within. Color whitish, with bands of pale brown.

NASSARIUS LUTEOSTOMA (Brod. & Sow.)   Pl. 59
Range: Gulf of California to Ecuador.
Habitat: Shallow water.
Description: About ¾ in. high, this is a rugged shell with an acutely pointed spire. There are 5 whorls, each bearing 6 or 7 prominent vertical ribs. The aperture is toothed; the outer lip has a distinct notch at the top. There is a short twisted canal at the base; the inner lip forms a broad layer of enamel over the body whorl. Color bluish gray, with brown bands; ribs and aperture white, with a bright yellow apertural callus.

NASSARIUS PAGODUS (Reeve)   Pl. 59
Range: Gulf of California to S. America.
Habitat: Shallow water.
Description: This shell may be an inch or so in height, but is usually smaller. There are 6 well-rounded whorls, each decorated with stout, rounded, vertical ridges, about 7 to a volution. Fine lines are present, encircling the whorls. The aperture is small; outer lip rather thin and sharp, and the inner lip is twisted as it joins the short curved canal. Color yellowish white, with brown bands.

NASSARIUS VERSICOLOR (C. B. Adams)   Pl. 59
Range: Gulf of California to Peru.
Habitat: Shallow water.

Description: About ½ in. high, this is a solid shell of 6 or 7 whorls. There are revolving lines and vertical ridges covering the surface, and there is a marked fold at the base of the shell. Sutures well impressed. The color is yellowish white, more or less banded with brown.

Family Buccinidae: Whelks

(see p. 92)

Genus *Cantharus* Röding 1798

CANTHARUS ELEGANS (Grif. & Pidg.)   Pl. 58
   Range: Gulf of California to Peru.
   Habitat: Moderately shallow water.
   Description: About 2 in. high, a sturdy shell of some 6 or 7 whorls. The surface bears strong and sharp revolving lines that are rather well spaced, and weak vertical folds. At the shoulders the crests of the folds form elongate knobs. Aperture moderately small; outer lip thin and crenulate, the inner lip is rolled over a deep fold at the base of the shell. Color yellowish brown, more or less variegated with white.

CANTHARUS GEMMATUS (Reeve)   Pl. 58
   Range: Mazatlán to Peru.
   Habitat: Moderately shallow water.
   Description: About 1 in. high, solid, and quite fusiform in shape. There are both revolving and vertical folds, but the prominent knobs at the shoulders of *C. elegans* (above) are lacking. The deep fold at the base of the shell is also missing, or poorly developed. Color dark brown.

CANTHARUS RINGENS (Reeve)   Pl. 58
   Range: Mazatlán to Ecuador.
   Habitat: Moderately shallow water.
   Description: This shell is about 1 in. high, ruggedly built, and has around 6 whorls. The surface bears revolving lines and weak vertical folds. Aperture rather small; outer lip thickened and crenulate, and there is a deep notch at the upper angle. Inner lip reflected over the columella, with a stout fold at the base. Color yellowish brown.

CANTHARUS SANGUINOLENTUS (Duc.)   Pl. 58
   Range: Gulf of California to Ecuador.
   Habitat: Moderately shallow water.
   Description: A rugged and colorful shell, in height averaging 1 in. and made up of 5 or 6 whorls. There are large swollen humps

encircling the shoulders, and obscure revolving lines. The outer lip is considerably thickened, and there is a noticeable notch at both ends of the rather small aperture. Color yellowish white, with a border all around the aperture that is red with white dots.

Genus *Engina* Gray 1839

ENGINA MAURA (Sow.)   Pl. 58
Range: San Pedro, California, to Ecuador.
Habitat: Shallow water.
Description: About ¾ in. high, a sturdy shell of 4 or 5 well-shouldered whorls, the sutures quite distinct. The surface bears vertical ribs that are rather widely spaced, and 3 or 4 rows of pointed knobs, placed precisely on the ribs, those at the shoulder most prominent. The aperture is narrow and small; lip toothed within; short, open canal. Color whitish, blotched and streaked with chocolate, aperture white.

ENGINA PULCHRA (Reeve)   Pl. 58
Range: Mazatlán to Panama.
Habitat: Shallow water.
Description: About 1 in. high, a fusiform shell of 5 whorls. Sculpture of revolving lines and vertical knobs. Outer lip thick, both lips well toothed within. Color brownish or yellowish; aperture bluish white.
Remarks: Formerly listed as *E. reeviana* (C. B. Adams).

Genus *Northia* Gray 1847

NORTHIA NORTHIAE (Grif. & Pidg.)   Pl. 55
Range: Gulf of California to Ecuador.
Habitat: Moderately shallow water.
Description: This snail is another favorite with collectors, perhaps because there is nothing else quite like it in the Gulf area. The height is about 2 in., and it has 8 or 9 rounded whorls and a fairly tall spire with the sutures well impressed. There is a marked twist at the base of the shell. Aperture moderately large; outer lip notched above and armed with numerous short spines at its edge. Surface smooth and shiny. Color olive-brown.
Remarks: Formerly placed in the family Nassariidae.

Family Melongenidae: Conchs

MODERATELY large and solid shells, living from the shoreline to moderate depths. They are carnivorous and predacious, and occur in temperate and tropic seas.

Genus *Melongena* Schumacher 1817

MELONGENA PATULA (Brod. & Sow.)   **Pl. 59**
Range: Gulf of California to Panama.
Habitat: Shallow water.
Description: This is a large, pyriform shell, usually from 4 to 7
in. high, but sometimes reaching a height of 10 in. There are
about 5 whorls, a very large body whorl, and a short but pointed
spire. The surface is fairly smooth, with a few obscure humps or
blunt spines at the shoulders in some specimens. Aperture large,
lip simple. The inner lip is polished and folded at the base.
Color rich brown, with a few encircling lines of yellow. In
life the shell is covered with a heavy, dark brown, fibrous
periostracum.
Remarks: Sometimes listed as *Galeodes patula* (Brod. & Sow.).

Family Fasciolariidae: Tulip Shells

GENERALLY large snails with strong, thick, fusiform shells. The
spire is elevated and sharply pointed, and there is no umbilicus.
These are predatory mollusks, slow and deliberate in their move-
ments. They are widely distributed in warm seas.

Genus *Pleuroploca* Fischer 1884

PLEUROPLOCA PRINCEPS (Sow.)   **Pl. 59**
Range: Gulf of California to Peru.
Habitat: Shallow water.
Description: Growing to a height of nearly 1 ft., this is the
largest gastropod found in the area. There may be as many as
8 whorls, the shoulders bearing large but low nodules. The spire
is elongate, and there is a sculpture of revolving ridges and
strong growth lines. Aperture oval and wide, contracted at the
base to form a narrow open canal. The columella is pleated, and
the ridged operculum is leathery. Color brown; aperture
orange-red.
Remarks: This is the Pacific analogue of *P. gigantea* (Kiener),
the well-known Horse Conch of the West Indies and Florida.

Genus *Latirus* Montfort 1810

LATIRUS CERATUS (Wood)   **Pl. 59**
Range: Gulf of California to Peru.
Habitat: Moderately shallow water.
Description: Attaining a height of nearly 3 in., this species has
about 7 whorls, the sutures indistinct. At the shoulders there
is a row of large blunt nodules, the rest of the volution being
ornamented with revolving lines arranged so that a coarser,
ridgelike line alternates with several smaller ones. Aperture

narrow, notched at the top and leading into a rather short open canal below. Color brown, the nodules whitish; aperture bluish white.

LATIRUS MEDIAMERICANUS Hert. & Strong   Pl. 59
Range: Gulf of California to S. America.
Habitat: Moderately shallow water.
Description: Some 2 in. high, a sturdy shell of about 8 whorls. There is a tall spire and a long canal, the aperture rather small. Volutions but little rounded and sutures well impressed. The surface bears broad rounded folds, with weak ridges on the canal. Color rich chestnut-brown; aperture white.

Genus *Opeatostoma* Berry 1958

OPEATOSTOMA PSEUDODON (Bur.)   Pl. 60
Range: S. Gulf of California to Peru.
Habitat: Moderately shallow water.
Description: This is a sturdy shell of about 5 strongly shouldered whorls, the height about 2½ in. The surface bears widely spaced revolving lines that are dark brown, the spaces between them white or dirty gray. Aperture moderate in size; inner lip rolled over at its base, where there is a short twisted canal. The outer lip bears a notch at the upper angle; at the bottom there is a long, sharp, needlelike tooth.
Remarks: Formerly known, incorrectly, as *Leucozonia cingulata* Lam.

Family Fusinidae: Spindle Shells
(see p. 97)

Genus *Fusinus* Rafinesque 1815

FUSINUS AMBUSTUS (Gould)   Pl. 59
Range: Gulf of California.
Habitat: Moderately shallow water.
Description: This spindle shell is nearly 2 in. high and has about 8 rounded whorls, a tallish spire, and a moderate canal. The sculpture consists of rather prominent vertical folds crossed by strong revolving lines. Color yellowish brown, the vertical ribs paler in tone.

FUSINUS CINEREUS (Reeve)   Pl. 59
Range: Gulf of California.
Habitat: Moderately shallow water.
Description: A sharply pointed shell of about 8 whorls, its height 1¼ in. Rounded vertical ridges are crossed by weak revolving lines. The canal is short and open. Color dull grayish, some of the encircling lines brown.

FUSINUS DUPETITTHOUARSI (Kiener)   Pl. 59
    Range: Gulf of California to Ecuador.
    Habitat: Moderately shallow water.
    Description: Sometimes reaches a height of 10 in., but averages
    about 6. A spindle-shaped shell of 9 or 10 whorls. The orna-
    mentation consists of coarse revolving lines. There is an acute
    angle at the shoulder which gives the spire a rounded-turret
    appearance, and at this angle there is a row of elongate, flattish
    knobs. Aperture small, lip simple; and there is a very long, open
    canal. Color yellowish brown.

FUSINUS FELIPENSIS Lowe   Pl. 59
    Range: N. Gulf of California.
    Habitat: Moderately shallow water.
    Description: A small spindle shell, its height generally less than
    1 in. There are about 6 whorls. The surface bears fairly strong
    encircling lines and vertical folds that are weak on the body
    whorl. Color grayish brown; aperture purplish.

Family Olividae: Olive Shells

(see p. 98)

Genus *Oliva* Bruguière 1789

OLIVA INCRASSATA (Sol.)   Pl. 60
    Range: Gulf of California to Peru.
    Habitat: Shallow water.
    Description: This is a strong and solid shell some 2 in. high,
    composed of about 5 whorls, the last one making up most of the
    shell. The sutures are deeply channeled. This species is dis-
    tinguished by an angular swelling of the body whorl at its center
    and by the unusual thickening of the outer lip. Aperture wider
    than in most olives. Color pinkish gray, flecked all over with
    pale lavender, and there are several irregular chocolate streaks
    arranged as broken vertical bars. As with all of the olives, the
    surface is highly polished. The inner lip is folded over at the
    columella and is grooved; this area is bright pink in fresh
    specimens.
    Remarks: One sometimes finds a pure yellowish example of this
    species, with no marks of any kind; such "golden olives" are
    eagerly sought by collectors. An example is also shown on
    Plate 60, No. 6.

OLIVA POLPASTA Duc.   Pl. 60
    Range: Gulf of California to Ecuador.
    Habitat: Shallow water.
    Description: About 1½ in. high, there is a moderate spire, and

about 5 whorls. Inner lip twisted over at the base, and strongly grooved. Color gray, profusely spotted with brown, with a circle of darker patches just below the suture. Highly polished.

OLIVA PORPHYRIA (Linné)   Tent Olive   Pls. 6, 60
Range: Mazatlán to Panama.
Habitat: Shallow water.
Description: The largest of the olive shells on our shores, attaining a height of 4 in. There is a short pointed spire. The shell has about 6 whorls, the sutures deeply impressed. Surface highly polished. Color pale pinkish lavender, overlain by a complicated pattern of thin zigzag lines of brown. These lines run together in places to form dark brown patches, but over most of the shell they give the appearance of triangular or steep-walled tents. Aperture long and narrow, outer lip simple; at base of columella the shell is rolled over to form a series of grooves. Inner lip strongly crenulate.

OLIVA SPICATA (Röd.)   Pl. 60
Range: Gulf of California.
Habitat: Shallow water.
Description: The height is about 1½ in. and there are 4 or 5 whorls. Sutures channeled; short pointed spire. There is a great deal of variation in color, but in general the pattern is yellowish gray, flecked with chestnut-brown.
Remarks: Probably the commonest olive shell in the Gulf of California. It is extremely variable, and several subspecies have been named, but it is now believed that they all represent a single species. Some of the published names are *O. cumingi* Reeve, *O. fuscata* Mar., *O. intertincta* Carp., *O. melchersi* Menke, *O. ustulata* Lam., and *O. venulata* Lam. Shown on Plate 60, No. 4, are an example of the typical form and one of the so-called varieties, *O. s. fuscata*, No. 2, which is brown all over.

Genus *Agaronia* Gray 1839

AGARONIA TESTACEA (Lam.)   Pl. 60
Range: N. Gulf of California to Peru.
Habitat: Shallow water.
Description: A sharply pointed, olive-shaped shell, differing from the genus *Oliva* in some respects. It has an operculum (not present in *Oliva*) and the aperture is somewhat widened below. There are about 5 whorls, the sutures deeply channeled; the height is about 2 in. Base of columella bears several oblique folds. Color yellowish gray, flecked with purplish spots and zigzag lines. The aperture is lavender, and the whole shell is moderately polished.

Genus *Olivella* Swainson 1840

OLIVELLA DAMA (Wood)   Pl. 60
  Range: Gulf of California to Mazatlán.
  Habitat: Shallow water.
  Description: The height from ½ to nearly 1 in., this is a highly
  polished shell of about 5 whorls. Sutures well marked, and there
  is a pointed spire. Aperture long and narrow; inner lip rolled
  over at the columella. Spire generally pale gray, overlain with
  a broad band of bluish having numerous paler spots. Rich brown
  streaks are present at the suture line. Aperture violet.

OLIVELLA GRACILIS (Brod. & Sow.)   Pl. 60
  Range: Guaymas to Panama.
  Habitat: Shallow water.
  Description: About ¾ in. high, a slender, sharply pointed shell
  of 4 or 5 whorls, the sutures fairly well impressed. As with all
  of this group, the surface is highly polished. Color ivory-white,
  with pale brownish zigzag markings and maculations.

OLIVELLA TERGINA (Duc.)   Pl. 60
  Range: S. Gulf of California to Peru.
  Habitat: Shallow water.
  Description: A neat little shell about ½ in. high, the whorl
  count 5. Aperture rather narrow; lip thin and sharp; sutures
  moderately distinct. The columella is rolled over at the base,
  the inner lip weakly plicate. Color pale gray, banded with
  irregular patches of purplish, commonly with a row of chestnut
  spots at the shoulder.

OLIVELLA ZANOETA (Duc.)   Pl. 60
  Range: Gulf of California to Ecuador.
  Habitat: Shallow water.
  Description: A fine shell of about ½ in. The body whorl takes
  up less of the shell than with many of this group, and a considerable portion of the shell is spire. As with all of the genus,
  there is a small operculum that is lacking in the true olive shells.
  The color of this species is white, with 2 or 3 broad bands of
  chocolate-brown.

Family Mitridae: Miters

(see p. 99)

Genus *Mitra* Röding 1798

MITRA BELCHERI Hinds   Pl. 60
  Range: Mazatlán to Panama.
  Habitat: Moderately deep water.

Description: Some 4 in. high, this splendid miter is eagerly sought by collectors. There are 8 or 9 flattish whorls, producing a tall spire. Surface bears numerous broad and flat revolving ribs. The color is whitish, but the shell is covered with a dark greenish periostracum.

MITRA DOLOROSA Dall   Pl. 60
Range: Gulf of California.
Habitat: Moderately shallow water.
Description: A slender gastropod, the sutures fairly well delineated. There are 6 flattish whorls, and the height is a bit more than 1 in. The surface is smooth. Color yellowish brown, with a distinct band of bluish white on upperpart of each volution. Narrow aperture lavender.

MITRA EFFUSA Brod.   Pl. 60
Range: S. Gulf of California to Galápagos Is.
Habitat: Moderately deep water.
Description: A slender shell 1½ in. high. There are about 6 whorls that are quite flat, the sutures scarcely discernible. Surface decorated with sharp closely spaced encircling lines, generally shiny. Aperture narrow; columella pleated, and the outer lip sharp. Color deep yellowish brown.

MITRA LENS Wood   Pl. 60
Range: Gulf of California to Peru.
Habitat: Moderately shallow water.
Description: A rugged shell some 2 in. high. There are 6 or 7 rather flattish whorls, the sutures moderately distinct. The sculpture consists of deep vertical grooves and widely spaced revolving lines. Aperture narrow; inner lip strongly plicate. Color rusty brown.

MITRA SULCATA Sow.   Pl. 60
Range: S. Gulf of California to Ecuador.
Habitat: Moderately deep water.
Description: A trim small shell of 5 or 6 whorls, the sutures very indistinct. Attaining a height of ¾ in., the shell is fusiform in shape, tapering to a sharp apex and a blunt base. Sculpture consists of strong revolving cords. The color is pale brown, sometimes lightly spotted with darker brown.

MITRA TRISTIS Brod.   Pl. 60
Range: N. Gulf of California to Ecuador.
Habitat: Moderately shallow water.
Description: A blocky little shell just over 1 in. high, the 5 or 6 whorls slightly shouldered, so that the sutures are plainly observed. The surface bears weak vertical ribs that are noticeable

on the shoulders but fade out on the volutions. Color brown, usually with a paler band toward the upperpart of each whorl.

MITRA ZACA (Strong, Hanna, & Hert.)   Pl. 60
   Range: S. Gulf of California to Mazatlán.
   Habitat: Deep water.
   Description: A large miter shell, reaching a height of close to 5 in. There are 8 slightly shouldered whorls, and the surface is generally smooth, although there may be weak spiraling lines. The shell itself is white, but in life it is covered by a blackish periostracum.

Family Vasidae: Vase Shells

CONFINED to tropical or semitropical waters, these are usually heavy shells, often ponderous, with strong plications on the columella. The operculum is clawlike. Only 1 representative of the family lives on this coast.

Genus *Vasum* Röding 1798

VASUM CAESTUS (Brod.)   Pl. 60
   Range: La Paz to Panama.
   Habitat: Moderately deep water.
   Description: A heavy and rugged shell about 3 in. high, shaped like an inverted vase. There are 6 or 7 whorls, the last one decorated with strong revolving lines and with blunt spines at the shoulder. There may be a 2nd row of spines midway of the whorl. There is a deep fold at the base of the columella. Aperture white; inner lip plicate; and there is a heavy, fibrous, brown periostracum over the rest of the shell.

Family Harpidae: Harp Shells

SHELLS large, swollen, with flaring apertures. Vertically ribbed, the columellar lip is smooth and polished. There is no operculum. These very ornate shells occur chiefly in the South Pacific and Indian Oceans. There is but a single representative in N. America.

Genus *Harpa* Röding 1798

HARPA CRENATA Swain.   Pl. 59
   Range: S. Gulf of California to Panama.
   Habitat: Moderately shallow water.
   Description: A handsome shell 2 to 3 in. high. There are about 5 whorls. The swollen body whorl makes up most of the shell,

but there is a short and pointed spire. Aperture flaring; the lip thickens slightly at the edge and is slightly notched below. There are about 12 rather broadly flattened vertical ribs, with wide spaces between, the ribs forming points at the shoulder. Color pale pinkish flesh, with squarish spots of purplish brown on the ribs. The spaces between are decorated with chevronlike marks of lavender and chocolate. Whole shell more or less polished.

Family Volutidae: Volutes

THE volutes are attractive, colorful shells, and have always been great favorites with collectors, sharing top honors with the cones and the cowries. Shells somewhat vase-shaped, and exhibit a wide assortment of ornamentation and color. Group noted for having a large, often bulbous, initial whorl (or protoconch) at the apex. Well distributed in warm seas, chiefly in deep waters, although no species of the genus *Voluta* occur in area covered by this *Field Guide*.

Genus *Lyria* Gray 1847

LYRIA CUMINGI (Brod.)   **Pl. 59**
   Range: Gulf of California to Peru.
   Habitat: Shallow water; sandy mud.
   Description: Somewhat under 2 in. high as a rule, a neat shell of about 5 whorls. Surface usually polished and bears broad vertical ribs that rise into little knobs at the shoulders. Aperture narrow; outer lip somewhat thickened; and there are 4 distinct pleats on the columella. Color pinkish gray, more or less mottled with brown.

Family Cancellariidae: Nutmegs
(see p. 100)

Genus *Cancellaria* Lamarck 1799

CANCELLARIA CASSIDIFORMIS Sow.   **Pl. 61**
   Range: San Felipe to Peru.
   Habitat: Moderately deep water.
   Description: Growing to a height of 1½ in. but generally aver-aging about 1 in., the shell is helmet-shaped, with 5 or 6 whorls, the sutures indistinct. The shell is largely body whorl, with a short, gently sloping spire. Surface with vertical ribs, about 12 to a volution, and these are crossed by cordlike revolving lines. At the sharply angular shoulder the ribs develop rather sharp spines. Aperture moderately large; inner lip ribbed within. Base

of shell slightly twisted. Color pale yellow, sometimes weakly banded.

CANCELLARIA CLAVATULA Sow.   Pl. 61
Range: Mazatlán to S. America.
Habitat: Moderately deep water.
Description: This species is tall and slender, in marked contrast to the other members of *Cancellaria*. Height about 1 in. and whorl count 6. The volutions are well inflated and slightly flattened on top, producing a turreted, well-elevated spire that is capped by a sharp apex. The surface bears strong vertical ribs and closely spaced threadlike revolving lines. Aperture rather small, with a pair of pleats on the columella; short open canal. Color yellowish brown, weakly banded with white.

CANCELLARIA OBESA Sow.   Pl. 61
Range: Gulf of California to Ecuador.
Habitat: Moderately deep water.
Description: A heavy and solid shell of about 7 rounded whorls, its height a full 2 in. Shoulders slightly flattened, the sutures well impressed. The surface bears rather strong revolving ribs and weaker vertical lines. Aperture moderate; outer lip simple but strongly ribbed inside, the inner lip bearing several strong folds. A prominent layer of enamel is spread over the front of the body whorl. Base of shell strongly twisted, leaving a small umbilicus. Color pale yellowish white, streaked and obscurely banded with orange-brown.

CANCELLARIA PULCHRA Sow.   Pl. 61
Range: Guaymas to Peru.
Habitat: Moderately deep water.
Description: About 1 in. high, this is a stubby shell of 6 or 7 swollen whorls, the sutures distinct and the apex sharply pointed. The surface is ornamented by robust revolving lines and even stronger vertical ribs, so that the shell has a cancellate appearance. Aperture moderately large; outer lip ribbed on inside. The whole base of the shell is severely twisted and the short canal bent back a little. There are 3 sturdy pleats on the columella. Color pale yellow, with orange bands.

CANCELLARIA URCEOLATA Hinds   Pl. 61
Range: Gulf of California to Ecuador.
Habitat: Moderately deep water.
Description: Nearly 1 in. high, there are 7 whorls, the sutures well defined. The volutions bear strong vertical ribs crossed by sharp revolving lines. Inner lip very strongly plicate, and there is a sharp twist at the base of the columella. The color is creamy white to pale brown.

Genus *Trigonostoma* Blainville 1827

TRIGONOSTOMA BULLATUM (Sow.)   Pl. 61
Range: Acapulco to Panama.
Habitat: Deep water.
Description: A loosely coiled shell with well-shouldered whorls.
There is a moderate spire, a deep umbilicus, and a wide aperture
with the inner lip strongly reflected. Height about 1 in., whorl
count 4 or 5. Weak nodes encircle the shoulders. Color yellowish
brown, sometimes weakly banded.

Family Marginellidae: Marginellas
(see p. 100)

Genus *Marginella* Lamarck 1799

MARGINELLA ALBUMINOSA Dall   Pl. 60
Range: S. Gulf of California.
Habitat: Shallow water.
Description: A full inch in height, this shell is smooth and pure
white or ivory-white, and has a low spire and a very high polish.
It is egg-shaped in outline, the inner lip bearing 4 strong pleats.
Largest member of the family on the western coast of N. America.

MARGINELLA CURTA Sow.   Pl. 60
Range: Gulf of California to Chile.
Habitat: Shallow water.
Description: About ¾ in. high, this is a solid shell that is nearly
all body whorl, with a very short spire. There are about 4 whorls,
capped by a small pointed apex. Surface smooth and polished.
Aperture long and narrow; outer lip considerably thickened, and
there are 4 sharp pleats on the inner lip. Color white or gray.

Family Conidae: Cone Shells
(see p. 101)

Genus *Conus* Linné 1758

CONUS BRUNNEUS Wood   **Brown Cone**   Pl. 62
Range: Gulf of California to Ecuador.
Habitat: Moderately shallow water.
Description: Some 2 in. high with 8 tightly coiled whorls. Spire
moderately pointed but low and very strongly tuberculated.
Shoulders somewhat rounded. Surface smooth, excepting the
spire. The color is mottled chestnut and darker brown, some-
times with an interrupted paler band encircling the body whorl.

CONUS DALLI Stearns   **Dall's Cone**   Pl. 62
  Range: Gulf of California to Galápagos Is.
  Habitat: Moderately deep water.
  Description: Height about 2 in., including a short pointed spire.
  The color pattern reminds one of fabric and follows the general
  style of the well-known (and highly poisonous) *C. textile* Linné
  (Cloth-of-Gold Cone; see p. 250) of the South Pacific. Browns
  and yellows are overlain by darker zigzag markings, enclosing
  numerous white triangles. There is a suggestion of brown band-
  ing, and the aperture is a delicate rosy pink.

CONUS GLADIATOR Brod.   **Gladiator Cone**   Pl. 62
  Range: Gulf of California to Ecuador.
  Habitat: Moderately shallow water.
  Description: This species is about 1½ in. high and has 8 or 9
  whorls, with nodular shoulders. The spire is low, the sutures
  indistinct. Surface bears numerous revolving lines that are
  likely to be quite pronounced on the lower part of the shell.
  Color brown, with vertical streaks; single band of white on the
  body whorl.

CONUS LUCIDUS Wood   **Spiderweb Cone**   Pl. 62
  Range: Gulf of California to Ecuador.
  Habitat: Moderately deep water.
  Description: About 2 in. high, this shell has a well-developed
  spire and about 8 whorls. Color pale lavender, decorated by
  numerous hairlike lines of brown, giving the surface an appearance of cracked china.

CONUS NUX Brod.   **Nut Cone**   Pl. 62
  Range: Gulf of California to Ecuador.
  Habitat: Shallow water.
  Description: A small cone, seldom as much as ¾ in. high. The
  spire is rather flat, with the shoulders slightly knobby, so that
  the top of the shell is somewhat nodular. Color whitish, variously
  mottled or marbled with brown. Commonly there is a whitish
  band at the upperpart of the body whorl, and the base of the
  shell is tinged with purple.

CONUS PATRICIUS Hinds   **Patrician Cone**   Pl. 62
  Range: Gulf of California to Ecuador.
  Habitat: Moderately deep water.
  Description: A large and solid shell, its height about 4 in. The
  top is rather flattish, but there is a pointed apex. Young indi-
  viduals are yellowish to orange, more or less banded; adults
  white. In life there is a velvety brown periostracum.
  Remarks: Formerly listed as *C. pyriformis* Reeve.

CONUS PERPLEXUS Sow.   **Puzzling Cone**   Pl. 62
  Range: Gulf of California to S. America.
  Habitat: Moderately shallow water.
  Description: In height averaging about 1 in., a neat little shell
  of 8 closely coiled whorls. The spire is moderately elevated and
  usually rather blunt on top. Color gray or pinkish, with numerous tiny brown dots and with 3 interrupted bands of purplish
  brown. Spire strongly blotched with brown and white; aperture
  pale violet.

CONUS PRINCEPS Linné   **Princely Cone**   Pls. 6, 62
  Range: Gulf of California to Ecuador.
  Habitat: Moderately shallow water.
  Description: About 2½ in. high, this cone has a low spire and
  about 8 whorls. Sides straight and sloping, the surface smooth.
  The color is yellowish brown, with irregular vertical chocolate
  lines that are sometimes straight and sometimes wavy. During
  life there is a heavy brownish periostracum.
  Remarks: A variety that has the vertical lines very thin and
  close together has been named *C. p. lineolatus* Val.; see Plate 62,
  No. 2.

CONUS PURPURASCENS Sow.   **Purple Cone**   Pl. 62
  Range: Gulf of California to Ecuador.
  Habitat: Moderately shallow water.
  Description: A sturdy shell of 8 whorls, its height about 2 in.
  The spire is but slightly elevated. Shell smooth in texture and
  violet-gray in color, heavily clouded and streaked with brown
  and black. Sometimes there is an obscure paler band at the
  center. A rough brownish periostracum covers the shell during
  life.

CONUS REGULARIS Sow.   **Regular Cone**   Pl. 62
  Range: Gulf of California to Panama.
  Habitat: Shallow water.
  Description: From 2 to 2½ in. high with a sharply pointed spire,
  this cone has about 10 whorls. A moderately slender shell, pale
  ivory-white, with orange-brown maculations arranged in revolving series.
  Remarks: This gastropod may be considered the Pacific counterpart of the Alphabet Cone of the West Indies, *C. spurius* Gmel.

CONUS VIRGATUS Reeve   Pl. 62
  Range: Gulf of California to Ecuador.
  Habitat: Moderately shallow water.
  Description: A rather slender cone with a short but sharply
  pointed spire. Surface smooth. Color pinkish gray, with broad,
  wavy vertical streaks of brown. The height is about 2 in., the
  whorl count about 8.

CONUS VITTATUS Brug. **Ribboned Cone** Pl. 62
  Range: Guaymas to S. America.
  Habitat: Moderately shallow water.
  Description: About 1½ in. high, a rather flat-topped shell of 7 or 8 whorls. The surface bears fine revolving lines, and the color may be anything from white to yellow or orange. At the middle there is a broad band of brown, broken by white marks, and the top of the shell is decorated with brown and white maculations.

CONUS XIMENES Gray **Interrupted Cone** Pl. 62
  Range: Gulf of California to Panama.
  Habitat: Shallow water.
  Description: About 1½ in. high, with 10 whorls, the shell is long and slender. A well-elevated spire is capped by a sharp apex. Color pale pinkish white, with numerous encircling rows of tiny purplish dots. On some individuals traces of purplish bands are discernible. Spire decorated with chocolate and purplish dots and splashes.
  Remarks: Formerly listed as *C. interruptus* Brod. A somewhat smaller and slimmer form, commonly darker in tone but with a lighter aperture, is known as *C. x. mahogani* Reeve; see Plate 62, No. 11.

Family Terebridae: Auger Shells

(see p. 102)

Genus *Terebra* Bruguière 1789

TEREBRA HINDSI Carp. **Hinds' Auger** Pl. 61
  Range: Gulf of California to Panama.
  Habitat: Moderately shallow water.
  Description: A high-spired, spikelike shell, 1½ in. tall, with from 10 to 12 flattish whorls. There are small knobs at the shoulders that produce a noticeable spiral up the spire. Color pale gray, more or less spotted with brown.

TEREBRA ROBUSTA Hinds **Robust Auger** Pl. 61
  Range: Guaymas to Galápagos Is.
  Habitat: Moderately shallow water.
  Description: A strong and solid shell of 4 or 5 in., with 18 to 20 rather flattish whorls, the sutures clearly marked. The early volutions are well sculptured with rounded vertical ridges but they tend to fade out as the shell grows, and the later volutions are relatively smooth. Whorls encircled just above center by a spiral groove. Aperture small and narrow; columella twisted

at its base. Color yellowish, vertically striped with chestnut-brown.

TEREBRA STRIGATA Sow.   **Pls. 6, 61**
  Range: Gulf of California to Panama.
  Habitat: Moderately shallow water; sandy bottoms.
  Description: Height about 4 in., whorl count 16 to 18. Sutures rather well marked, and there is a weak indentation below each suture. Volutions flatter than in *T. robusta* (above), and the shell is relatively stouter in proportion. Aperture moderately wide; columella twisted at base. Color yellowish brown, with heavy vertical streaks of chestnut-brown.

TEREBRA VARIEGATA Gray   Variegated Auger   **Pl. 61**
  Range: Gulf of California to Peru.
  Habitat: Moderately shallow water.
  Description: From 3 to 4 in. high, and with up to 25 whorls, this is a tall, spikelike shell with distinct sutures. Some of the early volutions may show vertical ridges, but for the most part the surface is smooth. The aperture is small, the columella twisted. Color ivory-white, with vertical bars of chocolate-brown, and there may be 1 or 2 revolving bands of whitish on the last few whorls.

Genus *Hastula* H. & A. Adams 1853

HASTULA LUCTUOSA (Hinds)   **Pl. 61**
  Range: Mazatlán to Panama.
  Habitat: Shallow water.
  Description: A small shell, seldom more than 1 in. high. It is slender and spikelike, with about 10 flattish whorls, the sutures scarcely indented. The upper half of each volution bears closely spaced vertical lines, with the bottom half smooth. Aperture small; columella only slightly twisted. The color is purplish brown.

Family Turridae: Slit Shells or Tower Shells

(see p. 102)

Genus *Knefastia* Dall 1919

KNEFASTIA DALLI Bar.   **Pl. 61**
  Range: Gulf of California.
  Habitat: Moderately shallow water.
  Description: A robust shell of about 2½ in. There are some 9

whorls, a tall spire, and a short open canal. Surface sculptured with strong revolving ribs, and by elongate vertical knobs, about 10 to a volution. The whorls are shouldered, the sutures distinct. The inner lip is plastered on the parietal wall, and the outer lip bears a deep notch, or slit, at its upper angle. Color yellowish brown; interior violet.

KNEFASTIA FUNICULATA (Kiener)   Pl. 61
Range: Gulf of California to Panama.
Habitat: Moderately shallow water.
Description: About 2 in. high, a somewhat more slender shell than *K. dalli* (above), with 9 or 10 whorls. Strong encircling lines cross over stout vertical ribs. Aperture small; outer lip with deep notch above. Color yellowish brown. Operculum horny.
Remarks: This is a common form of the genus in the Gulf of California. *K. olivacea* (Sow.) is a more southern species.

Genus *Clavus* Montfort 1810

CLAVUS AEOLIUS (Dall)   Pl. 61
Range: Gulf of California to Panama.
Habitat: Moderately deep water.
Description: A small shell, only about ¼ in. high, composed of 9 or 10 rounded whorls, each ornamented by several stout, slanting ridges and weak spiral lines. Aperture small; outer lip thin and sharp. Color pale brown, the surface generally quite shiny.

Genus *Crassispira* Swainson 1840

CRASSISPIRA ATERRIMA (Sow.)   Pl. 61
Range: Gulf of California to Panama.
Habitat: Moderately deep water.
Description: A rather unattractive shell, its height about ½ in. There are 8 or 9 whorls, the sutures indistinct. The base of each volution shows a few small beads. Aperture small; outer lip deeply notched. Color dark brown, sometimes with a narrow paler band at the suture.

CRASSISPIRA BOTTAE (Kiener)   Pl. 61
Range: Gulf of California.
Habitat: Moderately shallow water.
Description: A larger shell than *C. aterrima* (above), attaining a height of 1½ in. There are 8 whorls, the sutures plainly marked by a small spiral ridge. The sculpture consists of strong vertical ridges. Aperture moderately large; lip well notched above. Color rich brown, with a periostracum that is nearly black. Aperture white.

CRASSISPIRA COLLARIS (Sow.)   Pl. 61
   Range: Mazatlán to Panama.
   Habitat: Shallow water.
   Description: Fusiform, the apex sharply pointed, aperture small
   and narrow. Height ¾ in., whorl count about 7. Surface with
   revolving elongate beads. Color dark brown, with narrow bands
   of yellowish.

CRASSISPIRA MARTINENSIS Dall   Pl. 61
   Range: Gulf of California.
   Habitat: Moderately deep water.
   Description: About 1 in. high, with 8 whorls, the sutures plainly
   marked. Aperture small and narrow. Sculpture of distinct
   revolving cords made bumpy by crossing vertical lines. Color
   brownish.

CRASSISPIRA NYMPHIA Pils. & Lowe   Pl. 61
   Range: Guaymas to Panama.
   Habitat: Moderately shallow water.
   Description: A small high-spired shell of about 8 whorls, its
   height ¾ in. There is a strong series of beads at the periphery,
   with smaller beaded rows between. Aperture small; outer lip
   with a notch at suture line. Color pale greenish brown, the
   encircling knobs white.

Genus *Hormospira* Berry 1958

HORMOSPIRA MACULOSA (Sow.)   Pl. 61
   Range: Gulf of California to Colombia.
   Habitat: Moderately shallow water.
   Description: From 1 to 1½ in. high, this is a high-spired shell
   of about 9 whorls. The shape is fusiform. Each volution bears
   a row of rounded knobs at the periphery, and from this row the
   whorl slopes abruptly to the suture. Aperture long and narrow,
   with a short open canal. Color whitish or bluish gray, speckled
   and spotted with chestnut-brown.

Genus *Pleuroliria* Gregorio 1890

PLEUROLIRIA PICTA (Reeve)   Pl. 61
   Range: Guaymas to Panama.
   Habitat: Moderately shallow water.
   Description: Another fusiform shell that is high-spired, its
   height 1¼ in. There are about 10 whorls, decorated with revolving cordlike ridges. Aperture small; canal open and long. There
   is a noticeable slit in the outer lip. Color white, the ridges spotted
   with brown.

Genus *Pseudomelatoma* Dall 1918

PSEUDOMELATOMA PENICILLATA (Carp.)   Pl. 61
  Range: Gulf of California.
  Habitat: Moderately shallow water.
  Description: Growing to a height of nearly 2 in., the shell has about 8 whorls, rather strongly marked by vertical ribs. Aperture small and narrow. Color dark brown.

Family Bullidae: True Bubble Shells
(see p. 110)

Genus *Bulla* Linné 1758

BULLA PUNCTULATA A. Adams   Pl. 62
  Range: Gulf of California to Peru.
  Habitat: Shallow water.
  Description: An oval, bubble-shaped shell about 1 in. high. The shell is thin and light, and during life is partly covered by the animal. It is rolled up like a scroll, with the spire depressed. The aperture is longer than the body whorl and widest at the bottom; the lip thin and sharp. Color pinkish gray, flecked and mottled with brown; columella white.

Family Siphonariidae: False Limpets

THE resemblance of these snails to limpets explains the common name for the family. Shell roughly circular and conical, with a deep groove on one side that makes a distinct projection on that margin. The animals possess both gills and lungs and spend their time between the tide limits, living a somewhat amphibious life. Thus they form a connecting link between the purely aquatic snails and the more highly developed air-breathing mollusks.

Genus *Siphonaria* Sowerby 1824

SIPHONARIA MAURA Sow.   Pl. 62
  Range: Gulf of California to Chile.
  Habitat: Between tide limits.
  Description: About 1 in. long, the shell is quite flat (only slightly arched), with the apex at the center. The ornamentation consists of radiating ribs that are rounded, generally a larger rib alternating with a smaller one. Margins slightly scalloped, and there is a prominent bulge on one side. Mottled-gray color; interior rich brown, the border spotted with white.

Family Aplysiidae: Dolabella

COMMONLY called sea hares. The animal is sluglike, with distinct head, tentacles, and eyes. Sides with extensive lobes, with which the mollusk swims freely. There is an internal, flattish, calcareous shell.

Genus *Dolabella* Lamarck 1801

DOLABELLA CALIFORNICA Stearns   Pl. 62
  Range: Gulf of California.
  Habitat: Buried in upper surface of a pelagic mollusk related to the sea hares; found in drift along shores.
  Description: A flattish, hook-shaped shell. It is white on one side and covered by a brown chitinous film on the other.
  Remarks: Although an internal shell and not especially common, this is included in the *Field Guide* because it is now and then picked up on the beach and is baffling to identify.

VI

Hawaiian Pelecypods

Family Arcidae: Ark Shells

(see p. 5)

Genus *Arca* Linné 1758

ARCA KAUAIA Dall, Bar. & Reh.　　　　　　　　**Pl. 63**

Habitat: Deep water.

Description: A small shell, generally less than ¾ in. long, the anterior end rounded and the posterior end indented. Hinge line straight and long, the beaks fairly well elevated. A prominent ridge runs from the umbo to the basal posterior end. Surface with fine radiating lines. Color yellowish gray, with wavy bands and blotches of reddish brown.

ARCA VENTRICOSA Lam.　**Ventricose Ark**　　　**Pl. 63**

Habitat: Moderately deep water; rocks.

Description: A large and rough shell attaining a length of about 3 in. The shape is elongate, the anterior end rounded and the posterior end prolonged and somewhat rostrate at tip. Beaks fairly low and close to front end, and well separated, with a broad flat area between them. Valves gape widely at basal margin. Surface with radiating lines, fine at center of shell, coarser at ends. Color yellowish brown, with wavy streaks of reddish brown, the area between the beaks (hinge area) streaked with chocolate.

Genus *Acar* Gray 1857

ACAR HAWAIENSIS Dall, Bar., & Reh.　　　　　**Pl. 63**

Reticulate Ark

Habitat: Shallow water.

Description: About 1 in. long, this is a somewhat oblong shell with low beaks, a short and rounded anterior end, and a prolonged posterior end. Surface bears both concentric and radiating lines that produce a network pattern over the shell. Color yellowish white.

Remarks: Formerly listed as *Arca reticulata* Gmel.

Genus *Barbatia* Gray 1847

BARBATIA HAWAIA Dall, Bar., & Reh. Pl. 63
 Habitat: Moderately shallow water.
 Description: An elongate oval shell 1½ in. long. Both ends rounded, the posterior somewhat longer than the anterior. Beaks rounded and low. The sculpture consists of radiating and concentric lines, rendering the surface somewhat cancellate. Color white, with brownish periostracum.

BARBATIA OAHUA Dall, Bar., & Reh. Pl. 63
 Habitat: Shallow water.
 Description: A sizable shell some 2½ in. long, oval in outline and rather compressed. Beaks rounded but low, set close to anterior end. There is a sculpture of moderately strong radiating lines and weaker concentric lines. The hinge teeth are small at center of line, larger at the ends. Color white, with brownish periostracum; interior porcelaneous.

Family Glycymeridae: Bittersweet Shells
(see p. 6)

Genus *Glycymeris* Da Costa 1778

GLYCYMERIS DIOMEDEA Dall, Bar., & Reh. Pl. 63
Button Shell
 Habitat: Moderately shallow water.
 Description: A nearly circular shell, small but solid, about ¾ in. long. There are about 25 radiating ribs, wider than the spaces between them. There is also a concentric sculpture of fine lines that cut across the ribs. Margins scalloped, and hinge bears a curving row of teeth. Color yellowish white, heavily blotched and spotted with light brown.

Family Mytilidae: Mussels
(see p. 7)

Genus *Septifer* Récluz 1848

SEPTIFER RUDIS Dall, Bar., & Reh. **Platform Mussel** Pl. 63
 Habitat: Shallow water.
 Description: An angular, almost black shell, pinched out at the beak and rather broad and flaring at the other end. About 1 in. long, the valves well inflated; the surface bears strong wavy ribs that radiate from the umbo. Under the beak is a small, white,

shelly platform (septum) that gives the genus its name of *Septifer*.
Remarks: This small mussel is found attached to stones and other objects by a strong byssus.

Genus *Modiolus* Lamarck 1799

MODIOLUS MATRIS Pils.　**Smooth Mussel**　　　Pl. 63

Habitat: Moderately deep water.

Description: About ¾ in. long, this is a smooth-shelled mussel, considerably inflated, with beaks that are subterminal. Posterior end broadly rounded; anterior end extremely short. Color yellowish brown, some examples showing rays of darker hue; the shell bears a thin but hairy periostracum.

Genus *Brachidontes* Swainson 1840

BRACHIDONTES CREBRISTRIATUS (Con.)　　　Pl. 63

Striate Mussel

Habitat: Shallow water.

Description: This little mussel has its beaks at the tip of the pointed end, and from this point the shell slopes gently for a distance and then drops off abruptly to a rounded margin, giving the shell a sort of bent look. The surface is ornamented with numerous very fine radiating lines. Color purplish gray; interior dark. About 1 in. long, this mussel is generally found in clusters close to shore.

Genus *Musculus* Röding 1798

MUSCULUS AVIARIUS Dall, Bar., & Reh.　　　Pl. 63

Habitat: Moderately deep water.

Description: A small, inflated mussel, the length about ¼ in. There is a sculpture of weak radiating lines on both ends, with an area between where they are lacking. Beaks prominent, situated close to anterior end. There is a thin yellowish-brown periostracum.

Family Isognomonidae: Purse Shells

(see p. 12)

Genus *Isognomon* Solander 1786

ISOGNOMON COSTELLATUM (Con.)　　　Pl. 64

Costellate Purse Shell

Habitat: Shallow water.

Description: About 3 in. long and somewhat circular in outline.

The valves are much compressed, and are decorated with radiating lines, often rather obscure. Color yellowish gray; inside of shell with a pearly layer that does not extend all the way to the margin.

Remarks: This group has been listed as *Pedalion, Melina,* and *Perna.*

ISOGNOMON INCISUM (Con.) Pl. 64

Habitat: Shallow water.

Description: Elongate, oval, and flattish, with an oblique hinge bearing vertical grooves. It attains a length of 2 or 3 in., although most examples are smaller. Surface with concentric wrinkles. Color purplish brown.

Remarks: This group has been listed as *Pedalion, Melina,* and *Perna.*

Family Pteriidae: Pearl Oysters

(see p. 12)

Genus *Pteria* Scopoli 1777

PTERIA NEBULOSA Con. Little Pearl Oyster Pl. 64

Habitat: Moderately shallow water.

Description: A rather common shell about 3 in. long. The shape is somewhat squarish, with a straight hinge line and 2 small wings, or ears. One valve is a bit more inflated than the other, but both are rather flat. Surface bears concentric wrinkles but is relatively smooth. Color yellowish green, with broad radiating bands of brown; interior very pearly.

Genus *Pinctada* Röding 1798

PINCTADA GALTSOFFI Bar. Pl. 64
Black-lipped Pearl Oyster

Habitat: Moderately deep water.

Description: A large and heavy shell some 8 in. long. Shape oval, with a short but thick hinge line. Young specimens are greenish brown, the surface covered with thin scales arranged concentrically and forming a fringe around the margins of the shell. The interior is very pearly, and is used commercially.

Remarks: Valuable pearls are sometimes found under the mantle of this bivalve.

Family Pinnidae: Pen Shells
(see p. 13)

Genus *Pinna* Linné 1758

PINNA SEMICOSTATA Con.   **Costate Pen**   **Pl. 63**
    Habitat: Moderately shallow water.
    Description: The average length of this bivalve is from 6 to 10 in., but the species grows quite a bit larger. It is an elongate, triangular shell, thin and semitransparent when young. Gapes at posterior end. Surface with a series of folds radiating from the tip of the triangle, the latter portions covered with scales. There is a faint suggestion of concentric lines as well. Color yellowish tan.

Genus *Atrina* Gray 1847

ATRINA NUTTALLI (Con.)   **Bent Pen**   **Pl. 63**
    Habitat: Moderately shallow water.
    Description: This shell is in the neighborhood of 8 in. long, and the shape is more irregular than that of *Pinna semicostata* (above). Instead of being a long, sharply pointed triangle, it is rather blunt at the beaks, with the rest of the shell compressed and somewhat twisted. Posterior gapes widely. Surface with wavy folds. Color yellowish tan, shading to dark brown.

Family Pectinidae: Scallops
(see p. 13)

Genus *Chlamys* Röding 1798

CHLAMYS COOKEI Dall, Bar., & Reh.   **Pl. 64**
Cooke's Scallop
    Habitat: Shallow water.
    Description: An elongate-oval shell, rather thin and delicate, attaining a length of about 1½ in. Wings subequal in size. Shell but little inflated, and decorated with radiating lines that are small and somewhat crowded. Color yellowish, shading to orange on some individuals; there may be darker mottlings.
    Remarks: Formerly listed as *C. albolineata* (Sow.).

Genus *Haumea* Dall et al. 1938

HAUMEA JUDDI Dall, Bar., & Reh.   **Judd's Scallop**   **Pl. 64**
    Habitat: Moderately shallow water.
    Description: This shell is seldom more than 1 in. long. Equi-

valve, with both valves moderately inflated, the general outline obliquely circular. Wings small and nearly equal. The sculpture consists of prominent radiating ribs, and the margins of the shell are distinctly scalloped. Color white, variously mottled with red and orange. Lower valve paler, often unspotted.

Remarks: Formerly listed as *Chlamys loxoides* Hert.

Genus *Nodipecten* Dall 1898

NODIPECTEN LANGFORDI Dall, Bar., & Reh.   Pl. 64
Langford's Scallop

Habitat: Moderately deep water.

Description: A solid shell, 1½ in. long. Valves moderately inflated, the wings equally developed. There are about 8 very strong, rounded, radiating ribs that are distinctly nodular, and the spaces between them bear fine threadlike lines. Color red or orange, more or less flecked with white; interior often deep rose color.

Remarks: Formerly listed as *Chlamys noduliferus* Hert.

Family Spondylidae: Spiny Oysters
(see p. 128)

Genus *Spondylus* Linné 1758

SPONDYLUS HAWAIENSIS Dall, Bar., & Reh.   Pl. 63
Hawaiian Spiny Oyster

Habitat: Moderately shallow water.

Description: A large and ponderous shell, roughly oval, and 7 or 8 in. long. There is a straight and thick hinge area, and the 2 valves are fixed together by interlocking teeth in such a fashion that they can be opened only so far. Outer surface weakly ribbed when young, but old specimens are almost invariably eroded, drilled, and incrusted, and whitish in color. Interior pearly, with a dark marginal border, and the muscle scar is very prominent.

SPONDYLUS SPARSISPINOSUS Dall, Bar., & Reh.   Pl. 63
Weak-Spiny Oyster

Habitat: Moderately deep water.

Description: A smaller shell than *S. hawaiensis* (above), more circular in outline and diam. measuring about 3 in. Hinge line straight, with a pair of small wings. The sculpture consists of prominent radiating ribs, some of them bearing scattered short spines. Color reddish brown; interior pearly gray.

Family Ostreidae: Oysters
(see p. 17)

Genus *Ostrea* Linné 1758

OSTREA SANDWICHENSIS Sow.   **Hawaiian Oyster**   **Pl. 64**
 Habitat: Shallow water; rocky bottoms.
 Description: This is the common native oyster of the Islands.
A small bivalve seldom more than 2 in. long and growing in
clusters, so its shape is somewhat unpredictable. One valve
considerably larger than its mate. The surface bears several distinct folds. Color yellowish gray; inside dull and lusterless white.

Genus *Crassostrea* Sacco 1897

CRASSOSTREA GIGAS (Thun.)   **Japanese Oyster**   **Pl. 64**
 Habitat: Shallow water; rocky bottoms.
 Description: A large species, up to 12 in. long. Shape very
irregular but commonly elongate. Surface may be relatively
smooth or heavily fluted. Color gray; interior white. Lower
valve usually cupped and upper valve generally quite flat and
smaller.
 Remarks: Introduced in Hawaii and on our West Coast, where
it occurs from B.C. to California.

Family Anomiidae: Jingle Shells
(see p. 17)

Genus *Anomia* Linné 1758

ANOMIA NOBILIS Reeve   **Jingle Shell**   **Pl. 64**
 Habitat: Moderately shallow water.
 Description: From 2 to 3 in. long, this is a rather circular shell.
Upper valve well inflated and bearing irregular radiating
wrinkles; lower valve flat, with a round hole near beak for
passage of a byssus. The hinge is very weak, and after the
mollusk dies the upper valve soon becomes disengaged and
washes ashore; the perforated lower valve is not so often seen.
Shell thin and brittle, golden yellow, and has a waxy luster.

Family Carditidae: Carditas
(see p. 19)

Genus *Arcinella* Oken 1815

ARCINELLA THAANUMI Dall, Bar., & Reh.   Pl. 65
Thaanum's Arcinella
   Habitat: Moderately shallow water.
   Description: A small, somewhat rectangular shell, its length
   about ½ in. The shell is almost all posterior end, with the beaks
   very close to the front, and the shell has a pronounced dorsal
   curve. Surface marked by strong radiating ribs, crossed by
   sharp scalelike lines, and the outer margins are well scalloped.
   Color yellowish gray; interior white.

Family Lucinidae: Lucines
(see p. 21)

Genus *Anodontia* Link 1807

ANODONTIA HAWAIENSIS Dall, Bar., & Reh.   Pl. 65
   Habitat: Moderately shallow water.
   Description: Shell small, thin, inflated, and somewhat globular.
   Length about ½ in., color white or yellowish white. Surface
   smooth, with faint radiating striae and occasional concentric
   lines of growth. Interior with a yellowish tinge. No teeth in
   hinge.

Genus *Ctena* Mörch 1861

CTENA BELLA (Con.)   **Reticulate Saucer Shell**   Pl. 65
   Habitat: Moderately shallow water.
   Description: This is a circular shell about 1½ in. long. Valves
   strong and solid but only slightly inflated, so that the whole
   shell is rather thin. Beaks small and centrally located. The
   surface bears numerous fine radiating and concentric lines, giving the shell a reticulate pattern. Color white, sometimes
   yellowish; interior with a rosy area close to the margin.

Genus *Codakia* Scopoli 1777

CODAKIA THAANUMI Pils.   **Ribbed Saucer Shell**   Pl. 65
   Habitat: Moderately shallow water.
   Description: This shell is shaped like *Ctena bella* (above) but is
   larger — in length averaging about 2 in. — and its valves are
   slightly more inflated. Sculpture consists of radiating impressed

lines that are well separated, the spaces between them relatively broad at the margins. Color white; a broad marginal band of pink on the interior of the shell.

Family Chamidae: Jewel Boxes

(see p. 22)

Genus *Chama* Linné 1758

CHAMA HENDERSONI Dall, Bar., & Reh.   **Pl. 64**
Henderson's Jewel Box
   Habitat: Coral Reefs.
   Description: A small species, its length about ¾ in. The fixed (or bottom) valve is cup-shaped and frequently twisted, the upper valve fitting like a cap. The sculpture consists of numerous radiating lines that are scaly. Color whitish; interior white, no colored border.

CHAMA IOSTOMA Con.   **Violet-mouthed Jewel Box**   **Pl. 64**
   Habitat: Coral Reefs.
   Description: A thick and heavy oysterlike bivalve some 2 in. long. The shell is irregularly rounded in outline, and is attached to stones, corals, and other shells. The adhering valve is large and deep, flattened on one side where it is attached, and frequently so squeezed that its shape is uneven. Upper valve smaller and more regular in outline. Color pinkish gray, but the shell is usually overgrown with algae. Interior white, with a broad marginal band of violet. There are 2 very prominent muscle scars.

Family Cardiidae: Cockles

(see p. 23)

Genus *Trachycardium* Mörch 1853

TRACHYCARDIUM HAWAIENSIS Dall, Bar., & Reh.   **Pl. 65**
Hawaiian Cockle
   Habitat: Moderately shallow water.
   Description: A large and strong shell some 3 in. long. Shell oval, deeper than broad, the valves equal in size and shape and well inflated. The surface bears strong and sharp radiating ribs marked by numerous evenly spaced curving scales. On the posterior slope the scales are larger and more prominent. Color yellowish white, blotched with chestnut-brown. Interior shiny white, with a purple rim at the scalloped margin.

Remarks: This is the common cockle of the Islands, formerly listed as *Cardium orbiter* Sow.

Genus *Fragum* Röding 1798

FRAGUM THURSTONI Dall, Bar., & Reh.   **Pl. 65**
Blunt Cockle
   Habitat: Moderately deep water.
   Description: Generally less than ½ in. long, this bivalve has a short and regularly rounded anterior end; its posterior end is broader and rather abruptly chopped off and compressed to form a noticeable lateral slope. Beaks prominent. Surface bears numerous radiating ribs, each with a series of rather sharp but minute scales. Color yellowish white.

Family Pleurophoridae: Trapezium

SHELLS solid, equivalve, transversely elongated. The anterior end is short, posterior with angular ridge.

Genus *Trapezium* Mühlfeld 1811

TRAPEZIUM CALIFORNICUM (Con.)   **Pl. 65**
   Habitat: Shallow water; rocks.
   Description: An oblong shell, the anterior end extremely short and rounded, the posterior long and broadly rounded. Length nearly 2 in. Beaks low and inconspicuous, basal margin rather straight. Valves well inflated, and marked by both radiating and concentric lines, but they are usually quite faint. There is an angular ridge running from the beak to the posterior basal tip. Color yellowish white.

Family Veneridae: Venus Clams
(see p. 26)

Genus *Periglypta* Jukes-Browne 1914

PERIGLYPTA EDMONDSONI Dall, Bar., & Reh.   **Pl. 65**
Reticulate Venus
   Habitat: Moderately shallow water.
   Description: A rugged and solid shell, about 2 in. long, sometimes a bit larger. Anterior end short and rounded, posterior long and somewhat squarish. Beaks prominent. Valves well inflated. The surface bears sharp radiating lines that are crossed by equally sharp concentric lines, so that the pattern is reticu-

late. On the posterior slope the concentric ridges develop thin scalelike frills. Color yellowish gray, with scattered spots of pale orange. Interior white, stained with salmon-pink on teeth of hinge.

Remarks: Formerly listed as *Antigona reticulata* Linné.

Genus *Lioconcha* Mörch 1853

LIOCONCHA HIEROGLYPHICA (Con.)   Pl. 65
Hieroglyphic Venus
  Habitat: Shallow water.
  Description: An attractive shell, slightly more than 1½ in. long. Both ends are regularly rounded and about equal in length, the posterior end bearing the broadest curve. Beaks small but prominent. Surface smooth and shiny. Color ivory-white, with scattered dots, scrawls, and unusual markings that certainly do suggest hieroglyphics.

Genus *Meretrix* Lamarck 1799

MERETRIX MERETRIX (Linné)   Pl. 65
  Habitat: Moderately shallow water.
  Description: Nearly 3 in. long, this shell has a roughly triangular shape and well-inflated valves. There is a regular slope from the beaks to the ends, and the basal margin is gently rounded. Posterior end slightly the longer. Surface smooth and polished. Color yellowish gray, marked near beaks with a patch of orange-brown, and commonly a few scattered concentric streaks of same shade. Interior white.
  Remarks: This is a native of Asiatic waters that has been introduced in Hawaii.

Genus *Tapes* Mühlfeld 1811

TAPES JAPONICA (Desh.)   **Japanese Littleneck**   Pl. 65
(see p. 29)

Family Tellinidae: Tellins
(see p. 32)

Genus *Tellina* Linné 1758

TELLINA CRASSIPLICATA Sow.   **Sunset Tellin**   Pl. 65
  Habitat: Shallow water.
  Description: About 1½ in. long. The anterior end is somewhat longer than the posterior, and is regularly rounded; the posterior

end slopes gradually to a truncate tip. The valves are but little inflated and bear very fine and sharp concentric lines. Color yellowish, with pink radiating bands of varying widths. Interior pinkish, the bands showing through weakly.

TELLINA DISPAR Con.   White Tellin   Pl. 65
  Habitat: Shallow water.
  Description: A small oval shell ¾ in. long. The ends are nearly equal in size and both are regularly rounded. There is a slight fold on the posterior slope. Surface smooth and shiny. Color white, with a suggestion of rose near beaks.

TELLINA ELIZABETHAE Pils.   Rasp Tellin   Pl. 65
  Habitat: Moderately shallow water.
  Description: A roundish shell, strong and solid, its length about 2 in. The valves are moderately thick, but not much inflated. Both ends rounded, and about equal in size. Surface exceedingly rough, almost rasplike, with rounded but sharp scales arranged in concentric rings. Color pale yellow, white near the margin.
  Remarks: Formerly listed as *T. scobinata* Linné.

TELLINA OBLIQUILINEATA Con.   Pl. 65
  Habitat: Shallow water.
  Description: Just over ½ in. long. Beaks close to the short and acutely rounded anterior end, the posterior end broadly rounded. The surface is smooth. Color white, rayed with rose. Interior yellowish.

TELLINA PALATAM Ire.   Rough Tellin   Pl. 65
  Habitat: Shallow water.
  Description: A solid shell, but little inflated. Length about 2 in. The posterior end is noticeably pointed and somewhat twisted, the anterior end rounded. The surface is roughened by numerous wrinkled concentric lines. Color yellowish white; interior bright yellow in fresh specimens.
  Remarks: Formerly listed as *T. rugosa* Born.

TELLINA VENUSTA Desh.   Long Tellin   Pl. 65
  Habitat: Moderately shallow water.
  Description: In length about 2½ in., this is an elongate shell, very much compressed. The anterior end is the longer, and is rather broadly rounded. The posterior end is more pointed, and pinched out at the tip. Surface smooth and highly polished. Color white, tinged with ivory. Interior white, stained more or less with pale yellow.

Family Gastrochaenidae: Gaping Clams
(see p. 148)

Genus *Rocellaria* Blainville 1828

ROCELLARIA HAWAIENSIS Dall, Bar., & Reh.   Pl. 64
Habitat: Coral.
Description: A boring clam, 1½ in. long. The oval shell gapes widely, and is somewhat twisted in appearance. Beaks close to anterior end, and that end slopes sharply back to the basal margin. The valves are thin and fragile. Color yellowish white.

VII

Hawaiian Gastropods

Family Fissurellidae: Keyhole Limpets
(see p. 54)

Genus *Diodora* Gray 1821

DIODORA GRANIFERA (Pease) **Little Keyhole Limpet Pl. 66**
Habitat: Shallow water; rocks.
Description: A conical, well-elevated shell, oval in outline at the base, and only about ¼ in. long. Apex somewhat in front of middle, with a slitlike opening at the summit. Sculpture consists of radiating lines and weak concentric lines, the color whitish, often more or less marked with green.
Remarks: The Fissurellidae are not very well represented in Hawaii, this tiny shell being the most abundant example.

Family Patellidae: Limpets
(see p. 151)

Genus *Cellana* H. Adams 1869

CELLANA ARGENTATA (Sow.) **Kneecap Shell** **Pl. 66**
Habitat: Near shore; rocks.
Description: A fine large shell, the largest Hawaiian species of this group, attaining a length of nearly 4 in. The shape is dome-like, with the slopes convex, and the apex is nearly central. Surface decorated with numerous unequal ribs, the larger ones often notched, so that they appear beaded. Color brown, often coppery where worn a little. The interior has a jug-shaped central callus of white, bordered by a zone of dull lusterless white; the rest of the interior shines with a silvery sheen.

CELLANA EXARATA (Nutt.) **Black Limpet** **Pl. 66**
Habitat: Near shore; rocks.
Description: The shape is oval and conical, with the apex slightly closer to the anterior end. Length about 1½ in. Shell moder-

ately arched, and sculptured with numerous distinct black radiating ribs that render margins more or less scalloped. Between the ribs the surface is paler in tone. An area near the apex is often destitute of ribs, and a few weaker riblets are sometimes present between the main ones. Interior silvery, often lead-colored, with the dark ribs sometimes showing through, and there is a central patch of black or purplish blue.

Remarks: Commonly eaten, and fine specimens are often seen in Hawaiian fish markets, where they are called *opihi*.

Family Trochidae: Pearly Top Shells
(see p. 59)

Genus *Trochus* Linné 1758

TROCHUS INTEXTUS Kiener　**Hawaiian Top**　　Pls. 7, 8, 66
Habitat: Coral reefs.
Description: A neat and attractive shell, conical in shape, with a flat base, and slightly more than 1 in. high. There are about 8 partly flattened whorls, leading to a sharp apex. Sculpture consists of spiral series of very regular, deeply rounded granules, 5 or 6 to a volution, with more on the body whorl. Aperture small, and pearly within. Pinkish white, sometimes strongly marked with broad vertical bands of red or purplish, the bands commonly covering upper half of whorls.
Remarks: Another name, by which this shell has been known for years, is *T. sandwichensis* Soul.

Family Turbinidae: Turbans
(see p. 64)

Genus *Turbo* Linné 1758

TURBO INTERCOSTALIS Menke　**Green Turban**　　Pl. 66
Habitat: Moderately shallow water.
Description: A stoutly conic shell of 6 convex whorls, its height about 2 in. Sutures well defined, the aperture large and flaring a little at the base. The surface bears revolving ribs. Color greenish gray, with interrupted vertical bars of chocolate-brown. Aperture silvery white; operculum calcareous, its outside granulose.

Family Neritidae: Nerites
(see p. 156)

Genus *Nerita* Linné 1758

NERITA PICEA Réc.   **Common Nerite**   **Pl. 66**
  Habitat: Sea walls and rocks at high-tide line.
  Description: A small, roundish shell of 3 or 4 whorls, the body whorl making up most of the shell. About ½ in. high. Surface bears fine revolving lines but appears rather smooth. The outer lip is without teeth, but there are weak denticulations on the broad inner lip. Color shiny black, sometimes flecked with gray; aperture polished white.
  Remarks: The commonest nerite along Hawaiian shores.

NERITA PLICATA Linné   **Plicate Nerite**   **Pl. 66**
  Habitat: Intertidal stones.
  Description: A solid shell about 1 in. high, ridged with equal revolving lines, about 20 on the last whorl. Columellar area strongly wrinkled; inner lip armed with distinct teeth. Outer lip considerably thickened, with a large squarish tooth at each end and 4 narrow teeth between these. Color uniformly yellowish white in majority of specimens, but some individuals marked with black.

NERITA POLITA Linné   **Polished Nerite**   **Pls. 8, 66**
  Habitat: Shallow water.
  Description: An attractive and colorful shell of about 1½ in. There are 3 or 4 whorls, but the body whorl is so enlarged that it appears as if the snail is made up of but 1 volution. There is a tightly coiled spire not elevated at all. Shell thick and solid, smooth and polished, and extremely variable in color. It may be flecked, spotted, or banded with white, pink, orange, red, or black, and very commonly it shows most of these hues at once. Aperture white; outer lip thick but smooth, the inner lip feebly toothed. There is no umbilicus.

Genus *Neritina* Lamarck 1816

NERITINA CARIOSA Gray   **Winged Nerite**   **Pl. 66**
  Habitat: Brackish water.
  Description: Somewhat squarish in outline and about 1 in. high. The swollen body whorl is dilated into wings on each side of the beaklike apex. Color black or very dark brown, and there is a thin periostracum. Aperture bluish white, sometimes tinged with yellow.

Remarks: The wings are not developed until the mollusk is fully grown.

NERITINA GRANOSA Lam.　**Black Nerite**　　　**Pl. 66**
Habitat: Freshwater streams; stones.
Description: A greatly depressed shell, from 1 to 2 in. high. There is no spire, the whole shell being body whorl with a small beak at one end. The upper surface is covered with wartlike protuberences and is black. On the other side the shell is all aperture, with a greatly expanded columellar area; this side is bluish white, with more or less orange-yellow on the inner lip.
Remarks: This gastropod lives on rocks in swiftly flowing streams, and is not a marine mollusk. It is shown here because specimens are present in nearly all collections of Hawaiian shells.

NERITINA TAHITENSIS Less.　**Tahitian Nerite**　　**Pl. 66**
Habitat: Brackish water; stones at mouths of streams.
Description: This shell is shaped much like *N. granosa* (above), being rather flat and practically all body whorl, but it is smaller and more elongate. The height is about 1 in. Color brownish olive; aperture bluish white. There is a thin brownish periostracum, and the surface is smooth.
Remarks: A common shell in Hawaii, Samoa, and Tahiti.

Family Littorinidae: Periwinkles
(see p. 66)

Genus *Littorina* Férussac 1822

LITTORINA PICTA Phil.　**Painted Periwinkle**　　**Pl. 67**
Habitat: Rocks between tides.
Description: About ¾ in. tall, this periwinkle has 4 or 5 whorls, a well-developed spire, and a sharp apex. The surface is marked with revolving ribs that are somewhat roughened by granules. Color brownish, spotted and marbled with white; aperture purplish.

LITTORINA PINTADO Wood　**Dotted Periwinkle**　　**Pl. 67**
Habitat: Rocks between tides.
Description: Less than 1 in. high, with about 5 whorls, this shell tapers very regularly to a sharp apex. Sutures rather indistinct. The color is yellowish to bluish white, and the surface is marked by minute brown dots. Aperture reddish brown.

LITTORINA SCABRA (Linné)　**Variegated Periwinkle**　**Pl. 67**
Habitat: Shoreline; rocks and vines.
Description: This shell is 1 in. or more high, and is quite variable in color. It may be gray, reddish, yellowish, or purplish, varie-

gated with dark oblique markings. The shell is rather thin, with 6 or 7 whorls terminating in a sharp apex. Sutures slightly channeled. Aperture large and oval; operculum horny.

Remarks: This species is found all over the Pacific Ocean, as well as in the Atlantic. It used to be listed as *L. angulifera* Lam.

Family Architectonicidae: Sundials

(see p. 159)

Genus *Architectonica* Röding 1798

ARCHITECTONICA PERSPECTIVA (Linné)   **Pls. 7, 67**
Sundial

Habitat: Moderately shallow water.

Description: A circular shell, diam. from 1 to 2 in., occasionally larger. There are 6 or 7 whorls, the apex only slightly elevated, and the base is flat. Surface finely checked by crossing spiral lines, and each volution bears a pair of strong revolving ridges. Color yellowish gray, spotted and marbled with brown and purple. Aperture oval, the operculum horny, and the umbilicus is wide and deep and strongly crenulate.

Remarks: This gastropod occurs throughout the Indo-Pacific area, and a very similar form is found in the West Indies.

Genus *Torinia* Gray 1847

TORINIA VARIEGATA Gmel.   **Variegated Sundial**   **Pls. 8, 67**

Habitat: Moderately deep water.

Description: This is a smaller shell than *A. perspectiva* (above), the diam. some ¾ in. and its apex somewhat higher. About 6 whorls, decorated with strongly cut revolving lines, and by distinct vertical lines as well. The umbilicus extends through to the apex, and is rather strongly crenulate; the operculum is conically elevated. Color whitish, with numerous streaks of brown.

Remarks: The form found in Hawaii is sometimes listed as *T. v. depressa* Phil.

Family Modulidae: Modulus

(see p. 160)

Genus *Modulus* Potiez & Michaud 1838

MODULUS TECTUM Gmel.   **Knobby Snail**   **Pl. 67**

Habitat: Near shore; reefs.

Description: A short and bulbous shell, the diam. about 1 in. There are 4 or 5 whorls forming a depressed, flattish spire, the body whorl being relatively large. Aperture almost circular; lip thin and sharp. Sculpture consists of revolving ridges, some of them nodular, and strong vertical knobs on the shoulders. Color whitish, more or less clouded with brown.

Family Cerithiidae: Horn Shells

(see p. 69)

Genus *Cerithium* Bruguière 1789

CERITHIUM BAETICUM Pease   **Banded Horn Shell**   Pl. 67
   Habitat: Weedy shallow water.
   Description: A pretty shell about ½ in. high, with approximately 8 well-rounded whorls, the sutures impressed. Aperture small, canal short. The sculpture consists of vertical ribs that are low and encircling rows of tiny beads. Color white to yellowish, with a band of chocolate on each volution.

CERITHIUM COLUMNA Sow.   **Columnar Horn Shell**   Pl. 67
   Habitat: Weedy shallow water.
   Description: From 1 to 1½ in. high, this species is stoutly elongate, with about 9 whorls and indistinct sutures. The surface is sculptured with alternate larger and smaller encircling ridges that cross over prominent vertical ribs. A small notchlike canal at both ends of aperture; outer lip crenulate. Color grayish white, sometimes lightly mottled with brown.

CERITHIUM NASSOIDES Sow.   **Spotted Horn Shell**   Pl. 67
   Habitat: Shallow water.
   Description: A short and stout species about ⅓ in. high. Surface bears vertical ridges and knobby spiral bands, especially on the shoulders. There are about 6 whorls; the aperture is oval, the outer lip thickened. Color yellowish white, spotted or clouded with brown.

CERITHIUM NESIOTICUM Pils. & Van.   Pl. 67
Island Horn Shell
   Habitat: Shallow water.
   Description: A solid shell of 8 or 9 rather flattish whorls, the sutures shallow. Height about ¾ in. Surface bears weak encircling ridges that alternate in size. Color whitish, sometimes with a few faint brown spots at the sutures.

CERITHIUM OBELISCUS Brug.   **Obelisk Horn Shell**   Pl. 67
   Habitat: Weedy shallow water.
   Description: This shell is nearly 2 in. high and stoutly elongate. About 11 whorls that are rather straight-sided and decorated at the shoulders by knobby spiral bands, with a number of en-

circling beaded lines below. Aperture relatively small; inner lip plastered on the body whorl and the columella twisted backward to form a short canal. Color yellowish white, spotted and clouded with purplish brown.

CERITHIUM THAANUMI Pils.   **Thaanum's Horn Shell   Pl. 67**
Habitat: Weedy shallow water.
Description: A fairly rugged shell, nearly 1 in. high and consisting of 6 or 7 whorls, the sutures not very distinct. Surface with encircling lines of tiny beads. Aperture moderately large, outer lip somewhat expanded. Color whitish, sometimes spotted with reddish brown.

Family Triphoridae: Left-handed Snails
(see p. 70)

Genus *Triphora* Blainville 1828

TRIPHORA INCISUS Pease   **Pl. 67**
Habitat: Moderately shallow water.
Description: About ¼ in. high, this little shell has some 10 to 12 whorls. The whorls are rather flattish, and sculptured with revolving lines and weak vertical striations. Color yellowish, mottled with brown and purple.
Remarks: Snails in this group are left-handed (sinistral), coiling in the opposite direction to most of our gastropods. They are all small, many-whorled mollusks.

TRIPHORA PALLIDUS Pease   **Pl. 67**
Habitat: Moderately shallow water.
Description: Less than ¼ in. high, with about 12 roundish whorls. There are 3 rows of tiny beads encircling each volution. Color white, often with a brownish central band; surface quite shiny.
Remarks: Snails in this group are left-handed (sinistral), coiling in the opposite direction to most of our gastropods. They are all small, many-whorled mollusks.

Family Epitoniidae: Wentletraps
(see p. 70)

Genus *Epitonium* Röding 1798

EPITONIUM LAMELLOSUM (Lam.)   **Pl. 66**
Banded Wentletrap
Habitat: Limestone benches and coral reefs.

Description: A tall shell, the height about 1 in. and the whorl count about 9. Whorls well rounded, each decorated with about 12 thin and bladelike varices. During rest periods in shell growth, snails of this group develop a thickened outer lip, and as the mollusk increases in size these features become vertical ribs. Aperture round. Color white when found on the beach, but living specimens are apt to be flesh-colored, with a darker band at the suture.

Family Janthinidae: Violet Snails
(see p. 72)

Genus *Janthina* Röding 1798

JANTHINA GLOBOSA Blain. **Round Violet Snail**   Pls. 8, 66
(see p. 72)

JANTHINA JANTHINA (Linné) **Violet Snail**   Pl. 66
(see p. 72)

Family Hipponicidae: Hoof Shells
(see p. 73)

Genus *Hipponix* Defrance 1819

HIPPONIX PILOSUS (Desh.) **Hoof Shell**   Pl. 66
(see p. 164)

Family Calyptraeidae: Cup-and-Saucer Limpets and Slipper Shells
(see p. 74)

Genus *Crucibulum* Schumacher 1817

CRUCIBULUM SPINOSUM (Sow.)   Pl. 67
Cup-and-Saucer Limpet
(see p. 74)

Genus *Crepidula* Lamarck 1799

CREPIDULA ACULEATA (Gmel.) **Prickly Slipper Shell**   Pl. 67
(see p. 75)

Family Strombidae: Strombs
(see p. 165)

Genus *Strombus* Linné 1758

STROMBUS DENTATUS Linné   **Toothed Stromb**   **Pl. 67**
    Habitat: Moderately shallow water.
    Description: About 2 in. high when mature, this shell has 6 or 7 whorls, a rather tall spire, and a small elongate aperture. Sculpture consists of distinct vertical folds on upper half of each volution. Outer lip strongly grooved within, and there are 3 prominent teeth projecting from the edge toward its base. Inner lip rolled over on body whorl. Color yellowish, spotted with buffy orange; inside of aperture dark brown.
    Remarks: Formerly listed as *S. samar* Dill.

STROMBUS FRAGILIS Röd.   **Fragile Stromb**   **Pl. 67**
    Habitat: Shallow water.
    Description: A rather thin-shelled member of this group, attaining a height of about 1½ in. There are 4 or 5 whorls, a moderately sharp apex, and an elongate aperture, the lip thin and sharp. Surface smooth, often shiny. Color yellowish, lightly blotched with orange-brown.

STROMBUS HAWAIENSIS Pils.   **Hawaiian Stromb**   **Pl. 67**
    Habitat: Deep water.
    Description: A large and solid shell, from 2 to 3 in. high. There are 6 or 7 whorls, each decorated with revolving lines and by a single row of blunt knobs at the shoulder. Outer lip greatly expanded above, where it extends halfway up the spire, and is rather strongly ribbed within. Color yellowish white, flecked with orange-brown.
    Remarks: This is an uncommon species, generally obtained only by dredging.

STROMBUS HELLI Kiener   **Hell's Stromb**   **Pl. 67**
    Habitat: Moderately deep water.
    Description: Small but solid, the height no more than 1 in. About 6 whorls, the body whorl large and the spire tapering rapidly to a blunt point. The aperture is narrow and elongate. Inner lip ridged within; the outer lip thickened. Surface with vertical ridges. Color yellowish; aperture purplish.

STROMBUS MACULATUS Sow.   **Spotted Stromb**   **Pls. 8, 67**
    Habitat: Shallow water.
    Description: Seldom more than 1 in. high. There are 6 whorls,

the body whorl making up most of the shell. A short pointed spire. Surface smooth, sometimes with faint bumps at the shoulders. Aperture long and wide at base; inner lip reflected on body whorl and the outer lip considerably thickened. Color creamy white, variously speckled and spotted with yellowish brown.

Family Naticidae: Moon Shells

(see p. 77)

Genus *Natica* Scopoli 1777

NATICA MAROCHIENSIS Gmel.   **Moon Shell**   **Pl. 67**
Habitat: Shallow water; sandflats.
Description: A globular shell 1 in. or so in diam. Spire low, the whorl count about 4, the body whorl making up most of the shell. Aperture semilunar, outer lip simple. There is a well-developed umbilicus, and an operculum that is shelly. Surface smooth. Variable in color; commonly yellowish gray, with interrupted bands or blotches of reddish brown; often a whitish band at the suture.
Remarks: Gastropods of this family are noted for the large foot, used in plowing through the muds and sands in search of prey, chiefly small bivalves.

Genus *Polinices* Montfort 1810

POLINICES MELANOSTOMA (Gmel.)   **Pl. 67**
Black-mouthed Moon Shell
Habitat: Shallow water.
Description: A thin-shelled snail of 3 or 4 whorls, its height about 1 in. as a rule. There is a small pointed apex and a rather large aperture, the lip thin and sharp. Strong columellar callus and horny operculum. Surface smooth, with very fine revolving lines. The color is variable, usually white or yellowish white, more or less marked with pale purplish-brown streaks, with a heavy chocolate stain on the columella.

POLINICES PYRIFORMIS (Réc.)   **White Moon Shell**   **Pl. 67**
Habitat: Moderately shallow water.
Description: About 2 in. high when fully grown, this species is slightly taller than it is wide. There are 3 or 4 whorls, rising to a pointed apex. The columellar callus is very thick, completely covering the umbilicus. Operculum horny. Surface smooth and polished. Color pure white.
Remarks: A characteristic moon snail of many Pacific islands. Formerly called *Natica mammila* Linné.

Family Cypraeidae: Cowries
(see p. 79)

Genus *Cypraea* Linné 1758

CYPRAEA ANNULUS Linné **Ringed Cowry** Pl. 68
Habitat: Moderately shallow water.
Description: About ¾ in. long, a solid shell flat on the bottom and somewhat humped on the top. Color smoky white all over, with a distinct orange or yellow ring encircling the upper surface, and sometimes enclosing a bluish center.
Remarks: This cowry is commonly used for neckaces and shell jewelry.

CYPRAEA ARABICA Linné **Arabian Cowry** Pl. 68
Habitat: Moderately shallow water; reefs.
Description: From 2 to 2½ in. long. A solid shell distributed throughout the Indo-Pacific area. Like all the cowries, it is highly polished. Color on upper surface brownish, heavily marked with paler spots and interrupted wavy longitudinal lines. Lower surface whitish, the spaces between the teeth brown.

CYPRAEA CAPUTSERPENTIS Linné Pl. 68
Serpent's-head Cowry
Habitat: Shallow water.
Description: Heavy and solid, the length about 1½ in. Color reddish brown on upper surface, liberally sprinkled with white dots of various sizes. There is a conspicuous bluish-white patch at each end of the shell, the sides are dark brown, and the lower surface is grayish white.
Remarks: The commonest cowry in Hawaii.

CYPRAEA CARNEOLA Linné **Orange-banded Cowry** Pl. 68
Habitat: Moderately shallow water.
Description: Quite variable in size, the average less than 2 in. but occasional specimens more than 3 in. Shape less variable, but the larger individuals are often more swollen. Upper surface pale flesh color, sometimes tinged with violet on the back, and there are 4 (sometimes 5) broad bands of orange encircling the shell. Lower surface white, the teeth sometimes purplish.

CYPRAEA EROSA Linné **Eroded Cowry** Pl. 68
Habitat: Moderately shallow water.
Description: Oval and somewhat flattened, the base swollen at the margin. About 2 in. long. Color grayish above, covered with small white specks and a few larger brownish spots. A rather large dark patch is present at the sides. Lower side whitish.

CYPRAEA ESONTROPIA Duc.   Pl. 68
   Habitat: Moderately shallow water.
   Description: A pear-shaped shell, very well inflated, the length
   about 1 in. Color pale orange-yellow, thickly covered with
   roundish white spots. A few scattered reddish-brown dots are
   present along the sides. Base white.

CYPRAEA FIMBRIATA Gmel.   **Fringed Cowry**   Pl. 68
   Habitat: Moderately shallow water.
   Description: Length about 1 in. Shape oval, the top well
   arched. Aperture widens at the front, the teeth relatively small.
   Color light bluish gray above, more or less clouded with brownish
   scrawls, with a marked brownish patch at the center and sides.
   Underneath whitish.

CYPRAEA HELVOLA Linné   **Red Cowry**   Pl. 68
   Habitat: Shallow water.
   Description: A solid shell about 1 in. long, often somewhat less.
   Color orange-yellow above, rather thickly speckled with bluish
   white. Sides deep orange-red.
   Remarks: This is a very common cowry on many of the islands
   of the Pacific and Indian Oceans. Examples left on the beach
   fade in the sun and commonly take on a solid lavender color
   on the upper surface.

CYPRAEA ISABELLA Linné   **Isabel's Cowry**   Pl. 68
   Habitat: Moderately shallow water.
   Description: An elongate, rather cylindrical shell in length
   averaging about 1 in., sometimes a bit more. Upper surface
   ashy gray, with longitudinal black scrawls that are fine and delicate. The ends are stained orange-red; the lower surface is
   white. Teeth numerous and small.

CYPRAEA LYNX Linné   **Lynx Cowry**   Pl. 68
   Habitat: Moderately shallow water.
   Description: A well-known cowry throughout the Pacific, its
   length almost 2 in. when mature. Color pale gray above, clouded
   and spotted with brownish and yellowish blotches and a few
   scattered dark spots. Sides and bottom white, often stained
   with reddish between the teeth.

CYPRAEA MACULIFERA Schil.   **Reticulate Cowry**   Pl. 68
   Habitat: Moderately shallow water.
   Description: From 2 to 3 in. long. The color is dark brown,
   sometimes almost black, with bluish-white spots often closely
   crowded. Sides lavender, darker toward base, with irregular

brownish spots. Base violet, teeth brown. Young shells are bluish, clouded and banded with brown.

Remarks: Formerly listed as *C. reticulata* Mtyn.

CYPRAEA MAURITIANA Linné **Mourning Cowry** Pl. 68
Habitat: Near surf line; reefs.
Description: A large and solid shell up to 4 in. long. Upper surface somewhat humped, the sides thickened and flaring a little, the base quite flat. Color rich brown above, heavily marked with paler spots. Sides deep brown to nearly black; lower surface also very dark. Interior paler, so the strong teeth are very conspicuous.
Remarks: This shell is perhaps the most rugged and sturdy of the whole genus.

CYPRAEA MONETA Linné **Money Cowry** Pl. 68
Habitat: Moderately shallow water.
Description: About 1 in. long. The shape is somewhat triangular, the back quite bumpy, and the margins considerably thickened. The color ranges from nearly white to deep yellow.
Remarks: This well-known Money Cowry is abundant over a large part of the Pacific and Indian Oceans. Many hundreds of tons were shipped to Africa in the old days and used for currency. They are still so used in some parts of the Dark Continent, 100 shells equaling one English penny. It is an extremely variable shell, and several subspecies have been named.

CYPRAEA PEASEI Sow. **Pease's Cowry** Pl. 68
Habitat: Moderately shallow water.
Description: A pretty cowry about ¾ in. long. It is fairly well inflated. Pale yellowish color, spotted on the back with numerous round dots of white and a few reddish-brown dots along the sides. The lower surface is white.
Remarks: Some authorities regard this as *Cypraea gaskoini* Reeve.

CYPRAEA SCHILDERORUM Ire. **Sand Cowry** Pl. 68
Habitat: Shallow water.
Description: A small but unusually solid and heavy shell, the length about 1½ in. The shape is somewhat flattened, the sides greatly thickened. Color dusky above, with 4 rather broad reddish-brown bands. Sides grayish, with fine vertical lines of white. Underside white.
Remarks: Formerly listed as *C. arenosa* Gray.

CPYRAEA SCURRA Gmel. **Jester Cowry** Pl. 68
Habitat: Moderately shallow water.
Description: An elongate, nearly cylindrical shell, the length

about 1½ in. Top orange-brown, thickly covered with moderately large pale blue spots that occasionally run together. Sides pinkish brown, with a few scattered black dots. Lower surface pinkish brown. Aperture quite narrow; teeth small but numerous.

CYPRAEA SEMIPLOTA Mig.   **Little Spotted Cowry**   **Pls. 8, 68**
Habitat: Moderately deep water.
Description: Not much more than ½ in. long. A well-inflated shell, its color pale brown or fawn, generously sprinkled with minute whitish dots on the upper surface. Underside white; teeth often yellowish.

CYPRAEA TALPA Linné   **Mole Cowry**   **Pl. 68**
Habitat: Moderately shallow water.
Description: Attaining a length of between 3 and 4 in., this is a cylindrical shell, ranging throughout the Pacific and Indian Oceans. Color pale yellow above, with 3 broad bands, of paler shade. Underneath, the shell is very dark brown or black; sides and ends also dark. The aperture and teeth are lighter.

CYPRAEA TERES Gmel.   **Tapering Cowry**   **Pl. 68**
Habitat: Moderately shallow water.
Description: An elongate species, the length about 1½ in. Yellowish-white color, with weak bands of wavy longitudinal brown scrawls. Commonly a single irregular patch of brown near top. Underside whitish; aperture narrow, and teeth small.
Remarks: Formerly listed as *C. tabescens* Sol.

CYPRAEA TESSELLATA Mig.   **Tessellate Cowry**   **Pls. 7, 68**
Habitat: Moderately deep water.
Description: A little more than 1 in. long, this shell is considerably swollen and solid in substance. Color pale yellow, with 3 broad but rather faint bands, slightly darker in shade. Sides with 2 rather large, squarish spots of rich brown. Lower surface white, with pale orange bands; teeth orange.
Remarks: This is an uncommon species, much sought by collectors. There is evidence that it occurs nowhere but in the Hawaiian Is.

CYPRAEA TIGRIS Linné   **Tiger Cowry**   **Pl. 68**
Habitat: Moderately deep water.
Description: Up to 5 in. long, the shape swollen and the base rather flat. Color whitish to creamy whitish, covered all over the top with irregular spots and blotches of black, and sometimes purplish and brownish spots. Underside white. Aperture wide and curved, teeth robust.
Remarks: This is probably the best known of any cowry ranging throughout the Pacific and Indian Oceans. Attains its greatest size in the deep waters off Hawaii.

CYPRAEA VITELLUS Linné   Calf Cowry   Pl. 68
  Habitat: Moderately shallow water.
  Description: From 2 to 2½ in. long, a solid shell that is well
  inflated, the underside rather rounded. Color olive-gray above,
  decorated with numerous white spots of varying sizes. Lower
  surface white. Teeth numerous and rather large.

Genus *Pustularia* Swainson 1840

PUSTULARIA CICERCULA (Linné)   Pls. 8, 68
Chick Pea Cowry
  Habitat: Moderately shallow water.
  Description: About ¾ in. long, globular shape, with the ends
  drawn out very noticeably. A weak groove is present along the
  top; the base is rather flat; aperture narrow and bearing fine
  teeth. Color glossy yellowish, blotched with reddish brown, the
  sides dotted with brown.

Genus *Staphylaea* Jousseaume 1884

STAPHYLAEA GRANULATA (Pease)   Pl. 68
Granulated Cowry
  Habitat: Moderately shallow water.
  Description: Length somewhat more than 1 in., shell rather
  depressed, top not arched to any extent. Upper surface bears
  sharply cut transverse ribs in addition to numerous very pronounced pustules, and there is a median furrow running length-
  wise on the shell. Underside decorated with rather distant but
  strong transverse lines that render the margins more or less
  scalloped. Color yellowish white, often clouded with orange-
  brown.
  Remarks: Formerly listed as *Cypraea madagascarensis* Gmel.

STAPHYLAEA NUCLEUS (Linné)   **Nuclear Cowry**   Pl. 68
  Habitat: Moderately shallow water.
  Description: About ¾ in. long and slightly more arched than
  S. granulata (above). White, sometimes tinged with yellow.
  Ends somewhat drawn out. Upper surface bearing a distinct
  median furrow, the ornamentation consisting of prominent
  raised dots, or pustules, those near the margins commonly
  running together to form ridges. Lower surface with strong
  transverse ridges.

Family Eratoidae: Sea Buttons
(see p. 79)

Genus *Trivia* Broderip 1837

TRIVIA EXIGUA Gray   Pl. 68
  Habitat: Shallow water.
  Description: Less than ¼ in. long and considerably inflated. Decorated with transverse ribs that continue around the shell and into the aperture, and there is a well-defined median furrow. Color whitish, generally with a pair of rosy spots on the back (sometimes with a rosy ring encircling them).

TRIVIA INSECTA Mig.   Pl. 68
  Habitat: Shallow water.
  Description: A tiny shell, only about ⅛ in. long. Color white, and, like all of this genus, the transverse ribs continue around the shell to the base, and into the aperture.
  Remarks: Probably the most abundant of the group in Hawaii.

TRIVIA ORYZA Lam.   Pl. 68
  Habitat: Shallow water.
  Description: About ¼ in. long, sometimes a little more, this shell is a bit more inflated than *T. insecta* (above). The median furrow is rather obscure. Decorated like the others of the genus, perhaps rather less distinctly. Color white.

Family Cassididae: Helmets
(see p. 170)

Genus *Cassis* Scopoli 1777

CASSIS CORNUTA Linné   Horned Helmet   Pl. 69
  Habitat: Moderately deep water; sandy bottoms.
  Description: A large and ponderous shell, the largest of the group commonly known as helmet shells; attains height of 12 in. The shell is chiefly body whorl, with a flat spire of 6 or 7 volutions. Surface bears 3 rows of nodes, those on the shoulder enlarged to sturdy blunt spines. Both lips are enlarged and flattened to form a shelflike base for the shell, and both are toothed near the center. Color grayish white, often marked with brown. Lower surface yellowish orange (darker near aperture) and well polished.

Genus *Phalium* Link 1807

PHALIUM FORTISULCATA (Smith)   Grooved Helmet   Pl. 69
  Habitat: Moderately deep water; sandy bottoms.

Description: From 1 to 2 in. high, a sturdy shell of about 4 whorls, the surface marked with strong revolving ribs. Outer lip thickened and rolled over, strongly toothed along its inner margin; inner lip plastered on body whorl. Color creamy whitish, faintly marked with brown in the form of scattered dots.

PHALIUM VIBEX (Linné)   **White Helmet**   Pl. 69
Habitat: Moderately deep water.
Description: Some 3 in. high, this shell has about 5 whorls, the shoulders being decorated with knobby folds. Outer lip thickened at edge and rolled over; flares at base, where there are 3 or 4 short spines. No teeth on either lip. Surface usually polished. Color white, sometimes with a few pale orange streaks. Back of outer lip heavily spotted with chocolate-brown.

Family Cymatiidae: Tritons

(see p. 81)

Genus *Cymatium* Röding 1798

CYMATIUM GEMMATUM (Reeve)   **Gem Triton**   Pl. 69
Habitat: Moderately deep water.
Description: About 1½ in. high, a sturdy shell of 6 whorls. The surface bears rather strong revolving ribs and weak vertical lines, and there is a single stout varix on each volution. Outer lip greatly thickened and toothed within. Canal moderately long, open, and slightly bent. Color yellowish white.

CYMATIUM MURICINUM Röd.   **White-mouthed Triton** Pl. 69
Habitat: Moderately deep water.
Description: Averaging in height about 2 in., this is a rugged and strong shell with about 5 whorls and a sharply pointed apex. Surface sculptured with revolving nodular ribs, and there is a prominent varix on each volution. Aperture large, notched at upper end; outer lip toothed within. Canal moderately long and slightly curved. Color gray, spotted — and sometimes banded — with brown. Aperture pure white and shiny.
Remarks: This species occurs in the West Indies also. It used to be listed as *C. tuberosum* Lam.

CYMATIUM NICOBARICUM Röd.   Pls. 7, 69
Orange-mouthed Triton
Habitat: Moderately deep water.
Description: From 2 to 3 in. high and a soiled-white color, more or less mottled with brown. Aperture bright orange. The shell is rugged and solid, with about 5 whorls, a short spire, and a strong varix on each whorl. The surface is divided into squares by the crossing of horizontal and vertical ribs. Outer lip thick

and heavy, with a double row of teeth on the inner margin. Canal short and curved.

Remarks: This species occurs in the West Indies also. It used to be listed as *C. chlorostomum* Lam.

CYMATIUM PILEARE (Linné)   **Hairy Triton**   Pl. 69
Habitat: Moderately deep water.
Description: This species is from 3 to 5 in. high and rather slender in build. About 7 whorls, each with a robust varix. Surface sculptured with nodular revolving ribs. Outer lip bluntly toothed within; inner lip strongly plicate. Color yellowish white, the thickened outer lip and the varices barred with orange-brown. In life the shell is covered with a thick and hairy brown periostracum.

CYMATIUM RUBECULUM (Linné)   **Red Triton**   Pl. 69
Habitat: Moderately deep water.
Description: A solid shell of 4 or 5 whorls, its height about 1½ in. Surface with spiral ribs that are granulose, and prominent beaded varices. Canal short, aperture moderately large. The color ranges from yellow to orange-red, often with a whitish band at center of body whorl. Generally a few white patches on each varix.

Genus *Charonia* Gistel 1848

CHARONIA TRITONIS (Linné)   **Trumpet Shell**   Pl. 69
Habitat: Shallow bays.
Description: A large shell, up to 18 in. high. It is richly variegated with buff, brown, purple, and red, in crescentic patterns suggestive of the plumage of pheasants. Aperture pale orange. Shell strong and solid, gracefully elongate, the apex bluntly pointed. There are 8 or 9 whorls, the sutures plainly marked. Widely spaced rounded ribs encircle the shell, and each volution bears a prominent varix. Inner lip reflected and stained a dark purplish brown, crossed by whitish wrinkles.
Remarks: The largest univalve to be found on Hawaiian shores, this big gastropod shell is often made into a trumpet. In some South Sea islands it is used for a teakettle.

Family Bursidae: Frog Shells

(see p. 81)

Genus *Bursa* Röding 1798

BURSA AFFINIS Brod.   **Frog Shell**   Pl. 69
Habitat: Moderately shallow water.
Description: Some 2 in. high, with about 6 whorls. There is a prominent varix on opposite sides of each volution, making a

rounded ridge ascending the spire on each side. The sculpture consists of encircling rows of beads, with 1 row near the shoulder larger than the others. Aperture moderately large, notched at each end; outer lip strongly toothed within. Color yellowish brown, marked with orange, brown, and white.

BURSA BUFONIA (Gmel.)   **Toad Shell**   **Pl. 69**
   Habitat: Moderately shallow water.
   Description: A rough and bumpy shell some 3 in. high, unusually thick and solid. About 6 whorls, with poorly defined sutures. The sculpture consists of broad encircling ridges, plus scattered knobs and innumerable small beadlike pustules. Color grayish white; aperture sometimes yellowish.

BURSA SIPHONATA (Reeve)   **Spouted Triton**   **Pl. 69**
   Habitat: Moderately shallow water.
   Description: Some 2 in. high, with about 4 stout whorls. Sculpture of revolving warty ribs and rounded knobby varices. Aperture moderately large; outer lip thickened, and both lips strongly toothed. Canal short and nearly closed, and there is a distinct notch at the upper angle of the aperture. Color whitish; columella purplish.

Genus *Distorsio* Röding 1798

DISTORSIO ANUS Linné   **Warped Shell**   **Pls. 7, 69**
   Habitat: Moderately deep water.
   Description: This oddly shaped shell is about 3 in. high and has about 8 whorls that are decorated with rather sharp vertical ridges and weaker revolving lines. Aperture small and constricted, with a deep groove at center of columella. Inner lip reflected and expanded, and plastered on front of shell so as to hide all but top of the spire. Outer lip strongly toothed, the canal bent backward at a sharp angle. Color yellowish white, lightly banded with orange-brown; aperture, usually polished, stained bright orange-brown.

Family Colubrariidae: Curved Shells

(see p. 173)

Genus *Colubraria* Schumacher 1817

COLUBRARIA DISTORTA (Schu. & Wag.)   **Pl. 69**
Crooked Shell
   Habitat: Moderately deep water.
   Description: This is indeed a crooked shell. It is about 2½ in. high and elongate, with 8 or 9 rounded whorls, each with a single varix. The varices are disposed in a continuous line, which causes the spire to bend noticeably in that direction. Surface

bears fine vertical lines as well as revolving lines, so is more or less reticulate. Color pale yellowish brown, clouded with orange.

Family Tonnidae: Tun Shells
(see p. 173)

Genus *Tonna* Brünnich 1772

TONNA OLEARIUM (Linné)   **Tun Shell**   Pl. 69
Habitat: Moderately deep water.
Description: A large but thin-shelled snail, rather globular in shape. The height is from 3 to 5 in., with about 4 whorls. Spire short and body whorl very large; aperture wide and deep. Sutures depressed. The surface bears rounded revolving ribs, spaces between them narrow. Color yellowish brown, more or less clouded with reddish brown.

TONNA PERDIX (Linné)   **Partridge Shell**   Pl. 69
Habitat: Moderately deep water.
Description: This species grows to be about 7 in. high. The shell is rather thin but sturdy, and the spire is short. Aperture large, lip thin and sharp. There are well-defined revolving lines. The color is pale to rich brown, heavily mottled with crescent-shaped patches of white, so that the surface does indeed remind one of the plumage of a partridge.

Genus *Malea* Valenciennes 1832

MALEA POMUM Linné   **Apple Tun Shell**   Pl. 69
Habitat: Moderately deep water.
Description: A light but sturdy shell about 3 in. high, with 3 or 4 whorls, a short pointed spire, and a large body whorl. The surface bears about 12 low ribs encircling the last volution, separated by shallow grooves. The columella has a noticeable excavation at its lower center. Outer lip thickened at margin and strongly toothed within. Color creamy white, more or less streaked with orange.

Family Magilidae: Coral Snails
(see p. 178)

Genus *Coralliophila* H. & A. Adams 1853

CORALLIOPHILA DEFORMIS (Lam.)   Pl. 69
Habitat: Crevices of rocks and corals.
Description: About 1½ in. high, a rugged shell of 5 or 6 whorls.

The body whorl is swollen, and there is a short pointed spire. Vertical folds decorate the shoulders, and there are widely spaced revolving ridges on the lower half of the volutions. Color chalky white; aperture often rose or violet.

CORALLIOPHILA MADREPORARUM (Sow.)   **Pl. 69**
     (see p. 178)

CORALLIOPHILA NERITOIDEA (Lam.)   **Pl. 69**
     Habitat: Coral growths.
     Description: A solid and rough shell, its height 1½ in. Spire short, body whorl large. Surface coarsely wrinkled. Outer lip thickened and toothed within. Color whitish; aperture purple.
     Remarks: With all of these coral-dwelling gastropods, the outer surface is likely to be incrusted with coralline growths.

Family Thaididae: Dye Shells
(see p. 87)

Genus *Thais* Röding 1798

THAIS APERTA (Blain.)   **Wide-mouthed Thais**   **Pl. 67**
     Habitat: Rocks in shallow water; surf.
     Description: This shell appears to be nearly all aperture. It is from 2 to 3 in. high and has 3 or 4 whorls, the last one making up most of the shell. There is a very short spire. Sculpture consists of revolving ribs of varying sizes, some of which are decorated with moderately long tubercles. Color white or yellowish white; large aperture often stained with orange. Inner lip very broad, and highly polished.

THAIS HARPA (Con.)   **Harp Thais**   **Pl. 67**
     Habitat: Rocks in shallow water; surf.
     Description: Slightly more than 1 in. high, this shell has about 4 whorls, a moderate spire, and a sharp apex. Body whorl large, the lip flaring. Surface bears revolving ridges crossed by oblique vertical lines. Color brown, with scattered white spots; columella and the thickened outer lip rich chocolate-brown.

THAIS INTERMEDIA (Kiener)   **Intermediate Thais**   **Pl. 67**
     Habitat: Rocks in shallow water; surf.
     Description: A solid shell about 2 in. high, composed of about 4 whorls. Aperture broad and flaring. There are 3 rows of short and blunt nodes encircling the shell, with obscure lines between them. Color yellowish white, mottled with brown. Both lips are stained dark purplish brown; inside of aperture bluish white.

Genus *Drupa* Röding 1798

DRUPA GROSSULARIA Röd. **Finger Drupe** Pls. 8, 70
 Habitat: Moderately shallow water.
 Description: About 1 in. high, a solid shell of 4 whorls. Surface with revolving lines, but generally rough and unattractive. Outer lip considerably thickened, and ornamented by flattened, frondlike protuberances. Aperture narrow, strongly toothed. Color whitish; aperture bright orange.
 Remarks: Formerly listed as *Sistrum digitatum* Lam.

DRUPA MORUM Röd. **Mulberry Drupe** Pl. 70
 Habitat: Moderately shallow water.
 Description: From 1 to 1½ in. high, a very sturdy and robust shell, rather squat in appearance. There are 3 or 4 whorls, the last one very large. Shell ornamented with 3 or 4 rows of short, thick, blunt spines. Aperture small and narrow, with teeth of outer lip grouped in little bundles. The columella bears 4 plications. Color grayish white; tips of spines darker, often nearly black. Aperture deep purple.
 Remarks: Formerly listed as *Sistrum horridum* Lam.

DRUPA RICINA (Linné) **Spotted Drupe** Pl. 70
 Habitat: Moderately shallow water.
 Description: This species is about 1 in. high and has about 4 whorls. The body whorl has 4 rows of encircling nodes, those along the outer lip appearing as extended fronds. The long and narrow aperture is all but closed by the grouped teeth of the outer lip. Color whitish, the nodes black.

Genus *Morula* Schumacher 1817

MORULA ELATA (Blain.) Pl. 70
 Habitat: Moderately shallow water.
 Description: This shell is more highly ornate than most of its group, being sculptured with strong revolving ribs and by vertical folds. Height about 1 in. and whorl count 5. Aperture moderately long; outer lip feebly toothed within but strongly scalloped on outer edge. Inner lip reflected on body whorl. Color buffy yellowish, the vertical ridges darker in tone. Aperture yellowish.
 Remarks: Formerly listed as *M. ochrostoma* (Blain.).

MORULA FISCELLA Gmel. **Basket Morula** Pl. 70
 Habitat: Moderately shallow water.
 Description: About ¾ in. high, this species bears both vertical and horizontal ridges, producing a reticulated pattern with deep

pits. The aperture is relatively large, the lip thickened. Color grayish white; aperture purple.

MORULA GRANULATA (Duc.)   **Granulate Morula**   **Pl. 70**
    Habitat: Moderately shallow water.
    Description: A spindle-shaped shell about 1 in. high, consisting of about 4 whorls, the sutures indistinct. Outline somewhat variable, with some specimens more shouldered and possessing taller spines than others. There are 4 or 5 rows of black tubercles encircling the shell, the spaces between them dull gray. Aperture very small, strongly toothed, and purple.
    Remarks: Formerly listed as *M. tuberculata* (Blain.).

MORULA PORPHYROSTOMA (Reeve)   **Pl. 70**
    Habitat: Moderately shallow water.
    Description: About ½ in. high, rather spindle-shaped, with 4 whorls. Spire pointed. Sculpture of rather strong vertical folds and very fine revolving lines. Aperture relatively large. Color yellowish or whitish; aperture violet.

MORULA UVA Röd.   **Grape Morula**   **Pls. 8, 70**
    Habitat: Moderately shallow water.
    Description: About ¾ in. high, a solid shell of 4 whorls, decorated with encircling rows of stout nodes. Color grayish; nodes shiny black. Aperture narrow, purple, showing a pair of stout teeth inside the outer lip.
    Remarks: Formerly listed as *M. nodus* St. V.

Genus *Nassa* Röding 1798

NASSA SERTUM (Brug.)   **Garland Nassa**   **Pl. 70**
    Habitat: Moderately deep water.
    Description: About 2 in. high, composed of 4 or 5 whorls, the sutures not very distinct. Surface bears fine revolving lines but appears rather smooth. Outer lip somewhat thickened, aperture long and semilunar, with a small notchlike canal at upper angle. Color yellowish gray, streaked and clouded with reddish brown.
    Remarks: Sometimes listed as *Iopas sertum* (Brug.).

Genus *Vexilla* Swainson 1840

VEXILLA TAENIATA Gmel.   **Pl. 70**
    Habitat: Moderately shallow water.
    Description: A smooth shell of 4 or 5 whorls, the sutures indistinct. Apex sharply pointed. Height ¾ in. Color yellowish, with encircling brown lines; aperture purplish or brownish.

Family Columbellidae: Dove Shells
(see p. 89)

Genus *Pyrene* Röding 1798

PYRENE VARIANS (Sow.)   **Spotted Dove Shell**   Pl. 70
Habitat: Shallow water.
Description: A variable shell, sometimes rather squat and sometimes more elongate. Generally it is sturdy, the height about
½ in. Approximately 6 slightly shouldered whorls, a short spire,
and a pointed apex. Aperture long and narrow; outer lip thickened and weakly toothed within. Surface smooth, with a series
of blunt nodes encircling shoulders. Color creamy white, with
broken bands of brown spots.

PYRENE ZEBRA (Gray)   **Zebra Dove Shell**   Pl. 70
Habitat: Shallow water.
Description: A slightly larger shell than *P. varians* (above), just
just over ½ in. high. There are 4 or 5 whorls and a fairly tall
spire. Surface smooth; color white or yellowish white, decorated
with oblique zigzag streaks of brown that are sometimes broken
into elongate bars.

Family Nassariidae: Dog Whelks
(see p. 90)

Genus *Nassarius* Duméril 1805

NASSARIUS HIRTUS (Kiener)   **Rough Dog Whelk**   Pls. 8, 70
Habitat: Shallow water.
Description: A rather stout shell about 1 in. high. Approximately 6 whorls with well-defined sutures. The sculpture consists of vertical folds that become weaker toward the base of the
shell. Color yellowish or orange-brown, commonly with a paler
central band.

NASSARIUS PAPILLOSUS (Linné)   Pl. 70
Papillose Dog Whelk
Habitat: Shallow water.
Description: From 1 to 2 in. high, this is a solid shell of 6 or 7
whorls. There is a rather tall spire, capped by a pointed apex.
Body whorl bears 7 rows of encircling pustules, with usually 4
rows on each volution of the spire. Aperture moderately large,
with a deep notchlike excavation at base. Color white, sometimes tinged with yellow.

Family Buccinidae: Whelks

(see p. 92)

Genus *Pisania* Bivona 1832

PISANIA BILLETHEUSTI Petit   **Marbled Whelk**   **Pl. 70**
    Habitat: Moderately deep water.
    Description: A rather slender shell about 1 in. high, its whorl
count 8. Surface sculptured with vertical ribs and revolving
lines. Aperture moderately narrow. Color whitish, more or less
marked with reddish brown.

PISANIA TRITINOIDES Reeve   **Pisa Whelk**   **Pl. 70**
    Habitat: Moderately deep water.
    Description: A small elongate shell of about 7 whorls, the sutures
quite distinct. Height about 1 in. Surface ornamented with
weakly beaded revolving lines. Aperture narrow and moderately long; short, open canal. Color yellowish white, mottled
with pale orange.

Family Fasciolariidae: Tulip Shells

(see p. 188)

Genus *Latirus* Montfort 1810

LATIRUS NODATUS (Gmel.)   **Nodular Latirus**   **Pl. 70**
    Habitat: Moderately deep water.
    Description: A knobby shell, spindle-shaped and about 3 in.
high. There are 6 or 7 whorls, each with 6 rounded swollen areas,
so that the whole surface is a series of smooth, rounded knobs.
Canal long and open. Color pale orange, the nodes lighter
in tone.

Genus *Peristernia* Mörch 1852

PERISTERNIA CHLOROSTOMA Sow.   **Pl. 70**
    Habitat: Moderately shallow water.
    Description: A stoutly fusiform shell about ½ in. high. There
are 5 whorls, each decorated with strong vertical folds and by
fine revolving lines. The aperture is small; the inner lip reflected
and outer lip thin; there is a short, open canal. Color yellowish
white, marked with brownish spots.

Family Olividae: Olive Shells

(see p. 98)

Genus *Oliva* Bruguière 1789

OLIVA SANDWICHENSIS Pease **Hawaiian Olive** Pl. 70
  Habitat: Sandflats at low tide.
  Description: About 1 in. high, with 4 or 5 whorls, a short spire and a long body whorl that is cylindrical in shape. Aperture long and narrow. Surface smooth and polished. Color yellowish white, spotted with brown, commonly in the form of 3 irregular bands.
  Remarks: This olive shell varies widely in color, as do many of this group. Usually there is a row of dark marks along the suture line.

Family Mitridae: Miters

(see p. 99)

Genus *Mitra* Röding 1798

MITRA ASTRICTA Lam. **Smooth Miter** Pl. 70
  Habitat: Moderately shallow water.
  Description: About 1 in. high, with 6 sloping whorls. There is no evidence of shoulders, and the surface is quite smooth, although there are weak revolving lines. Aperture narrow; inner lip plicate. Color olive-gray, sometimes with narrow encircling lines of brown.

MITRA AURICULOIDES Reeve **Banded Miter** Pls. 8, 70
  Habitat: Moderately shallow water.
  Description: About 1 in. high, a fusiform shell of some 6 or 7 whorls, the sutures quite distinct. Surface smooth, with encircling rows of punctuate grooves. Shell very sturdy, colored yellow-orange, often with a single yellow band on upperpart of each volution.

MITRA BALDWINI Mel. **Baldwin's Miter** Pl. 70
  Habitat: Moderately shallow water.
  Description: This species gets to be almost 1 in. high, and has about 6 whorls, the sutures quite distinct. Surface smooth and polished, with longitudinal lines on the first few whorls only. Color creamy white, with vertical streaks of reddish brown. Aperture long and narrow, with strong pleats on inner lip.

MITRA BRUNNEA Pease   **Brown Miter**   Pl. 70
   Habitat: Moderately shallow water.
   Description: A rather slender species. Color dark brown, the aperture white. It attains a height of 1 in. and has about 6 shoulderless whorls. Surface fairly smooth, with only suggestions of revolving lines.

MITRA CONSANGUINEA Reeve   **Ribbed Miter**   Pl. 70
   Habitat: Moderately shallow water.
   Description: About ½ in. high and rather stout. Whorl count 6. There is a strong sculpture of vertical ribs, about 15 on the body whorl. Aperture narrow, the inner lip bearing the typical pleats of this group. Color yellowish orange, the ribs paler in tone.

MITRA CORONATA Lam.   **Crowned Miter**   Pl. 70
   Habitat: Moderately shallow water.
   Description: A stocky shell, generally about 1 in. high. There are 5 or 6 whorls, the sutures plainly marked. The surface bears both horizontal and vertical lines, the former more pronounced, and there is a series of beadlike nodes at the suture. Color orange-brown, flecked with white.

MITRA CUCUMERINA Lam.   **Ridged Miter**   Pl. 70
   Habitat: Moderately shallow water.
   Description: A neat little shell, very fusiform in shape, being rather sharply pointed at both ends and swollen in the middle. About ¾ in. high, with 7 whorls, the sutures indistinct. Surface sculptured with sharp revolving ridges, set close together. Color yellowish orange, more or less flecked with white.

MITRA LITTERATA Lam.   **Lettered Miter**   Pl. 70
   Habitat: Moderately shallow water.
   Description: A variable shell about 1 in. high, sometimes rather slender and sometimes quite stout. There are 5 or 6 whorls, the sutures clear-cut. Sculpture consists of fine encircling lines. The color is almost white, with very irregular markings of dark brown.
   Remarks: The markings often have the appearance of letters of the alphabet

MITRA NODOSA Swain.   **Nodular Miter**   Pl. 70
   Habitat: Moderately shallow water.
   Description: About ½ in. high. Stoutly fusiform, decorated with revolving rows of nodes. Whorl count 5. Aperture narrow; inner lip strongly plicate. Spire short and noticeably turreted. Color white, occasionally banded with brown.

Family Harpidae: Harp Shells

(see p. 194)

Genus *Harpa* Röding 1798

HARPA CONOIDALIS Lam. **Harp Shell** Pls. 7, 70
  Habitat: Moderately deep water.
  Description: A splendid shell some 2 in. high, with about 5
  whorls (the last one expanded) and a flaring aperture. There are
  about 12 rather broadly flattened vertical ribs on each whorl,
  with wide spaces between them. Spire short and pointed. The
  aperture has a small notch at its base. Color pinkish gray to
  bluish white, with squarish spots of violet on the ribs; the spaces
  between are decorated with chevronlike marks of brown and
  lavender. There are 2 strong patches of chocolate-brown on the
  inner lip, which is folded over at the base. The whole shell is
  rather well polished, and is one of the most attractive of our
  marine shells.

Family Marginellidae: Marginellas

(see p. 100)

Genus *Marginella* Lamarck 1799

MARGINELLA SANDWICHENSIS Pease Pl. 70
Hawaiian Marginella
  Habitat: Shallow water; tidepools.
  Description: A small oval shell generally no more than ¼ in.
  high. There are 3 or 4 whorls, with a very short rounded spire
  on top; the body whorl forms most of the shell. Aperture long
  and narrow, widest at the bottom; inner lip decorated with 4
  strong pleats. Color milky white; surface highly polished.

Family Conidae: Cone Shells

(see p. 101)

Genus *Conus* Linné 1758

CONUS ABBREVIATUS Reeve **Abbreviated Cone** Pl. 71
  Habitat: Moderately shallow water; reefs.
  Description: A sturdy shell slightly more than 1 in. high, with
  about 8 whorls. Spire rather flat, the shoulders strongly crenulate. Color bluish gray, with a paler central band and a 2nd

band at the shoulder. There is a pattern of small reddish-brown dots encircling the shell in regular and distinct rows.

CONUS CATUS Hwass **Cat Cone** Pl. 71
Habitat: Shallow water; reefs.
Description: About 1½ in. high, this is a strong cone of 6 or 7 whorls, the spire only slightly elevated. Surface with revolving lines that are most pronounced toward base of shell, that portion being spirally grooved. Color bluish gray, heavily splashed with patches of rich chocolate-brown.

CONUS CHALDEUS (Röd.) **Worm Cone** Pl. 71
Habitat: Shallow water; reefs.
Description: Usually less than 1 in. high. A rough and sturdy cone of about 7 whorls, the spire moderately elevated. The surface bears a number of vertical grooves. Color black, marked more or less by zigzag whitish streaks.
Remarks: Formerly listed as *C. vermicularis* Lam., this is regarded by many authorities as a subspecies of *C. ebraeus* Linné (below).

CONUS DISTANS Hwass **Knobby-top Cone** Pl. 71
Habitat: Moderately deep water; reefs.
Description: Height 1½ in., whorl count 7. The shoulders are decorated with a row of prominent knobs, and the short spire is ringed with a spiral of rounded knobs. Surface smooth. Color pale yellowish gray, generally with a central band of bluish white. Aperture shows a violet tinge.

CONUS EBRAEUS Linné **Hebrew Cone** Pl. 71
Habitat: Moderately shallow water; reefs.
Description: A distinctive shell about 1½ in. high. There are 6 or 7 whorls, producing a slightly domed spire. Surface with numerous revolving lines, strongest toward the base of shell. Color white, with 3 rows of angular, squarish black marks. Another row of smaller black marks encircles the shoulders, and the base of the shell is black. Aperture white, with clouded bands.
Remarks: There is considerable variation in individuals, some showing more of the white than others, but the patterns of many specimens do suggest printed Hebrew characters.

CONUS FLAVIDUS Lam. **Yellow-tinged Cone** Pl. 71
Habitat: Moderately shallow water; reefs.
Description: Some 2 in. high, with about 7 whorls. Spire domed. Color light yellowish olive, with a distinct band of bluish gray at center of body whorl. Top of shell white, the shoulders more or less clouded with bluish white. Aperture rich purple, streaked with white.

CONUS IMPERIALIS Linné   **Imperial Cone**   Pl. 71
  Habitat: Moderately deep water; reefs.
  Description: Height about 4 in., whorl count about 6. Shoulders strongly crenulate, and the whole surface bears fine revolving lines. Spire nearly flat. Color white, or pale bluish white, with many interrupted encircling lines and dots of purplish brown and 2 irregular light brownish bands.
  Remarks: When in fresh condition this is one of the most beautiful cones.

CONUS LEOPARDUS (Röd.)   **Many-spotted Cone**   Pl. 71
  Habitat: Moderately shallow water; reefs.
  Description: A large and sturdy shell, attaining a height of 6 in. There are 7 or 8 whorls but no spire, the top of the shell being nearly flat. Color white or creamy white, heavily spotted with brown or black. The spots are usually arranged as broken revolving bands, and sometimes a row of small spots alternates with one of larger spots.
  Remarks: Formerly listed as *C. millepunctatus* Lam.

CONUS LITHOGLYPHUS Meus.   **Pebble Carved Cone**   Pl. 71
  Habitat: Moderately deep waters; reefs.
  Description: A rather elongate shell some 3 in. high. There are about 8 whorls, the spire moderately elevated. Color olive-brown. At the shoulders and the middle of the body whorl are irregular whitish bands, often interrupted by orange scrawls.
  Remarks: Now listed by some authorities as *C. ermineus* Born.

CONUS LIVIDUS Hwass   **Spiteful Cone**   Pl. 71
  Habitat: Moderately shallow water; reefs.
  Description: This species is about 2 in. high and has 6 whorls. Spire rather low, but the apex is pointed. The shoulders bear rounded knobs. Color olive-tan, with a central band of bluish white and a narrower band at the shoulders.

CONUS MARMOREUS Linné   **Marbled Cone**   Pl. 71
  Habitat: Moderately deep water; reefs.
  Description: Height about 5 in. There are some 8 or 9 whorls and a low spire that is grooved and covered by tubercles. Color dark brown, well covered with whitish or pinkish triangular spots, sometimes arranged so as to suggest banding.
  Remarks: This is one of the several species of cone shells capable of inflicting a dangerous, perhaps fatal, wound.*

CONUS MILES Linné   **Soldier Cone**   Pl. 71
  Habitat: Moderately deep water; reefs.
  Description: A solid cone of some 4 in. and composed of about

*See William J. Clench and Yoshio Kondo, *The Poisonous Cones.*
Occasional Papers on Mollusks, Vol. 1 (1946), No. 7, Department of Mollusks, Museum of Comparative Zoology, Harvard University.

7 whorls, with the spire moderately elevated. The shoulder of the last whorl may be crenulate, whereas those of the spire are rather strongly plicate. Color yellowish brown, with a chocolate band on the body whorl. Above and below this band the shell may be marked with wavy, vertical streaks and narrow lines of chestnut. Base of shell chocolate. Aperture banded, brown and white.

CONUS NUSSATELLA Linné **Slender Cone** Pl. 71

Habitat: Moderately shallow water; reefs.
Description: A cylindrical shell some 2 in. high and composed of about 7 whorls. Shoulders rounded, the spire moderately high. Surface of the shell is sculptured with faintly beaded revolving lines. Color yellowish white, clouded with vertical streaks of orange; numerous tiny red-brown dots on the encircling lines.

CONUS OBSCURUS Sow. **Obscure Cone** Pl. 71

Habitat: Moderately deep water; reefs.
Description: A thin-shelled cone, light in weight and growing to a height of about 1¼ in. There is a well-developed spire. The aperture is quite wide, particularly at the base. Color yellowish brown, clouded and streaked with pale orange.

CONUS PENNACEUS Born **Pearled Cone** Pls. 7, 71

Habitat: Shallow water; reefs.
Description: A solid shell 2½ in. high, made up of about 7 whorls, the spire moderately elevated. Color variable but usually orange-brown, covered with small whitish spots and larger triangular patches of white, sometimes with a suggestion of banding.
Remarks: One of the commoner cones found on Hawaiian reefs.

CONUS PULICARIUS Brug. **Flea-bitten Cone** Pl. 71

Habitat: Moderately shallow water; reefs.
Description: From 1 to 2 in. high, this is a decorative shell of about 7 whorls. The shoulders bear rather strong nodules, and the spire is moderately elevated. Base of shell less pointed than in most cones, so that the shape is somewhat plump. Color white, heavily spotted with dark brown or black. Sometimes the spots are thicker in certain areas and suggest a pair of obscure bands. Aperture white.

CONUS QUERCINUS Sol. **Oak Cone** Pl. 71

Habitat: Moderately deep water; reefs.
Description: A rather solidly built shell that may be 5 in. high. There are 7 or 8 whorls, producing a spire that is well elevated and capped by a sharply pointed apex. Color lemon-yellow to white, often with numerous very fine and crowded lines of pale brown encircling the shell. Older specimens are likely to be paler in tone, and the encircling lines may be indefinite.

CONUS RATTUS Hwass   **Rat Cone**   Pl. 71
  Habitat: Shallow water; reefs.
  Description: A solid and stubby shell, the height about 2 in.
  The shell has a rather flat top and about 6 whorls. Color yellowish brown, with a large bluish-white band composed of interrupted blotches and spots at the center, and another at the
  shoulder.

CONUS SPONSALIS Hwass   Pl. 71
  Habitat: Intertidal beaches.
  Description: A thick and solid shell about 1 in. high. The spire
  is moderately elevated and the shoulders bear small tubercles.
  Color bluish white, paler near the upper portions, the base tipped
  with brownish purple. Young specimens may be dotted or
  streaked with reddish brown.

CONUS STRIATUS Linné   **Striate Cone**   Pl. 71
  Habitat: Moderately deep water; reefs.
  Description: A well-known species reaching a height of 5 in.
  Top of shell rather flat, the 7 or 8 volutions slightly channeled.
  Surface with many fine crowded lines. Color pinkish white,
  irregularly clouded with chocolate-brown.
  Remarks: A highly dangerous gastropod. When Clench and
  Kondo were preparing their work on the poisonous cones (see
  footnote, p. 248) they selected this species for dissection, since
  no other species exceeds it in size and development of the stinging
  and poisonous apparatus.

CONUS TESSULATUS Born   **Tessellate Cone**   Pl. 71
  Habitat: Deep water.
  Description: About 2 in. high, with 7 or 8 whorls. Apex moder-
  ately elevated. Color pale yellowish, with encircling rows of
  orange spots.
  Remarks: A common shell throughout the Pacific, but rare in
  Hawaii.

CONUS TEXTILE Linné   **Cloth-of-Gold Cone**   Pl. 71
  Habitat: Moderately deep water.
  Description: A large and colorful shell, attaining a height of 4 in.
  There are about 8 whorls, which form a short spire. Color yellowish brown, with wavy vertical lines of chocolate interrupted
  by sharp triangles of white. These latter are crowded at the
  shoulders, the center, and the base — suggesting irregular banding in many cases. Unlike spires of many cones, the spire is
  decorated the same as the body whorl.
  Remarks: Another poisonous and highly dangerous snail.

CONUS VEXILLUM Gmel.   **Flag Cone**   Pl. 71
  Habitat: Moderately deep water.
  Description: A heavy and sturdy shell reaching a height of 5 in.

There are 6 or 7 whorls, the spire only slightly elevated. The taper is quite rapid, so that the shell is very wide at the top in relation to its height. Color chestnut-brown, with a row of white blotches at the shoulders and another at center of last whorl. Top of shell white, strongly checked with large patches of brown. **Remarks:** Widespread in the Pacific, the Hawaiian shell is sometimes listed as *C. sumatrensis* Lam.

CONUS VITULINUS Hwass **Calf Cone** **Pl. 71**
  Habitat: Moderately deep water; reefs.
  Description: About 3 in. high, the whorl count 6. Spire rather low, but the apex is sharply pointed. Shoulders obscurely crenulate. Color olive-tan, with a central band of bluish white, and a 2nd band at the shoulder.

Family Terebridae: Auger Shells

(see p. 102)

Genus *Terebra* Bruguière 1789

TEREBRA CRENULATA Linné **Crenulate Auger** **Pls. 7, 72**
  Habitat: Shallow water; sand.
  Description: This shell attains a height of around 5 in. and has some 16 whorls. There is a row of small pointed nodules just below the sutures, giving a somewhat turreted appearance to the spire. Except for these nodules, the surface is smooth and shining. Aperture moderately small; inner lip twisted at base. The shell is cream-colored, streaked with lilac-brown between the nodules; bears 3 rows of small chestnut dots on the body whorl, 2 rows on the whorls of the spire.

TEREBRA DIMIDIATA Linné **Divided Auger** **Pls. 7, 72**
  Habitat: Shallow water.
  Description: A slender shell 5 in. high, made up of about 15 whorls. There is a spiral groove toward the bottom of each whorl, and the earlier volutions bear vertical ribs. Color reddish orange, with streaks and bands of white.

TEREBRA FELINA Dill. **Tiger Auger** **Pl. 72**
  Habitat: Shallow water.
  Description: Nearly 3 in. high, with some 15 or 16 whorls, each bearing an impressed line below the suture. Color pale gray or white, with a single row of small brown spots encircling the shell just above the suture line.
  Remarks: Formerly listed as *T. tigrina* Gmel.

TEREBRA GOULDI Desh. **Gould's Auger** **Pl. 72**
  Habitat: Shallow water.
  Description: About 2½ in. high, with some 12 whorls, each

marked toward its base by a spiral groove. Above the groove. the whorls are sculptured with close-set vertical ribs; below, they bear small knobs. Surface shiny. Color yellowish white, with rows of chestnut blotches.

TEREBRA GUTTATA Röd. **Eyed Auger** Pl. 72
Habitat: Shallow water.
Description: A fine, distinctive shell of about 20 whorls, reaching a height of 5 in. Sutures plainly marked, the shell's surface smooth. Color orange-brown, with 2 rows of large white spots on body whorl and a single row on shoulders of the volutions of the spire.
Remarks: Formerly listed as *T. oculata* Lam.

TEREBRA MACULATA Linné **Big Auger** Pl. 72
Habitat: Shallow water; sandy bottoms.
Description: A large, solid shell, the strongest and most sturdy of the genus. The height is from 5 to 8 in., and the whorls number about 16. The early volutions are vertically plicate, but most of the shell is quite smooth. Sutures distinct, but there are no shoulders, and the shell tapers gradually to a fine point. Aperture small, with the inner lip twisted at base. Color bluish white, broadly banded with purplish brown, the bands usually broken into squarish blotches; there may be various purplish vertical splashes.

TEREBRA NITIDA Hinds **Shining Auger** Pl. 72
Habitat: Shallow water.
Description: A very slender shell of some 14 flattish whorls, its height about 1½ in. The sutures are well marked, and each volution bears about 15 rounded vertical ribs. Aperture small; inner lip slightly twisted at base. Color yellowish gray, the ribs generally paler in tone. The shell has a fairly high gloss.

TEREBRA STRIGILATA Linné **Painted Auger** Pls. 8, 72
Habitat: Shallow water.
Description: A slender shell 1½ in. high. About 15 whorls, the sutures plainly impressed. The surface is sculptured with fine vertical ridges, and the whole shell is well polished. Color yellowish gray, with a distinct whitish band at the suture, and on this band is a series of square red-brown spots.
Remarks: If this shell were larger it would be considered one of the more showy of the tropical mollusks.

TEREBRA SUBULATA Linné **Spotted Auger** Pl. 72
Habitat: Shallow water.
Description: A slender spikelike shell of about 5 in. There may be as many as 20 whorls, the sutures well impressed. Each volu-

tion is flat-sided, so that its outline is somewhat squarish. The upper whorls bear vertical ridges, and also an impressed line at the suture, but both are lost on the later whorls. Color yellowish gray, with 2 rows of squarish chocolate spots on each volution of the spire and 3 on the body whorl.

Family Eulimidae: Obelisk Shells

(see p. 105)

Genus *Eulima* Risso 1826

EULIMA METCALFI (A. Adams)   **Mottled Eulima**   **Pl. 66**
   Habitat: Moderately shallow water.
   Description: An attractive shell, rather elongate in shape and measuring a trifle more than ¼ in. high. About 7 rather flattish whorls, the sutures not well defined. Aperture narrow and elongate, rounded at the base; outer lip thin and sharp. Color buffy yellow or gray, variously marked with reddish-brown scrawls; surface brightly polished.

Genus *Balcis* Gray 1847

BALCIS ACICULATA (Pease)   **Needle Balcis**   **Pl. 66**
   Habitat: Parasitical on echinoderms.
   Description: A slender high-spired shell of about 10 flattened whorls, the sutures scarcely discernible. Height about ½ in. Aperture small; outer lip thin and sharp. Color pure white; surface beautifully polished.

BALCIS CUMINGI (A. Adams)   **Cuming's Balcis**   **Pl. 66**
   Habitat: Parasitical on sea cucumbers.
   Description: A larger shell than *B. aciculata* (above), attaining a height of just over 1 in. The whorl count is about 10; sutures fairly well impressed. Surface highly polished. Color white. Aperture rather small; outer lip thin and sharp.

BALCIS PEASEI (Tryon)   **Pease's Balcis**   **Pl. 66**
   Habitat: Parasitical on echinoderms.
   Description: About ½ in. high, this shell has 7 or 8 whorls, the sutures being rather indistinct. The spire is noticeably curved to one side. Aperture small, apex somewhat blunt. The shell is glassy white.
   Remarks: Examples of these gastropods are often quite abundant among the fine beach litter but are easily overlooked by the casual collector. Under a hand lens many of them show considerable beauty.

Family Pyramidellidae: Pyramid Shells

(see p. 106)

Genus *Pyramidella* Lamarck 1799

PYRAMIDELLA SULCATA A. Adams   Pls. 8, 66
Sulcate Pyramidella
    Habitat: Shallow water; sandy bottoms.
    Description: Stoutly elongate, with about 10 rounded whorls,
the sutures well impressed. Height from 1 to 1½ in. Color shiny
white, clouded with vertical blotches of pale orange or brown.
Aperture small and oval; columella bears 3 distinct pleats; outer
lip strongly toothed within.

PYRAMIDELLA TEREBELLUM (Möll.)   Pl. 66
Ringed Pyramidella
    Habitat: Moderately shallow water; sandy bottoms.
    Description: About ¾ in. high, this shell is shaped like *P. sulcata*
(above). There are 8 or 9 whorls, rounded, with well-defined
sutures. Color yellowish white, with a series of chocolate lines
encircling each volution. The columella bears 2 pleats; the
aperture is rather small and oval. Surface highly polished.

Family Bullidae: True Bubble Shells

(see p. 110)

Genus *Bulla* Linné 1758

BULLA PEASIANA Pils.   **Bubble Shell**   Pl. 72
    Habitat: Mudflats.
    Description: This shell varies in size, its average height about
¾ in. Oval and inflated, with the spire depressed. The aperture
is higher than the shell, the outer lip rounded at both ends.
There is a reflected white shield at the base of the inner. Surface
smooth and shiny. Color mottled gray, brown, and white.

Family Scaphandridae: Canoe Shells

SHELL thin in substance but well inflated. Aperture wider at base.
Spire sunken.

Genus *Atys* Montfort 1810

ATYS SEMISTRIATA Pease   **Striate Bubble**   Pl. 72
 Habitat: Shallow water.
 Description: A thin, roundly oval, inflated shell about ½ in.
 high. The shell is involute, the spire concealed in a sunken top.
 Aperture wide, with outer lip rising above top of shell. The body
 whorl bears widely separated impressed lines at the base and a
 2nd series at the top, the surface between smooth and without
 lines. Color yellowish white.

Family Akeridae: Paper Bubble Shells
(see p. 110)

Genus *Haminoea* Turton & Kingston 1830

HAMINOEA CROCATA Pease   **Paper Bubble**   Pl. 72
 Habitat: Mudflats.
 Description: About ½ in. high, a glossy and tiny shell, shaped
 much like *Atys semistriata* and *Bulla peasiana* (above). Shell
 very thin and translucent, yellowish. The aperture is higher
 than the shell and widens noticeably at the base. The surface
 bears minute revolving lines, but the general appearance is
 smooth and glassy.
 Remarks: In life the animal is too large for its shell, which is
 partially imbedded in the mantle.

Family Hydatinidae: Bubble Shells

SHELL thin, nearly globular. Body whorl large and aperture wide.
Often brightly marked.

Genus *Hydatina* Schumacher 1817

HYDATINA ALBOCINCTA (Hoeven)   **Clown Bubble**   Pl. 72
 Habitat: Shallow water; sand.
 Description: A little smaller than *H. physis* (below), but otherwise very much like it. It is inflated, thin, and fragile, the top
 showing a small sunken spiral. The surface is polished. The
 color is pale brown, with 4 rather broad and sharply defined
 bands of white on the body whorl.

HYDATINA AMPLUSTRE (Linné)   **Pink Bubble**   Pls. 8, 72
 Habitat: Shallow water; sand.
 Description: A flat-topped shell about 1 in. high when fully
 grown. Whorls 5, the body whorl swollen and tapering below.

Aperture flaring; outer lip thin and sharp. Surface polished. Color rich pink, with revolving bands of brown and white in various combinations. Commonly there is a central band of white bordered by a pair of brown bands, and a single brown band at the shoulder and at the base. The pink is always the predominant color; a trayful of these shells stands out in any collection.

HYDATINA PHYSIS (Linné)   **Striped Bubble**   Pl. 72
Habitat: Shallow water; sand.
Description: A globose, well-inflated shell, thin in substance, attaining a height of 1½ in. The spire is not concealed as in *Bulla*, but the top of the shell is flattened, and shows a small, tight spiral. Surface smooth and polished. Color yellowish gray, with numerous thin wavy lines of brown encircling the shell, every 4th or 5th line heavier than the others.
Remarks: This snail enjoys a very wide distribution, being found in Africa, India, Australia, Japan, Hawaii, and in the West Indies and Florida.

Family Umbraculidae: Umbrella Shells

SHELL limpet-shaped, embedded in the upper surface of the much larger animal.

Genus *Umbraculum* Schumacher 1817

UMBRACULUM SINICUM (Gmel.)   **Umbrella Shell**   Pl. 72
Habitat: Shallow water.
Description: Shell roughly circular, or oval, some 3 in. long. It is considerably depressed, with the apex a small round nub somewhat to the left of the center of the dorsal surface. Inside the shell there is a large, rich-brown muscle scar that is radially ridged. Often there is a paler band, or halo, around this area. Upper surface white, sometimes stained with yellowish.
Remarks: In life the animal is never able to conceal itself under its shell, which merely forms a small cap over the body. In older books this gastropod may be found listed as *Umbrella indica* Lam.

Family Siphonariidae: False Limpets

(see p. 204)

Genus *Siphonaria* Sowerby 1824

SIPHONARIA NORMALIS Gould   **False Limpet**   Pl. 72
Habitat: Between tides; rocks.
Description: A limpet-like shell about ½ in. long. The apex is

moderately elevated, and the surface is sculptured with strong radiating ridges, a larger ridge alternating with a smaller one. A rather deep siphonal groove is present at the upper left. Color dark gray, the ridges of lighter hue. Inside of shell dark purplish brown, with radiating streaks of gray near margin.

Remarks: These mollusks possess both gills and lungs and spend their time between the tide limits, living a more or less amphibious life; thus they form a connecting link between the purely aquatic snails and the more highly developed air-breathing snails.

Family Ellobiidae: Marsh Snails

(see p. 111)

Genus *Melampus* Montfort 1810

MELAMPUS SEMIPLICATA Pease   Pl. 72
  Habitat: Grasses in salt marshes.
  Description: An oval shell with a sharp apex, the height about ½ in. The color is grayish brown, with a fairly strong brownish periostracum. The aperture is small and rather narrow, with weak teeth on both lips.

Family Achatinellidae: Tree Snails

BRIGHTLY colored tree or vine snails. Base of columella thickened, forming pronounced notch. Confined to the Hawaiian Islands.

Genus *Achatinella* Swainson 1828

ALTHOUGH this book is concerned exclusively with the marine snails and clams, no discussion of Hawaiian shells would be satisfactory without mentioning, at least briefly, the land snails of this interesting genus. The achatinellas are tree snails, at home in the bushes, vines, and trees throughout the Hawaiian group. There are several species and a great many varieties of the genus *Achatinella*, all of them confined exclusively to the Hawaiian Islands. A few examples are shown on Plate 8, No. 15. About 1 in. high, they have 6 or 7 rounded whorls which produce a moderately tall spire. The aperture is small, the inner lip often toothed or twisted. The shell is smooth and polished, and may be either sinistral or dextral. The colors, and the color combinations, are almost infinite.

Each isolated valley appears to have its own peculiar color forms, and it has been claimed that a specialist could tell what island he was on, and which particular valley he was in, merely by collecting a few shells of these tree snails.

Early writers attributed a "squeaking" in the treetops to these snails, believing that the sound was produced by the mollusks suddenly withdrawing into their shells, and the name "singing snails" is sometimes applied to them. The sounds from the treetops, however, upon careful investigation, turned out to be a chorus of tiny tree crickets.

Appendixes

Glossary of
Conchological Terms

Acuminate — tapering to a point.
Acute — sharply pointed.
Animal — the fleshy part of the mollusk.
Annulated — marked with rings.
Anterior — the forward end of a bivalve shell.
Aperture — the entrance or opening of the shell.
Apex — the tip of the spire in snail shells.
Apophysis — a peglike structure to support a muscle (also called myophore).
Axis — the central structure of a spiral shell.

Base — *snails*, the extremity opposite the apex; *clams*, the margin opposite the beaks.
Beaks — the initial, or earliest, part of a bivalve shell.
Bifid — cleft, divided into 2 parts.
Bivalve — a shell with 2 valves (or shell parts).
Body whorl — the last whorl of a snail shell.
Byssus — a series of threadlike filaments that serve to anchor the bivalve to some support.

Calcareous — composed of lime.
Callum — thin calcareous covering of the gape in some clams.
Callus — a calcareous deposit, such as enamel.
Canal — a tubular prolongation of the lip of the aperture, containing the siphon, in many snails.
Cancellate — longitudinal and spiral lines, or ribs, crossing.
Carinate — with a keel-like, elevated ridge.
Cartilage — an internal, elastic substance found in bivalves which controls the opening of the valves.
Chondrophore — a spoonlike projection in the hinge of some bivalves.
Columella — the pillar around which the whorls form their spiral circuit.
Concentric — applied to curved ridges on a bivalve shell, being arcs with the beaks at the center.
Conic — shaped like a cone.

Coronate — crowned.
Costate — ribbed.
Crenulate — notched or scalloped.
Cuspidate — prickly pointed.

Deck — a small platform under the beaks; also diaphragm.
Decussated — lines crossing at right angles.
Denticulate — toothed.
Dextral — turning from left to right; right-handed.
Diaphanous — transparent, clear.
Diaphragm — *see* Deck.
Discoidal — the whorls being coiled in one plane.
Dorsal — belonging to the back.

Ear — *see* Wing.
Epidermis — *see* Periostracum.
Equivalve — both valves the same size and shape.
Escutcheon — an elongated depression behind the beaks in a bivalve shell.

Fissure — a slit or cut.
Foot — muscular extension of the body used in locomotion.
Fusiform — spindle-shaped.

Gaping — the valves only partially closing.
Gastropod — a snail (or slug)
Genus — a separate group of species, distinguished from all others by certain permanent marks called generic characters.
Globose — rounded like a globe or ball.
Granulated — covered with minute grains or beads.
Growth lines — lines on the surface of a shell indicating rest periods during growth; also growth laminae.

Hinge — where the valves of a bivalve are joined.

Inequivalve — valves differing in size or shape.
Inner lip — portion of aperture adjacent to axis, or pillar.
Involute — rolled inward from each side, as in *Cypraea*.

Keel — a flattened ridge, usually at shoulder or periphery.

Lamellibranchia — an older name for pelecypods (bivalves).
Lanceolate — shaped like a lance.
Ligament — a cartilage that connects the valves.
Linear — very narrow.
Lineated — marked with lines.
Lips — the margins of the aperture.
Lirate — resembling fine incised lines.

Littoral — tidal zone.
Lunule — a depressed area, usually heart-shaped, in front of the beaks, in many bivalve shells.
Lyrate — shaped like a lyre.

Maculate — splashed or spotted.
Mantle — a membranous flap or outer covering of the soft parts of a mollusk; it secretes the material that forms the shell.
Margin — the edges of the shell.
Mesoplax — an accessory plate.
Mouth — aperture of a snail.
Myophore — *see* Apophysis.

Nacreous — pearly.
Nodose — having tubercles or knobs.
Nodule — knoblike projection.
Nucleus — the initial, or nuclear whorl.

Oblique — in a slanting direction.
Operculum — a plate or door that closes the aperture in many snails.
Orbicular — round or circular.
Outer lip — outer edge of the aperture.
Ovate — egg-shaped or oval.

Pallial line — a groove or channel near the inner base of a bivalve shell, where the mantle is made fast to the lower part of the shell.
Pallial sinus — a notch in same.
Parietal wall — area of inner lip.
Pelagic — inhabiting the open sea.
Penultimate whorl — next to the last whorl.
Periostracum — the noncalcareous covering on many shells; sometimes wrongly called the epidermis.
Peristome — edge of the aperture.
Pleat — applied to folds on the columella.
Plicate — folded or pleated.
Posterior — the backward end of a bivalve shell.
Produced — elongated.
Protoconch — the initial whorl of a snail shell.
Pyriform — pear-shaped.

Quadrate — of rectangular shape.

Radial — pertaining to a ray.
Radiating — applied to ribs or lines that start at the beak and extend fanwise to the margins.
Radula — "tongue" or dental apparatus of gastropods.
Recurved — turned backward.

Resilium — internal cartilage in bivalve hinge; causes shell to spring open when muscles relax.

Reticulate — crossed like network.

Rostrate — beaked.

Rostrum — a beak.

Rugose — rough or wrinkled.

Scabrous — rough.

Scalariform — loosely coiled.

Sculpture — ornamentation.

Semilunar — half-moon-shaped.

Septum — diaphragm, platform.

Sinistral — turning from right to left; left-handed.

Sinuate — excavated.

Sinus — a deep cut.

Siphon — the organ through which water enters or leaves the mantle cavity.

Species — the subdivision of a genus, distinguished from all others of the genus by certain permanent marks called specific characters.

Spire — the upper whorls, from the apex to the body whorl.

Striae — very fine lines.

Sulci — grooves or furrows.

Suture — the spiral line of the spire, where one whorl touches another.

Teeth — the pointed protuberences at the hinge of a bivalve shell; in snails, the toothlike structures in the aperture.

Truncate — having the end cut off squarely.

Tubercle — a knob.

Turbinate — top-shaped.

Turreted — the tops of the whorls flattened.

Umbilicus — a small hollow at the base of the shell in snails, visible from below.

Umbones (umbo) — the swelling part of bivalve shells, near the beaks.

Undulating — wavelike.

Univalve — a shell composed of a single piece, as a snail.

Valve — one part of a bivalve shell; one of the 8 plates that make up the dorsal shield of a chiton.

Varices (varix) — prominent raised ribs on surface of a snail shell, caused by a periodic thickening of the outer lip during rest periods in shell growth.

Varicose — bearing 1 varix or more.

Ventral — of or relating to the underside.

Ventricose — swollen or rounded out.

Volutions — the distinct turns of the spire, also called whorls.

Whorls — *see* Volutions.

Wing — a more or less triangular projection or expansion of the shell of a bivalve, either in the plane of the hinge or extending above it; also known as an "ear."

List of Authors

Adams, A. — Arthur Adams
Adams, C. B. — Charles B. Adams
Adams, H. — Henry Adams
Anton — Hermann E. Anton
Arn. — Ralph Arnold

Baily — Joshua L. Baily, Jr.
Baird — William Baird
Bar. — Paul R. Bartsch
Bayle — E. Bayle
Bellevue — Fleuriau de Bellevue
Ben. — W. H. Benson
Berry — S. Stillman Berry
Bivona — A. Bivona
Blain. — H. M. de Blainville
Born — Ignatius A. Born
Brod. — William J. Broderip
Bronn — Heinrich Georg Bronn
Brown — Thomas Brown
Brünnich — Morton T. Brünnich
Brug. — Joseph G. Bruguière
Bucquoy — Eugene Bucquoy
Bur. — E. J. Burrow
Burch — John Q. Burch

Carp. — Philip P. Carpenter
Chavan — André Chavan
Chem. — Johann H. Chemnitz
Chenu — Jean C. Chenu
Con. — Timothy A. Conrad
Cossmann — Maurice Cossmann
Couth. — Joseph P. Couthouy

Da Costa — E. Mendes da Costa
Dall — William H. Dall
Daudin — François M. Daudin
Dautzenberg — Philippe
  Dautzenberg

Defrance — M. Jacques Defrance
Desh. — Gérard P. Deshayes
Dill. — Lewis W. Dillwyn
Dixon — George Dixon
Dollfus — Gustave F. Dollfus
Duc. — P. L. Duclos
Duméril — André M. C. Duméril
Dun. — William B. Dunker
Dur. — J. Wyatt Durham

Esch. — Johann F. Eschscholtz

Fabr. — Otto Fabricius
Férussac — Jean B. Férussac
Fisch. — Paul Fischer
Fleming — John Fleming
For. — Edward Forbes
Friele — Herman Friele

Gabb — William M. Gabb
Gale — Hoyt R. Gale
Gistel — Johannes Gistel
Gmel. — Johann F. Gmelin
Gould — Augustus A. Gould
Grant — Ulysses S. Grant IV
Gray — John E. Gray
Greg. — Antonio de Gregorio
Grif. — Edward Griffith

Hald. — Samuel S. Haldeman
Han. — Sylvanus Hanley
Hanna — G. Dallas Hanna
Harmer — Frederic W. Harmer
Hemp. — Henry Hemphill
Herrmannsen — A. N.
  Herrmannsen
Hert. — Leo G. Hertlein
Hinds — Richard B. Hinds

Hoeven — H. van der Hoeven
Hol. — J. S. Holten
Hum. — George Humphrey
Hwass — Christian H. Hwass

Ino — Takashi Ino
Ire. — Tom Iredale

Jay — John C. Jay
Jonas — J. H. Jonas
Jouss. — Felix P. Jousseaume
Jukes-Browne — Alfred J. Jukes-Browne

Keen — A. Myra Keen
Keep — Josiah Keep
Kiener — Louis C. Kiener
King — Philip P. King
Kingston — J. F. Kingston
Koch — Carl Ludwig Koch
Koenen — Adolf von Koenen
Kröyer — Henrik Kröyer

Lam. — Jean-Baptiste Lamarck
Lamy — Edouard Lamy
Lea — Isaac Lea
Leach — William E. Leach
Lesueur — Charles A. Lesueur
Less. — René-P. Lesson
Link — Heinrich F. Link
Linné — Carl von Linnaeus
Lovén — Sven Lovén
Lowe — Herbert N. Lowe

Mar. — Frederick P. Marrat
Marks — Jay G. Marks
Mart. — Edward von Martens
Mawe — John Mawe
Meek — Fielding B. Meek
Mel. — J. Cosmo Melville
Ménard — G. de la Ménard
Menke — Karl T. Menke
Meus. — Frederich C. Meuschen
Mich. — H. Michelin
Michaud — André L. G. Michaud
Midd. — Alex T. von Middendorff
Mig. — Jesse W. Mighels
Mill. — K. Miller
Modeer — A. Modeer

Möll. — H. P. C. Möller
Mörch — Otto A. L. Mörch
Mol. — G. I. Molina
Mont. — Denys de Montfort
Mtg. — George Montagu
Mtyn. — Thomas Martyn
Mühl. — Megerle von Mühlfeld
Müll. — Otto F. Müller

Nardo — Giovanni D. Nardo
Nutt. — Thomas Nuttall

Odhner — Nils H. Odhner
Oken — Lorenz Oken
Old. — Ida. S. Oldroyd
Orb. — Alcide d'Orbigny

Pease — William H. Pease
Perry — George Perry
Petit — S. Petit de la Saussaye
Pfr. — Louis Pfeiffer
Phil. — Rudolf A. Philippi
Pidg. — Edward Pidgeon
Pils. — Henry A. Pilsbry
Potiez — V. Louis Victor Potiez
Powys — W. Lytellton Powys
Pusch — G. G. Pusch

Raf. — Constantine S. Rafinesque
Ray. — William J. Raymond
Réc. — C. A. Récluz
Red. — John H. Redfield
Reeve — Lovell A. Reeve
Reh. — Harald A. Rehder
Risso — Antoine Risso
Röd — Peter F. Röding (Roeding)
Römer — Edward Römer

Sacco — Federico Sacco
Salisbury — A. E. Salisbury
Sars — Georg Ossian Sars
Sassi — A. Sassi (or Sasso)
Say — Thomas Say
Schil. — Franz A. Schilder
Schm. — F. C. Schmidt
Schu. — Gotthilf H. Schubert
Schum. — Christian F. Schumacher

Scop. — Giovanni A. Scopoli
Smith — Edgar A. Smith
Sol. — Daniel Solander
Soot-Ryen — Tron Soot-Ryen
Soul. — F. L. A. Souleyet
Sow. — George B. Sowerby
Speng. — Lorenz Spengler
St. V. — Bory St. Vincent
Stearns — Robert E. C. Stearns
Steens. — Johannes S. Steenstrup
Stewart — Ralph B. Stewart
Stim. — William Stimpson
Stor. — D. Humphreys Storer
Strong — Archibald M. Strong
Swain. — William Swainson

Test — Avery R. Test
Thun. — Karl P. Thunberg

Tom. — John R. Tomlin
Troschel — Franz H. Troschel
Tryon — George W. Tryon
Turner — Ruth D. Turner
Turt. — William H. Turton

Val. — Achilles Valenciennes
Van. — Edward G. Vanatta
Ver. — Addisson E. Verrill

Wag. — Johann A. Wagner
Waldheim — Fischer von
  Waldheim
Whit. — Joseph F. Whiteaves
Will. — George Willett
Wood — Searless V. Wood

Yates — Lorenzo G. Yates

APPENDIX III

Bibliography

Abbott, R. Tucker. American Seashells. New York: Van Nostrand, 1954.

Dall, William H. Summary of the Marine Shellbearing Mollusks of the Northwest Coast of America. U.S. Natl. Museum Bull. 112 (1921).

Edmondson, Charles H. Reef and Shore Fauna of Hawaii. Honolulu: Bishop Museum, 1946.

Fitch, John E. Common Marine Bivalves of California. Calif. Dept. of Fish and Game, Fish Bull. 90 (1953).

Grau, Gilbert. Pectinidae of the Eastern Pacific. Los Angeles: Univ. So. Calif. Press, 1959.

Hirase, Shintaro, and Taki Isao. A Handbook of Illustrated Shells from the Japanese Islands and Adjacent Territory. Tokyo: Bunkyokaku Publ., 1951.

Johnson, Myrtle E., and Henry J. Snook. Seashore Animals of the Pacific Coast. New York: Macmillan, 1935.

Johnston, Kathleen Y. Sea Treasure. Boston: Houghton Mifflin, 1957.

Keen, A. Myra. Sea Shells of Tropical West America. Stanford University, Calif.: Stanford Univ. Press, 1958.

——, and Don L. Frizzell. Illustrated Key to West North American *Pelecypod* Genera. Rev. ed. Stanford University, Calif.: Stanford Univ. Press, 1953.

——, and John C. Pearson. Illustrated Key to West North American *Gastropod* Genera. Stanford University, Calif.: Stanford Univ. Press, 1952.

Keep, Josiah. West Coast Shells. Rev. by Joshua L. Baily, Jr. Stanford University, Calif.: Stanford Univ. Press, 1935.

Kira, Tetsuaki. Shells of Japan. Osaka, 1955.

La Rocque, Aurèle. Catalogue of the Recent Mollusca of Canada. Natl. Museum of Canada Bull. 129. Ottawa, 1953.

Light, Sol. F. Intertidal Invertebrates of the Central California Coast. Light's Laboratory and Field Text in Invertebrate Zoology. Rev. by Ralph I. Smith *et al*. Berkeley: Univ. of Calif. Press, 1954.

Oldroyd, Ida. S. Marine Shells of Puget Sound and Vicinity. Seattle: Univ. of Wash. Press, 1924. Vol. 4.

——. Marine Shells of the West Coast of North America. 4 parts. Stanford University, Calif: Stanford Univ. Press, 1924–27.

Palmer, Katherine van Winkle. Catalog of the First Duplicate Series of the Reigen Collection of Mazatlan Shells in the State Museum at Albany. New York State Bull. 342 (1951).

Quayle, Daniel B. The Intertidal Bivalves of British Columbia. B.C. Provincial Museum, Handbook 7 (1960).

Ricketts, Edward F., and Jack Calvin. Between Pacific Tides. Stanford University, Calif.: Stanford Univ. Press, 1939.

Rogers, Julia. The Shell Book. Garden City, N.Y.: Doubleday, Page, 1908. Reprinted 1951, C. T. Branford, Boston, with names brought up to date in an appendix by Harald A. Rehder.

Smith, Maxwell. Panamic Marine Shells. Winter Park, Florida: Tropical Photographic Lab., 1944.

———. World-wide Shells. Lantana, Florida: Tropical Photographic Lab., 1940.

Steinbeck, John, and Edward F. Ricketts. Sea of Cortez. New York: Viking, 1941.

Tinker, Spencer W. Pacific Sea Shells. Rev. ed. Rutland, Vt.: Tuttle, 1958.

Verrill, Alpheus H. Shell Collector's Handbook. New York: Putnam, 1950.

Webb, Walter F. Handbook for Shell Collectors. St. Petersburg, Fla.: Privately printed, 1948.

IN ADDITION

Indo-Pacific Mollusca: A series devoted to taxonomic revision of the mollusks of this vast area. Many illustrations in color. Published by Dept. of Mollusks, Acad. of Natural Sciences, Philadelphia, Penna., 19103.

How to Collect Shells: A publication written by dozens of experts in their fields. Subjects covered include shore collecting, reef collecting, dredging, collecting mollusks from fish, land collecting, freshwater collecting, and many others. Obtainable from the American Malacological Union (see The Nautilus, below).

The Nautilus: A quarterly journal written for and by conchologists. Technical and semipopular articles. The official organ of the American Malacological Union. Address: Acad. of Natural Sciences, Philadelphia, Penna. 19103.

Mr. Richard E. Petit, P.O. Box 133, Ocean Drive Beach, South Carolina 29582, publishes a yearly directory of conchologists, containing the names and addresses of hundreds of collectors, both here and abroad, with their particular interests. Ideal for building up a list of "swapping" friends.

The Annual Report of the American Malacological Union lists several hundred active members, with addresses and specialties.

APPENDIX IV

Some West Coast Shell Clubs

Conchological Club of Southern California, Los Angeles County Museum, Los Angeles, California 90007.

Hawaiian Malacological Society, Aquarium, 2777 Kalakaua Avenue, Honolulu, Hawaii 96815.

Long Beach Shell Club, Long Beach, California.

Northern California Malacozoological Club, Berkeley, California 94720.

Pacific Northwest Shell Club, Seattle, Washington 98105.

Pacific Shell Club, Los Angeles County Museum, Los Angeles, California 90007.

Sacramento Valley Conchological Society, Sonora, California.

Index

ONLY the main species description sections are covered by this index. When there is a combination of lightface roman and italic numbers for an entry the description is on the page indicated by the lightface roman figures. Illustrations are given in boldface type. In general the shells are to be found under their group classifications. If the English common name of a species incorporates a genus name, the shell will be found only under the anglicized genus name rather than under the larger group (family) name.